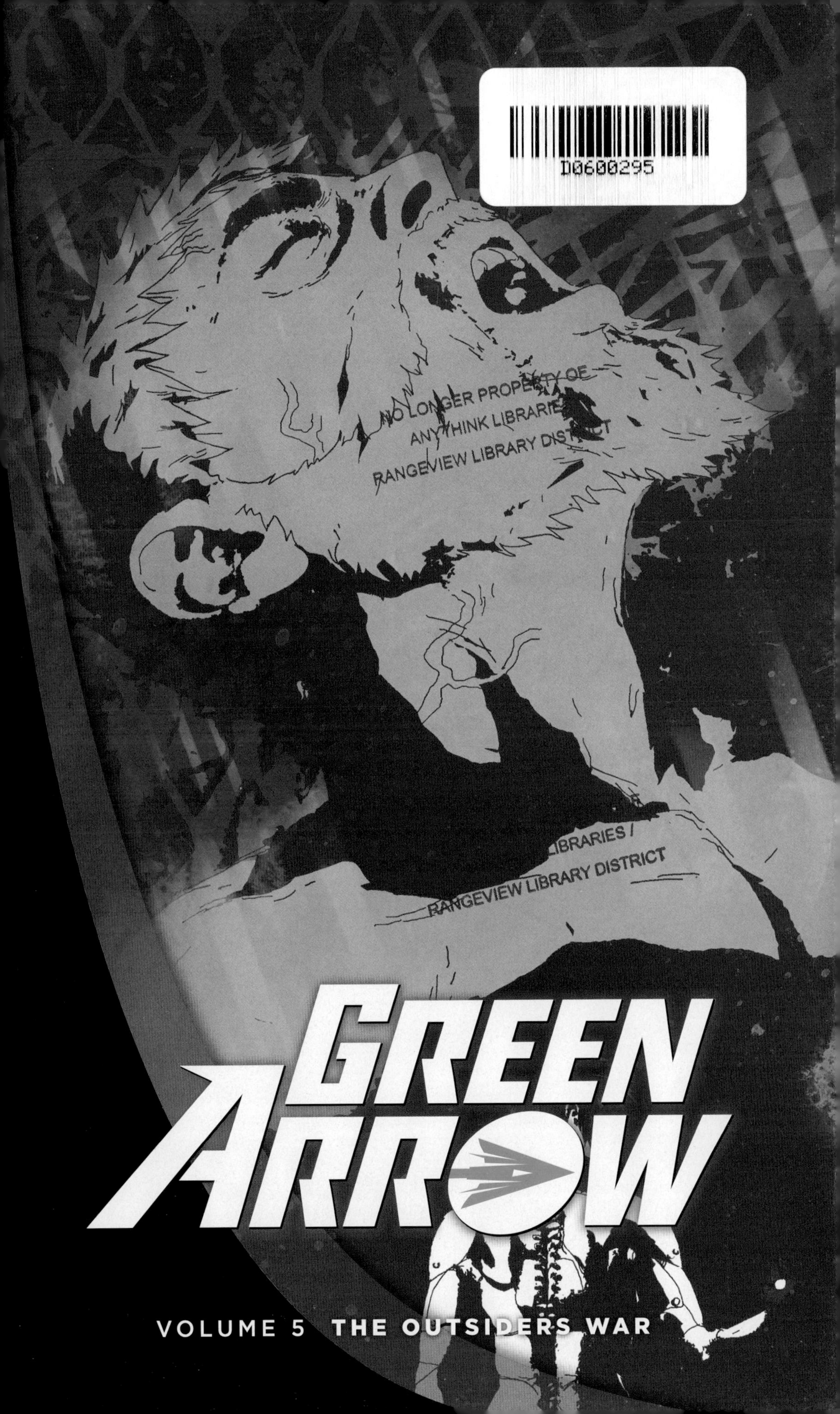
GREEN ARROW
VOLUME 5 THE OUTSIDERS WAR

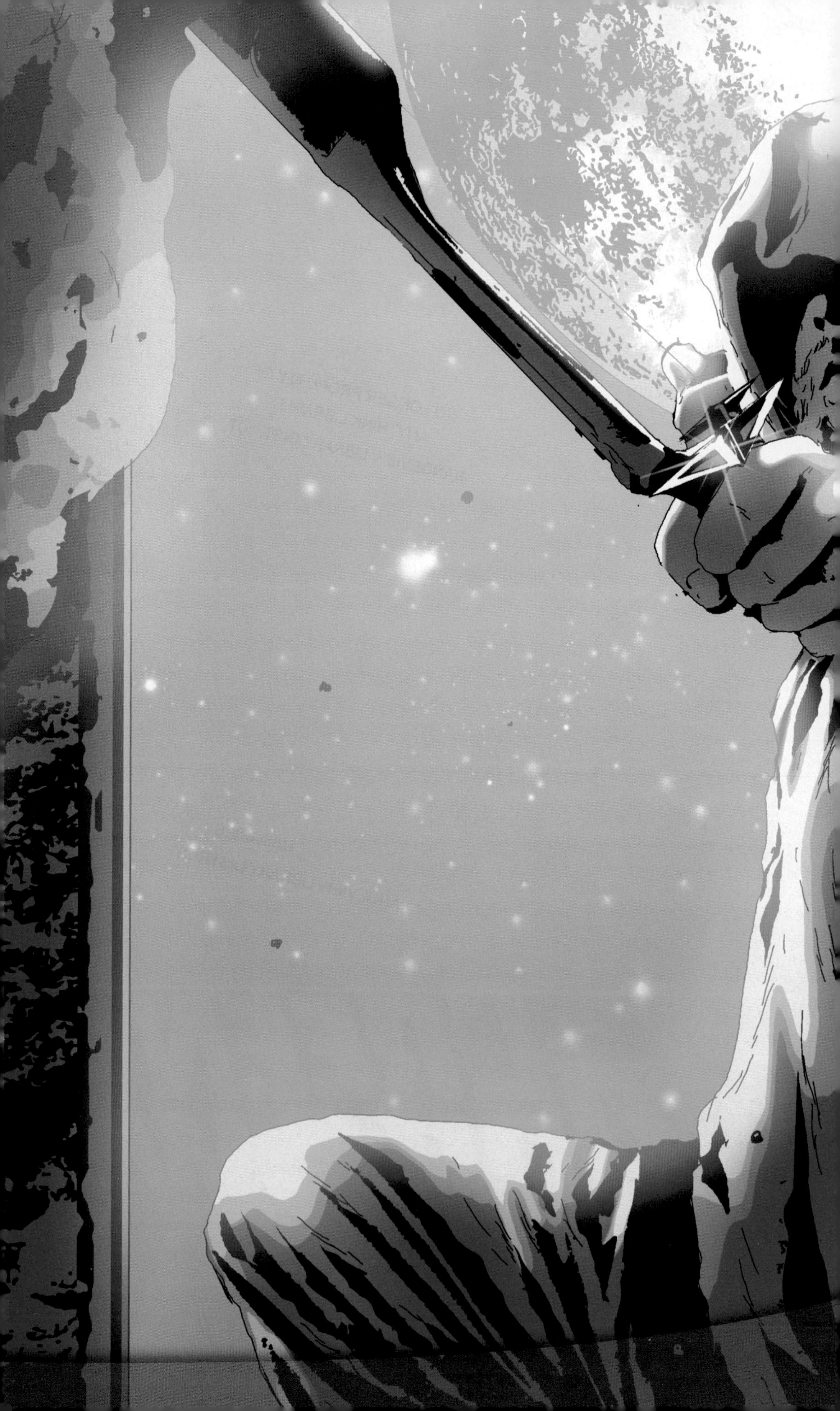

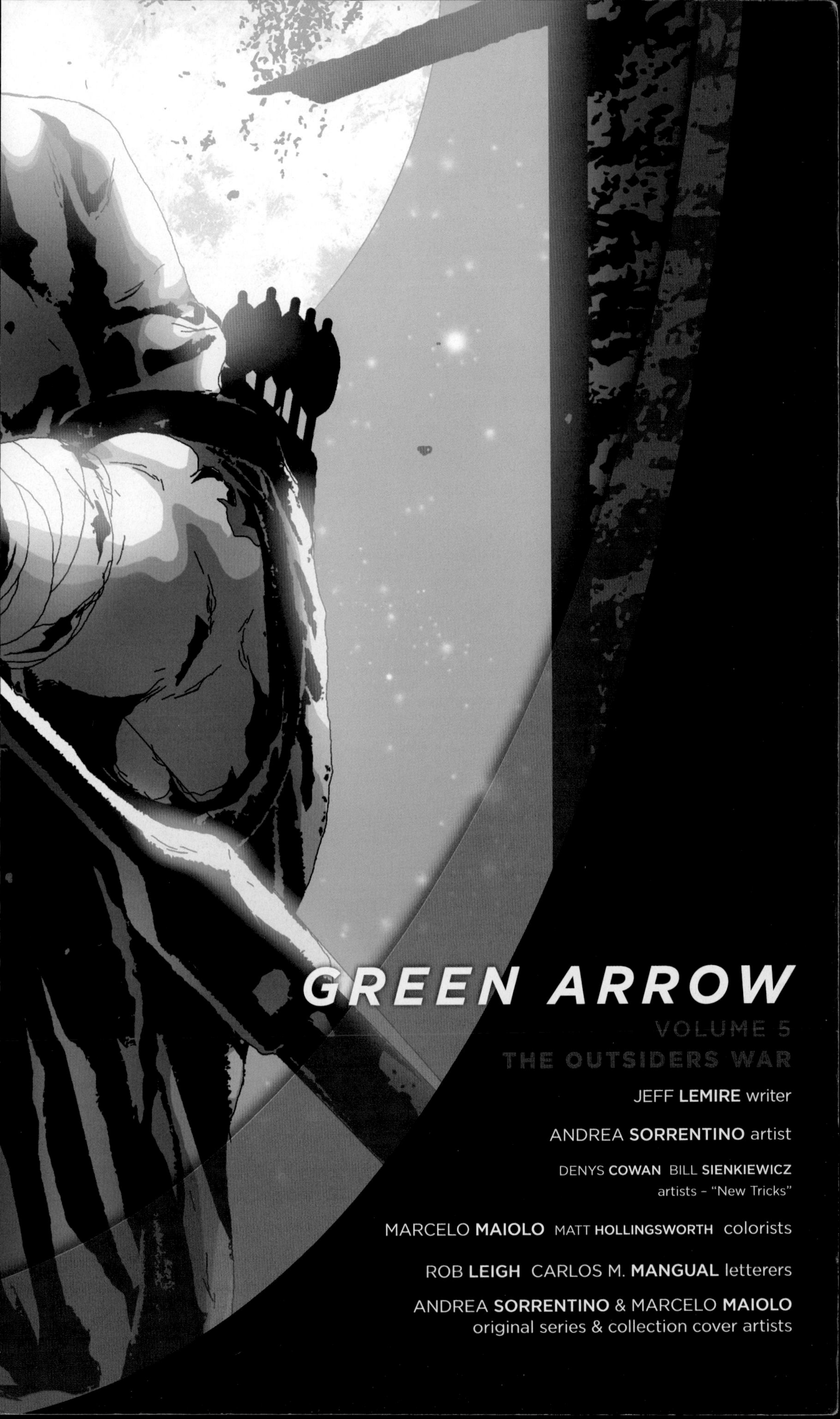

GREEN ARROW

VOLUME 5
THE OUTSIDERS WAR

JEFF **LEMIRE** writer

ANDREA **SORRENTINO** artist

DENYS **COWAN** BILL **SIENKIEWICZ**
artists – "New Tricks"

MARCELO **MAIOLO** MATT **HOLLINGSWORTH** colorists

ROB **LEIGH** CARLOS M. **MANGUAL** letterers

ANDREA **SORRENTINO** & MARCELO **MAIOLO**
original series & collection cover artists

WIL MOSS Editor – Original Series HARVEY RICHARDS Associate Editor – Original Series ROBIN WILDMAN Editor
ROBBIN BROSTERMAN Design Director – Books ROBBIE BIEDERMAN Publication Design

BOB HARRAS Senior VP – Editor-in-Chief, DC Comics

DIANE NELSON President DAN DIDIO and JIM LEE Co-Publishers GEOFF JOHNS Chief Creative Officer
AMIT DESAI Senior VP – Marketing and Franchise Management
AMY GENKINS Senior VP – Business and Legal Affairs NAIRI GARDINER Senior VP – Finance
JEFF BOISON VP – Publishing Planning MARK CHIARELLO VP – Art Direction and Design
JOHN CUNNINGHAM VP – Marketing TERRI CUNNINGHAM VP – Editorial Administration
LARRY GANEM VP – Talent Relations and Services ALISON GILL Senior VP – Manufacturing and Operations
HANK KANALZ Senior VP – Vertigo and Integrated Publishing JAY KOGAN VP – Business and Legal Affairs, Publishing
JACK MAHAN VP – Business Affairs, Talent NICK NAPOLITANO VP – Manufacturing Administration SUE POHJA VP – Book Sales
FRED RUIZ VP – Manufacturing Operations COURTNEY SIMMONS Senior VP – Publicity BOB WAYNE Senior VP – Sales

GREEN ARROW VOLUME 5: THE OUTSIDERS WAR

DC Comics, 1700 Broadway, New York, NY 10019
A Warner Bros. Entertainment Company.
Printed by RR Donnelley, Salem, VA, USA. 9/5/14. First Printing.
ISBN: 978-1-4012-5044-7

SUSTAINABLE
FORESTRY
INITIATIVE

Certified Chain of Custody
20% Certified Forest Content,
80% Certified Sourcing
www.sfiprogram.org
SFI-01042
APPLIES TO TEXT STOCK ONLY

Library of Congress Cataloging-in-Publication Data

Lemire, Jeff, author.
Green Arrow. Volume 5, The Outsiders War / Jeff Lemire, writer ; Andrea Sorrentino, artist.
pages cm. — (The New 52!)
ISBN 978-1-4012-5044-7 (paperback)
1. Graphic novels. I. Sorrentino, Andrea, illustrator. II. Title. III. Title: Outsiders War.
PN6728.G725L47 2014
741.5'973—dc23

2014014909

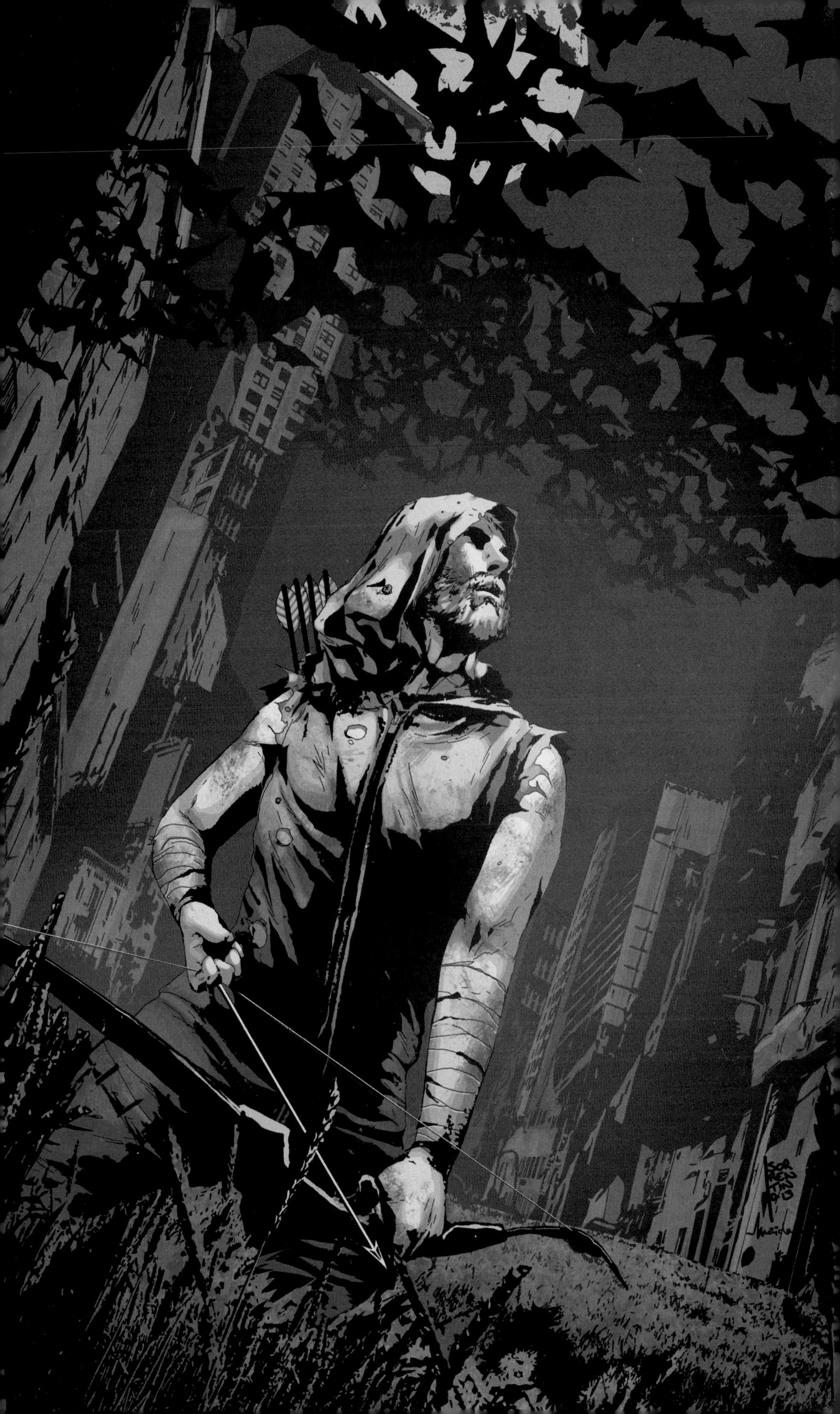

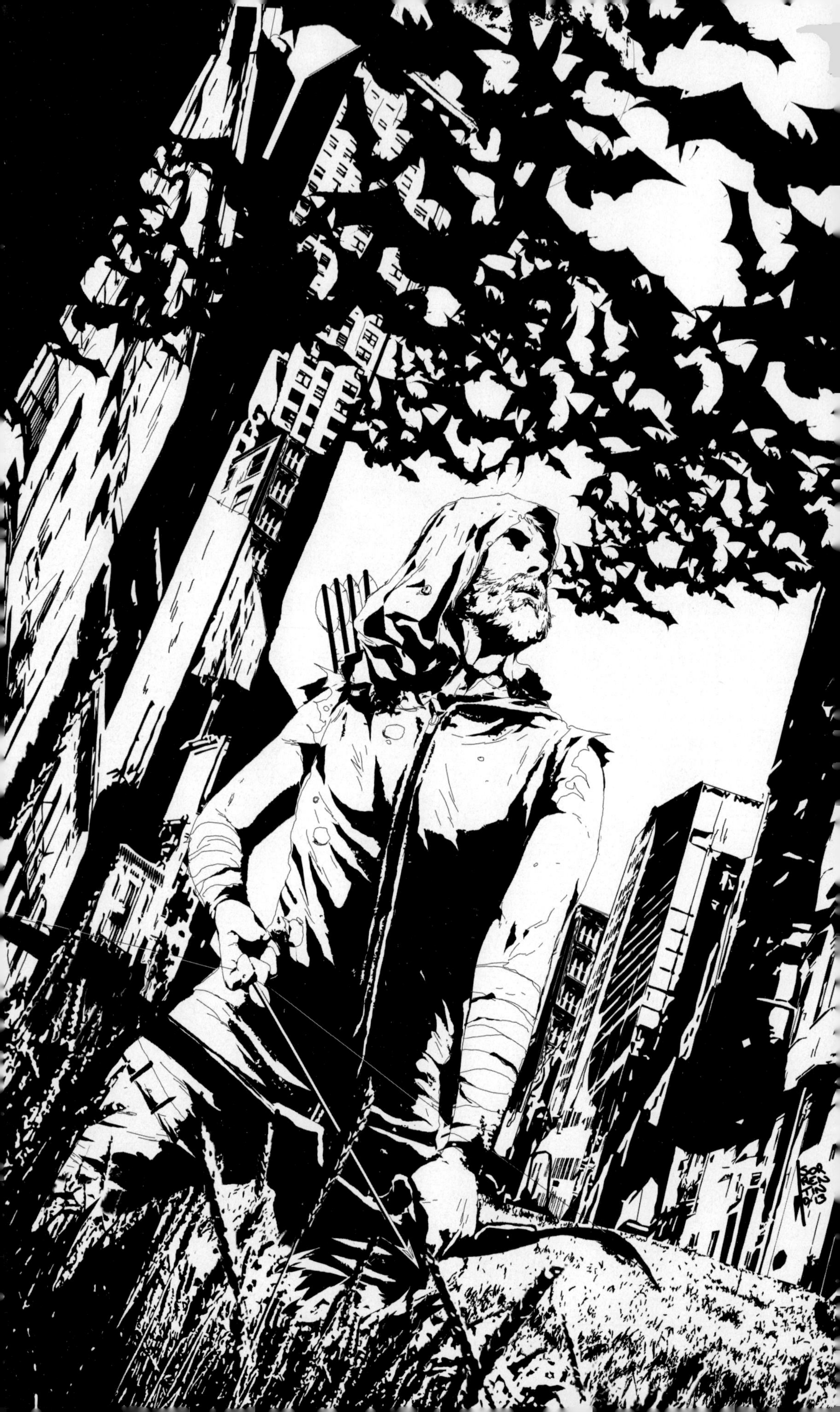

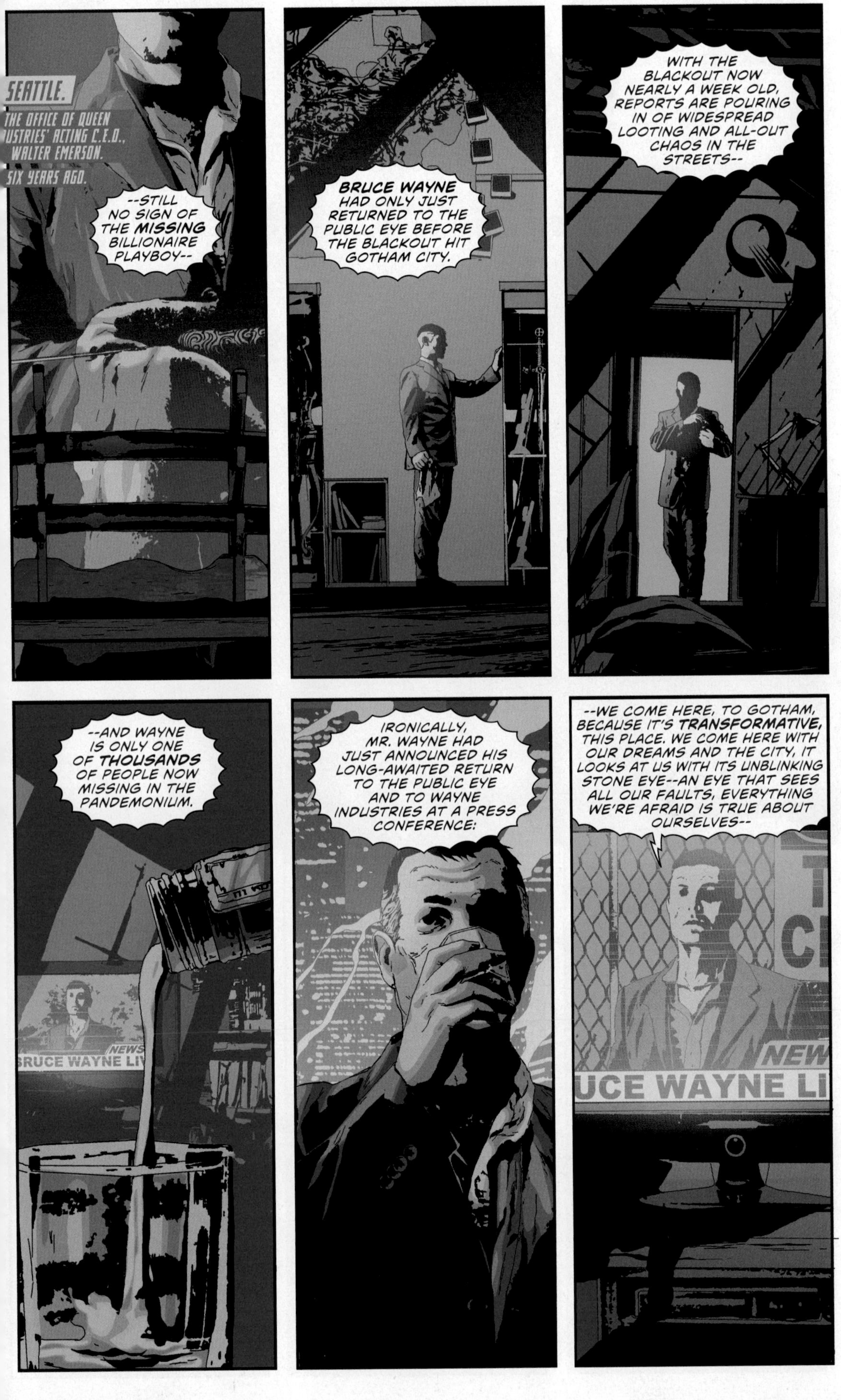
SEATTLE.
THE OFFICE OF QUEEN USTRIES' ACTING C.E.O., WALTER EMERSON.
SIX YEARS AGO.
--STILL NO SIGN OF THE MISSING BILLIONAIRE PLAYBOY--
BRUCE WAYNE HAD ONLY JUST RETURNED TO THE PUBLIC EYE BEFORE THE BLACKOUT HIT GOTHAM CITY.
WITH THE BLACKOUT NOW NEARLY A WEEK OLD, REPORTS ARE POURING IN OF WIDESPREAD LOOTING AND ALL-OUT CHAOS IN THE STREETS--
--AND WAYNE IS ONLY ONE OF THOUSANDS OF PEOPLE NOW MISSING IN THE PANDEMONIUM.
NEWS
BRUCE WAYNE LI
IRONICALLY, MR. WAYNE HAD JUST ANNOUNCED HIS LONG-AWAITED RETURN TO THE PUBLIC EYE AND TO WAYNE INDUSTRIES AT A PRESS CONFERENCE:
--WE COME HERE, TO GOTHAM, BECAUSE IT'S TRANSFORMATIVE, THIS PLACE. WE COME HERE WITH OUR DREAMS AND THE CITY, IT LOOKS AT US WITH ITS UNBLINKING STONE EYE--AN EYE THAT SEES ALL OUR FAULTS, EVERYTHING WE'RE AFRAID IS TRUE ABOUT OURSELVES--
NEWS
UCE WAYNE LI

--AND IT SAYS, "TRY. I DARE YOU."

I NEVER LIKED THAT GUY. ALWAYS STEALING MY HEADLINES.

AHH!

SIX YEARS AGO THE LEGEND OF BATMAN EMERGED AMIDST THE GREATEST CATASTROPHE GOTHAM HAD EVER ENDURED. A MANIAC CALLING HIMSELF THE RIDDLER HAS SHUT DOWN ALL ELECTRIC POWER MERE DAYS BEFORE A TERRIFYING SUPERSTORM. BUT THE DARK KNIGHT ISN'T THE ONLY HERO TO SURFACE DURING THIS MOMENT IN TIME KNOWN ONLY AS THE ZERO YEAR. OLIVER QUEEN, LONG THOUGHT DEAD, RETURNED HOME TO SEATTLE AND, SOON AFTER, GREEN ARROW WAS BORN...

DC COMICS PRESENTS GREEN ARROW A ZERO YEAR ADVENTURE:

the PRODIGAL

...O-OLIVER?

IT'S ME, EMERSON.

I'M BACK.

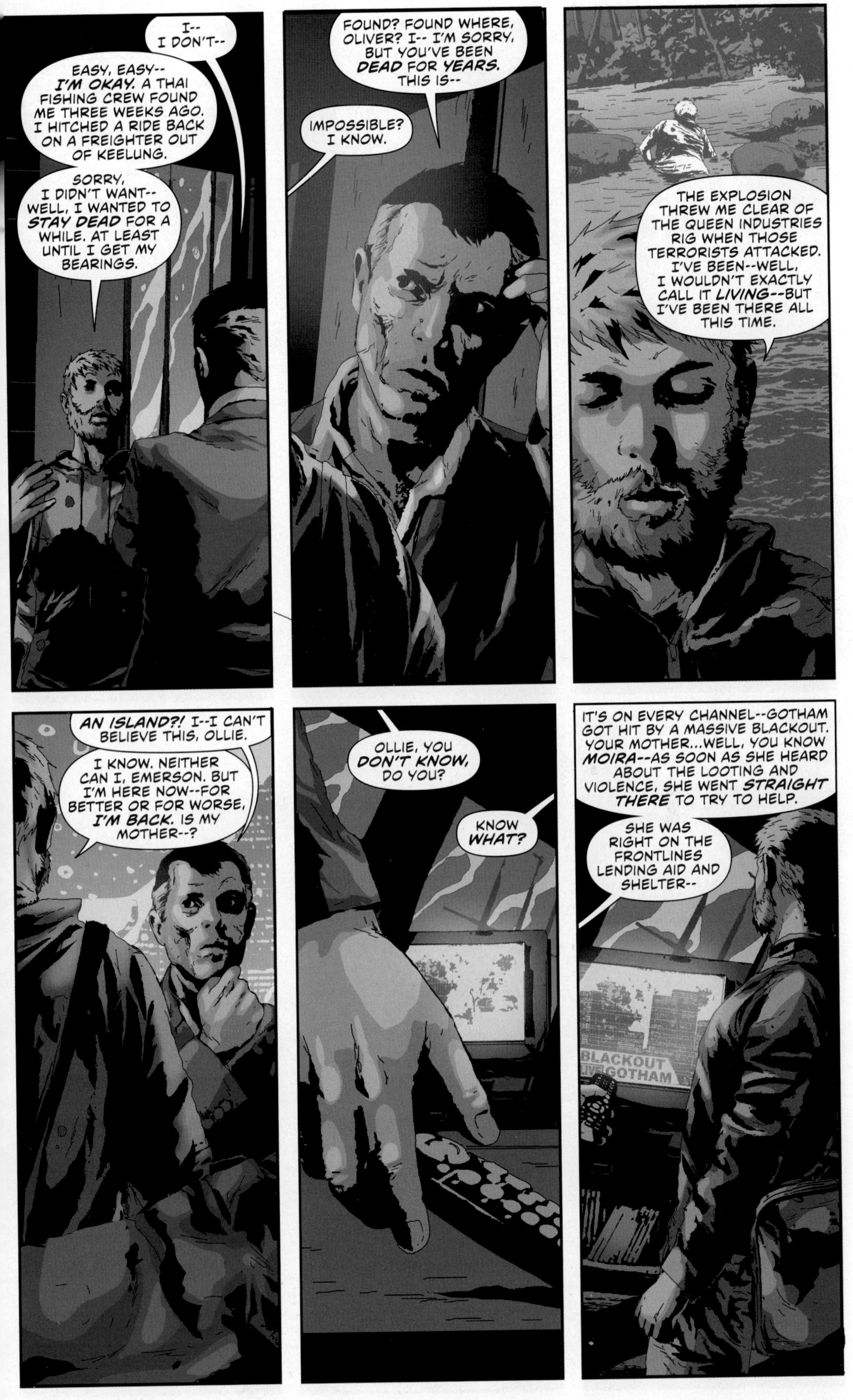
I--
I DON'T--
EASY, EASY-- I'M OKAY. A THAI FISHING CREW FOUND ME THREE WEEKS AGO. I HITCHED A RIDE BACK ON A FREIGHTER OUT OF KEELUNG.
SORRY, I DIDN'T WANT-- WELL, I WANTED TO STAY DEAD FOR A WHILE. AT LEAST UNTIL I GET MY BEARINGS.
FOUND? FOUND WHERE, OLIVER? I-- I'M SORRY, BUT YOU'VE BEEN DEAD FOR YEARS. THIS IS--
IMPOSSIBLE? I KNOW.
THE EXPLOSION THREW ME CLEAR OF THE QUEEN INDUSTRIES RIG WHEN THOSE TERRORISTS ATTACKED. I'VE BEEN--WELL, I WOULDN'T EXACTLY CALL IT LIVING--BUT I'VE BEEN THERE ALL THIS TIME.
AN ISLAND?! I--I CAN'T BELIEVE THIS, OLLIE.
I KNOW. NEITHER CAN I, EMERSON. BUT I'M HERE NOW--FOR BETTER OR FOR WORSE, I'M BACK. IS MY MOTHER--?
OLLIE, YOU DON'T KNOW, DO YOU?
KNOW WHAT?
IT'S ON EVERY CHANNEL--GOTHAM GOT HIT BY A MASSIVE BLACKOUT. YOUR MOTHER...WELL, YOU KNOW MOIRA--AS SOON AS SHE HEARD ABOUT THE LOOTING AND VIOLENCE, SHE WENT STRAIGHT THERE TO TRY TO HELP.
SHE WAS RIGHT ON THE FRONTLINES LENDING AID AND SHELTER--
BLACKOUT
LIVE GOTHAM

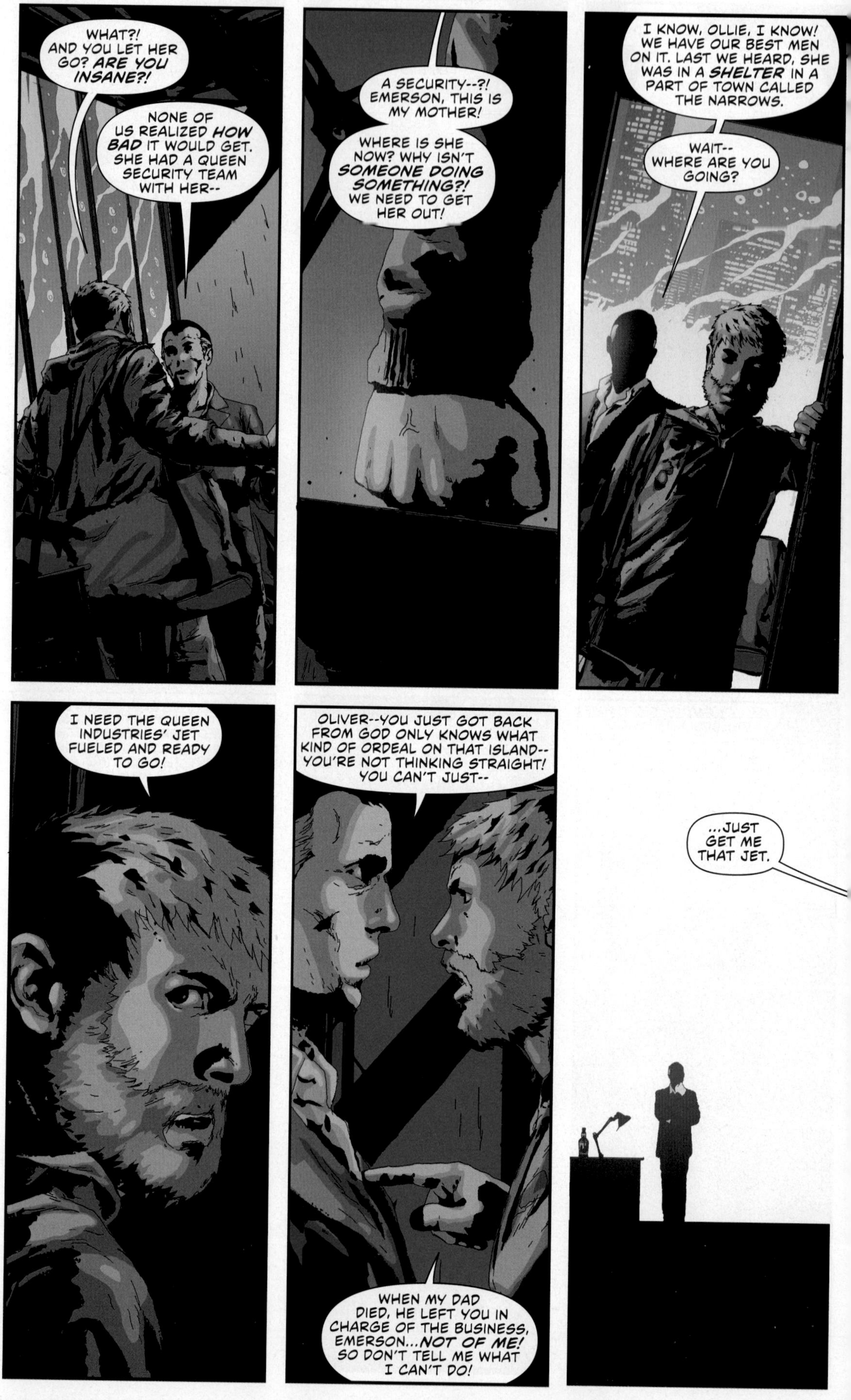
WHAT?! AND YOU LET HER GO? ARE YOU INSANE?!
NONE OF US REALIZED HOW BAD IT WOULD GET. SHE HAD A QUEEN SECURITY TEAM WITH HER--
A SECURITY--?! EMERSON, THIS IS MY MOTHER!
WHERE IS SHE NOW? WHY ISN'T SOMEONE DOING SOMETHING?! WE NEED TO GET HER OUT!
I KNOW, OLLIE, I KNOW! WE HAVE OUR BEST MEN ON IT. LAST WE HEARD, SHE WAS IN A SHELTER IN A PART OF TOWN CALLED THE NARROWS.
WAIT-- WHERE ARE YOU GOING?
I NEED THE QUEEN INDUSTRIES' JET FUELED AND READY TO GO!
OLIVER--YOU JUST GOT BACK FROM GOD ONLY KNOWS WHAT KIND OF ORDEAL ON THAT ISLAND--YOU'RE NOT THINKING STRAIGHT! YOU CAN'T JUST--
WHEN MY DAD DIED, HE LEFT YOU IN CHARGE OF THE BUSINESS, EMERSON...NOT OF ME! SO DON'T TELL ME WHAT I CAN'T DO!
...JUST GET ME THAT JET.

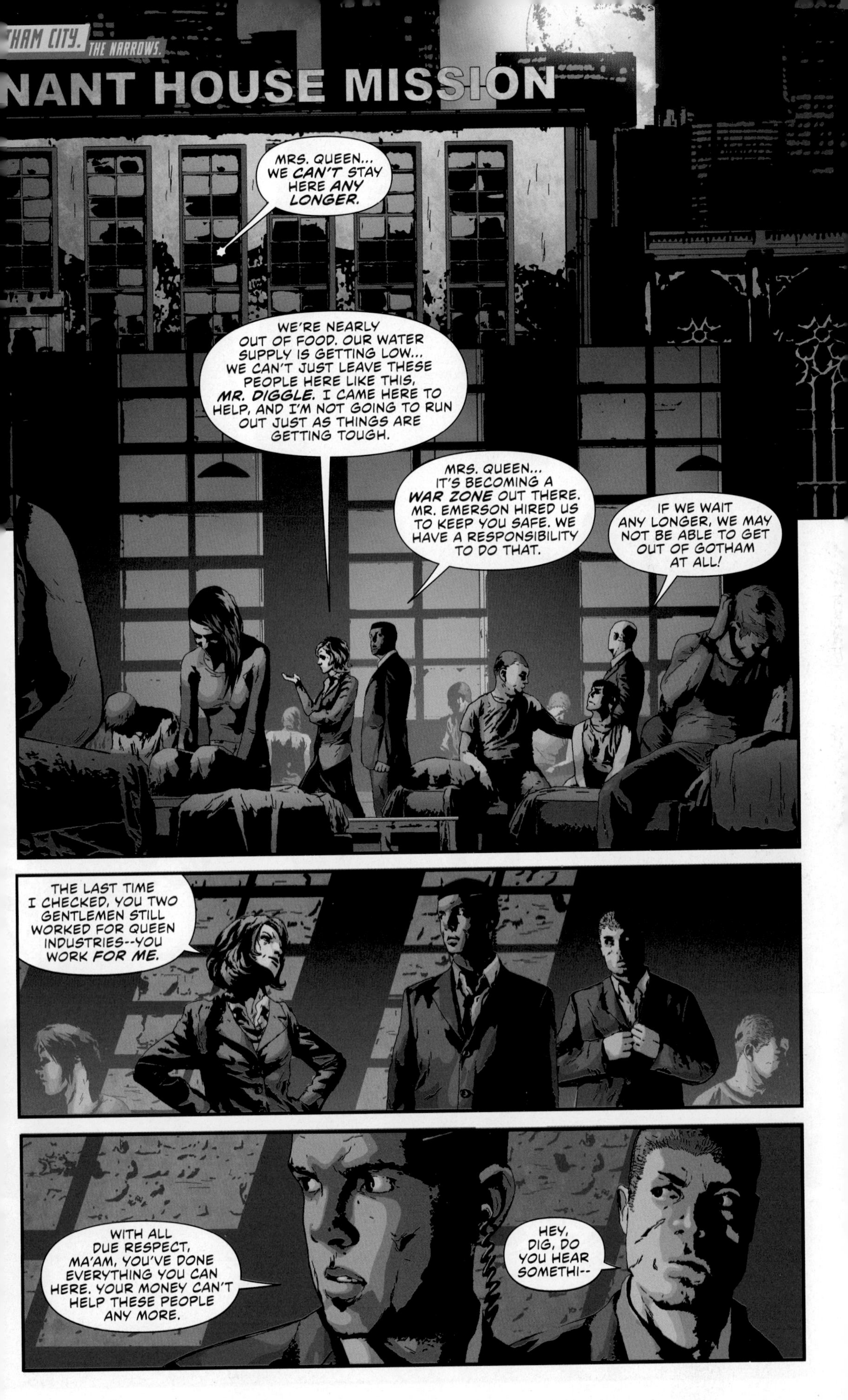
THAM CITY. THE NARROWS.
NANT HOUSE MISSION
MRS. QUEEN... WE CAN'T STAY HERE ANY LONGER.
WE'RE NEARLY OUT OF FOOD. OUR WATER SUPPLY IS GETTING LOW... WE CAN'T JUST LEAVE THESE PEOPLE HERE LIKE THIS, MR. DIGGLE. I CAME HERE TO HELP, AND I'M NOT GOING TO RUN OUT JUST AS THINGS ARE GETTING TOUGH.
MRS. QUEEN... IT'S BECOMING A WAR ZONE OUT THERE. MR. EMERSON HIRED US TO KEEP YOU SAFE. WE HAVE A RESPONSIBILITY TO DO THAT.
IF WE WAIT ANY LONGER, WE MAY NOT BE ABLE TO GET OUT OF GOTHAM AT ALL!
THE LAST TIME I CHECKED, YOU TWO GENTLEMEN STILL WORKED FOR QUEEN INDUSTRIES--YOU WORK FOR ME.
WITH ALL DUE RESPECT, MA'AM, YOU'VE DONE EVERYTHING YOU CAN HERE. YOUR MONEY CAN'T HELP THESE PEOPLE ANY MORE.
HEY, DIG, DO YOU HEAR SOMETHI--

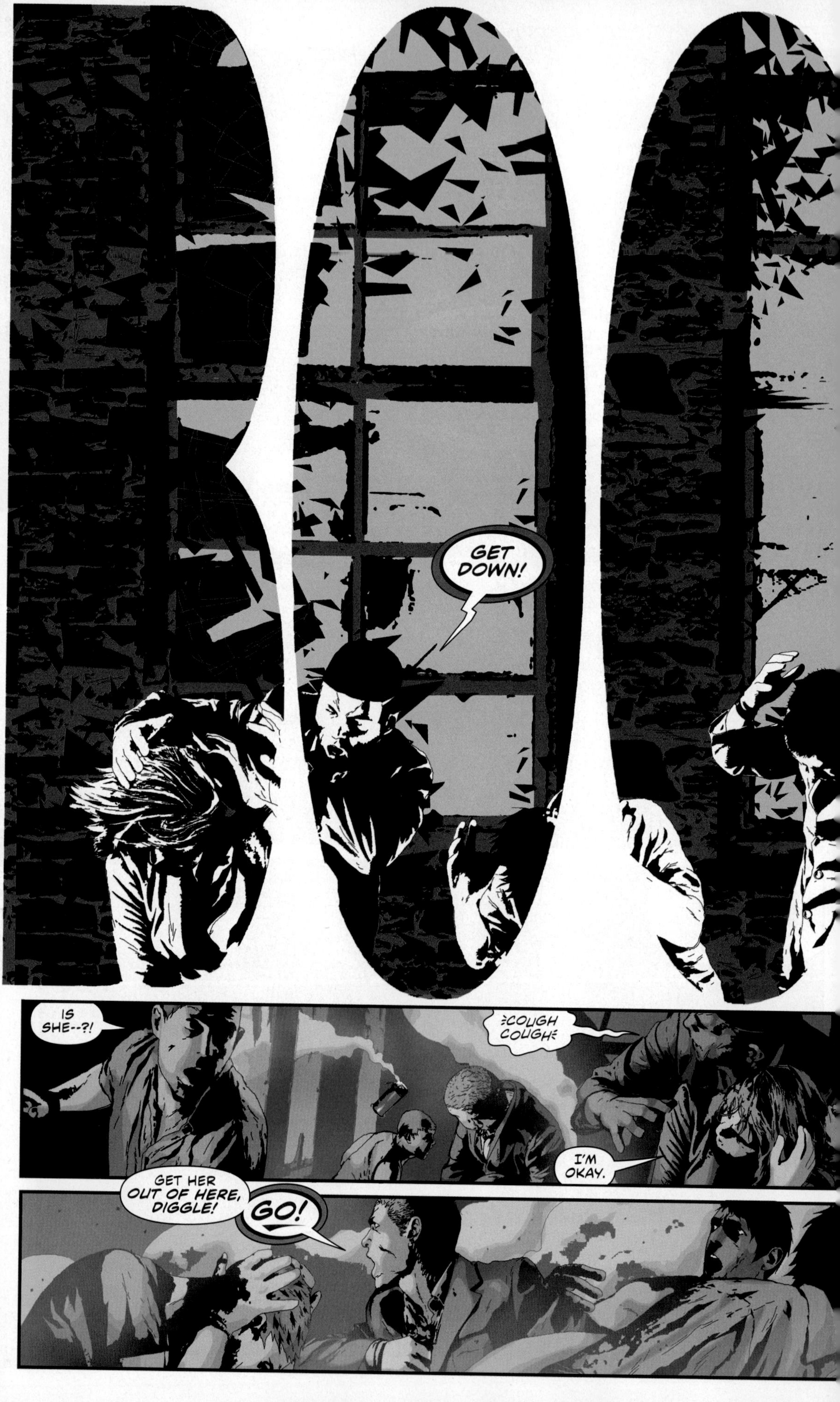
GET DOWN!
IS SHE--?!
≈COUGH COUGH≈
I'M OKAY.
GET HER OUT OF HERE, DIGGLE!
GO!

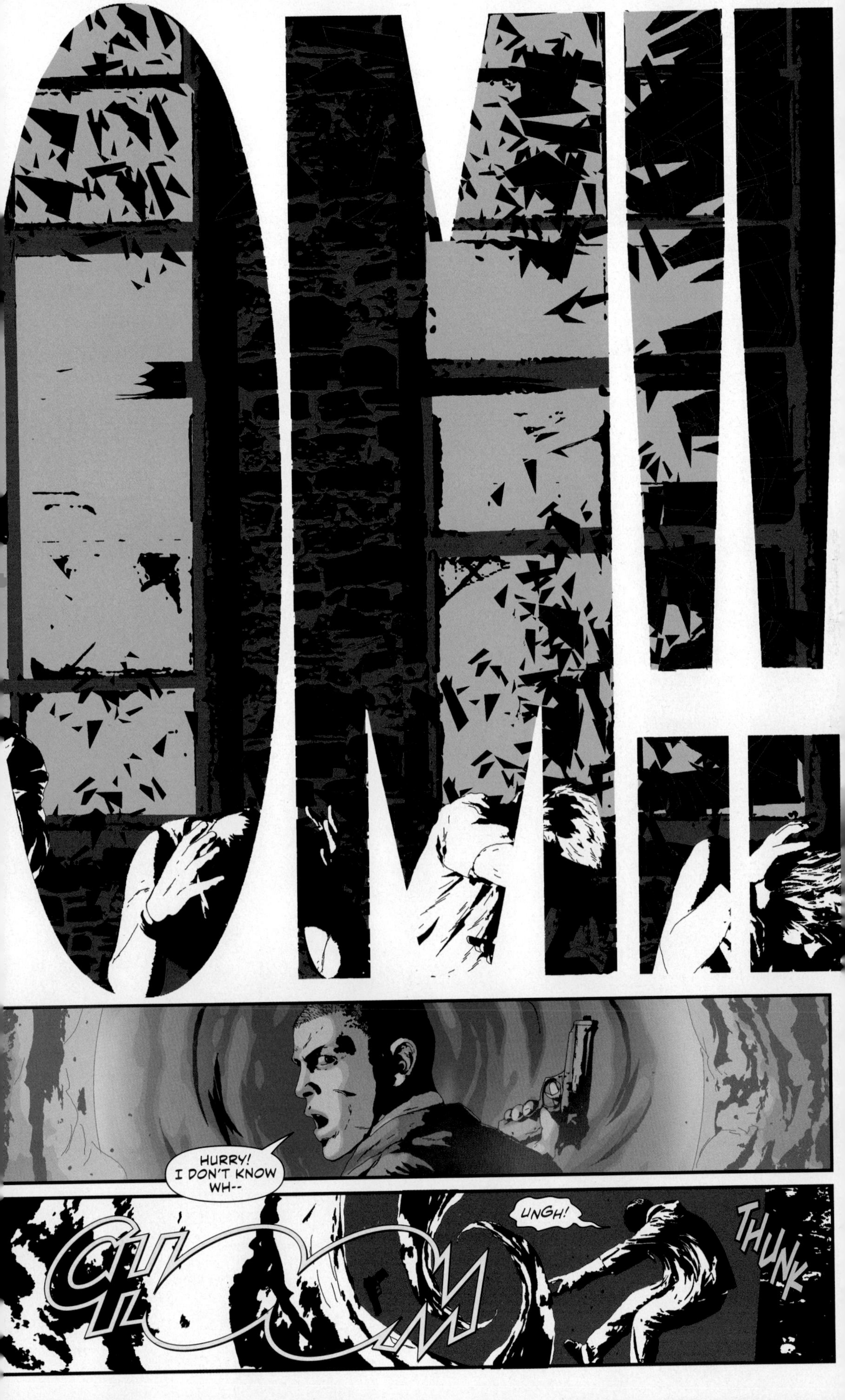
OM!!
HURRY! I DON'T KNOW WH--
CHUNK
UNGH!
THUNK

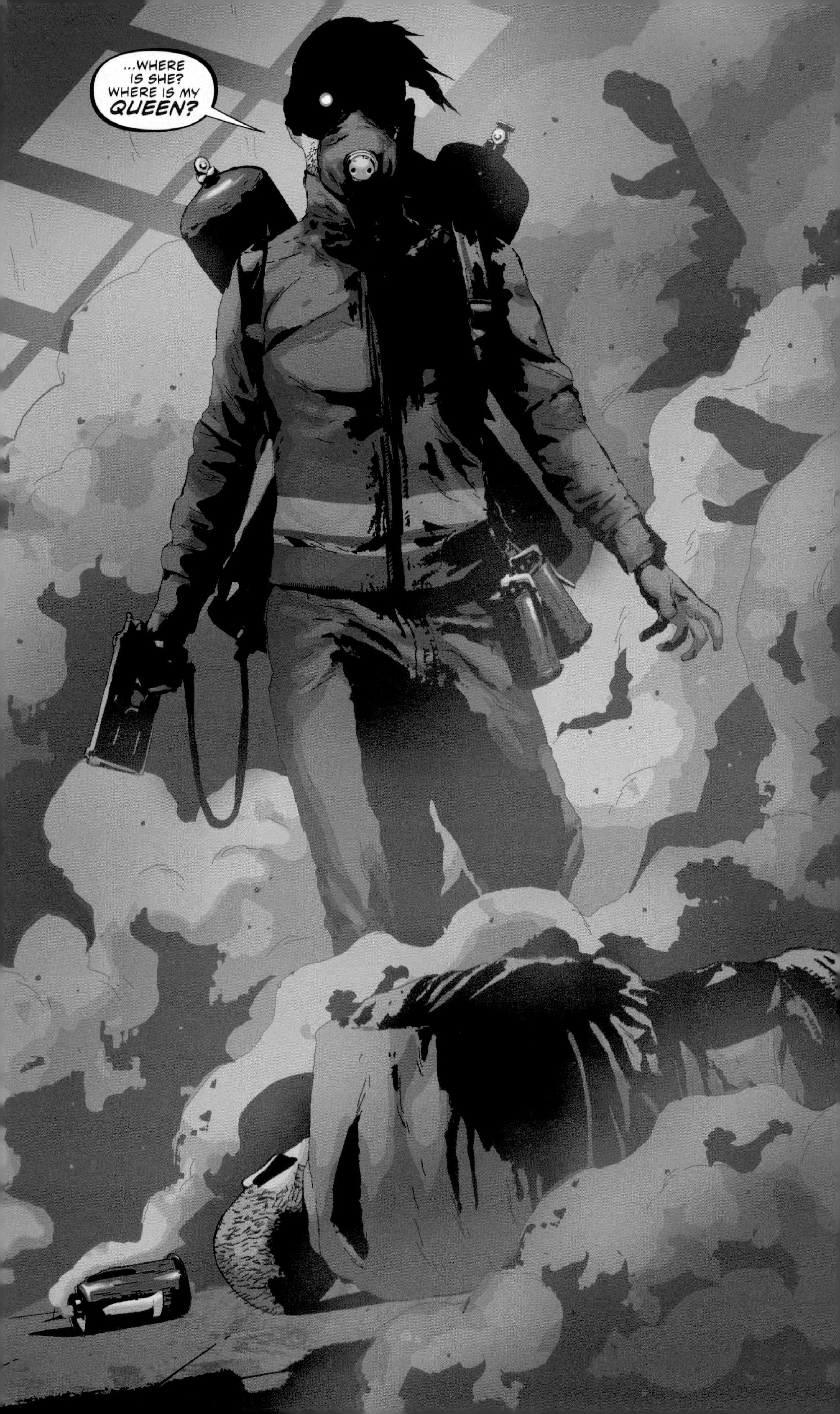
...WHERE IS SHE? WHERE IS MY QUEEN?

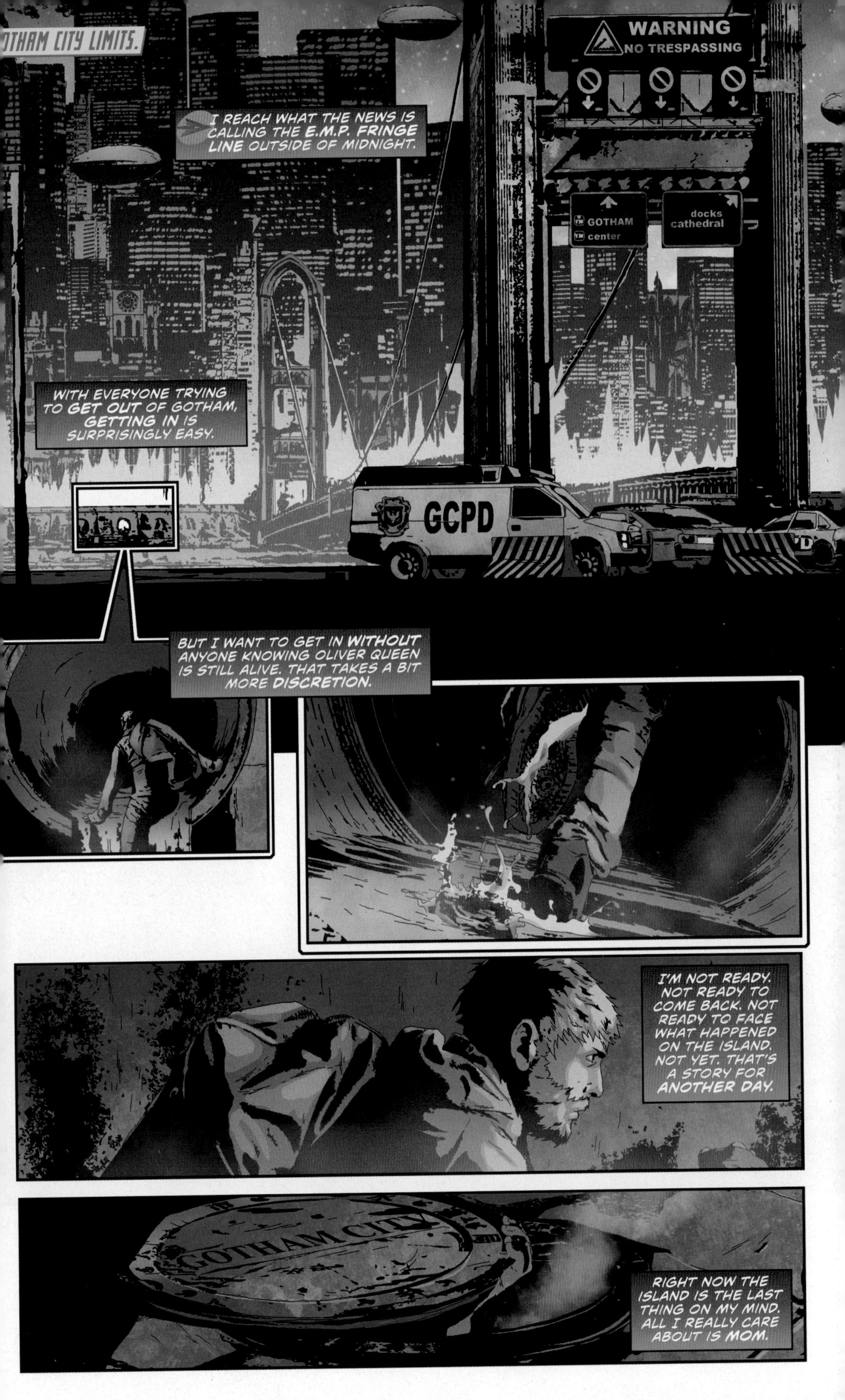
GOTHAM CITY LIMITS.
WARNING
NO TRESPASSING
I REACH WHAT THE NEWS IS CALLING THE E.M.P. FRINGE LINE OUTSIDE OF MIDNIGHT.
GOTHAM
center
docks
cathedral
WITH EVERYONE TRYING TO GET OUT OF GOTHAM, GETTING IN IS SURPRISINGLY EASY.
GCPD
BUT I WANT TO GET IN WITHOUT ANYONE KNOWING OLIVER QUEEN IS STILL ALIVE. THAT TAKES A BIT MORE DISCRETION.
I'M NOT READY. NOT READY TO COME BACK. NOT READY TO FACE WHAT HAPPENED ON THE ISLAND. NOT YET. THAT'S A STORY FOR ANOTHER DAY.
GOTHAM CITY
RIGHT NOW THE ISLAND IS THE LAST THING ON MY MIND. ALL I REALLY CARE ABOUT IS MOM.

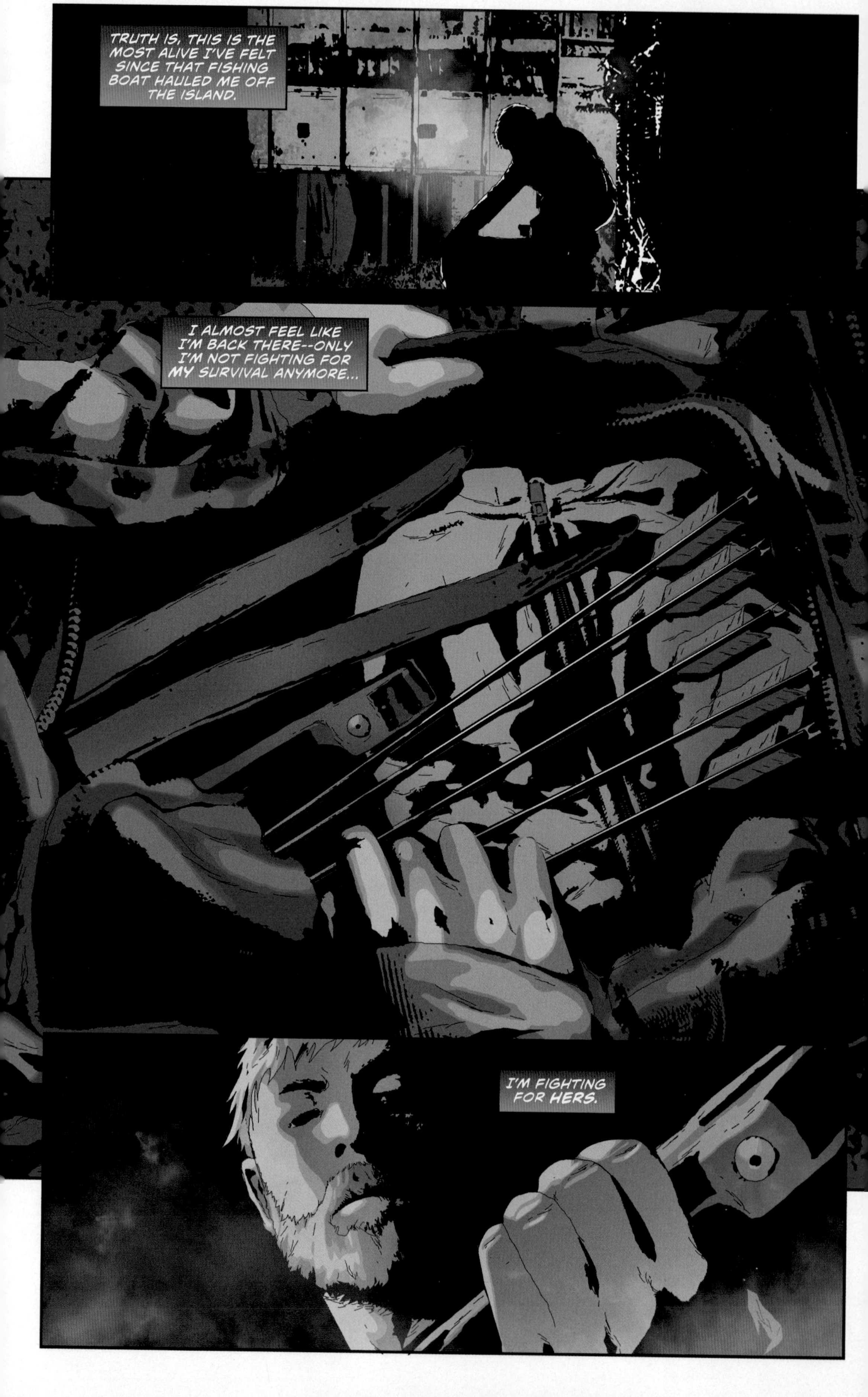
TRUTH IS, THIS IS THE MOST ALIVE I'VE FELT SINCE THAT FISHING BOAT HAULED ME OFF THE ISLAND.
I ALMOST FEEL LIKE I'M BACK THERE--ONLY I'M NOT FIGHTING FOR MY SURVIVAL ANYMORE...
I'M FIGHTING FOR HERS.

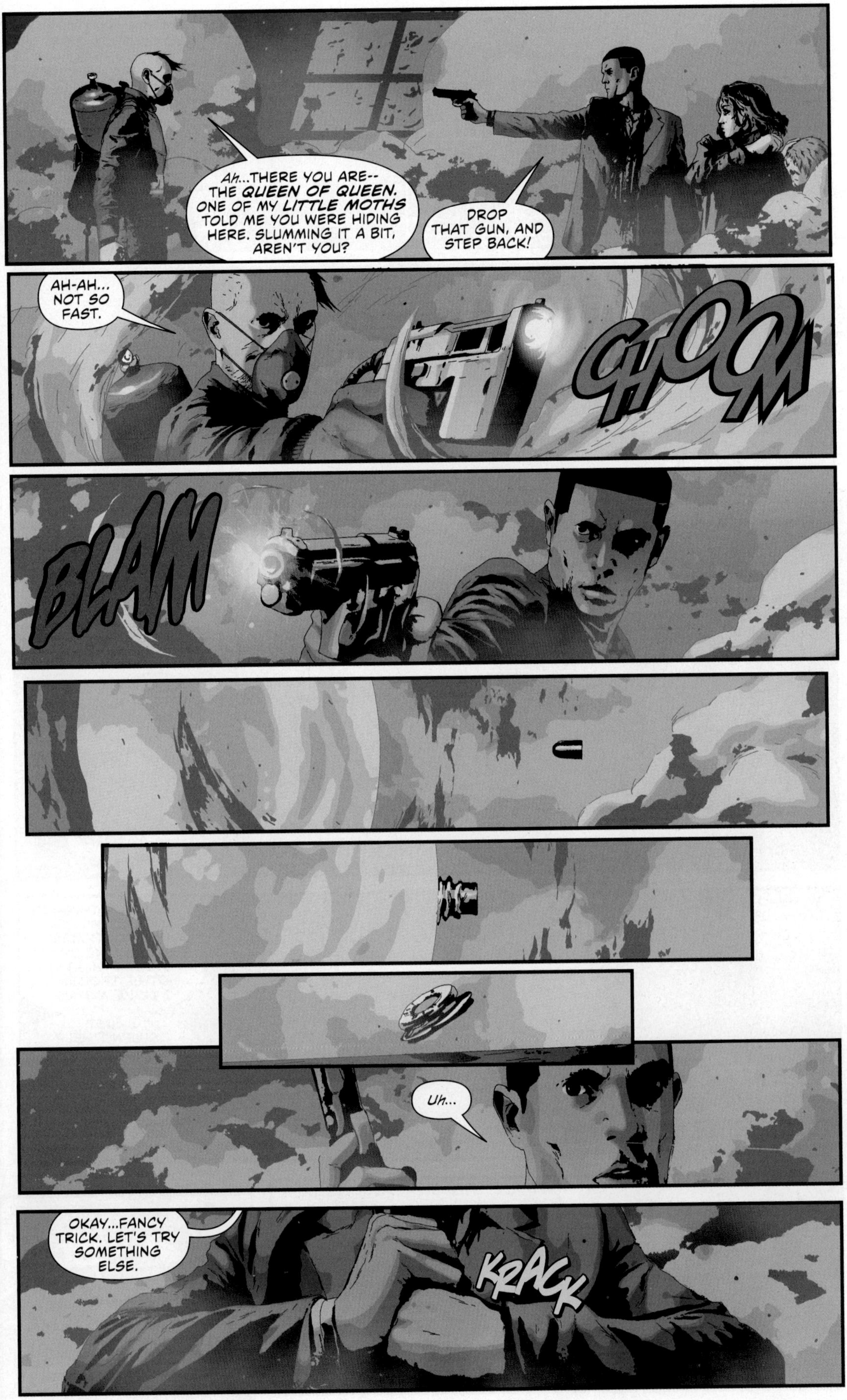
Ah...THERE YOU ARE-- THE QUEEN OF QUEEN. ONE OF MY LITTLE MOTHS TOLD ME YOU WERE HIDING HERE. SLUMMING IT A BIT, AREN'T YOU?
DROP THAT GUN, AND STEP BACK!
AH-AH... NOT SO FAST.
CHOOM
BLAM
Uh...
OKAY...FANCY TRICK. LET'S TRY SOMETHING ELSE.
KRACK

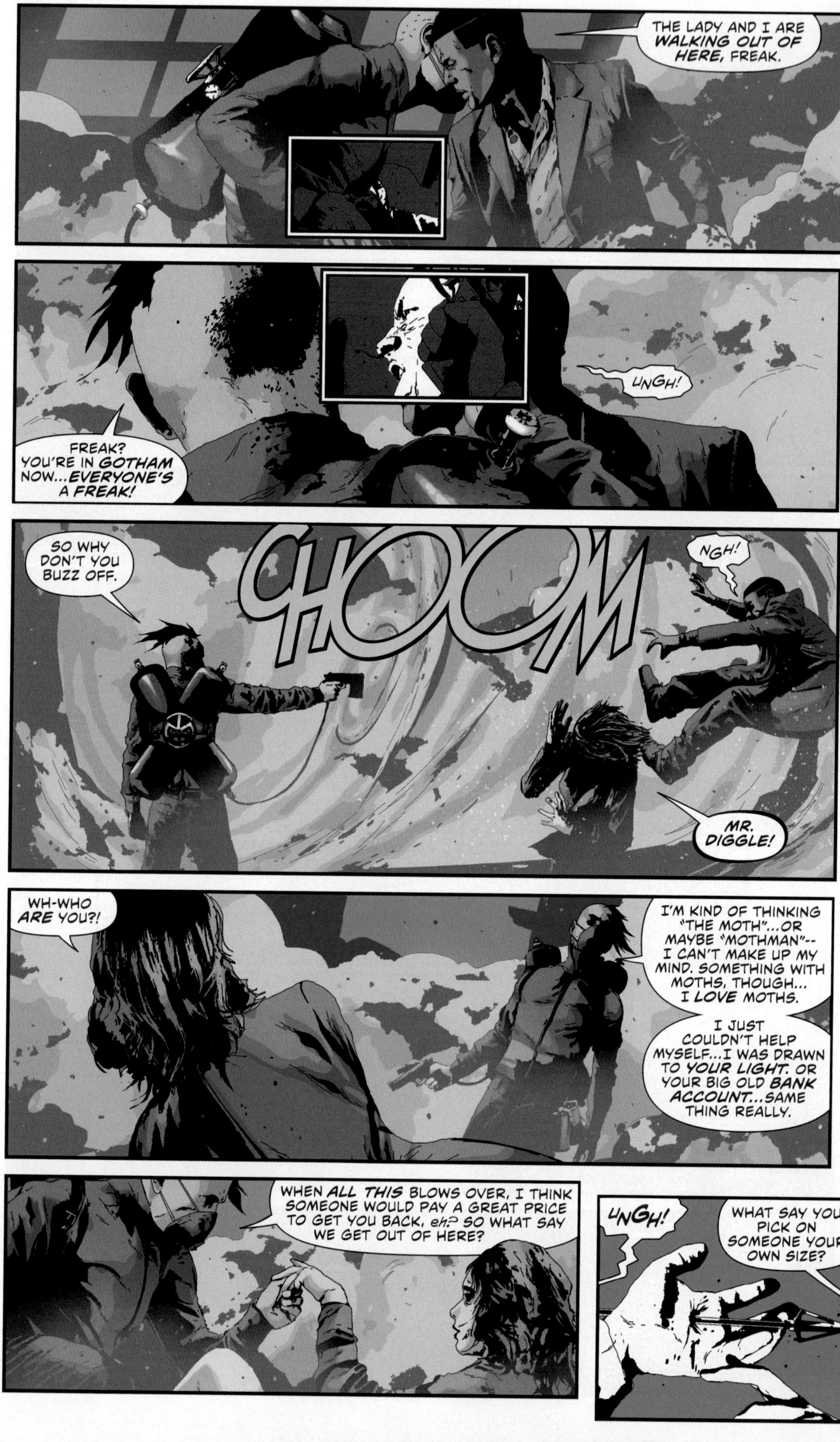

THE LADY AND I ARE WALKING OUT OF HERE, FREAK.
UNGH!
FREAK? YOU'RE IN GOTHAM NOW...EVERYONE'S A FREAK!
SO WHY DON'T YOU BUZZ OFF.
CHOOM
NGH!
MR. DIGGLE!
WH-WHO ARE YOU?!
I'M KIND OF THINKING "THE MOTH"...OR MAYBE "MOTHMAN"-- I CAN'T MAKE UP MY MIND. SOMETHING WITH MOTHS, THOUGH... I LOVE MOTHS.
I JUST COULDN'T HELP MYSELF...I WAS DRAWN TO YOUR LIGHT. OR YOUR BIG OLD BANK ACCOUNT...SAME THING REALLY.
WHEN ALL THIS BLOWS OVER, I THINK SOMEONE WOULD PAY A GREAT PRICE TO GET YOU BACK, eh? SO WHAT SAY WE GET OUT OF HERE?
UNGH!
WHAT SAY YOU PICK ON SOMEONE YOUR OWN SIZE?

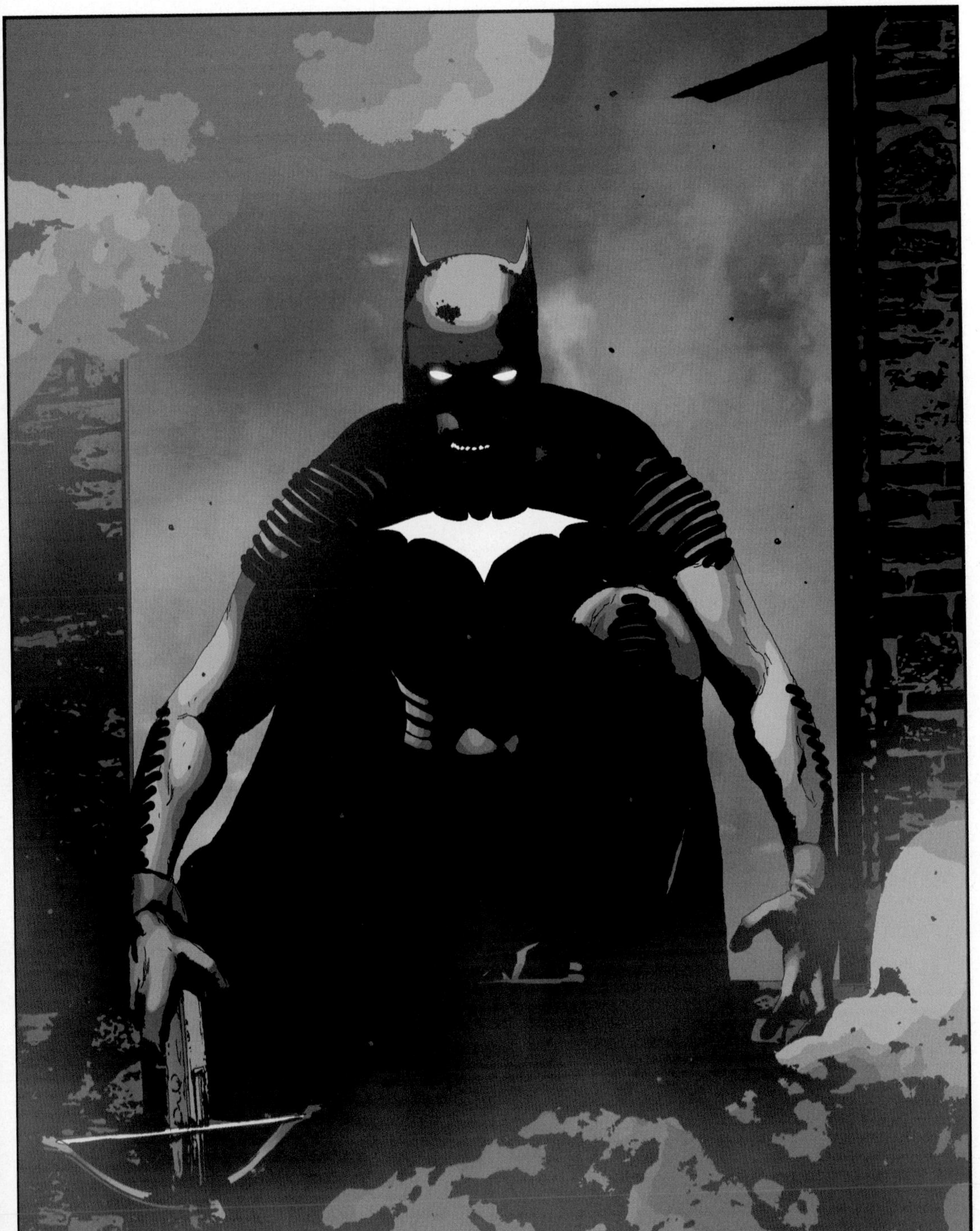
I HATE BUGS.
UNGH!

YOU!

THOCK

I WAS SO HOPING I'D RUN INTO YOU.

YOU'RE MY INSPIRATION, AFTER ALL!

WHIP

YOU'RE NOTHING LIKE ME.

WHAT, YOU WANT GOTHAM ALL TO YOURSELF? WHAT'S THE FUN IN THAT?

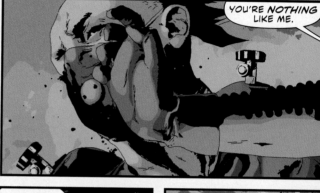

YOU NEED TO LEARN TO SHARE!

CHOOM

UNGH!

BET YOU WISH YOU HAD ONE OF THESE, eh? HIGHLY CONCENTRATED AIR BLASTS. TOYING WITH A FEW NAMES FOR IT...WHAT DO YOU THINK OF "THE STINGER"?

I KNOW, I KNOW...MOTHS DON'T STING.

NO... BUT I DO.

ARGHH!

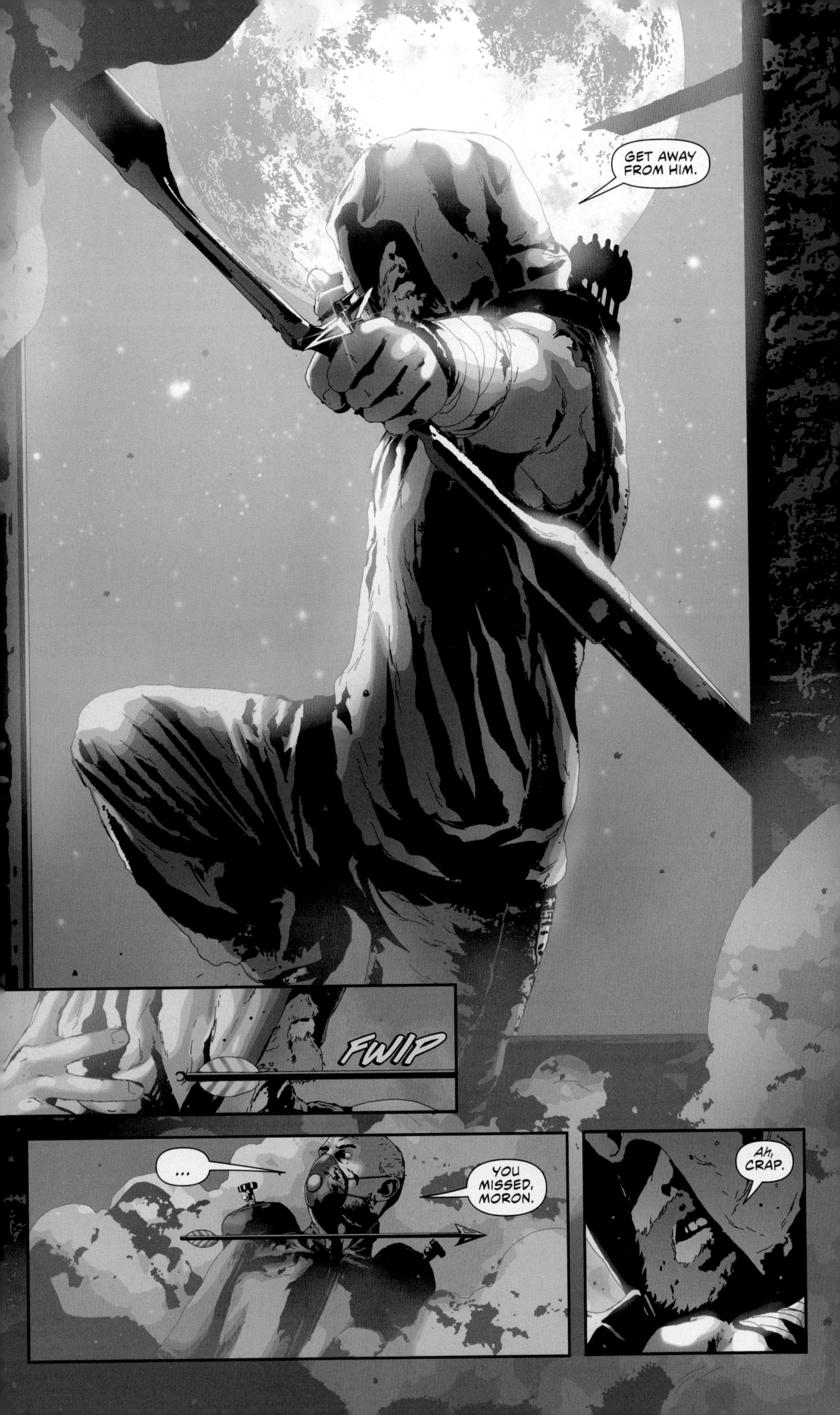
GET AWAY FROM HIM.
FWIP
...
YOU MISSED, MORON.
AH, CRAP.

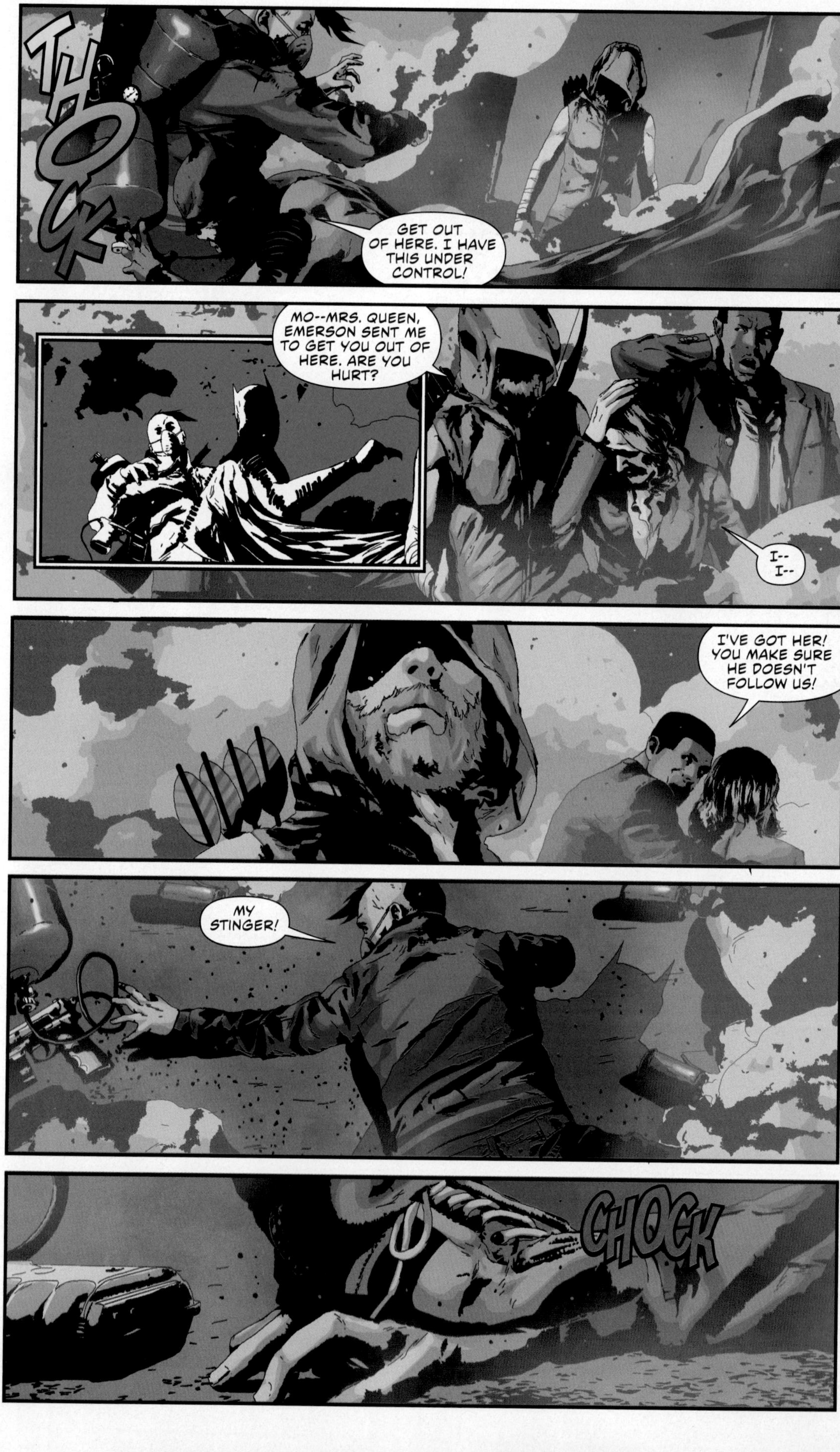
THOCK
GET OUT OF HERE. I HAVE THIS UNDER CONTROL!
MO--MRS. QUEEN, EMERSON SENT ME TO GET YOU OUT OF HERE. ARE YOU HURT?
I-- I--
I'VE GOT HER! YOU MAKE SURE HE DOESN'T FOLLOW US!
MY STINGER!
CHOCK

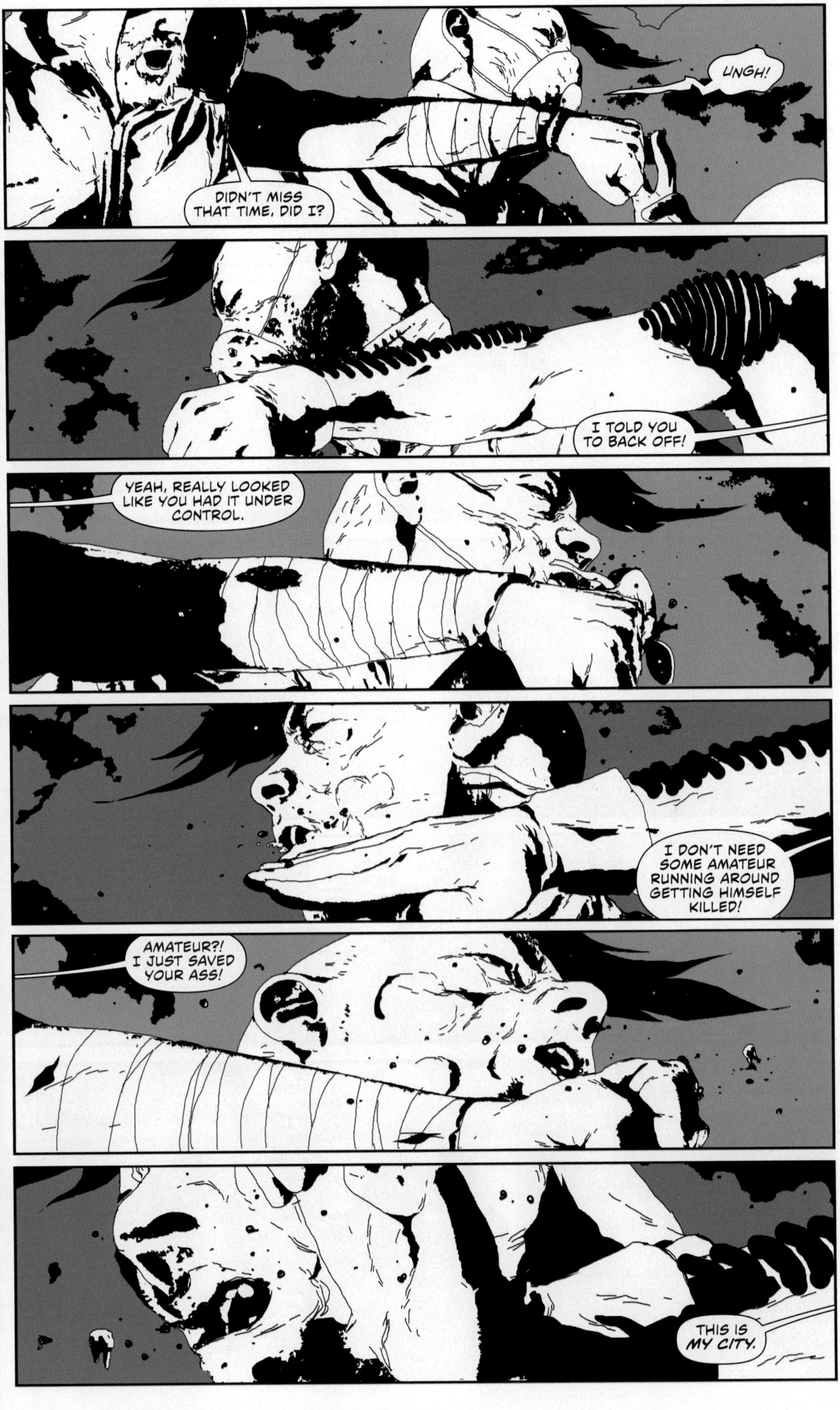
UNGH!
DIDN'T MISS THAT TIME, DID I?
I TOLD YOU TO BACK OFF!
YEAH, REALLY LOOKED LIKE YOU HAD IT UNDER CONTROL.
I DON'T NEED SOME AMATEUR RUNNING AROUND GETTING HIMSELF KILLED!
AMATEUR?! I JUST SAVED YOUR ASS!
THIS IS *MY CITY.*

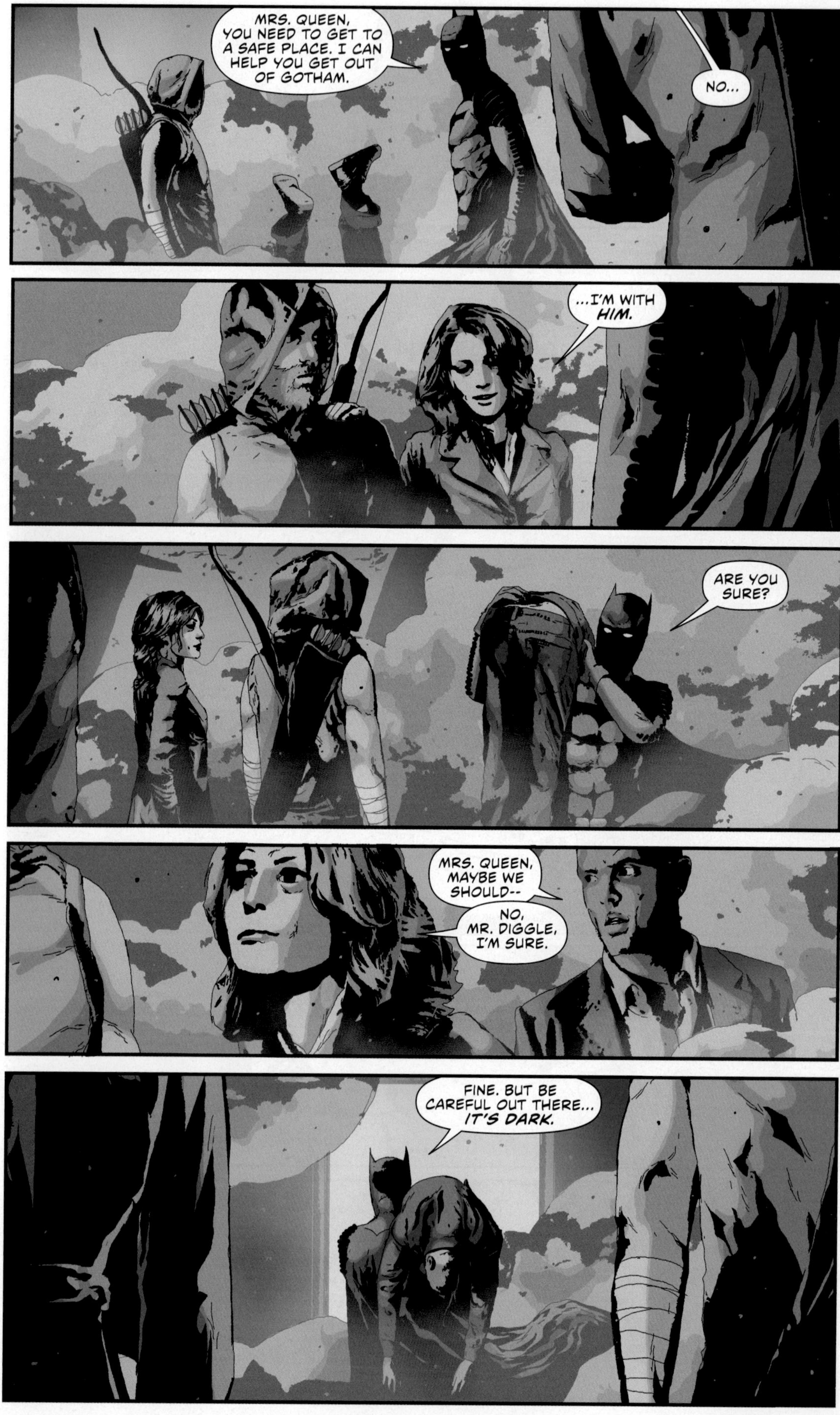
MRS. QUEEN, YOU NEED TO GET TO A SAFE PLACE. I CAN HELP YOU GET OUT OF GOTHAM.
NO...
...I'M WITH *HIM.*
ARE YOU SURE?
MRS. QUEEN, MAYBE WE SHOULD--
NO, MR. DIGGLE, I'M SURE.
FINE. BUT BE CAREFUL OUT THERE... *IT'S DARK.*

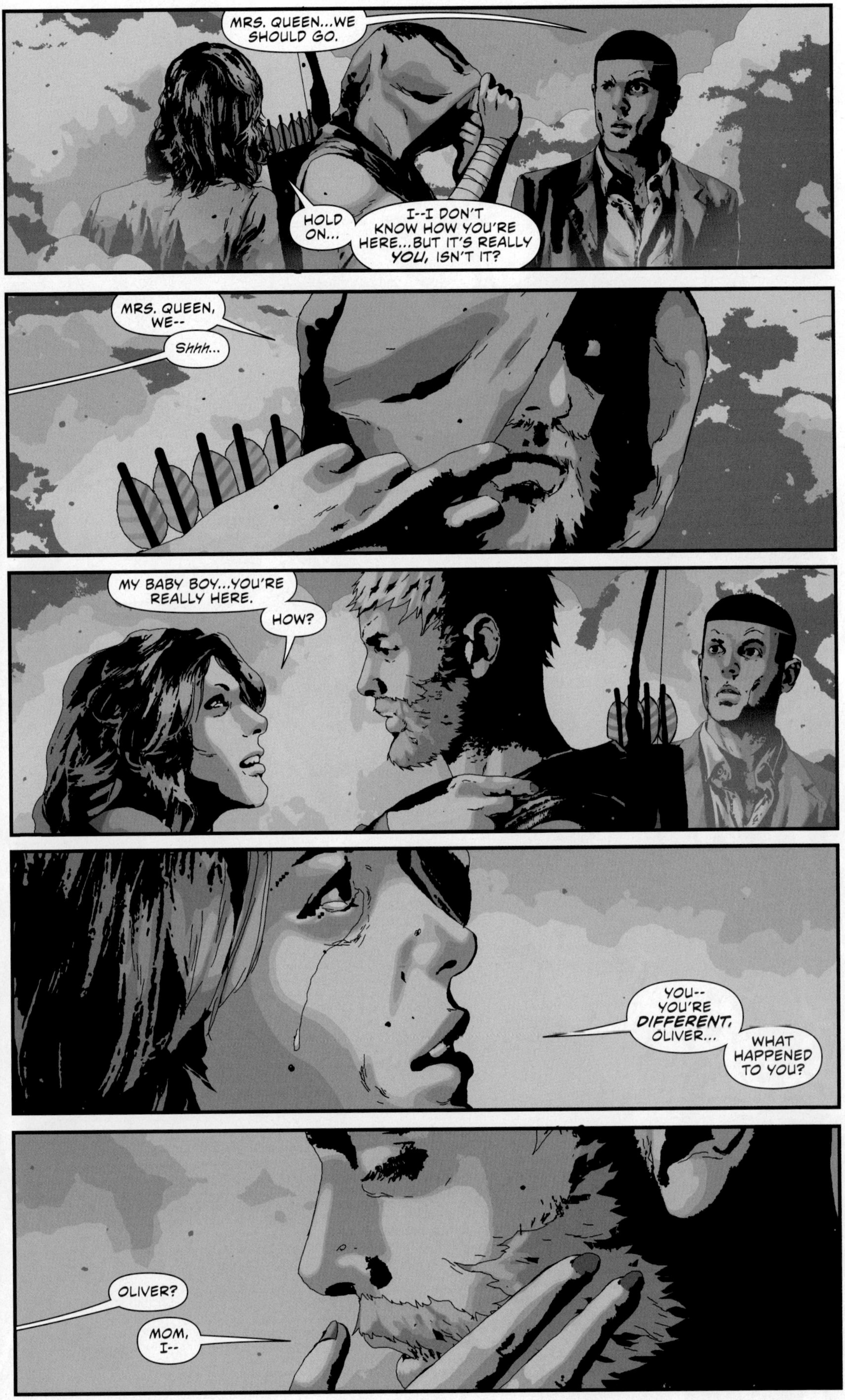

MRS. QUEEN...WE SHOULD GO.
HOLD ON...
I--I DON'T KNOW HOW YOU'RE HERE...BUT IT'S REALLY *YOU*, ISN'T IT?
MRS. QUEEN, WE--
Shhh...
MY BABY BOY...YOU'RE REALLY HERE.
HOW?
YOU--YOU'RE **DIFFERENT**, OLIVER...
WHAT HAPPENED TO YOU?
OLIVER?
MOM, I--

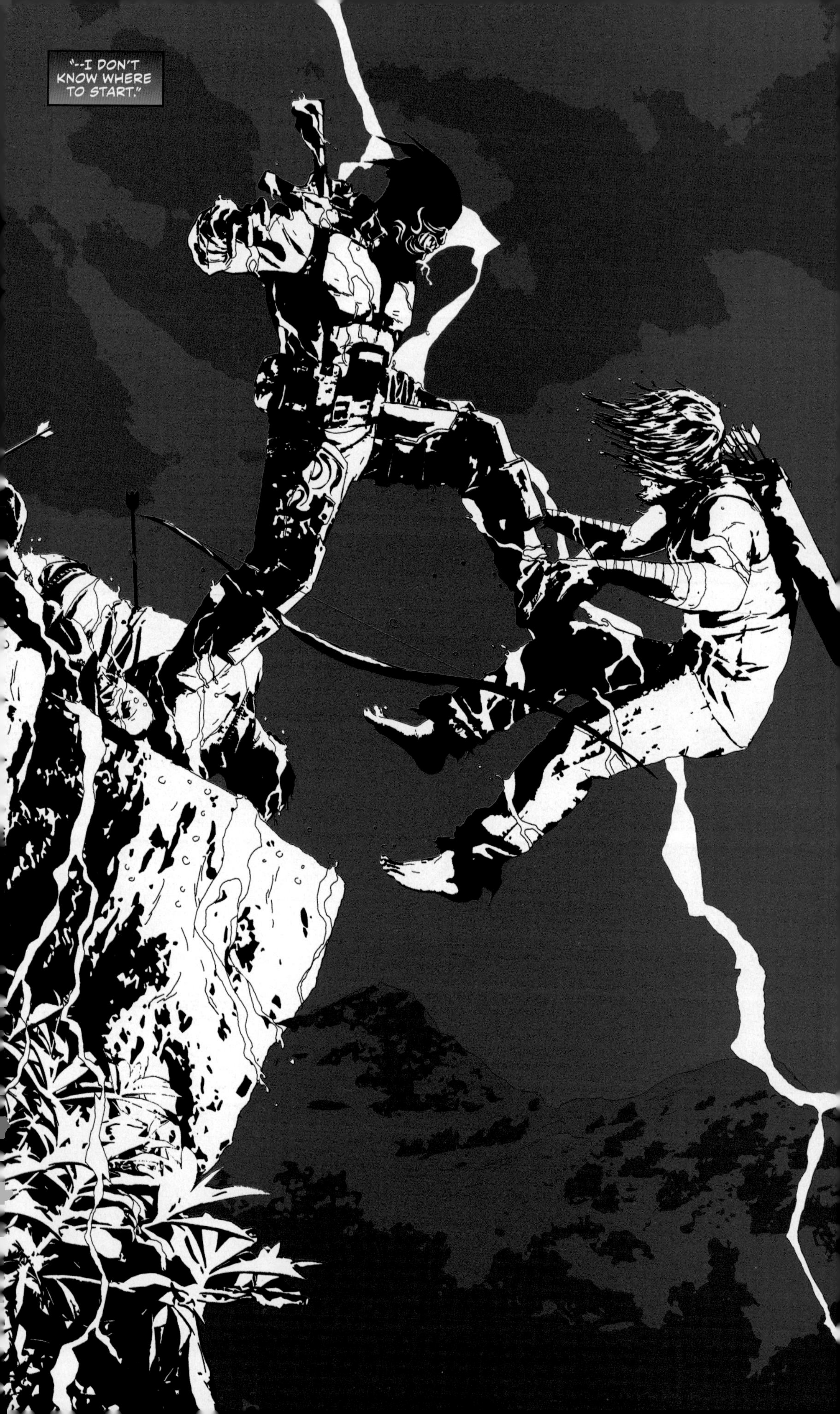
"--I DON'T KNOW WHERE TO START."

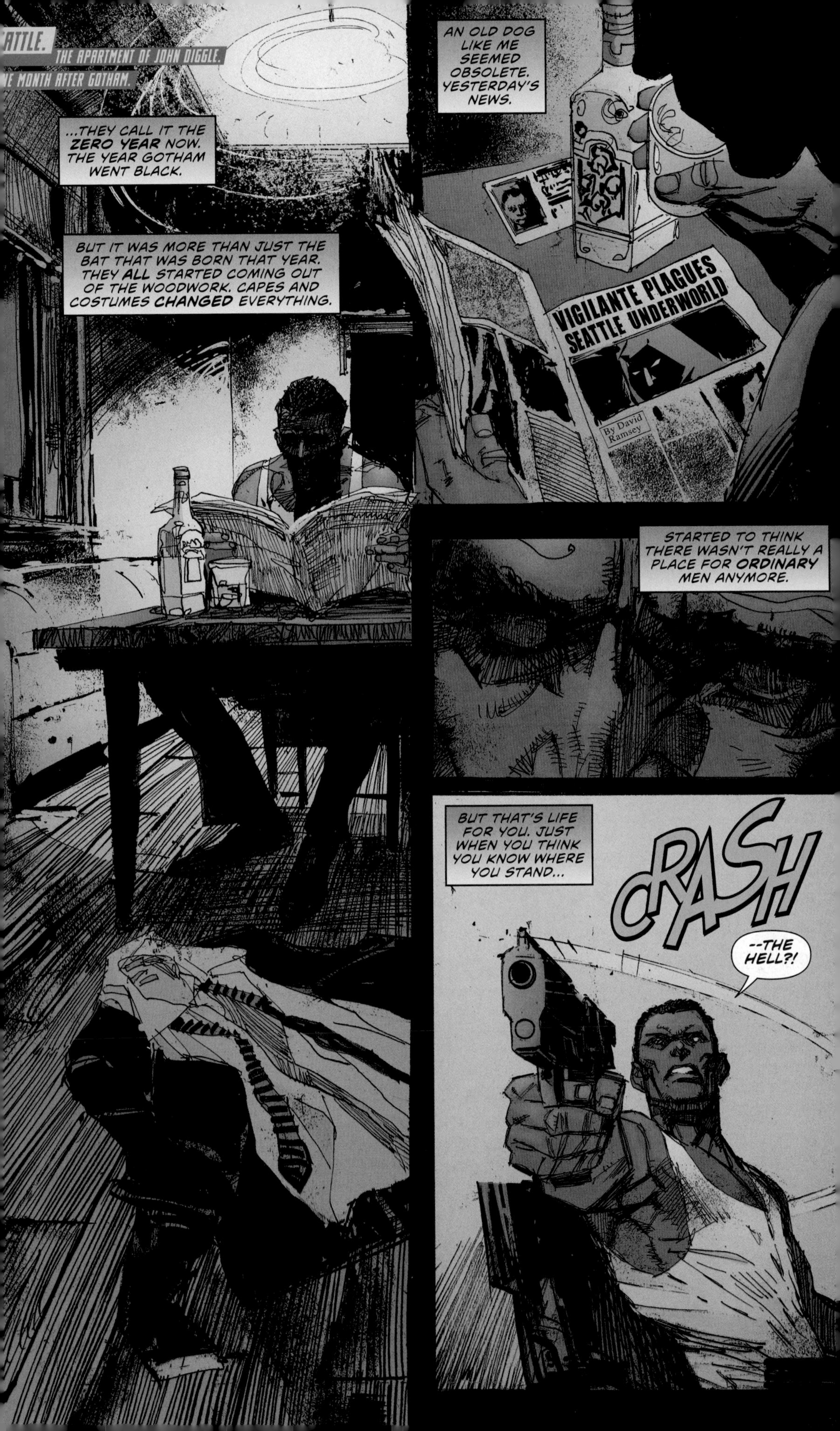
ATTLE.
THE APARTMENT OF JOHN DIGGLE.
E MONTH AFTER GOTHAM.
...THEY CALL IT THE ZERO YEAR NOW. THE YEAR GOTHAM WENT BLACK.
BUT IT WAS MORE THAN JUST THE BAT THAT WAS BORN THAT YEAR. THEY ALL STARTED COMING OUT OF THE WOODWORK. CAPES AND COSTUMES CHANGED EVERYTHING.
AN OLD DOG LIKE ME SEEMED OBSOLETE. YESTERDAY'S NEWS.
VIGILANTE PLAGUES SEATTLE UNDERWORLD
By David Ramsey
STARTED TO THINK THERE WASN'T REALLY A PLACE FOR ORDINARY MEN ANYMORE.
BUT THAT'S LIFE FOR YOU. JUST WHEN YOU THINK YOU KNOW WHERE YOU STAND...
CRASH
--THE HELL?!

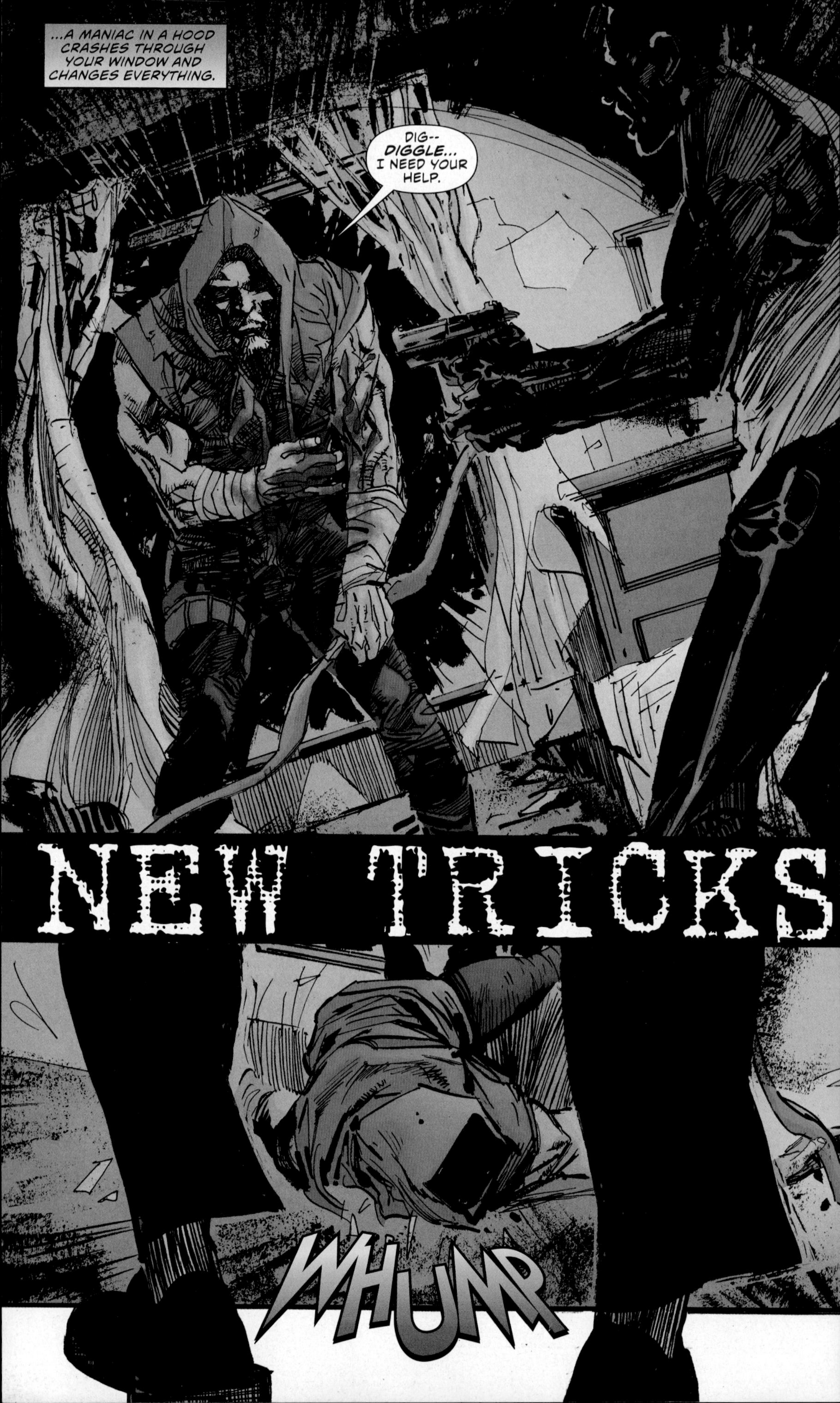

...A MANIAC IN A HOOD CRASHES THROUGH YOUR WINDOW AND CHANGES EVERYTHING.
DIG-- DIGGLE... I NEED YOUR HELP.
NEW TRICKS
WHUMP

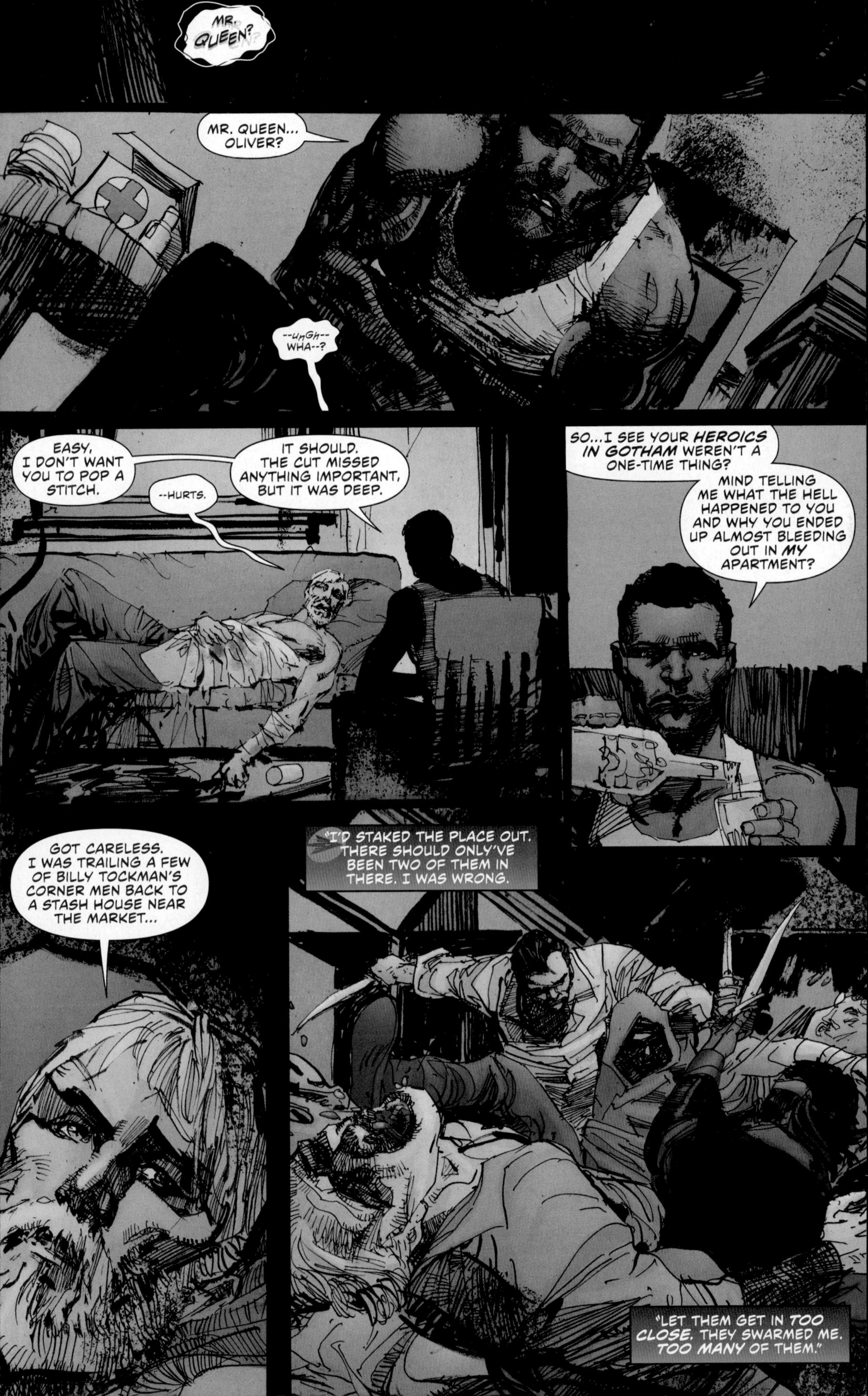
MR. QUEEN?
MR. QUEEN... OLIVER?
--UNGH-- WHA--?
EASY, I DON'T WANT YOU TO POP A STITCH.
--HURTS.
IT SHOULD. THE CUT MISSED ANYTHING IMPORTANT, BUT IT WAS DEEP.
SO...I SEE YOUR HEROICS IN GOTHAM WEREN'T A ONE-TIME THING?
MIND TELLING ME WHAT THE HELL HAPPENED TO YOU AND WHY YOU ENDED UP ALMOST BLEEDING OUT IN MY APARTMENT?
GOT CARELESS. I WAS TRAILING A FEW OF BILLY TOCKMAN'S CORNER MEN BACK TO A STASH HOUSE NEAR THE MARKET...
"I'D STAKED THE PLACE OUT. THERE SHOULD ONLY'VE BEEN TWO OF THEM IN THERE. I WAS WRONG.
"LET THEM GET IN TOO CLOSE. THEY SWARMED ME. TOO MANY OF THEM."

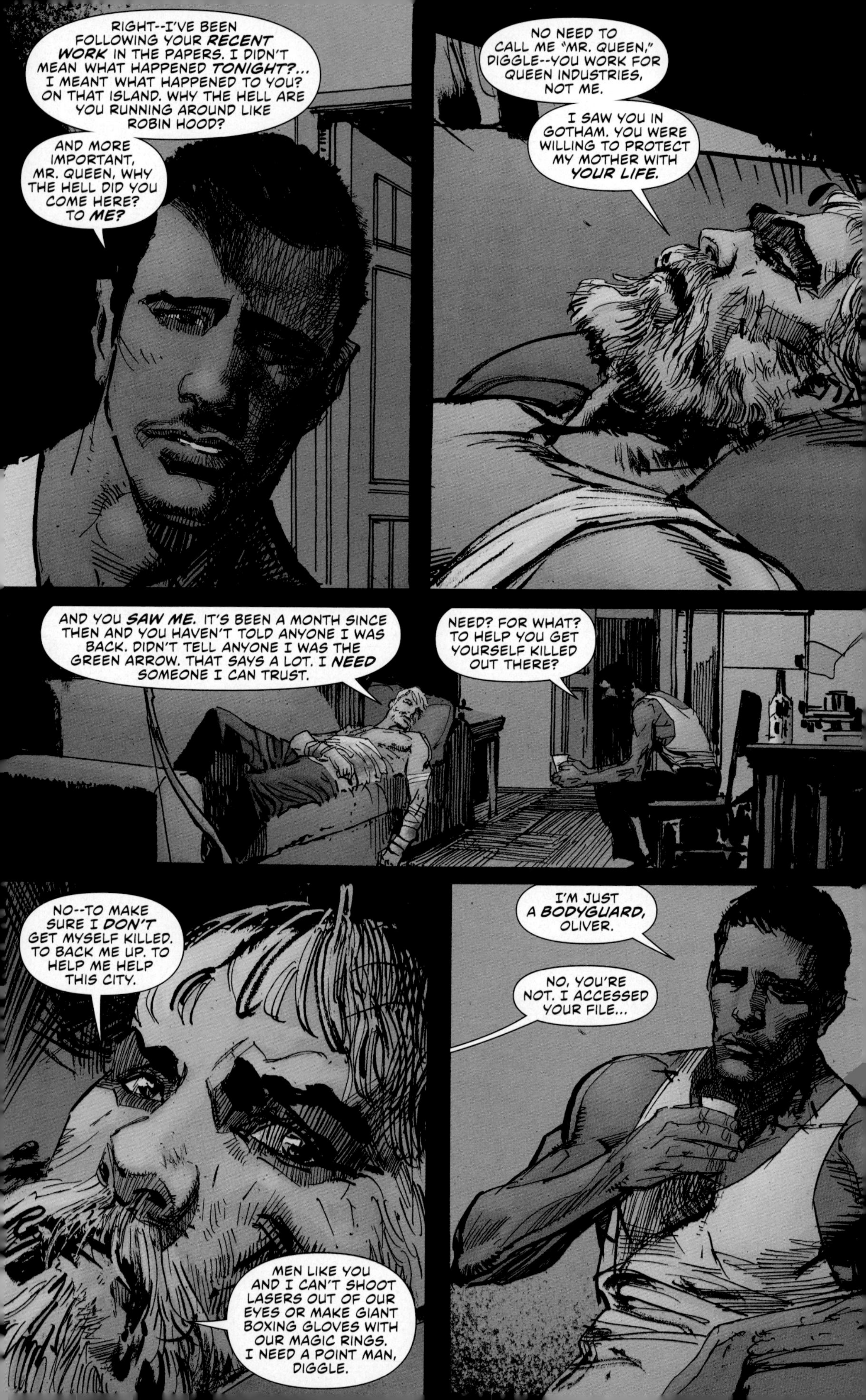
RIGHT--I'VE BEEN FOLLOWING YOUR RECENT WORK IN THE PAPERS. I DIDN'T MEAN WHAT HAPPENED TONIGHT?... I MEANT WHAT HAPPENED TO YOU? ON THAT ISLAND. WHY THE HELL ARE YOU RUNNING AROUND LIKE ROBIN HOOD?
AND MORE IMPORTANT, MR. QUEEN, WHY THE HELL DID YOU COME HERE? TO ME?
NO NEED TO CALL ME "MR. QUEEN," DIGGLE--YOU WORK FOR QUEEN INDUSTRIES, NOT ME.
I SAW YOU IN GOTHAM. YOU WERE WILLING TO PROTECT MY MOTHER WITH YOUR LIFE.
AND YOU SAW ME. IT'S BEEN A MONTH SINCE THEN AND YOU HAVEN'T TOLD ANYONE I WAS BACK. DIDN'T TELL ANYONE I WAS THE GREEN ARROW. THAT SAYS A LOT. I NEED SOMEONE I CAN TRUST.
NEED? FOR WHAT? TO HELP YOU GET YOURSELF KILLED OUT THERE?
NO--TO MAKE SURE I DON'T GET MYSELF KILLED. TO BACK ME UP. TO HELP ME HELP THIS CITY.
MEN LIKE YOU AND I CAN'T SHOOT LASERS OUT OF OUR EYES OR MAKE GIANT BOXING GLOVES WITH OUR MAGIC RINGS. I NEED A POINT MAN, DIGGLE.
I'M JUST A BODYGUARD, OLIVER.
NO, YOU'RE NOT. I ACCESSED YOUR FILE...

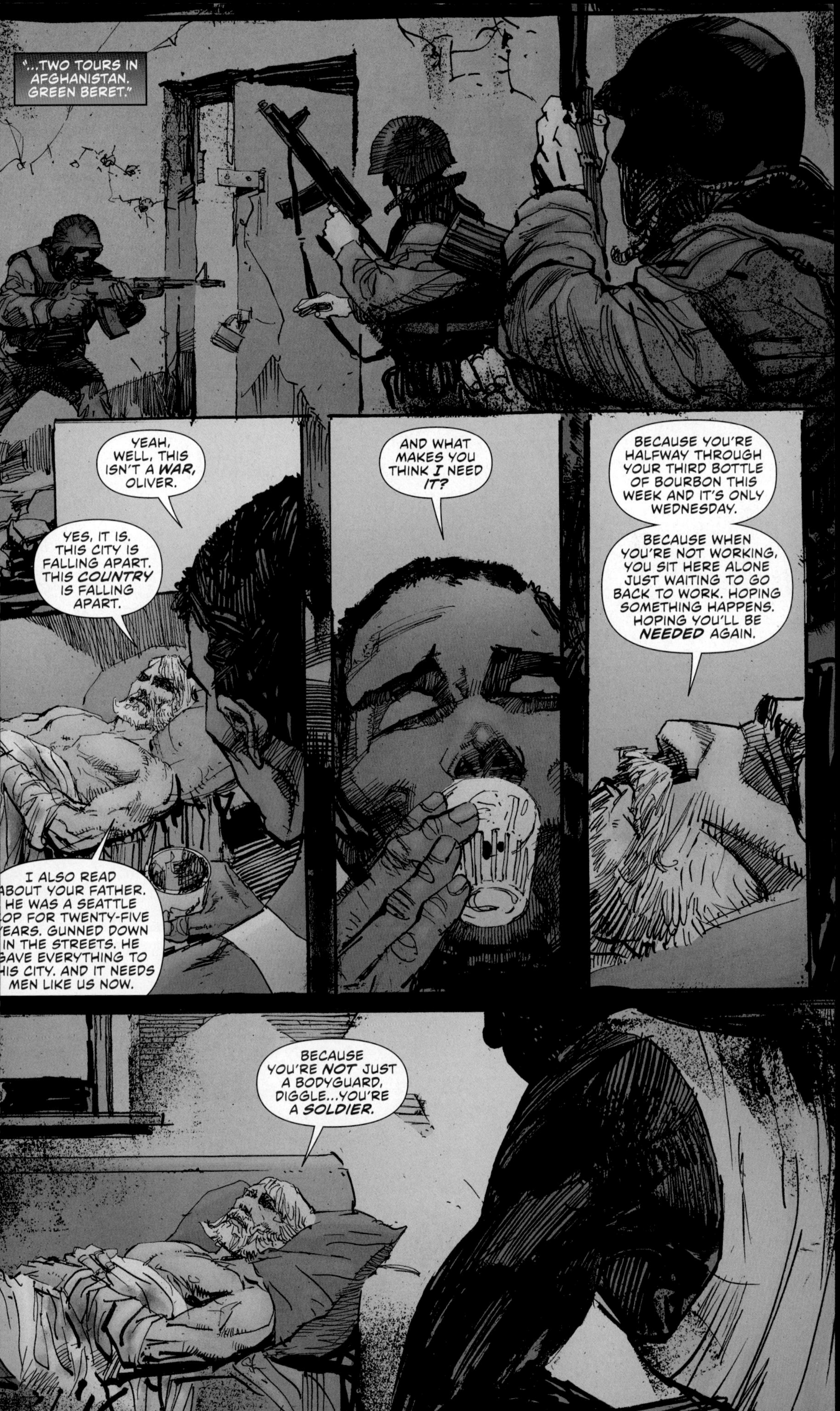
"...TWO TOURS IN AFGHANISTAN. GREEN BERET."
YEAH, WELL, THIS ISN'T A WAR, OLIVER.
YES, IT IS. THIS CITY IS FALLING APART. THIS COUNTRY IS FALLING APART.
I ALSO READ ABOUT YOUR FATHER. HE WAS A SEATTLE COP FOR TWENTY-FIVE YEARS. GUNNED DOWN IN THE STREETS. HE GAVE EVERYTHING TO THIS CITY. AND IT NEEDS MEN LIKE US NOW.
AND WHAT MAKES YOU THINK I NEED IT?
BECAUSE YOU'RE HALFWAY THROUGH YOUR THIRD BOTTLE OF BOURBON THIS WEEK AND IT'S ONLY WEDNESDAY.
BECAUSE WHEN YOU'RE NOT WORKING, YOU SIT HERE ALONE JUST WAITING TO GO BACK TO WORK. HOPING SOMETHING HAPPENS. HOPING YOU'LL BE NEEDED AGAIN.
BECAUSE YOU'RE NOT JUST A BODYGUARD, DIGGLE...YOU'RE A SOLDIER.

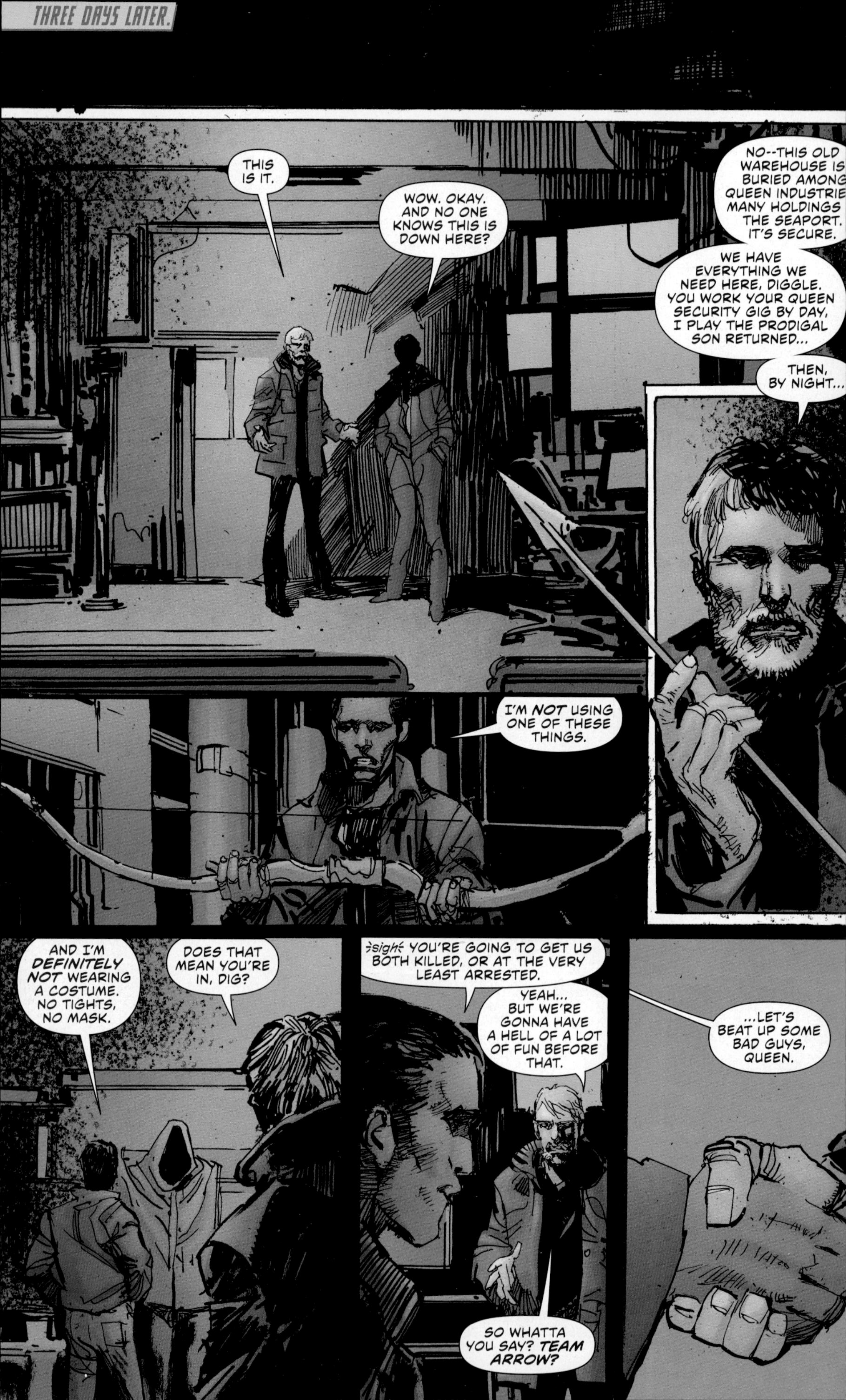
THREE DAYS LATER.
THIS IS IT.
WOW. OKAY. AND NO ONE KNOWS THIS IS DOWN HERE?
NO--THIS OLD WAREHOUSE IS BURIED AMONG QUEEN INDUSTRIE MANY HOLDINGS THE SEAPORT. IT'S SECURE.
WE HAVE EVERYTHING WE NEED HERE, DIGGLE. YOU WORK YOUR QUEEN SECURITY GIG BY DAY, I PLAY THE PRODIGAL SON RETURNED...
THEN, BY NIGHT...
I'M NOT USING ONE OF THESE THINGS.
AND I'M DEFINITELY NOT WEARING A COSTUME. NO TIGHTS, NO MASK.
DOES THAT MEAN YOU'RE IN, DIG?
sigh YOU'RE GOING TO GET US BOTH KILLED, OR AT THE VERY LEAST ARRESTED.
YEAH... BUT WE'RE GONNA HAVE A HELL OF A LOT OF FUN BEFORE THAT.
SO WHATTA YOU SAY? TEAM ARROW?
...LET'S BEAT UP SOME BAD GUYS, QUEEN.

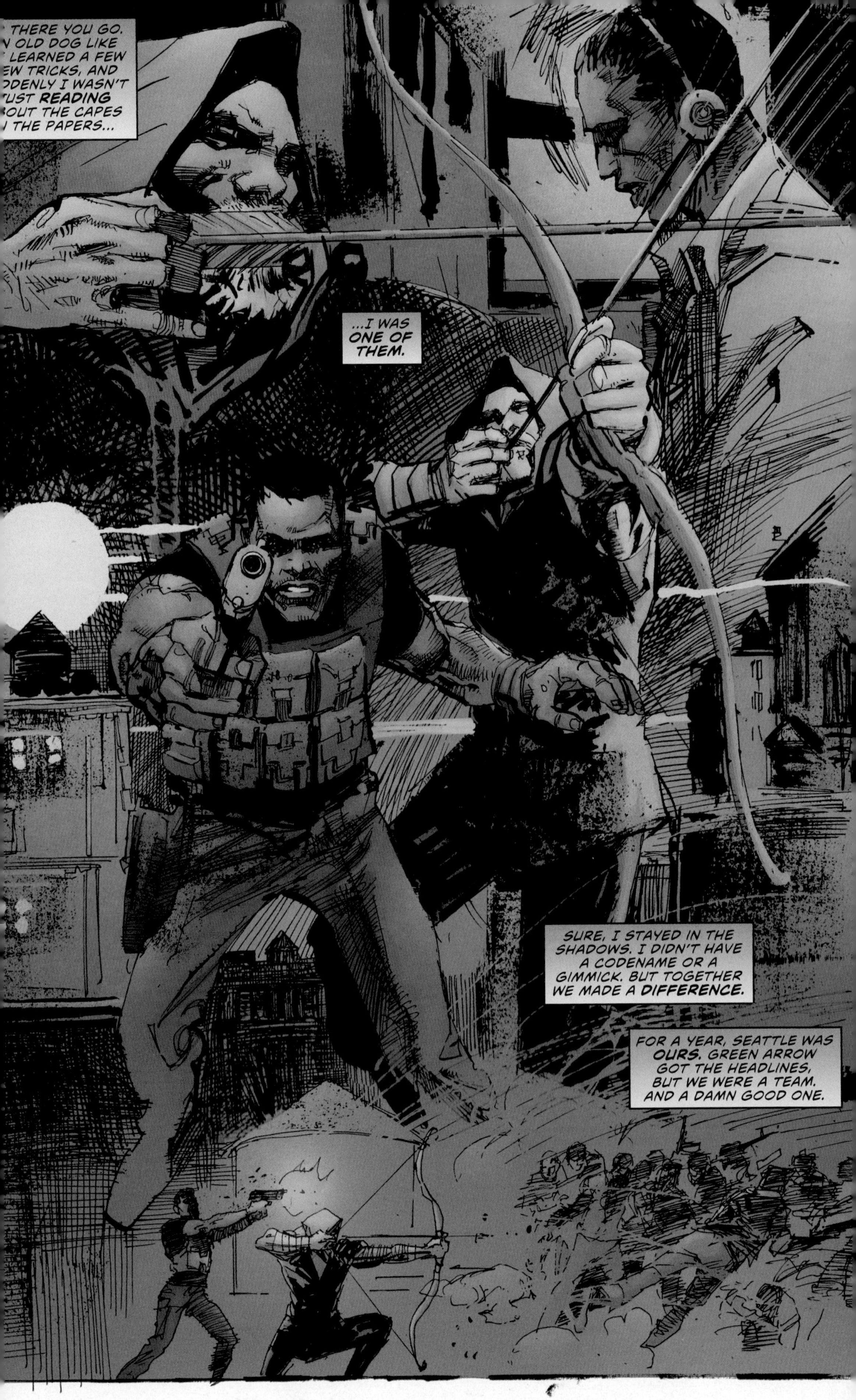
...THERE YOU GO. AN OLD DOG LIKE ME LEARNED A FEW NEW TRICKS, AND SUDDENLY I WASN'T JUST READING ABOUT THE CAPES IN THE PAPERS...
...I WAS ONE OF THEM.
SURE, I STAYED IN THE SHADOWS. I DIDN'T HAVE A CODENAME OR A GIMMICK. BUT TOGETHER WE MADE A DIFFERENCE.
FOR A YEAR, SEATTLE WAS OURS. GREEN ARROW GOT THE HEADLINES, BUT WE WERE A TEAM. AND A DAMN GOOD ONE.

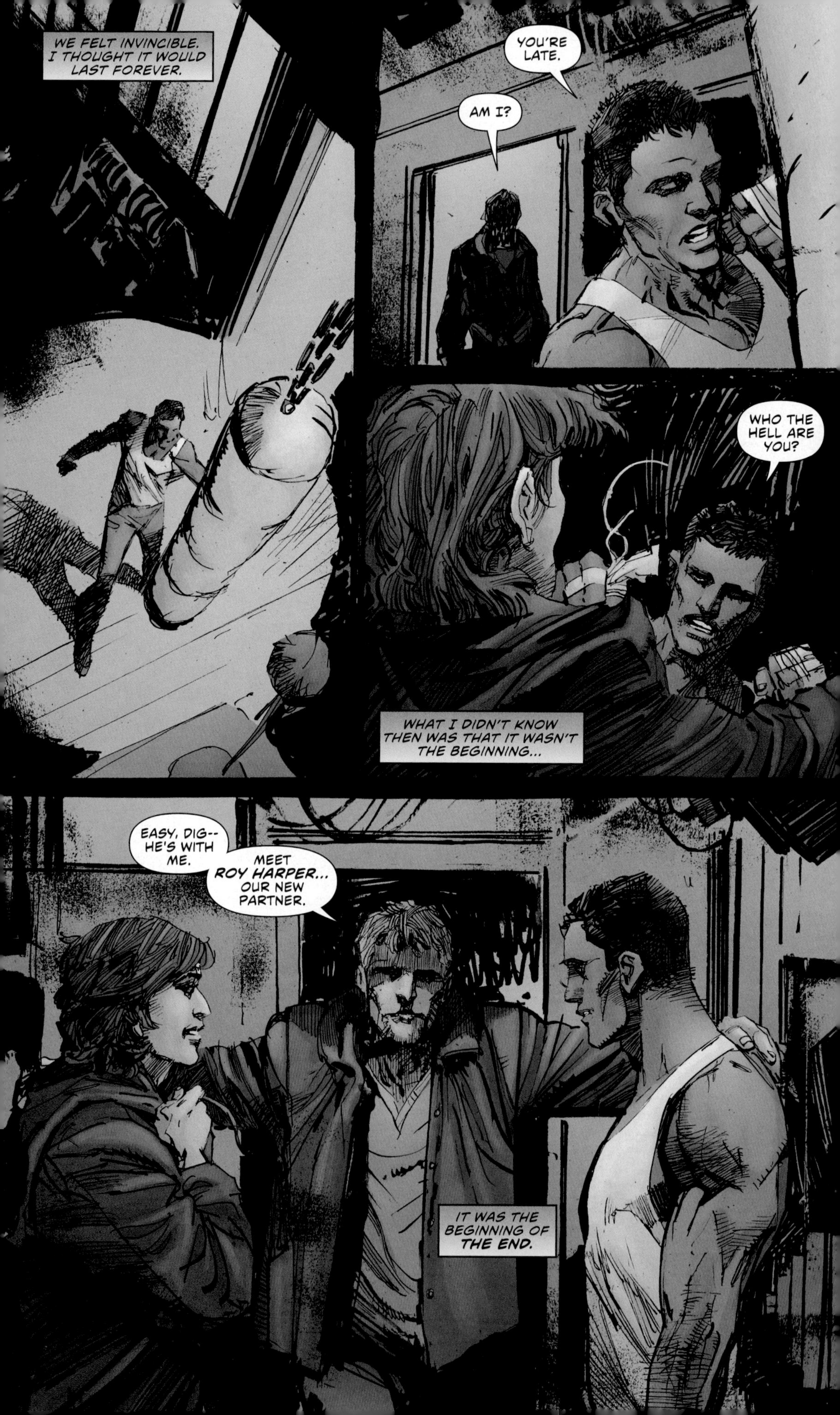
WE FELT INVINCIBLE. I THOUGHT IT WOULD LAST FOREVER.
YOU'RE LATE.
AM I?
WHO THE HELL ARE YOU?
WHAT I DIDN'T KNOW THEN WAS THAT IT WASN'T THE BEGINNING...
EASY, DIG-- HE'S WITH ME.
MEET ROY HARPER... OUR NEW PARTNER.
IT WAS THE BEGINNING OF THE END.

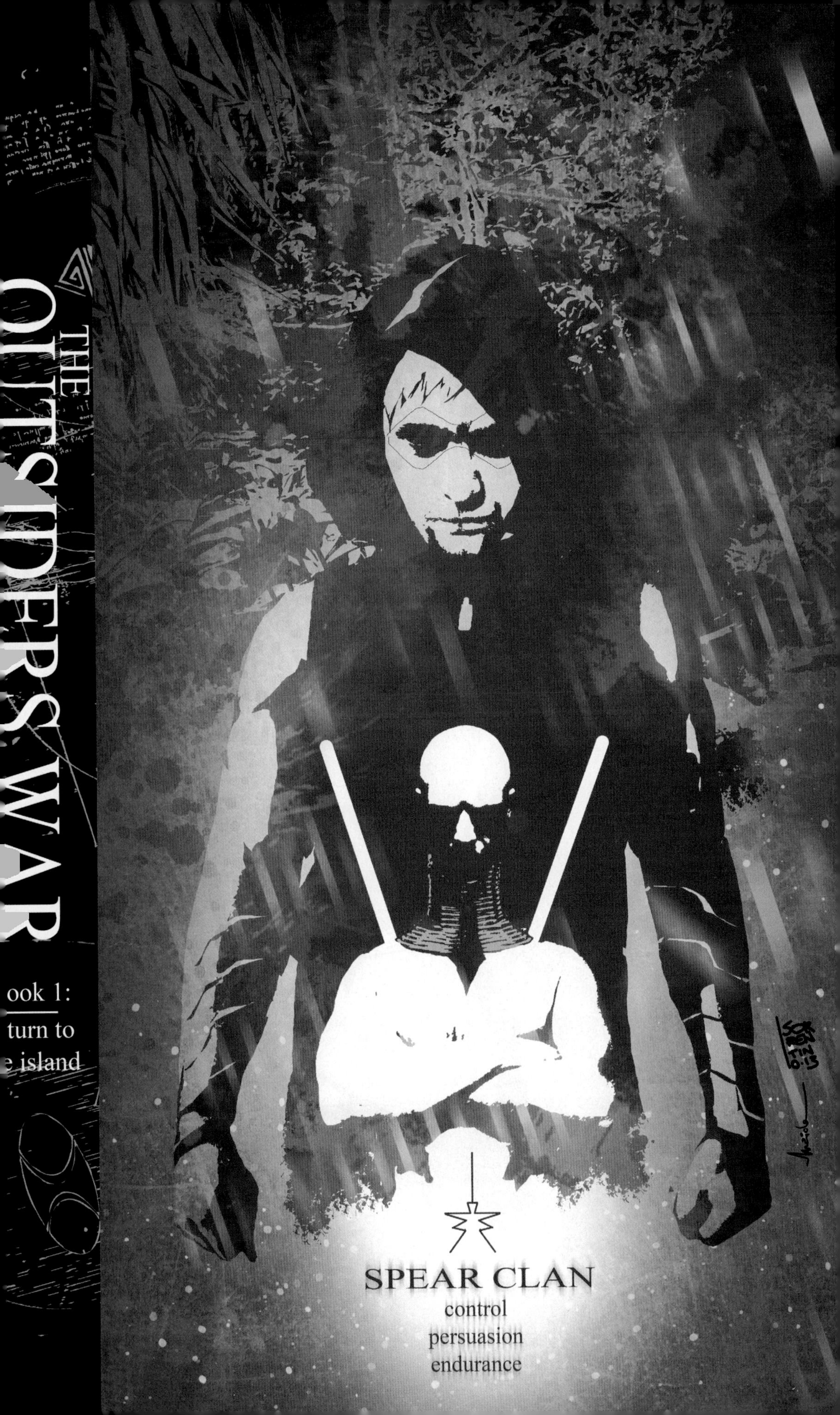
THE
ook 1:
turn to
island
SPEAR CLAN
control
persuasion
endurance

THE OUTSIDERS WAR

book 1:
return to
the island

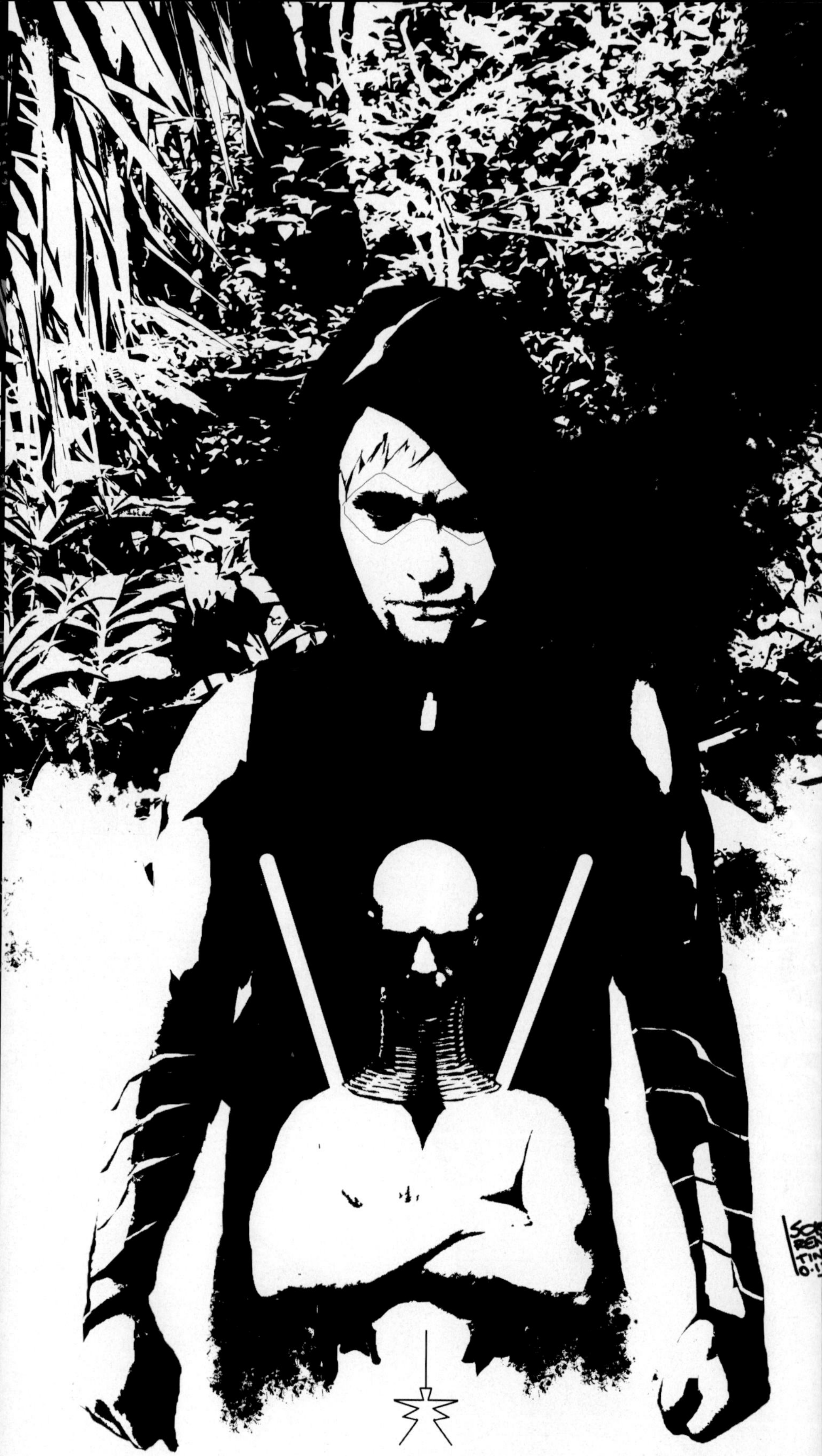

SPEAR CLAN
pride
ardor
devotion

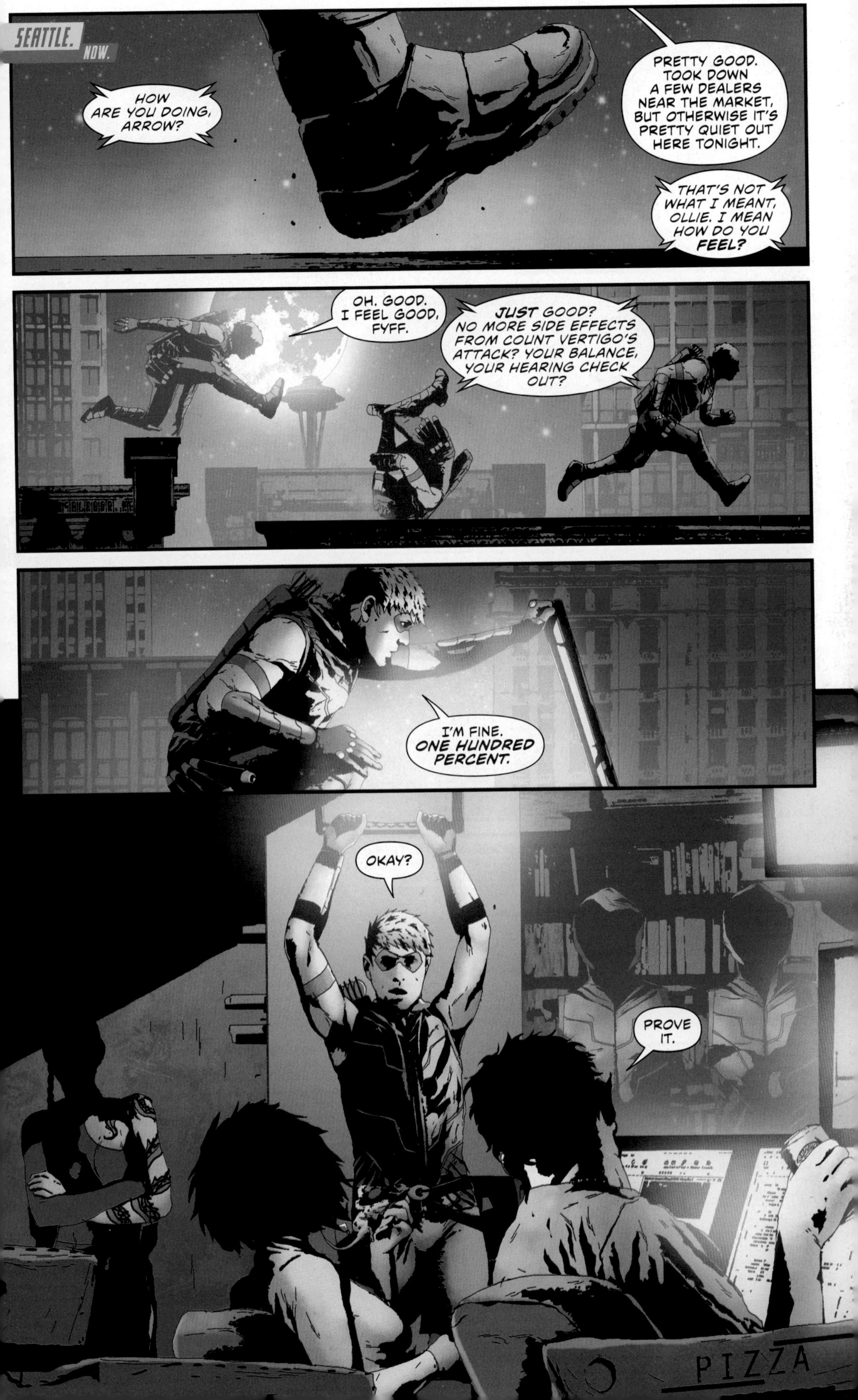
SEATTLE. NOW.
HOW ARE YOU DOING, ARROW?
PRETTY GOOD. TOOK DOWN A FEW DEALERS NEAR THE MARKET, BUT OTHERWISE IT'S PRETTY QUIET OUT HERE TONIGHT.
THAT'S NOT WHAT I MEANT, OLLIE. I MEAN HOW DO YOU FEEL?
OH. GOOD. I FEEL GOOD, FYFF.
JUST GOOD? NO MORE SIDE EFFECTS FROM COUNT VERTIGO'S ATTACK? YOUR BALANCE, YOUR HEARING CHECK OUT?
I'M FINE. ONE HUNDRED PERCENT.
OKAY?
PROVE IT.
PIZZA

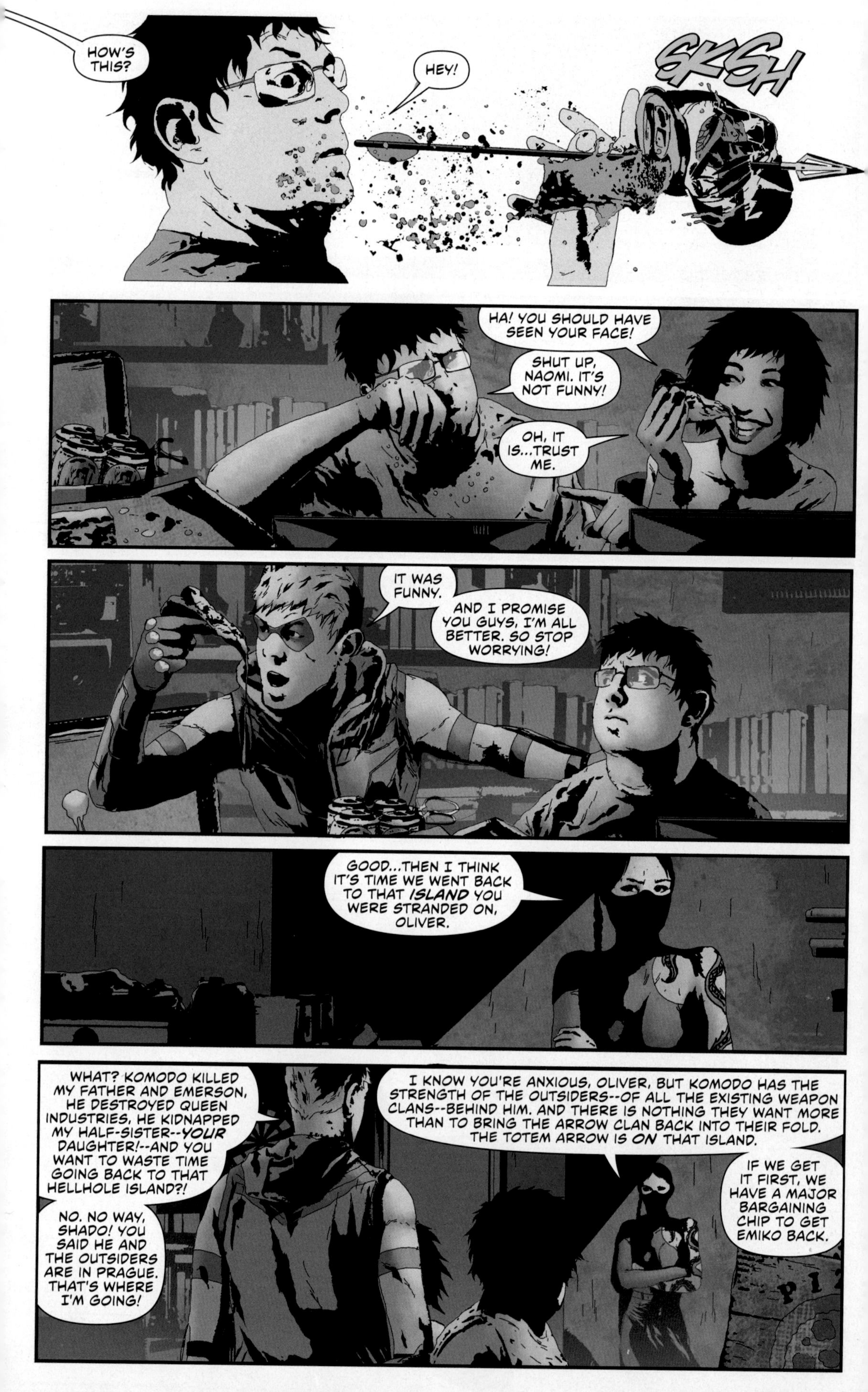
HOW'S THIS?
HEY!
SKSH
HA! YOU SHOULD HAVE SEEN YOUR FACE!
SHUT UP, NAOMI. IT'S NOT FUNNY!
OH, IT IS...TRUST ME.
IT WAS FUNNY.
AND I PROMISE YOU GUYS, I'M ALL BETTER. SO STOP WORRYING!
GOOD...THEN I THINK IT'S TIME WE WENT BACK TO THAT ISLAND YOU WERE STRANDED ON, OLIVER.
WHAT? KOMODO KILLED MY FATHER AND EMERSON, HE DESTROYED QUEEN INDUSTRIES, HE KIDNAPPED MY HALF-SISTER--YOUR DAUGHTER!--AND YOU WANT TO WASTE TIME GOING BACK TO THAT HELLHOLE ISLAND?!
NO. NO WAY, SHADO! YOU SAID HE AND THE OUTSIDERS ARE IN PRAGUE. THAT'S WHERE I'M GOING!
I KNOW YOU'RE ANXIOUS, OLIVER, BUT KOMODO HAS THE STRENGTH OF THE OUTSIDERS--OF ALL THE EXISTING WEAPON CLANS--BEHIND HIM. AND THERE IS NOTHING THEY WANT MORE THAN TO BRING THE ARROW CLAN BACK INTO THEIR FOLD. THE TOTEM ARROW IS ON THAT ISLAND.
IF WE GET IT FIRST, WE HAVE A MAJOR BARGAINING CHIP TO GET EMIKO BACK.

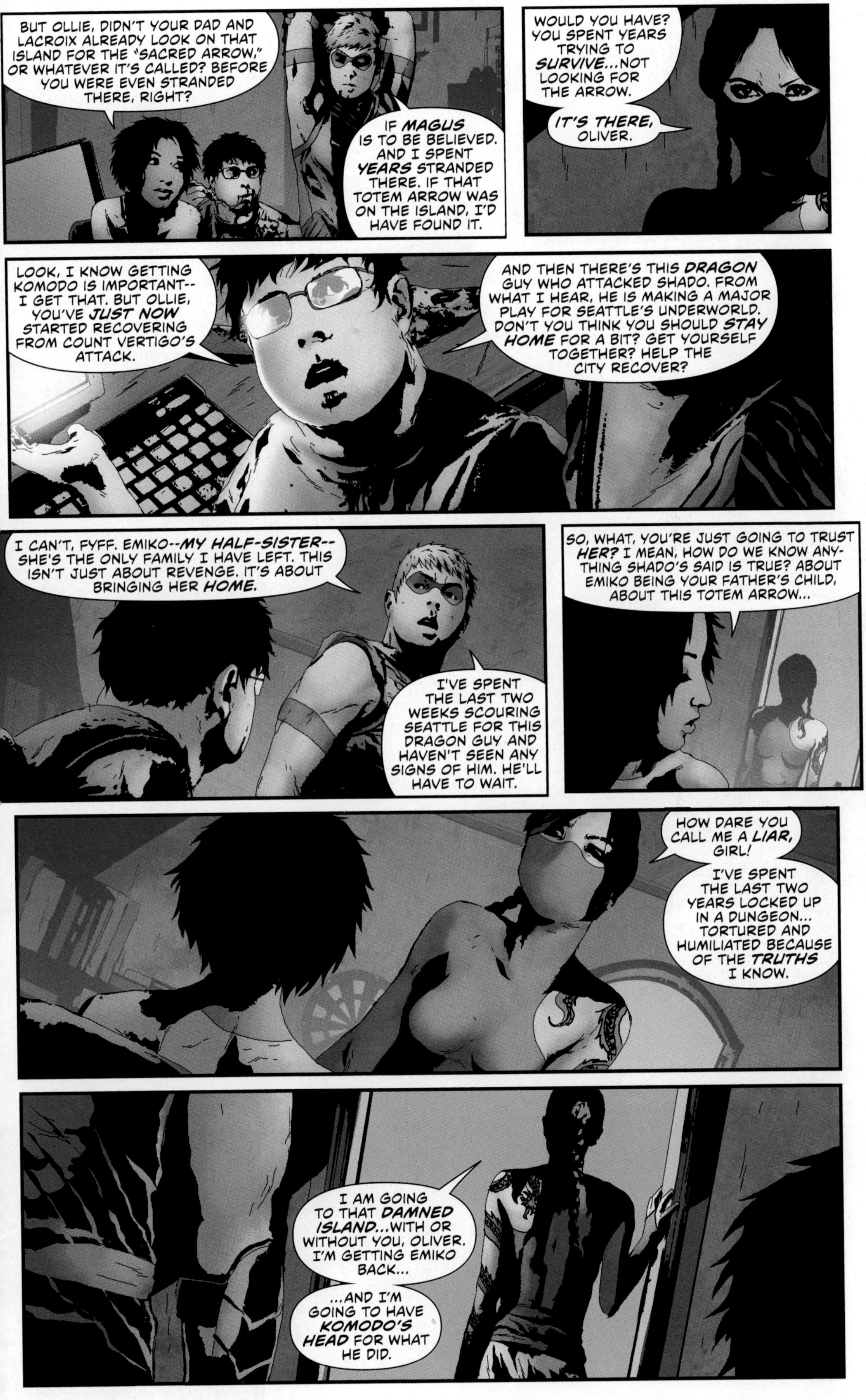
BUT OLLIE, DIDN'T YOUR DAD AND LACROIX ALREADY LOOK ON THAT ISLAND FOR THE "SACRED ARROW," OR WHATEVER IT'S CALLED? BEFORE YOU WERE EVEN STRANDED THERE, RIGHT?
IF MAGUS IS TO BE BELIEVED. AND I SPENT YEARS STRANDED THERE. IF THAT TOTEM ARROW WAS ON THE ISLAND, I'D HAVE FOUND IT.
WOULD YOU HAVE? YOU SPENT YEARS TRYING TO SURVIVE...NOT LOOKING FOR THE ARROW.
IT'S THERE, OLIVER.
LOOK, I KNOW GETTING KOMODO IS IMPORTANT-- I GET THAT. BUT OLLIE, YOU'VE JUST NOW STARTED RECOVERING FROM COUNT VERTIGO'S ATTACK.
AND THEN THERE'S THIS DRAGON GUY WHO ATTACKED SHADO. FROM WHAT I HEAR, HE IS MAKING A MAJOR PLAY FOR SEATTLE'S UNDERWORLD. DON'T YOU THINK YOU SHOULD STAY HOME FOR A BIT? GET YOURSELF TOGETHER? HELP THE CITY RECOVER?
I CAN'T, FYFF. EMIKO--MY HALF-SISTER-- SHE'S THE ONLY FAMILY I HAVE LEFT. THIS ISN'T JUST ABOUT REVENGE. IT'S ABOUT BRINGING HER HOME.
I'VE SPENT THE LAST TWO WEEKS SCOURING SEATTLE FOR THIS DRAGON GUY AND HAVEN'T SEEN ANY SIGNS OF HIM. HE'LL HAVE TO WAIT.
SO, WHAT, YOU'RE JUST GOING TO TRUST HER? I MEAN, HOW DO WE KNOW ANYTHING SHADO'S SAID IS TRUE? ABOUT EMIKO BEING YOUR FATHER'S CHILD, ABOUT THIS TOTEM ARROW...
HOW DARE YOU CALL ME A LIAR, GIRL!
I'VE SPENT THE LAST TWO YEARS LOCKED UP IN A DUNGEON... TORTURED AND HUMILIATED BECAUSE OF THE TRUTHS I KNOW.
I AM GOING TO THAT DAMNED ISLAND...WITH OR WITHOUT YOU, OLIVER. I'M GETTING EMIKO BACK...
...AND I'M GOING TO HAVE KOMODO'S HEAD FOR WHAT HE DID.

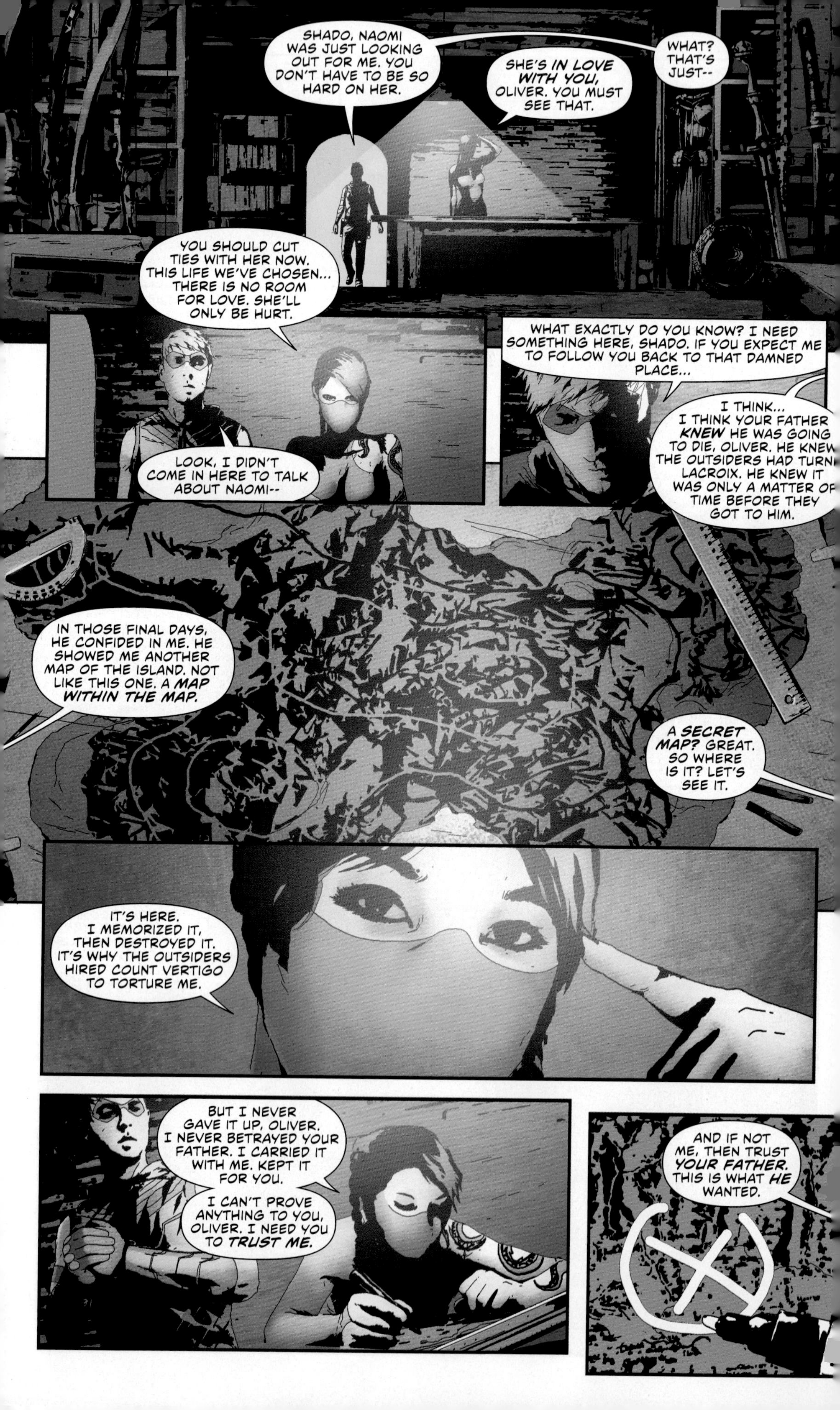

SHADO, NAOMI WAS JUST LOOKING OUT FOR ME. YOU DON'T HAVE TO BE SO HARD ON HER.
SHE'S *IN LOVE WITH YOU,* OLIVER. YOU MUST SEE THAT.
WHAT? THAT'S JUST--
YOU SHOULD CUT TIES WITH HER NOW. THIS LIFE WE'VE CHOSEN... THERE IS NO ROOM FOR LOVE. SHE'LL ONLY BE HURT.
LOOK, I DIDN'T COME IN HERE TO TALK ABOUT NAOMI--
WHAT EXACTLY DO YOU KNOW? I NEED SOMETHING HERE, SHADO. IF YOU EXPECT ME TO FOLLOW YOU BACK TO THAT DAMNED PLACE...
I THINK... I THINK YOUR FATHER *KNEW* HE WAS GOING TO DIE, OLIVER. HE KNEW THE OUTSIDERS HAD TURN LACROIX. HE KNEW IT WAS ONLY A MATTER OF TIME BEFORE THEY GOT TO HIM.
IN THOSE FINAL DAYS, HE CONFIDED IN ME. HE SHOWED ME ANOTHER MAP OF THE ISLAND. NOT LIKE THIS ONE. A *MAP WITHIN THE MAP.*
A *SECRET MAP?* GREAT. SO WHERE IS IT? LET'S SEE IT.
IT'S HERE. I MEMORIZED IT, THEN DESTROYED IT. IT'S WHY THE OUTSIDERS HIRED COUNT VERTIGO TO TORTURE ME.
BUT I NEVER GAVE IT UP, OLIVER. I NEVER BETRAYED YOUR FATHER. I CARRIED IT WITH ME. KEPT IT FOR YOU.
I CAN'T PROVE ANYTHING TO YOU, OLIVER. I NEED YOU TO *TRUST ME.*
AND IF NOT ME, THEN TRUST *YOUR FATHER.* THIS IS WHAT *HE* WANTED.

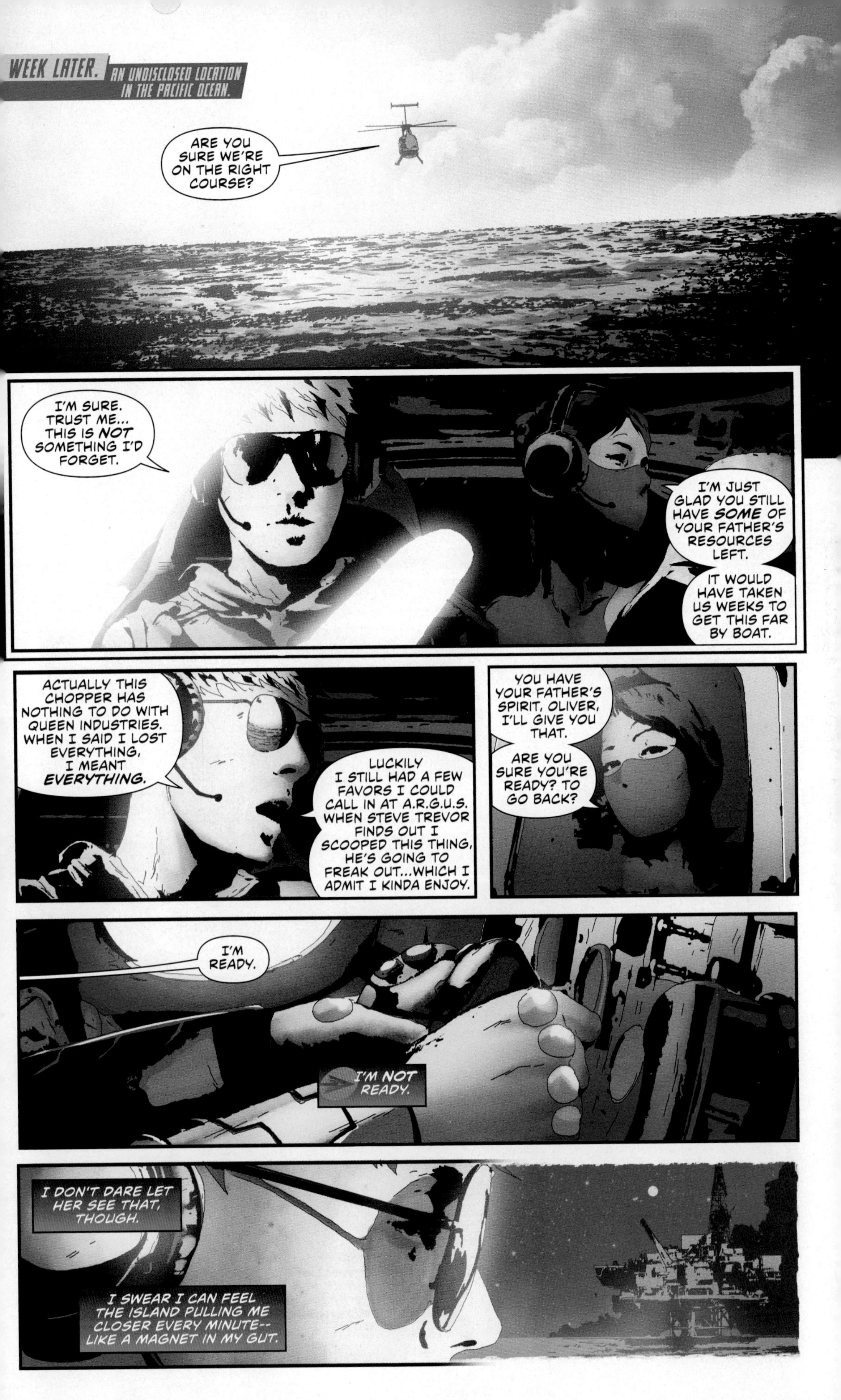
WEEK LATER.
AN UNDISCLOSED LOCATION IN THE PACIFIC OCEAN.
ARE YOU SURE WE'RE ON THE RIGHT COURSE?
I'M SURE. TRUST ME... THIS IS NOT SOMETHING I'D FORGET.
I'M JUST GLAD YOU STILL HAVE SOME OF YOUR FATHER'S RESOURCES LEFT.
IT WOULD HAVE TAKEN US WEEKS TO GET THIS FAR BY BOAT.
ACTUALLY THIS CHOPPER HAS NOTHING TO DO WITH QUEEN INDUSTRIES. WHEN I SAID I LOST EVERYTHING, I MEANT EVERYTHING.
LUCKILY I STILL HAD A FEW FAVORS I COULD CALL IN AT A.R.G.U.S. WHEN STEVE TREVOR FINDS OUT I SCOOPED THIS THING, HE'S GOING TO FREAK OUT...WHICH I ADMIT I KINDA ENJOY.
YOU HAVE YOUR FATHER'S SPIRIT, OLIVER, I'LL GIVE YOU THAT.
ARE YOU SURE YOU'RE READY? TO GO BACK?
I'M READY.
I'M NOT READY.
I DON'T DARE LET HER SEE THAT, THOUGH.
I SWEAR I CAN FEEL THE ISLAND PULLING ME CLOSER EVERY MINUTE-- LIKE A MAGNET IN MY GUT.

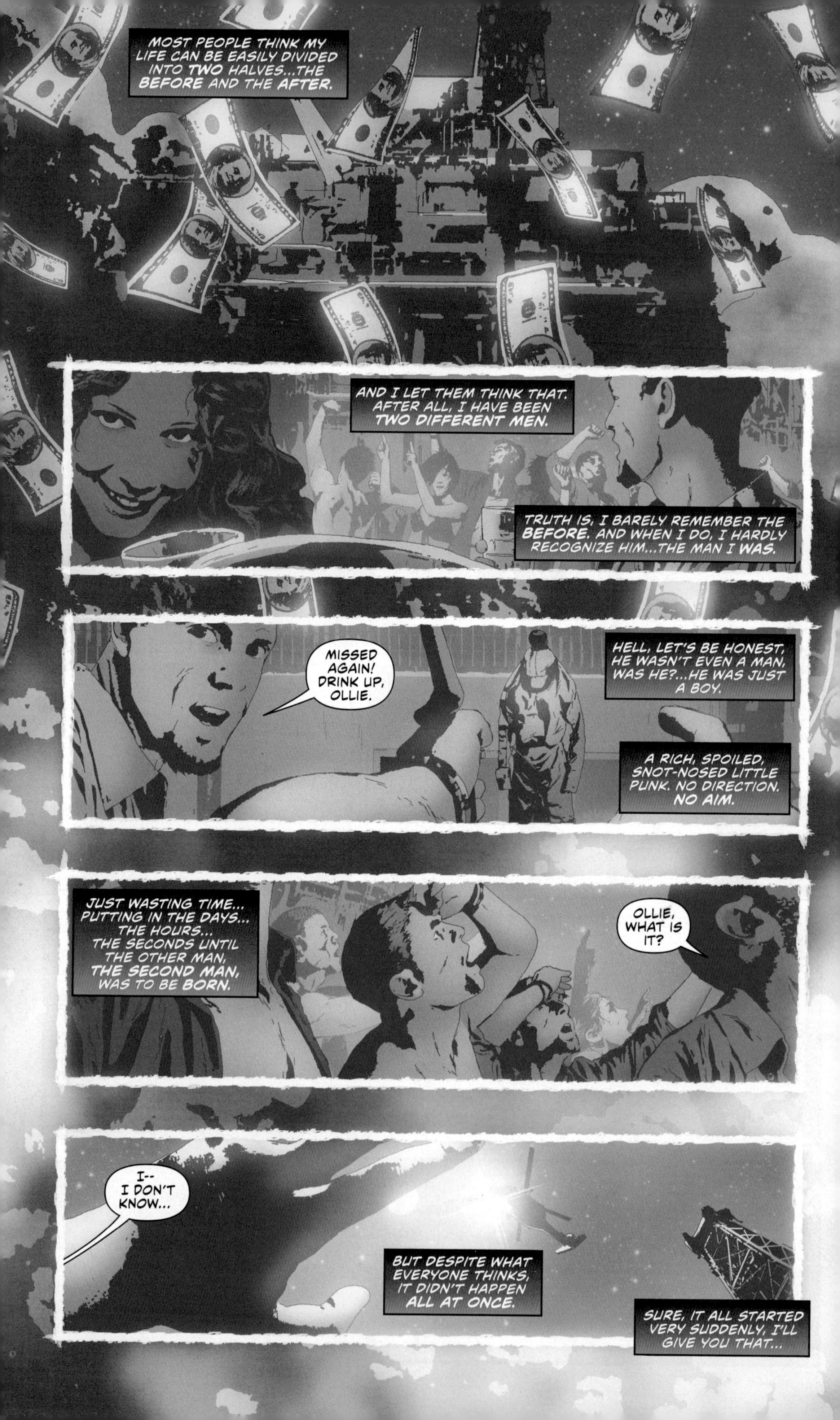
MOST PEOPLE THINK MY LIFE CAN BE EASILY DIVIDED INTO TWO HALVES...THE BEFORE AND THE AFTER.
AND I LET THEM THINK THAT. AFTER ALL, I HAVE BEEN TWO DIFFERENT MEN.
TRUTH IS, I BARELY REMEMBER THE BEFORE. AND WHEN I DO, I HARDLY RECOGNIZE HIM...THE MAN I WAS.
MISSED AGAIN! DRINK UP, OLLIE.
HELL, LET'S BE HONEST, HE WASN'T EVEN A MAN, WAS HE?...HE WAS JUST A BOY.
A RICH, SPOILED, SNOT-NOSED LITTLE PUNK. NO DIRECTION. NO AIM.
JUST WASTING TIME... PUTTING IN THE DAYS... THE HOURS... THE SECONDS UNTIL THE OTHER MAN, THE SECOND MAN, WAS TO BE BORN.
OLLIE, WHAT IS IT?
I-- I DON'T KNOW...
BUT DESPITE WHAT EVERYONE THINKS, IT DIDN'T HAPPEN ALL AT ONCE.
SURE, IT ALL STARTED VERY SUDDENLY, I'LL GIVE YOU THAT...

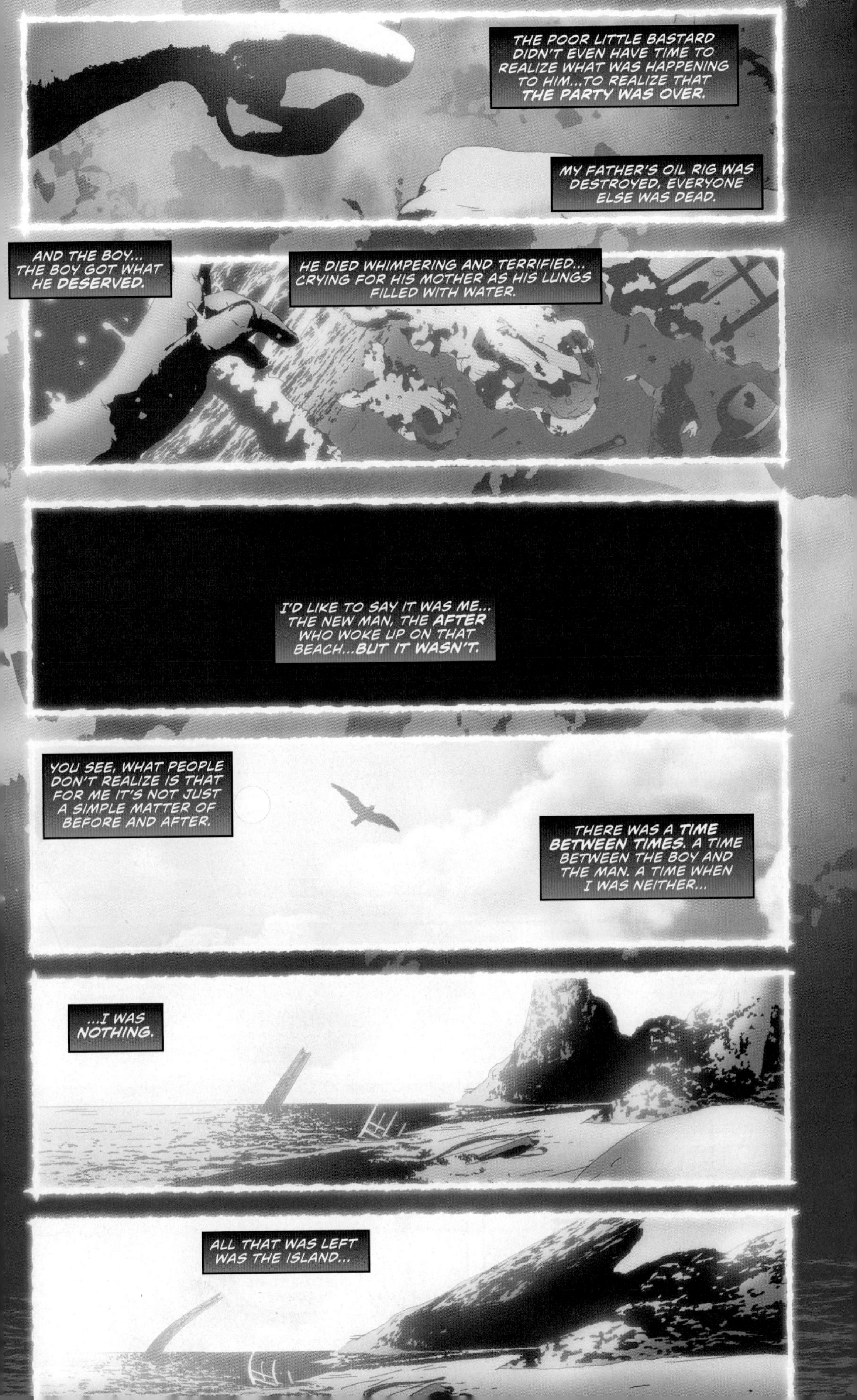
THE POOR LITTLE BASTARD DIDN'T EVEN HAVE TIME TO REALIZE WHAT WAS HAPPENING TO HIM...TO REALIZE THAT THE PARTY WAS OVER.
MY FATHER'S OIL RIG WAS DESTROYED, EVERYONE ELSE WAS DEAD.
AND THE BOY... THE BOY GOT WHAT HE DESERVED.
HE DIED WHIMPERING AND TERRIFIED... CRYING FOR HIS MOTHER AS HIS LUNGS FILLED WITH WATER.
I'D LIKE TO SAY IT WAS ME... THE NEW MAN, THE AFTER WHO WOKE UP ON THAT BEACH...BUT IT WASN'T.
YOU SEE, WHAT PEOPLE DON'T REALIZE IS THAT FOR ME IT'S NOT JUST A SIMPLE MATTER OF BEFORE AND AFTER.
THERE WAS A TIME BETWEEN TIMES. A TIME BETWEEN THE BOY AND THE MAN. A TIME WHEN I WAS NEITHER...
...I WAS NOTHING.
ALL THAT WAS LEFT WAS THE ISLAND...

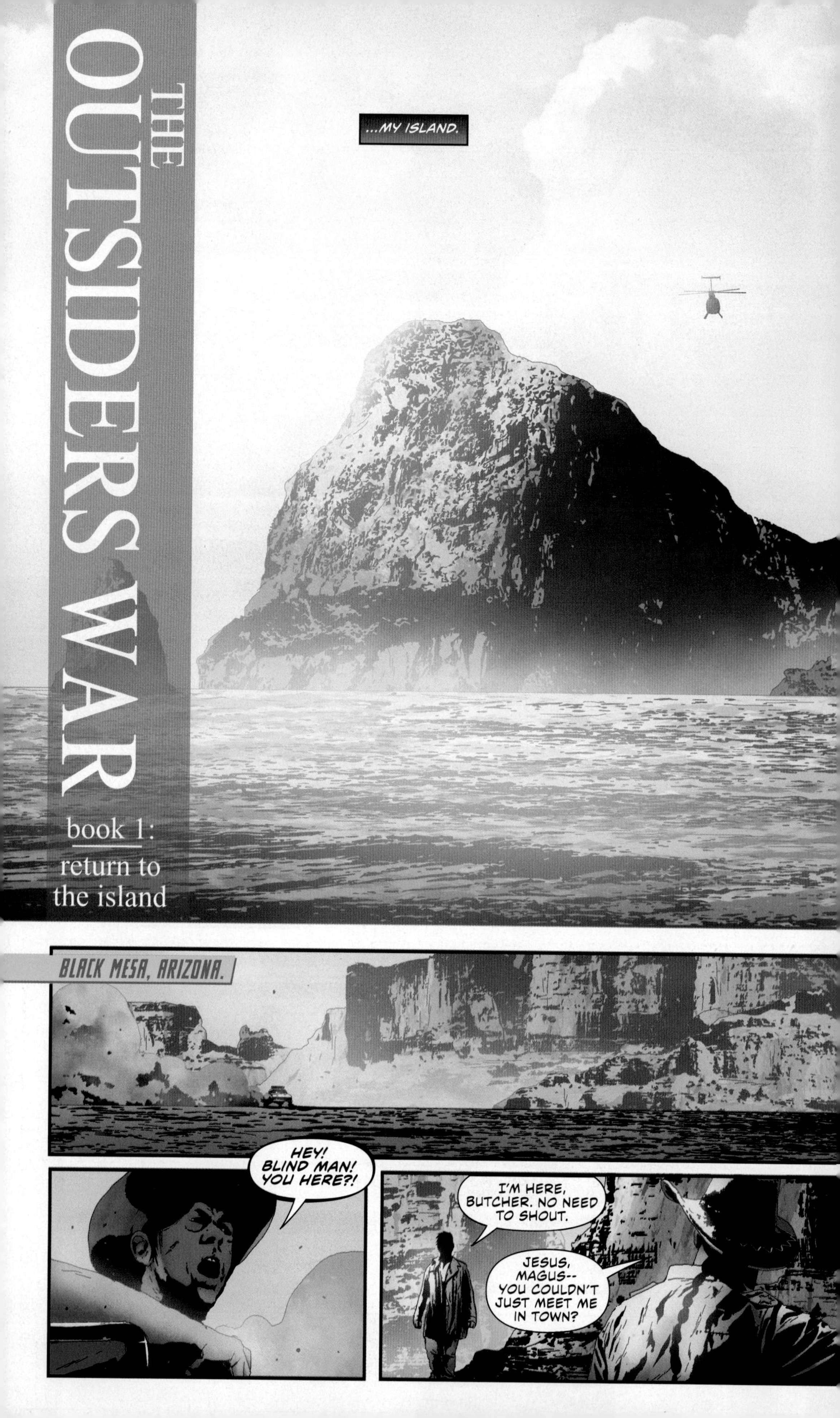

...MY ISLAND.
THE OUTSIDERS WAR
book 1:
return to the island
BLACK MESA, ARIZONA.
HEY! BLIND MAN! YOU HERE?!
I'M HERE, BUTCHER. NO NEED TO SHOUT.
JESUS, MAGUS-- YOU COULDN'T JUST MEET ME IN TOWN?

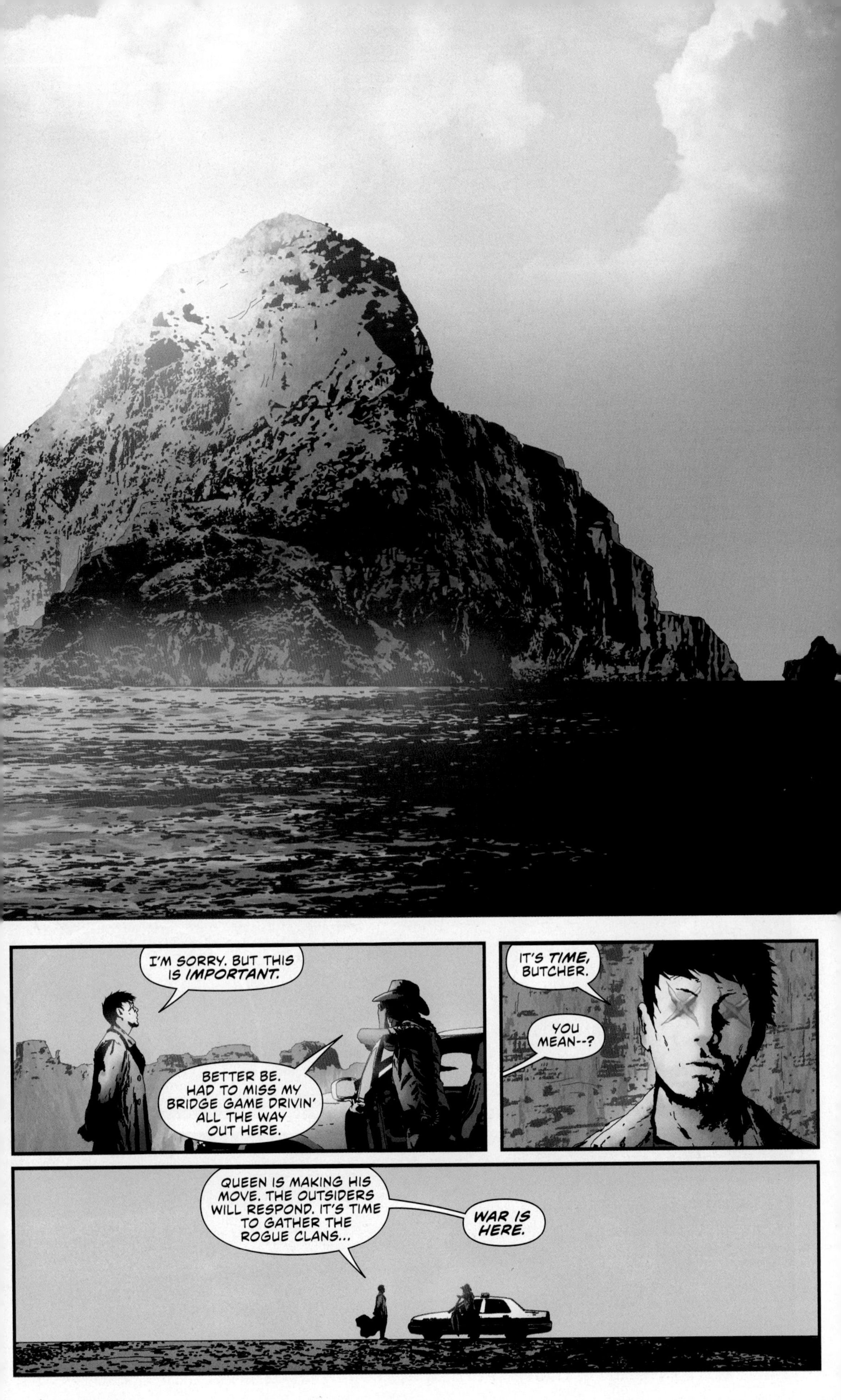
I'M SORRY. BUT THIS IS IMPORTANT.
BETTER BE. HAD TO MISS MY BRIDGE GAME DRIVIN' ALL THE WAY OUT HERE.
IT'S TIME, BUTCHER.
YOU MEAN--?
QUEEN IS MAKING HIS MOVE. THE OUTSIDERS WILL RESPOND. IT'S TIME TO GATHER THE ROGUE CLANS...
WAR IS HERE.

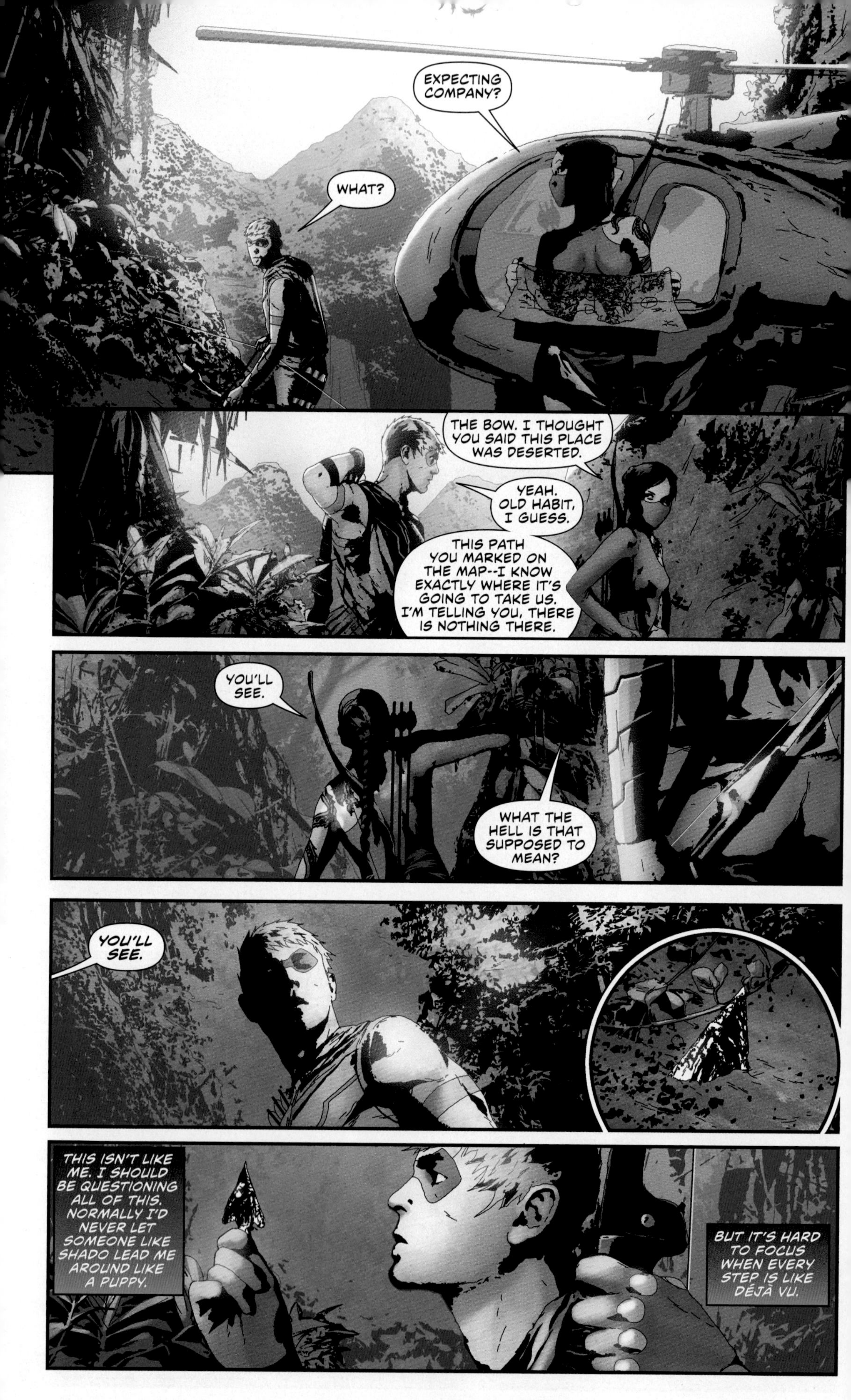
EXPECTING COMPANY?
WHAT?
THE BOW. I THOUGHT YOU SAID THIS PLACE WAS DESERTED.
YEAH. OLD HABIT, I GUESS.
THIS PATH YOU MARKED ON THE MAP--I KNOW EXACTLY WHERE IT'S GOING TO TAKE US. I'M TELLING YOU, THERE IS NOTHING THERE.
YOU'LL SEE.
WHAT THE HELL IS THAT SUPPOSED TO MEAN?
YOU'LL SEE.
THIS ISN'T LIKE ME. I SHOULD BE QUESTIONING ALL OF THIS. NORMALLY I'D NEVER LET SOMEONE LIKE SHADO LEAD ME AROUND LIKE A PUPPY.
BUT IT'S HARD TO FOCUS WHEN EVERY STEP IS LIKE DÉJÀ VU.

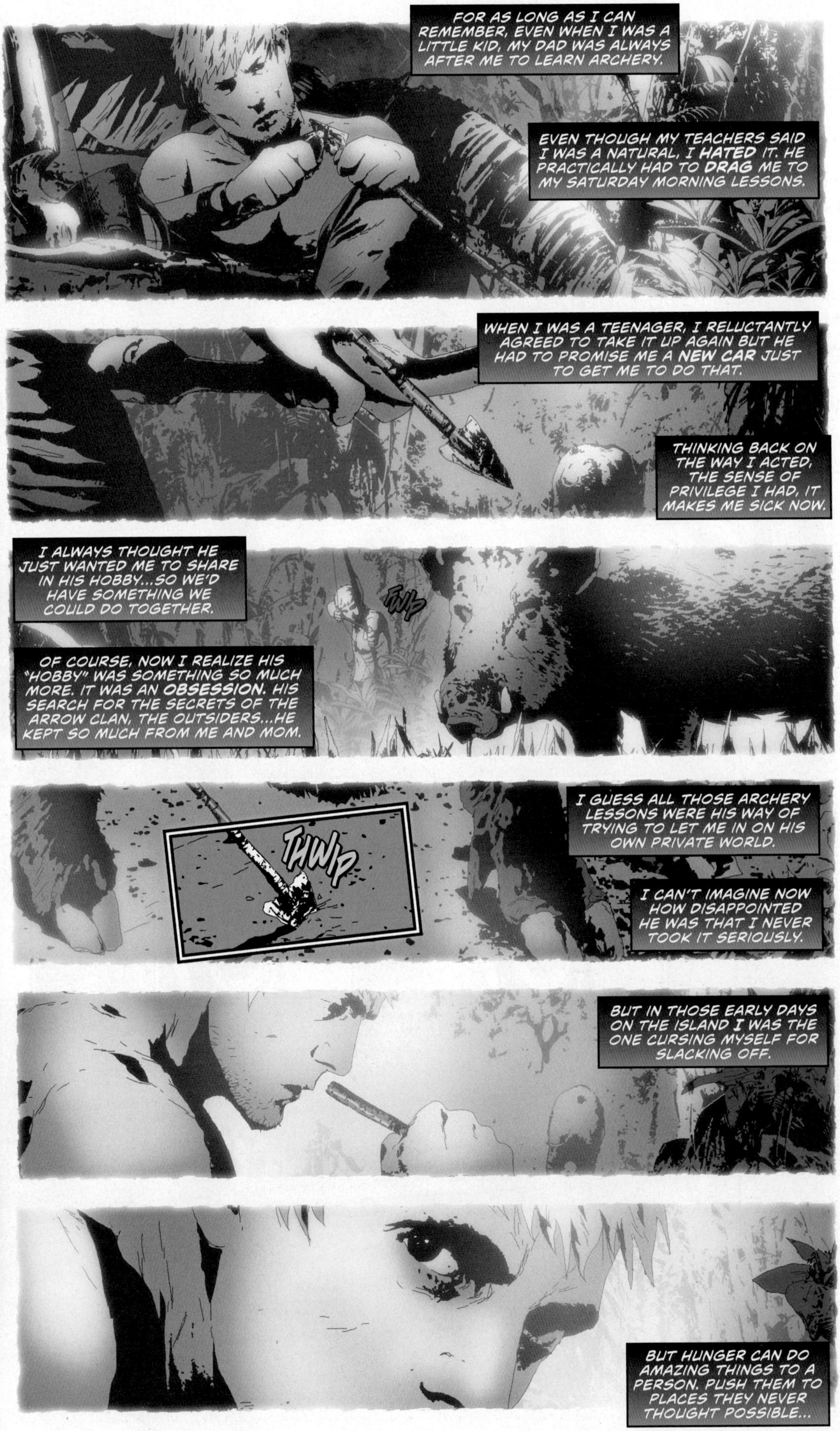
FOR AS LONG AS I CAN REMEMBER, EVEN WHEN I WAS A LITTLE KID, MY DAD WAS ALWAYS AFTER ME TO LEARN ARCHERY.
EVEN THOUGH MY TEACHERS SAID I WAS A NATURAL, I **HATED** IT. HE PRACTICALLY HAD TO **DRAG** ME TO MY SATURDAY MORNING LESSONS.
WHEN I WAS A TEENAGER, I RELUCTANTLY AGREED TO TAKE IT UP AGAIN BUT HE HAD TO PROMISE ME A **NEW CAR** JUST TO GET ME TO DO THAT.
THINKING BACK ON THE WAY I ACTED, THE SENSE OF PRIVILEGE I HAD, IT MAKES ME SICK NOW.
I ALWAYS THOUGHT HE JUST WANTED ME TO SHARE IN HIS HOBBY...SO WE'D HAVE SOMETHING WE COULD DO TOGETHER.
OF COURSE, NOW I REALIZE HIS "HOBBY" WAS SOMETHING SO MUCH MORE. IT WAS AN **OBSESSION.** HIS SEARCH FOR THE SECRETS OF THE ARROW CLAN, THE OUTSIDERS...HE KEPT SO MUCH FROM ME AND MOM.
FWIP
THWIP
I GUESS ALL THOSE ARCHERY LESSONS WERE HIS WAY OF TRYING TO LET ME IN ON HIS OWN PRIVATE WORLD.
I CAN'T IMAGINE NOW HOW DISAPPOINTED HE WAS THAT I NEVER TOOK IT SERIOUSLY.
BUT IN THOSE EARLY DAYS ON THE ISLAND **I** WAS THE ONE CURSING MYSELF FOR SLACKING OFF.
BUT HUNGER CAN DO AMAZING THINGS TO A PERSON. PUSH THEM TO PLACES THEY NEVER THOUGHT POSSIBLE...

IT'S ALL-CONSUMING.
EVERYTHING ELSE FADES.
ALL THAT MATTERS IS FINDING
FOOD. MAKING IT STOP.

THAT'S WHEN THE BOY REALLY
STARTED TO FADE. THAT'S WHEN
I BECAME SOMETHING ELSE...
A HUNTER.

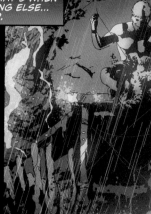

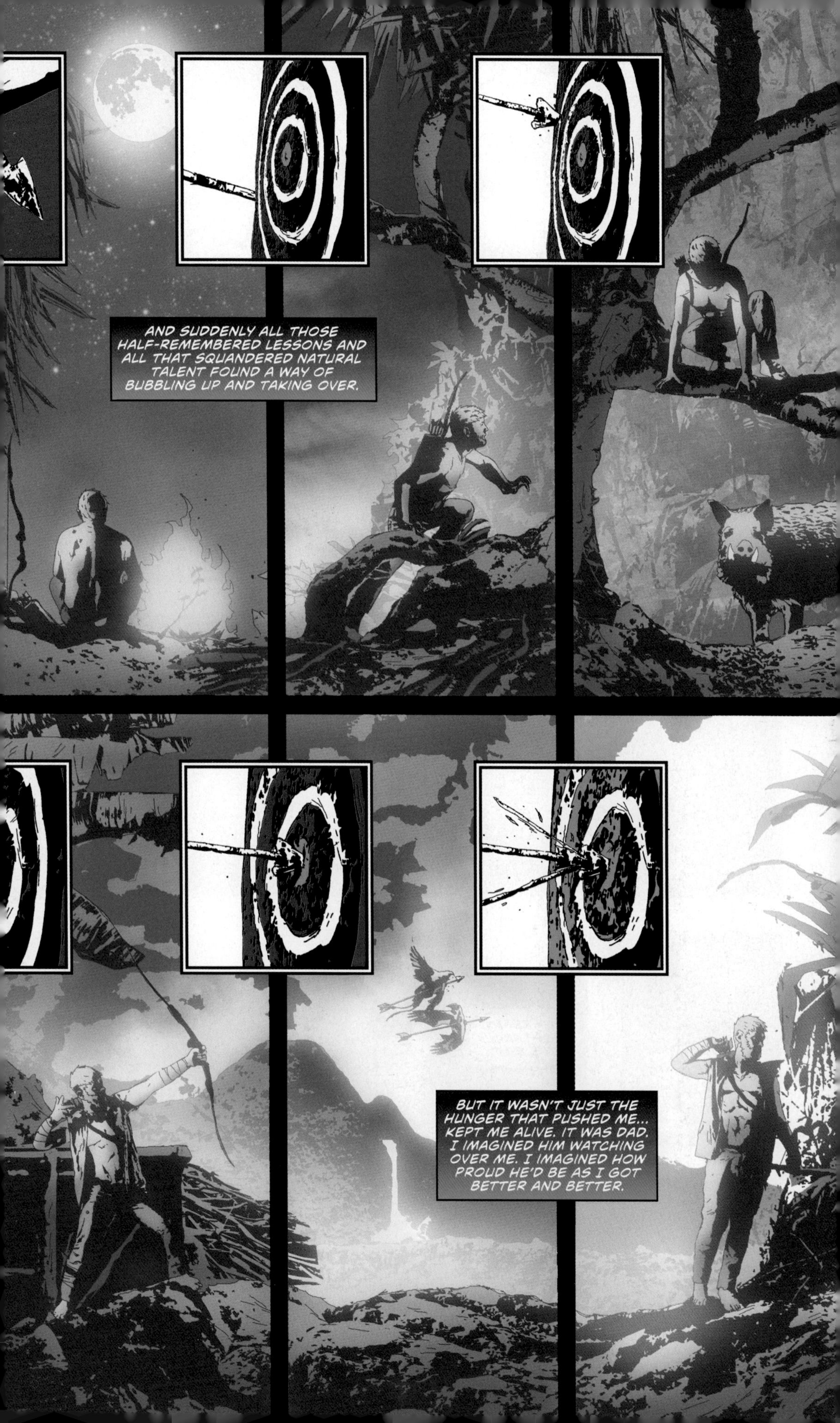
AND SUDDENLY ALL THOSE HALF-REMEMBERED LESSONS AND ALL THAT SQUANDERED NATURAL TALENT FOUND A WAY OF BUBBLING UP AND TAKING OVER.
BUT IT WASN'T JUST THE HUNGER THAT PUSHED ME... KEPT ME ALIVE. IT WAS DAD. I IMAGINED HIM WATCHING OVER ME. I IMAGINED HOW PROUD HE'D BE AS I GOT BETTER AND BETTER.

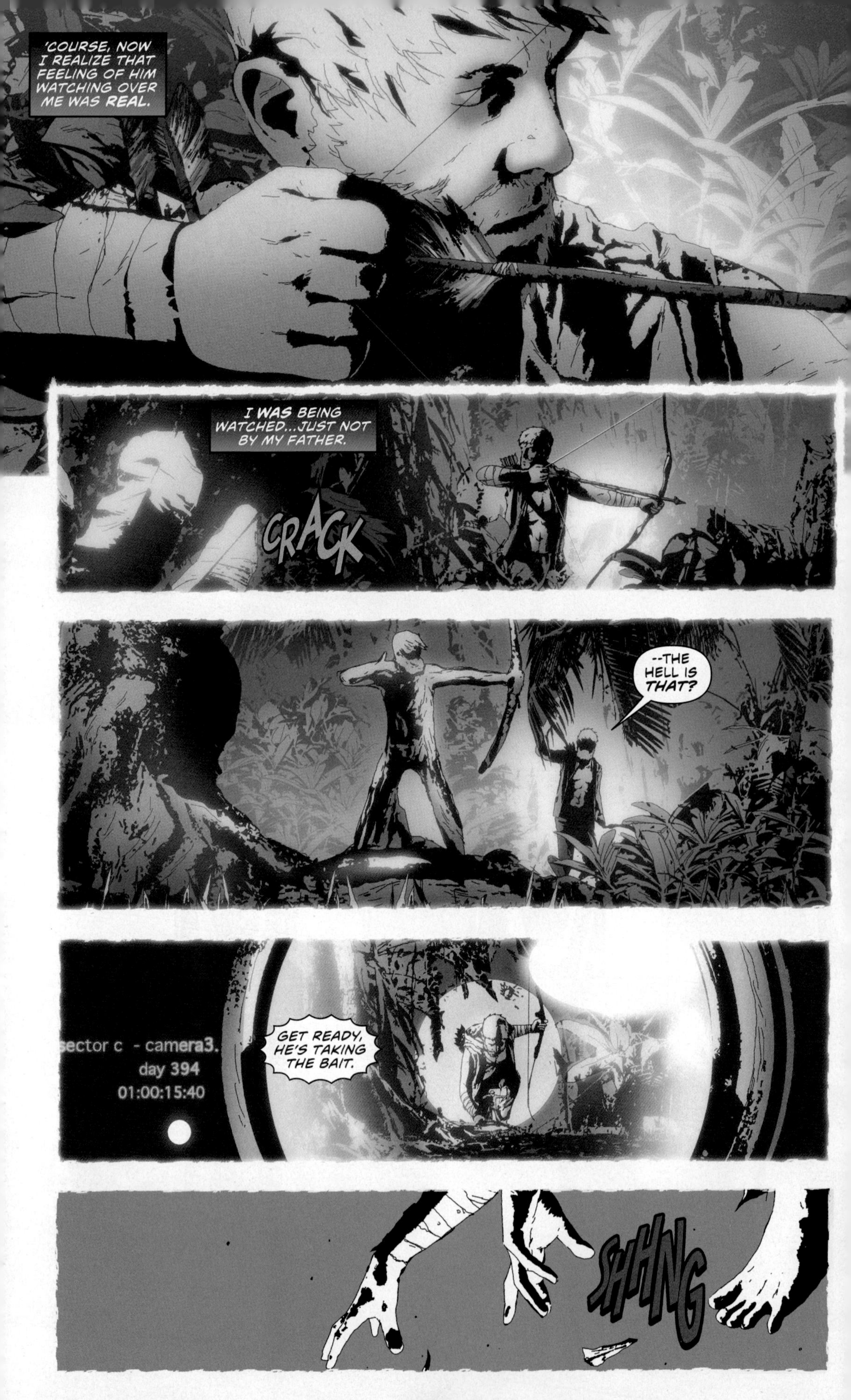
'COURSE, NOW I REALIZE THAT FEELING OF HIM WATCHING OVER ME WAS REAL.
I WAS BEING WATCHED...JUST NOT BY MY FATHER.
CRACK
--THE HELL IS THAT?
sector c - camera3.
day 394
01:00:15:40
GET READY, HE'S TAKING THE BAIT.
SHHNG

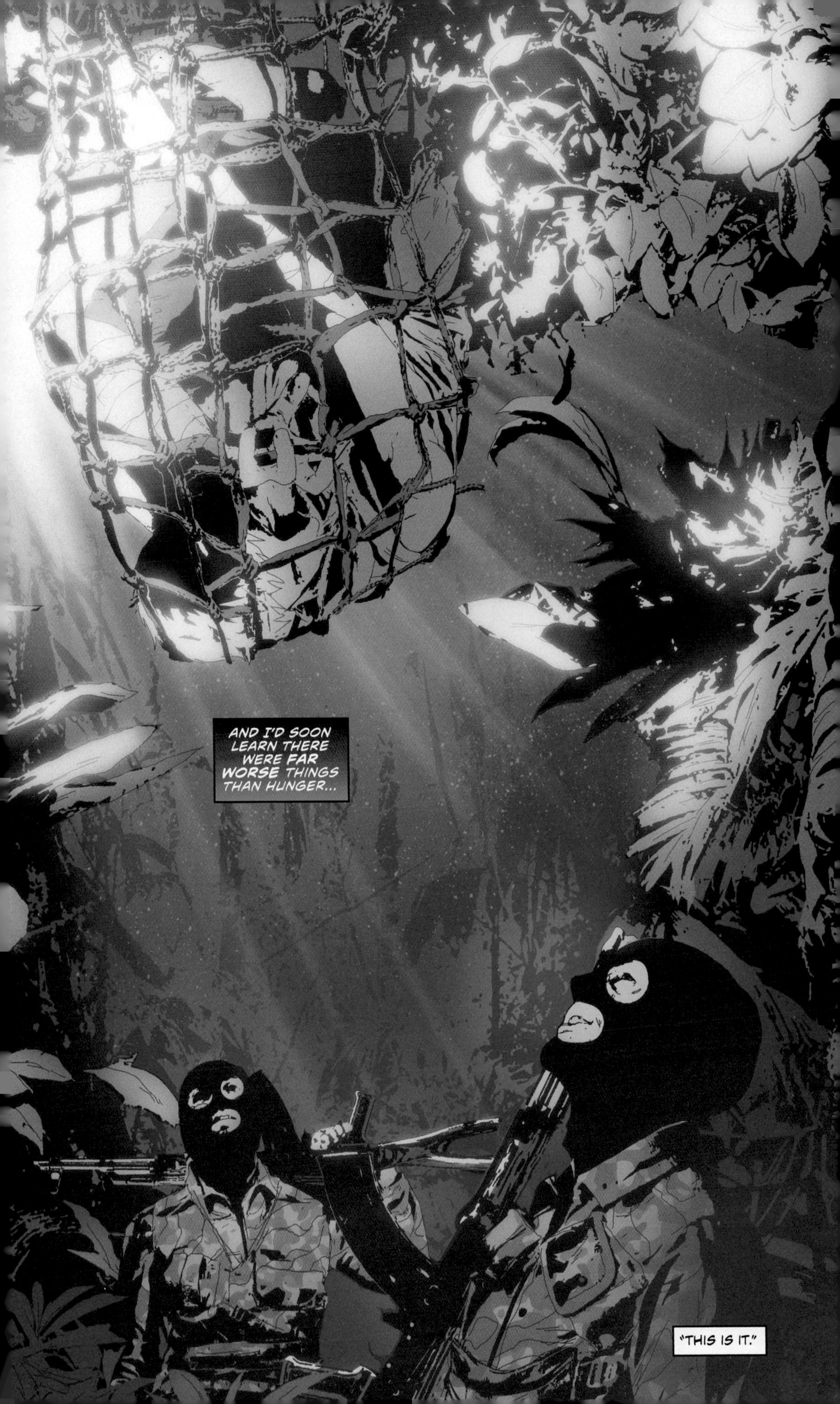
AND I'D SOON LEARN THERE WERE FAR WORSE THINGS THAN HUNGER...
"THIS IS IT."

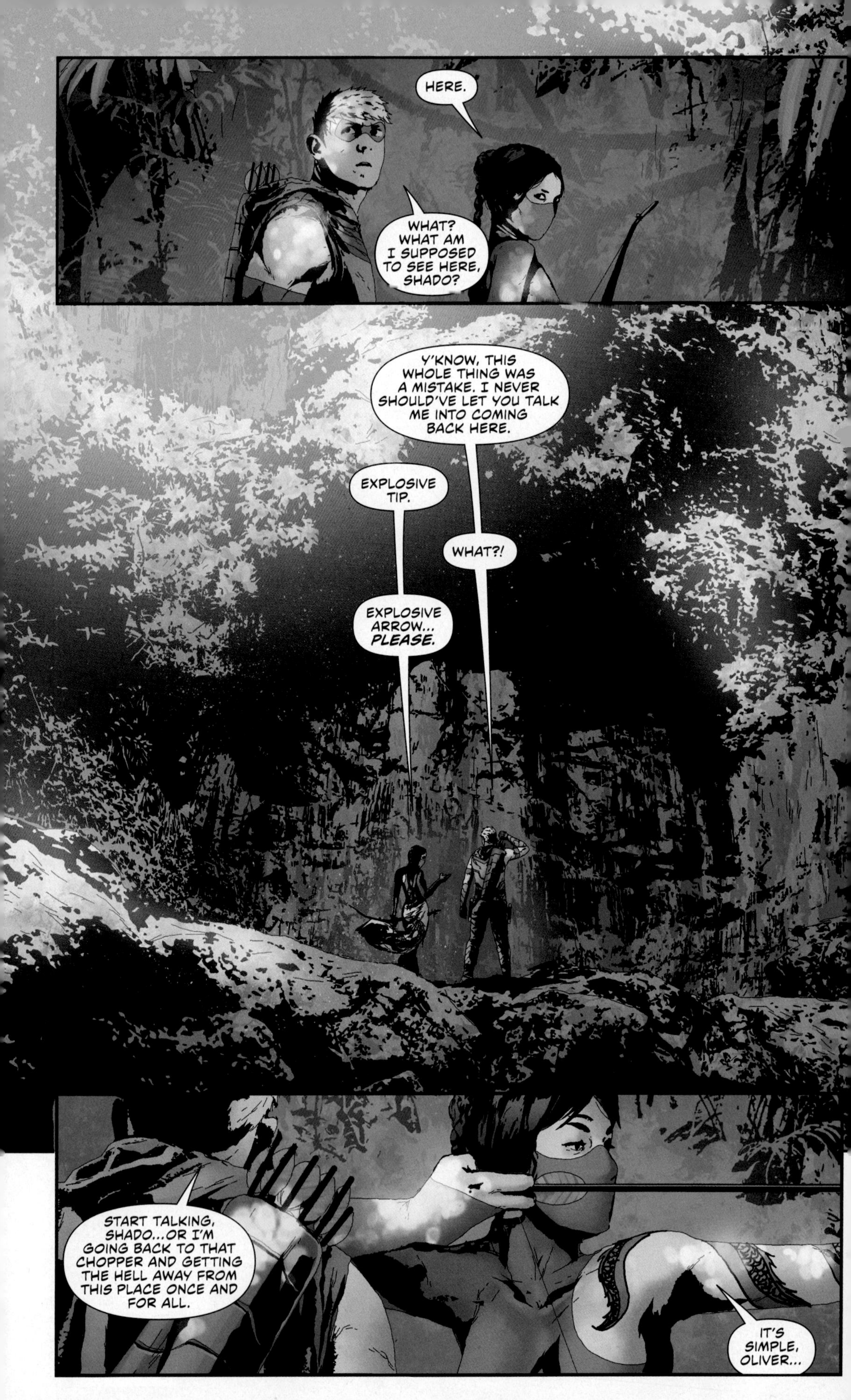
HERE.
WHAT? WHAT AM I SUPPOSED TO SEE HERE, SHADO?
Y'KNOW, THIS WHOLE THING WAS A MISTAKE. I NEVER SHOULD'VE LET YOU TALK ME INTO COMING BACK HERE.
EXPLOSIVE TIP.
WHAT?!
EXPLOSIVE ARROW... *PLEASE.*
START TALKING, SHADO...OR I'M GOING BACK TO THAT CHOPPER AND GETTING THE HELL AWAY FROM THIS PLACE ONCE AND FOR ALL.
IT'S SIMPLE, OLIVER...

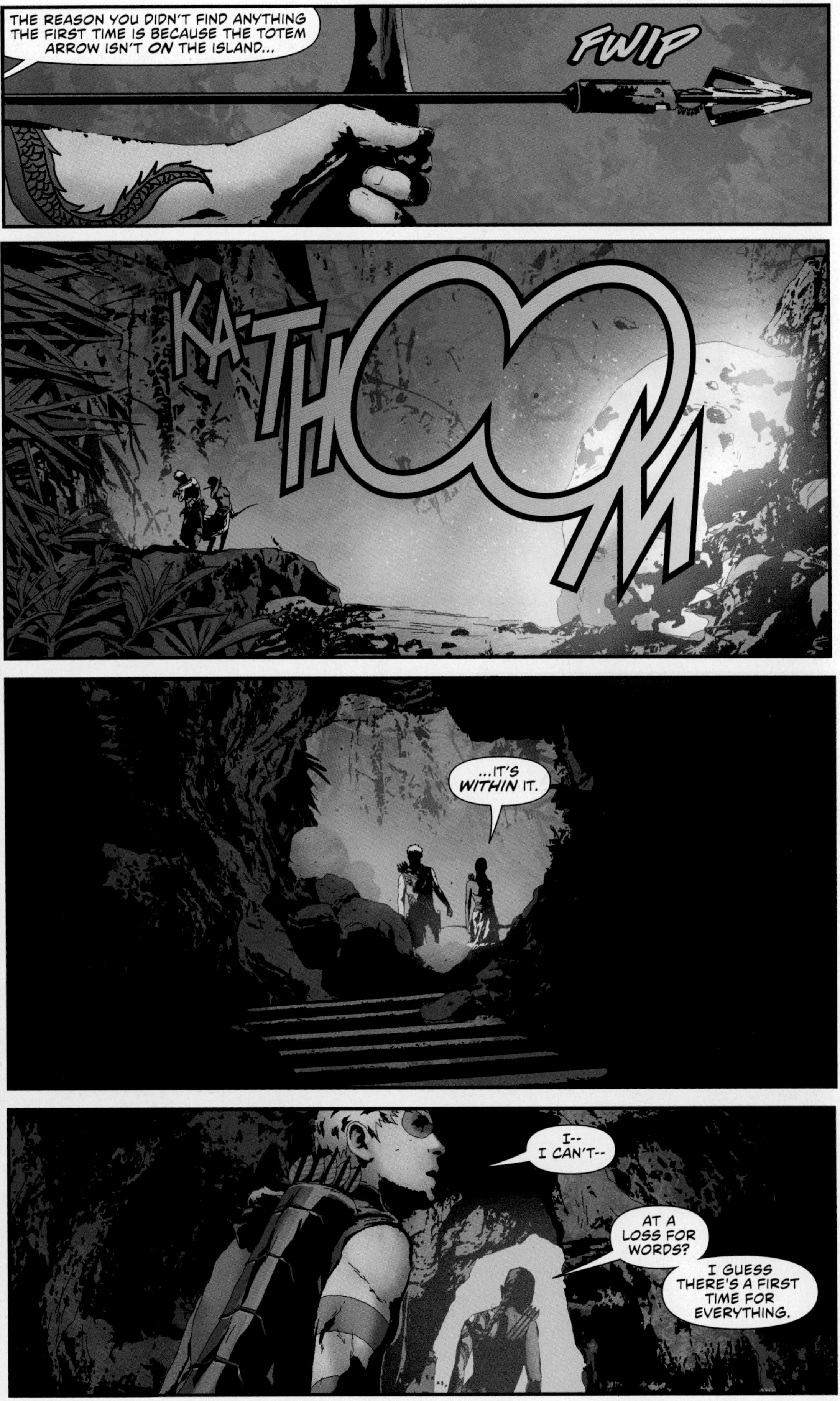
THE REASON YOU DIDN'T FIND ANYTHING THE FIRST TIME IS BECAUSE THE TOTEM ARROW ISN'T ON THE ISLAND...
FWIP
KA-THOOM
...IT'S WITHIN IT.
I-- I CAN'T--
AT A LOSS FOR WORDS?
I GUESS THERE'S A FIRST TIME FOR EVERYTHING.

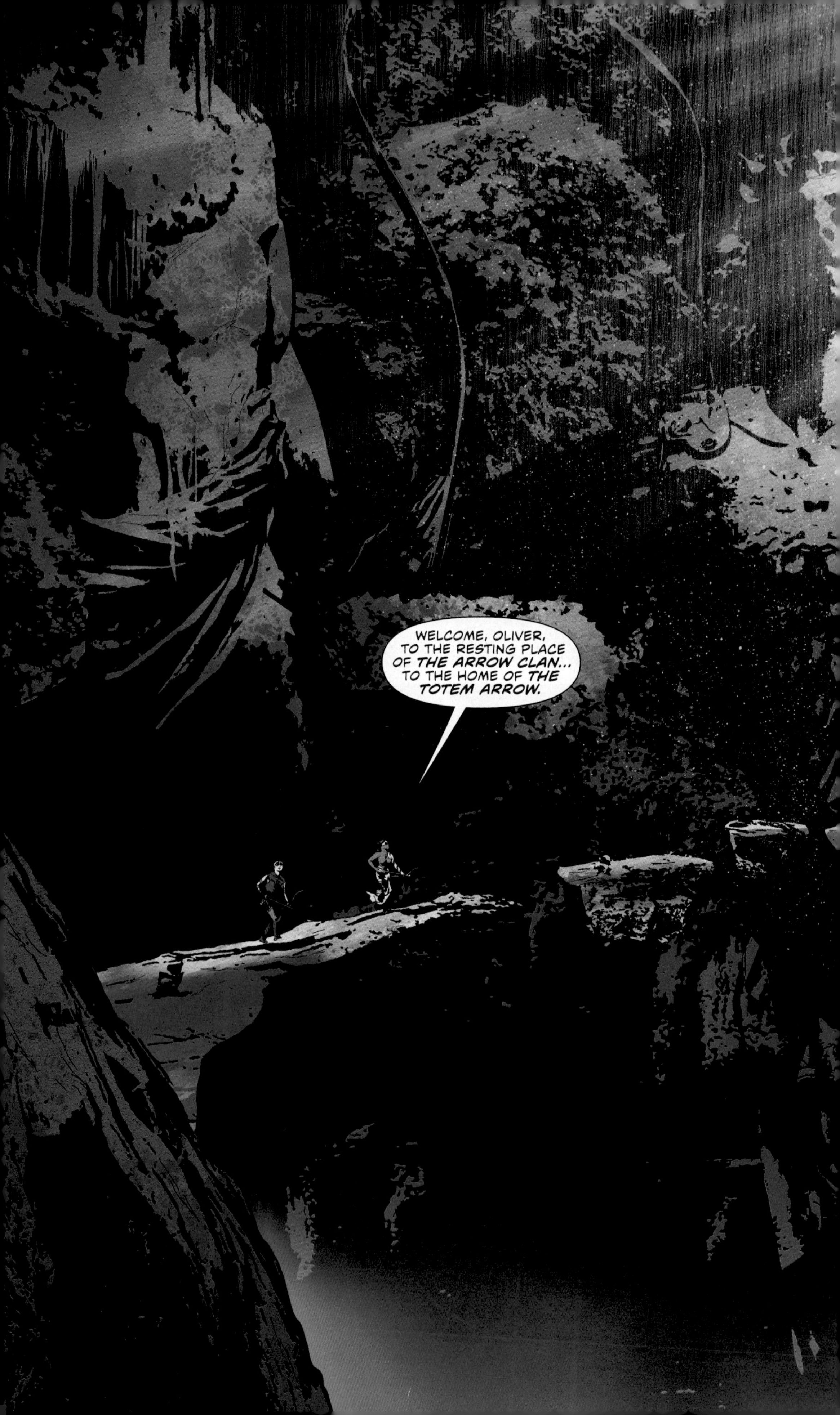
WELCOME, OLIVER, TO THE RESTING PLACE OF THE ARROW CLAN... TO THE HOME OF THE TOTEM ARROW.

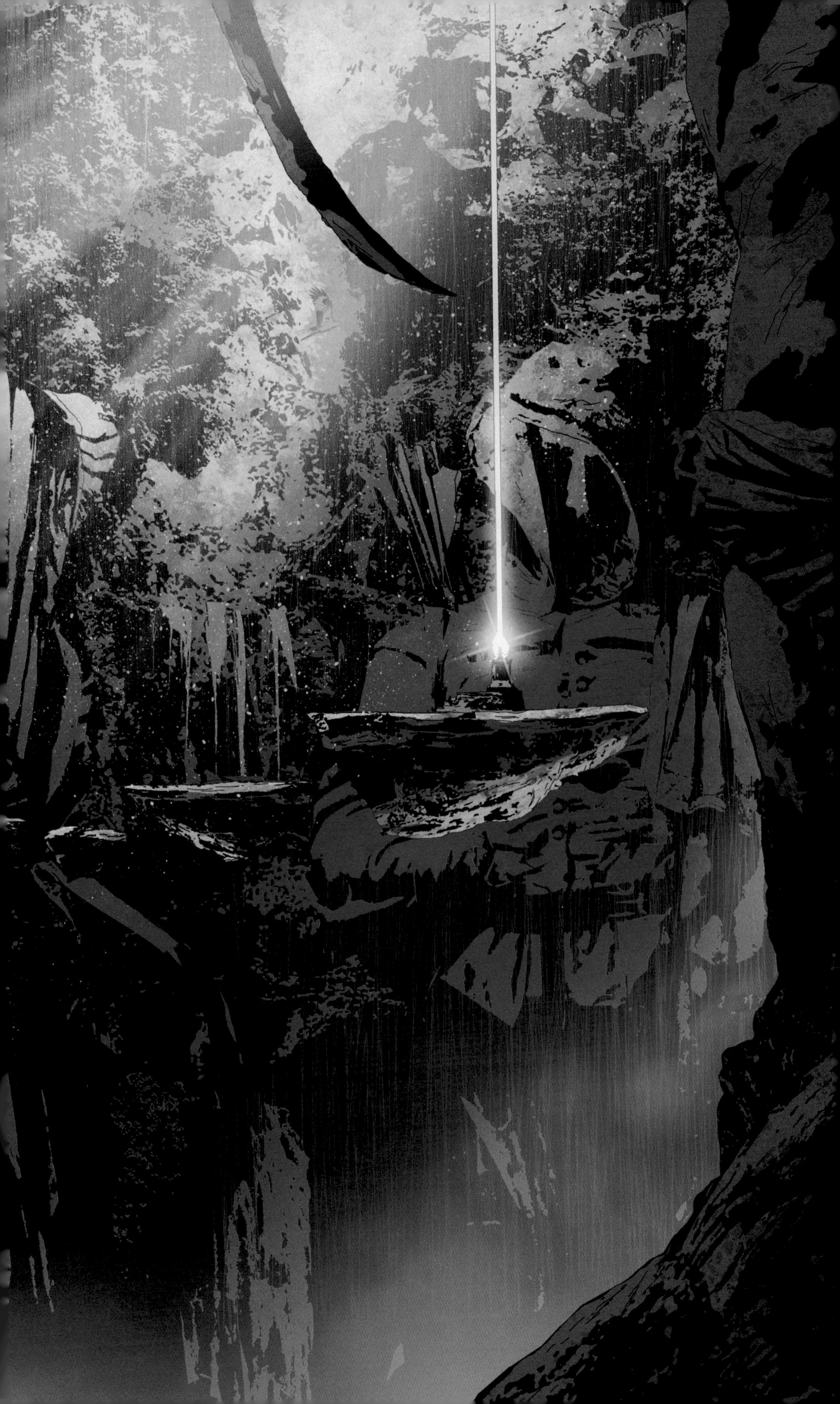

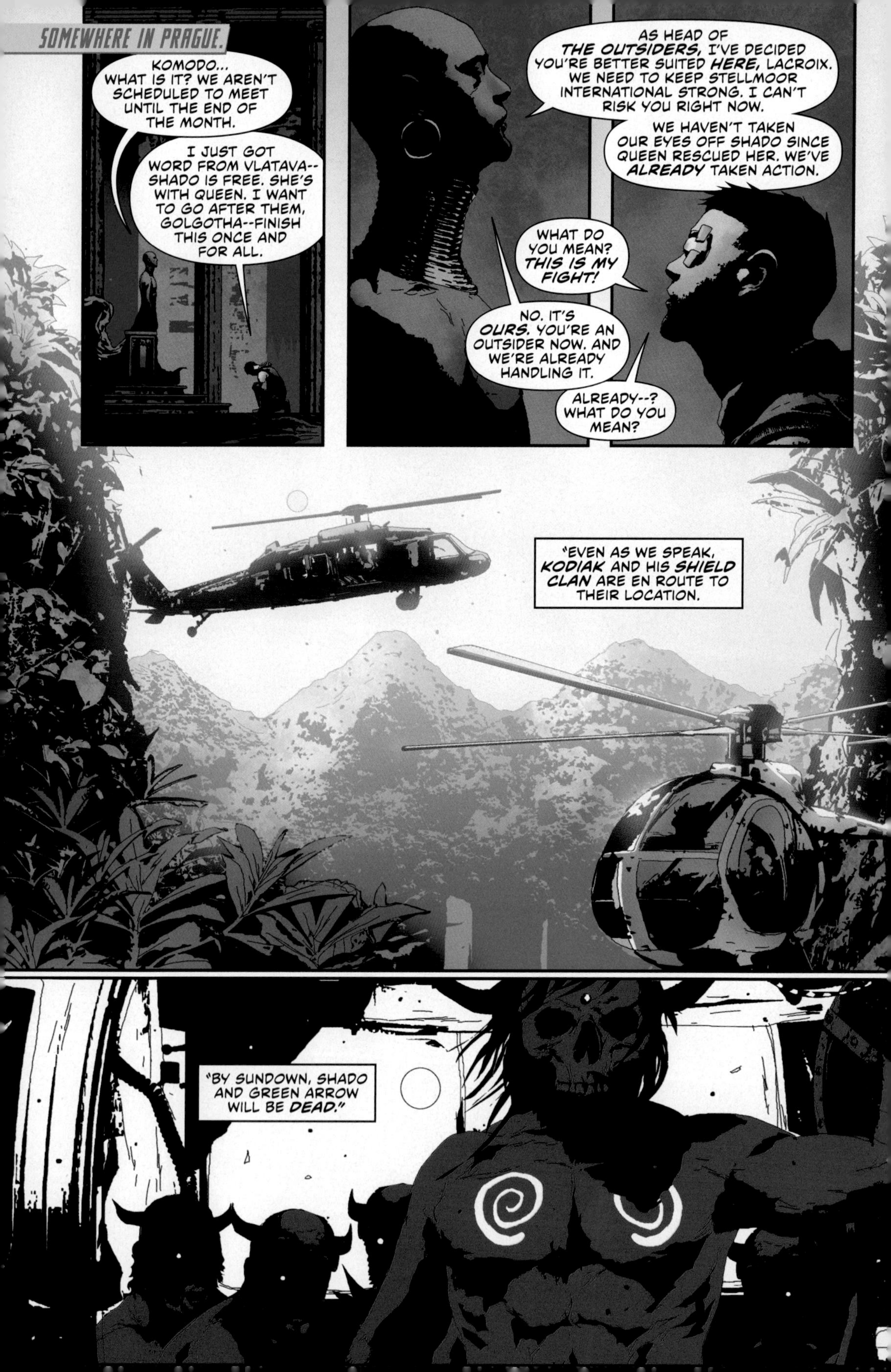
SOMEWHERE IN PRAGUE.
KOMODO... WHAT IS IT? WE AREN'T SCHEDULED TO MEET UNTIL THE END OF THE MONTH.
I JUST GOT WORD FROM VLATAVA-- SHADO IS FREE. SHE'S WITH QUEEN. I WANT TO GO AFTER THEM, GOLGOTHA--FINISH THIS ONCE AND FOR ALL.
AS HEAD OF THE OUTSIDERS, I'VE DECIDED YOU'RE BETTER SUITED HERE, LACROIX. WE NEED TO KEEP STELLMOOR INTERNATIONAL STRONG. I CAN'T RISK YOU RIGHT NOW.
WE HAVEN'T TAKEN OUR EYES OFF SHADO SINCE QUEEN RESCUED HER. WE'VE ALREADY TAKEN ACTION.
WHAT DO YOU MEAN? THIS IS MY FIGHT!
NO. IT'S OURS. YOU'RE AN OUTSIDER NOW. AND WE'RE ALREADY HANDLING IT.
ALREADY--? WHAT DO YOU MEAN?
"EVEN AS WE SPEAK, KODIAK AND HIS SHIELD CLAN ARE EN ROUTE TO THEIR LOCATION.
"BY SUNDOWN, SHADO AND GREEN ARROW WILL BE DEAD."

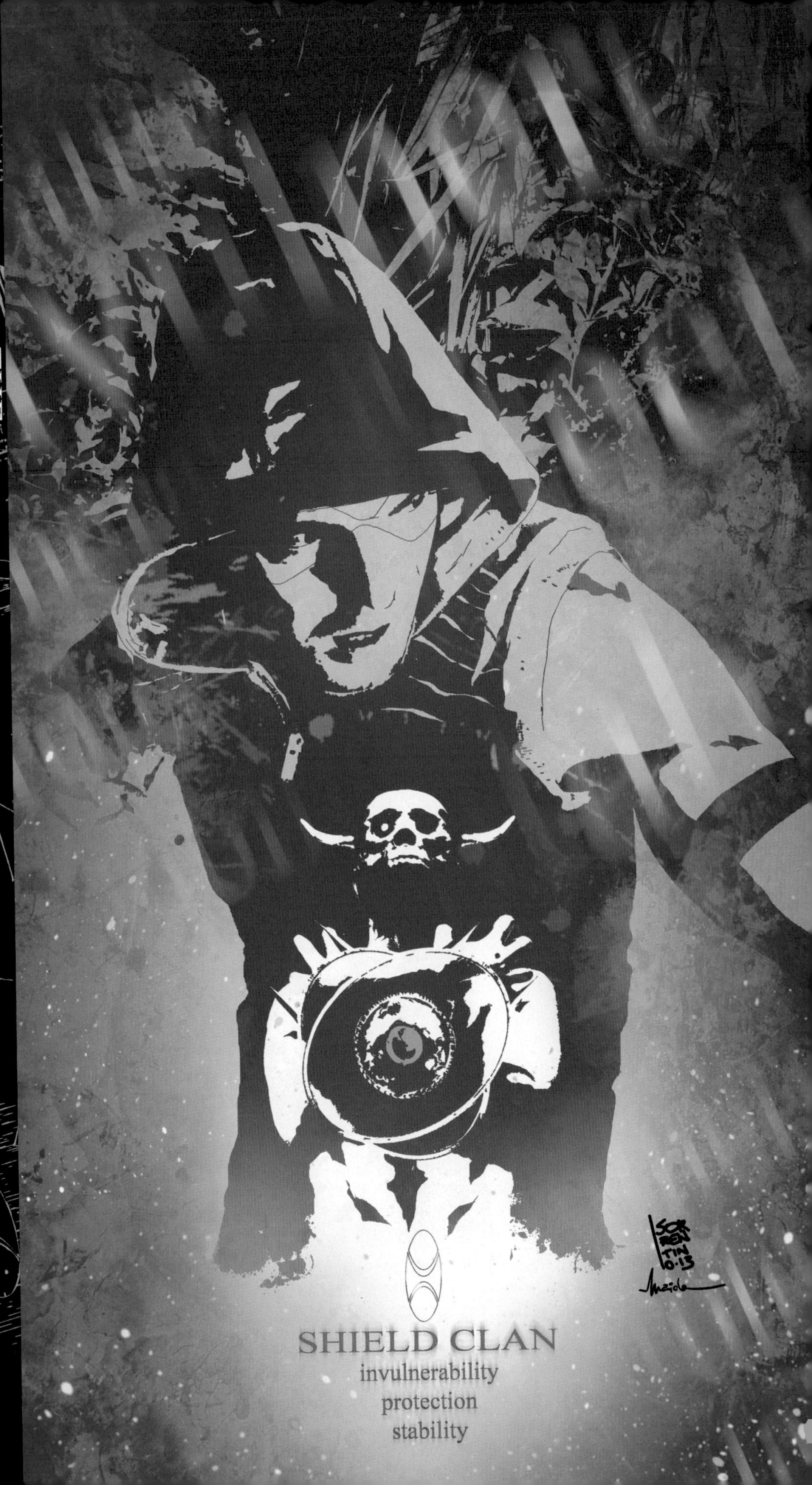
SHIELD CLAN
invulnerability
protection
stability

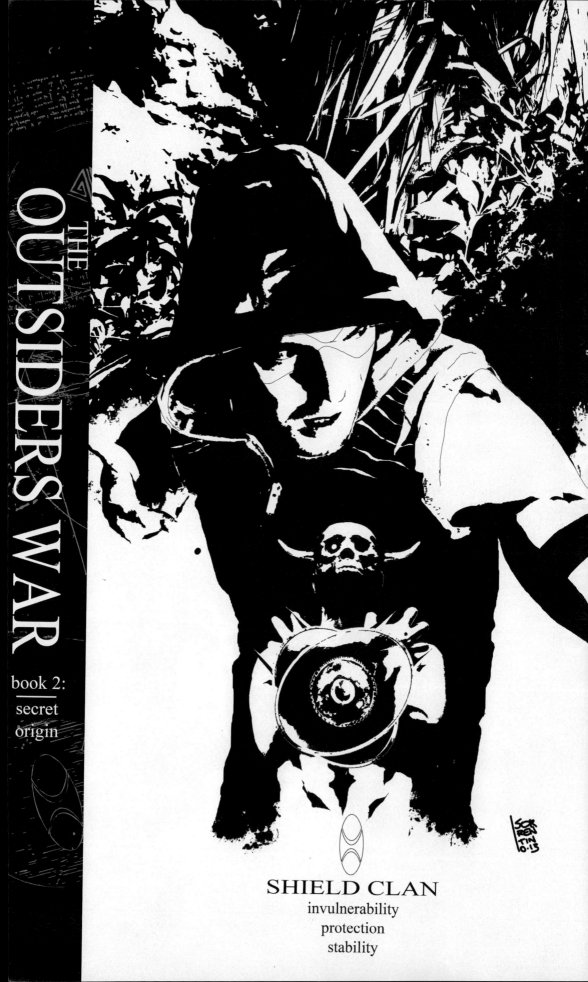

THE OUTSIDERS' WAR

book 2:
secret
origin

SHIELD CLAN
invulnerability
protection
stability

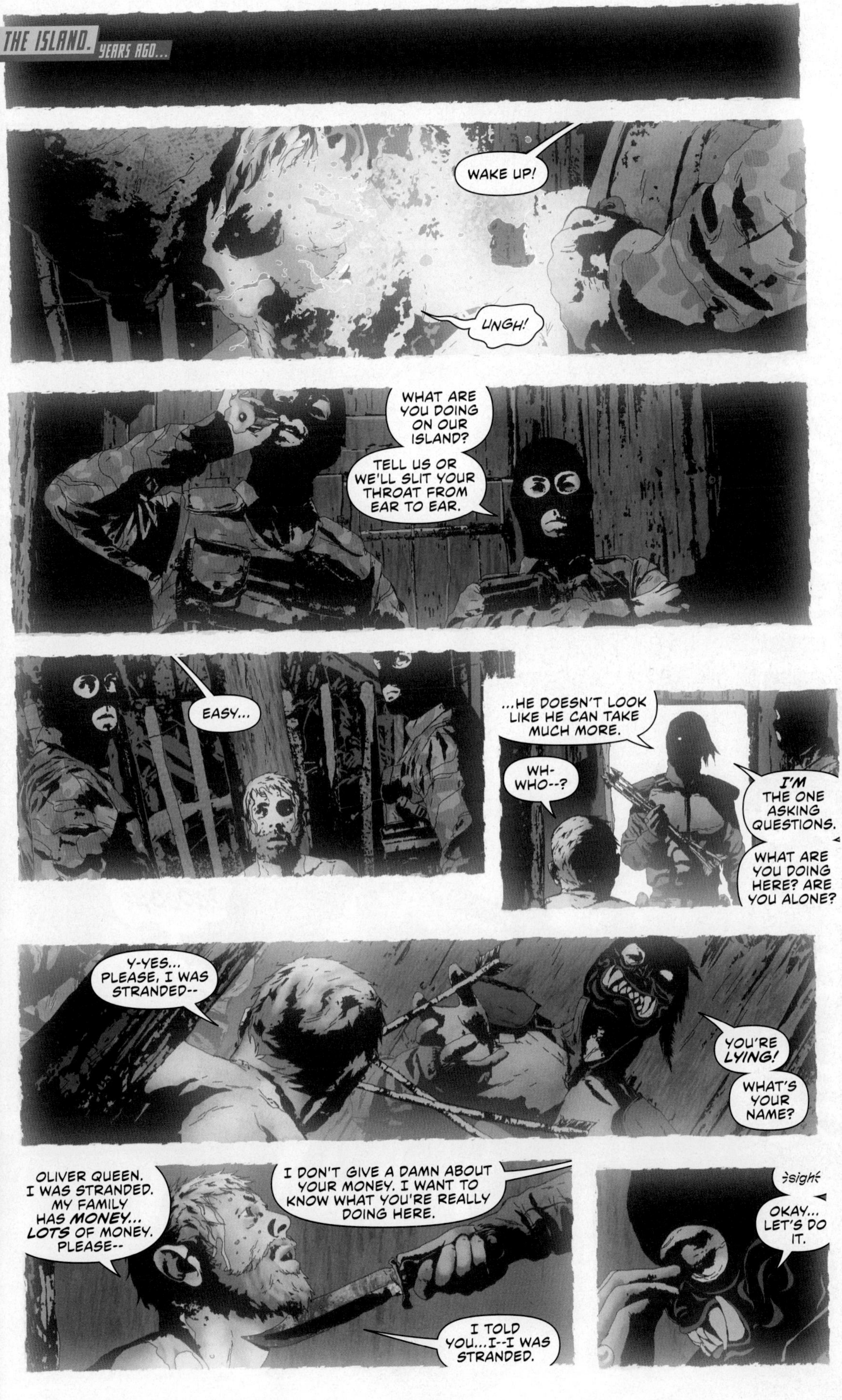
THE ISLAND.
YEARS AGO...
WAKE UP!
UNGH!
WHAT ARE YOU DOING ON OUR ISLAND?
TELL US OR WE'LL SLIT YOUR THROAT FROM EAR TO EAR.
EASY...
...HE DOESN'T LOOK LIKE HE CAN TAKE MUCH MORE.
WH- WHO--?
I'M THE ONE ASKING QUESTIONS.
WHAT ARE YOU DOING HERE? ARE YOU ALONE?
Y-YES... PLEASE, I WAS STRANDED--
YOU'RE LYING!
WHAT'S YOUR NAME?
OLIVER QUEEN. I WAS STRANDED. MY FAMILY HAS MONEY... LOTS OF MONEY. PLEASE--
I DON'T GIVE A DAMN ABOUT YOUR MONEY. I WANT TO KNOW WHAT YOU'RE REALLY DOING HERE.
I TOLD YOU...I--I WAS STRANDED.
sigh
OKAY... LET'S DO IT.

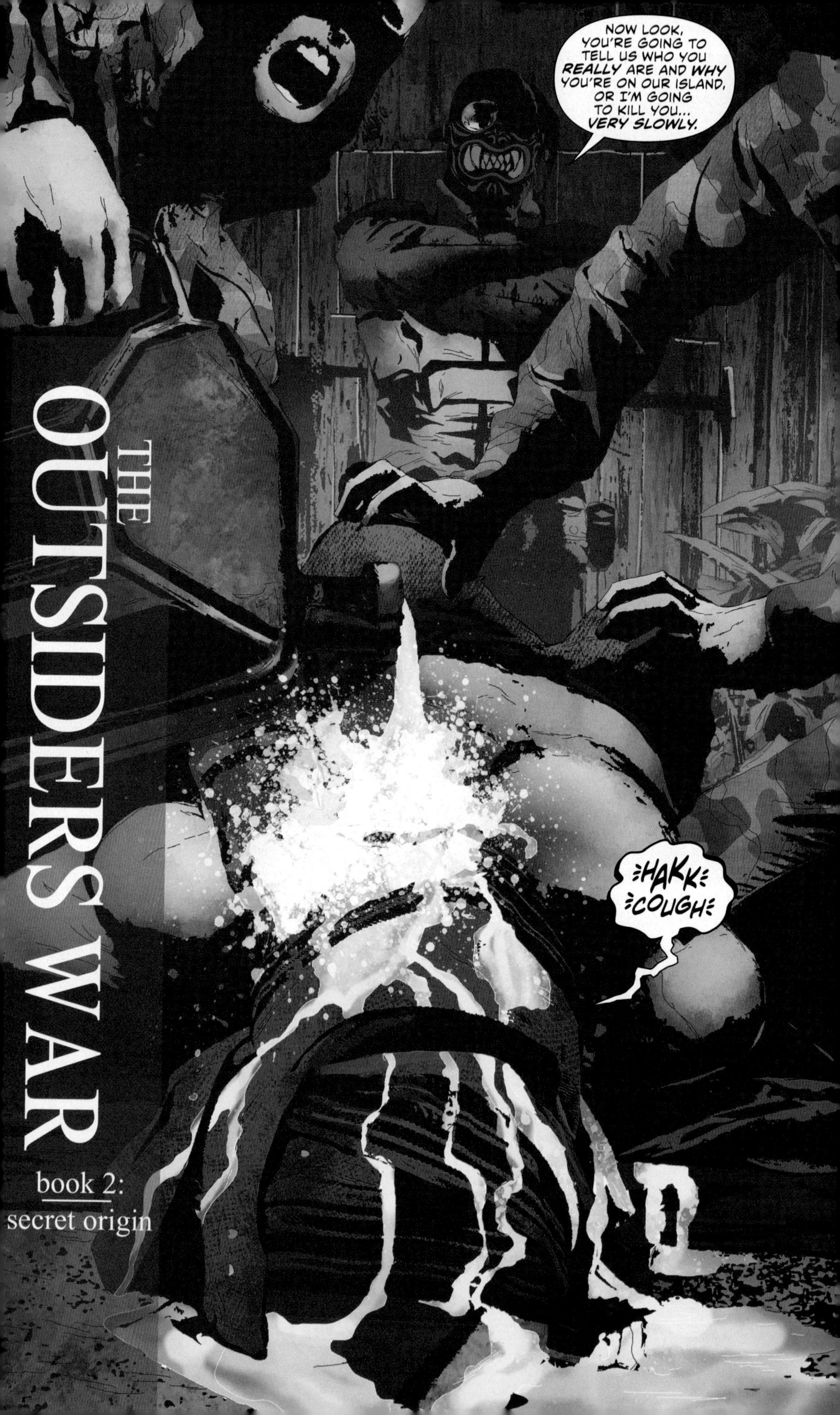
NOW LOOK, YOU'RE GOING TO TELL US WHO YOU REALLY ARE AND WHY YOU'RE ON OUR ISLAND, OR I'M GOING TO KILL YOU... VERY SLOWLY.
THE OUTSIDERS WAR
book 2: secret origin
HAKK COUGH

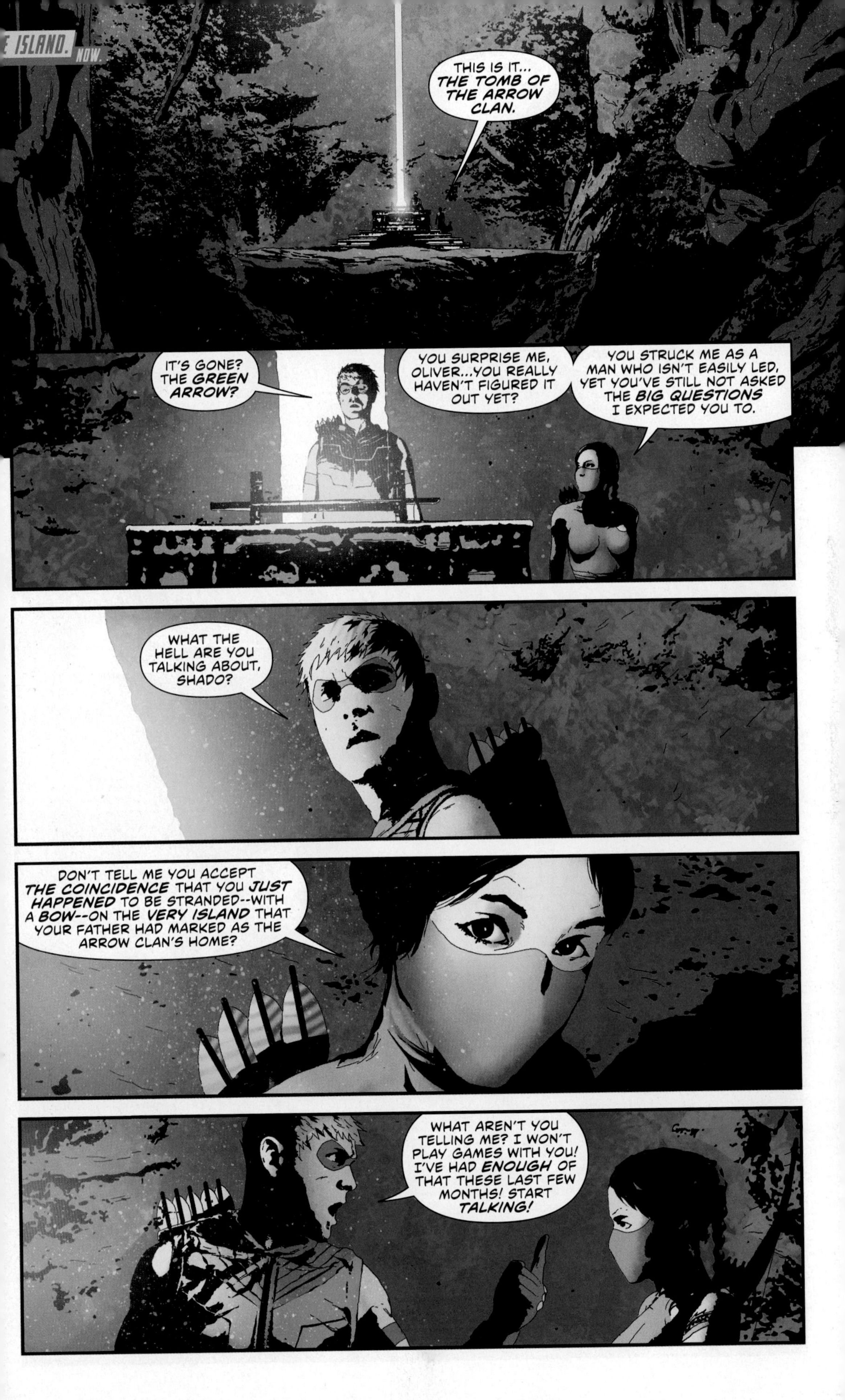

E ISLAND. NOW.
THIS IS IT... THE TOMB OF THE ARROW CLAN.
IT'S GONE? THE GREEN ARROW?
YOU SURPRISE ME, OLIVER...YOU REALLY HAVEN'T FIGURED IT OUT YET?
YOU STRUCK ME AS A MAN WHO ISN'T EASILY LED, YET YOU'VE STILL NOT ASKED THE BIG QUESTIONS I EXPECTED YOU TO.
WHAT THE HELL ARE YOU TALKING ABOUT, SHADO?
DON'T TELL ME YOU ACCEPT THE COINCIDENCE THAT YOU JUST HAPPENED TO BE STRANDED--WITH A BOW--ON THE VERY ISLAND THAT YOUR FATHER HAD MARKED AS THE ARROW CLAN'S HOME?
WHAT AREN'T YOU TELLING ME? I WON'T PLAY GAMES WITH YOU! I'VE HAD ENOUGH OF THAT THESE LAST FEW MONTHS! START TALKING!

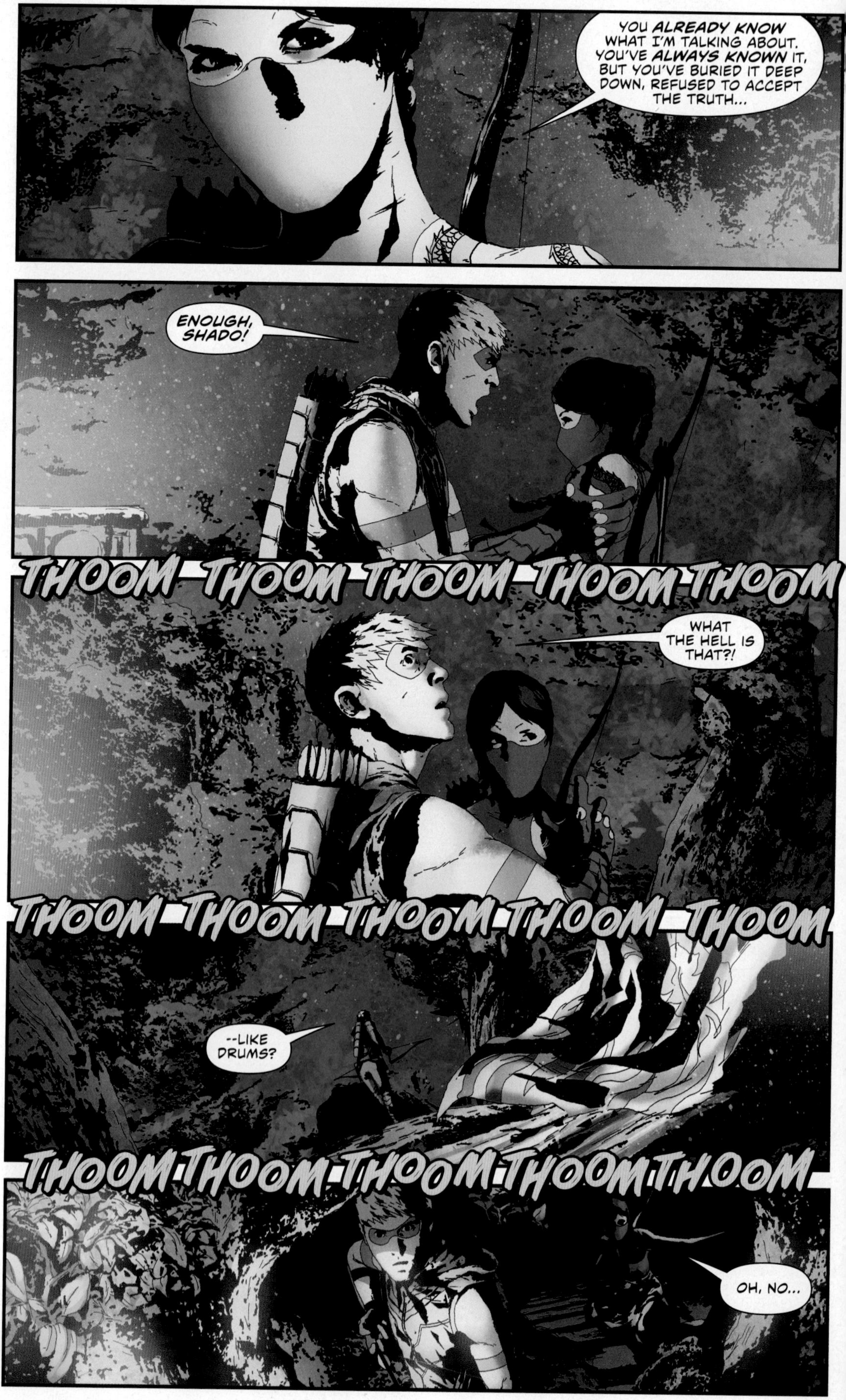
YOU ALREADY KNOW WHAT I'M TALKING ABOUT. YOU'VE ALWAYS KNOWN IT, BUT YOU'VE BURIED IT DEEP DOWN, REFUSED TO ACCEPT THE TRUTH...
ENOUGH, SHADO!
THOOM THOOM THOOM THOOM THOOM
WHAT THE HELL IS THAT?!
THOOM THOOM THOOM THOOM THOOM
--LIKE DRUMS?
THOOM THOOM THOOM THOOM THOOM
OH, NO...

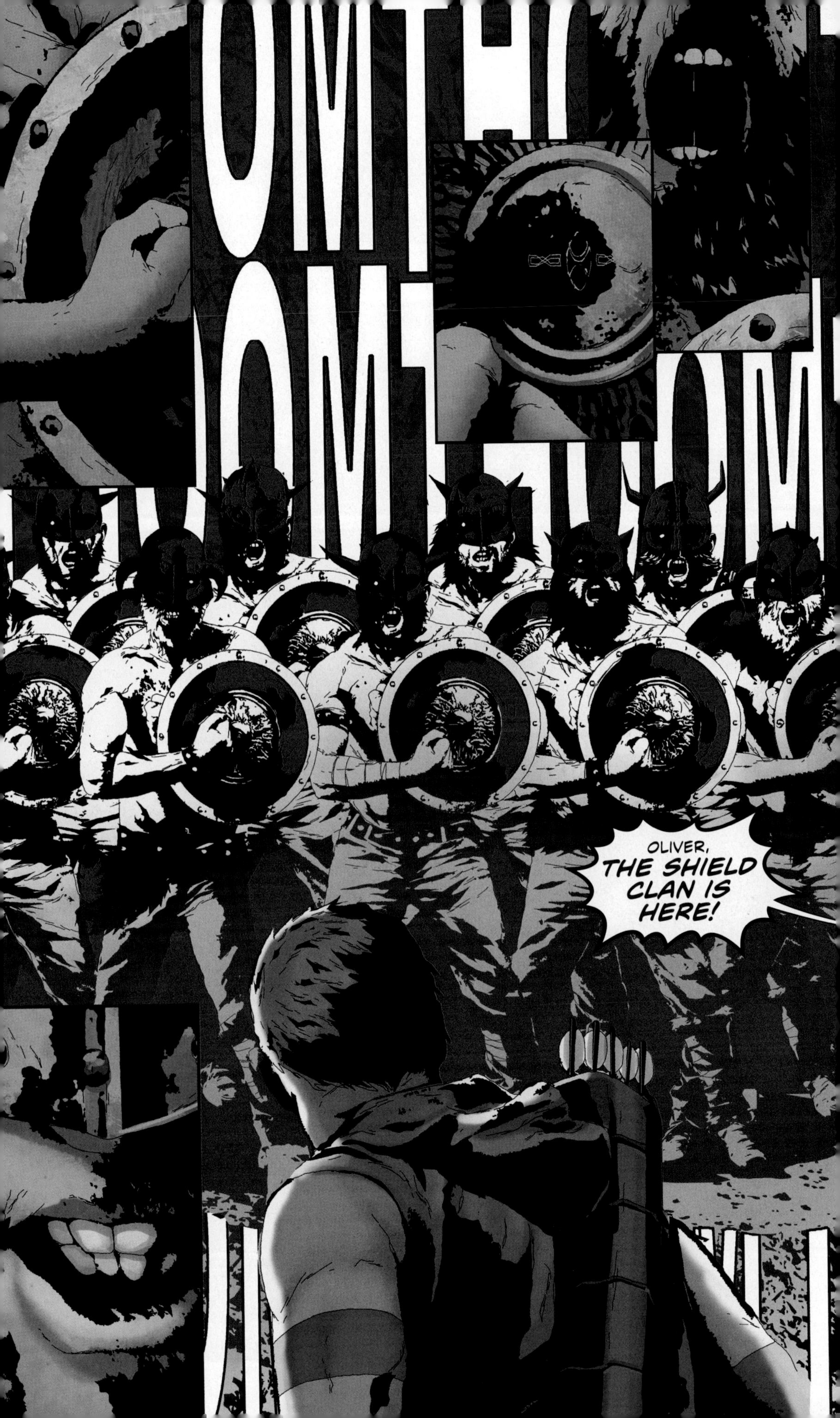
OLIVER, THE SHIELD CLAN IS HERE!

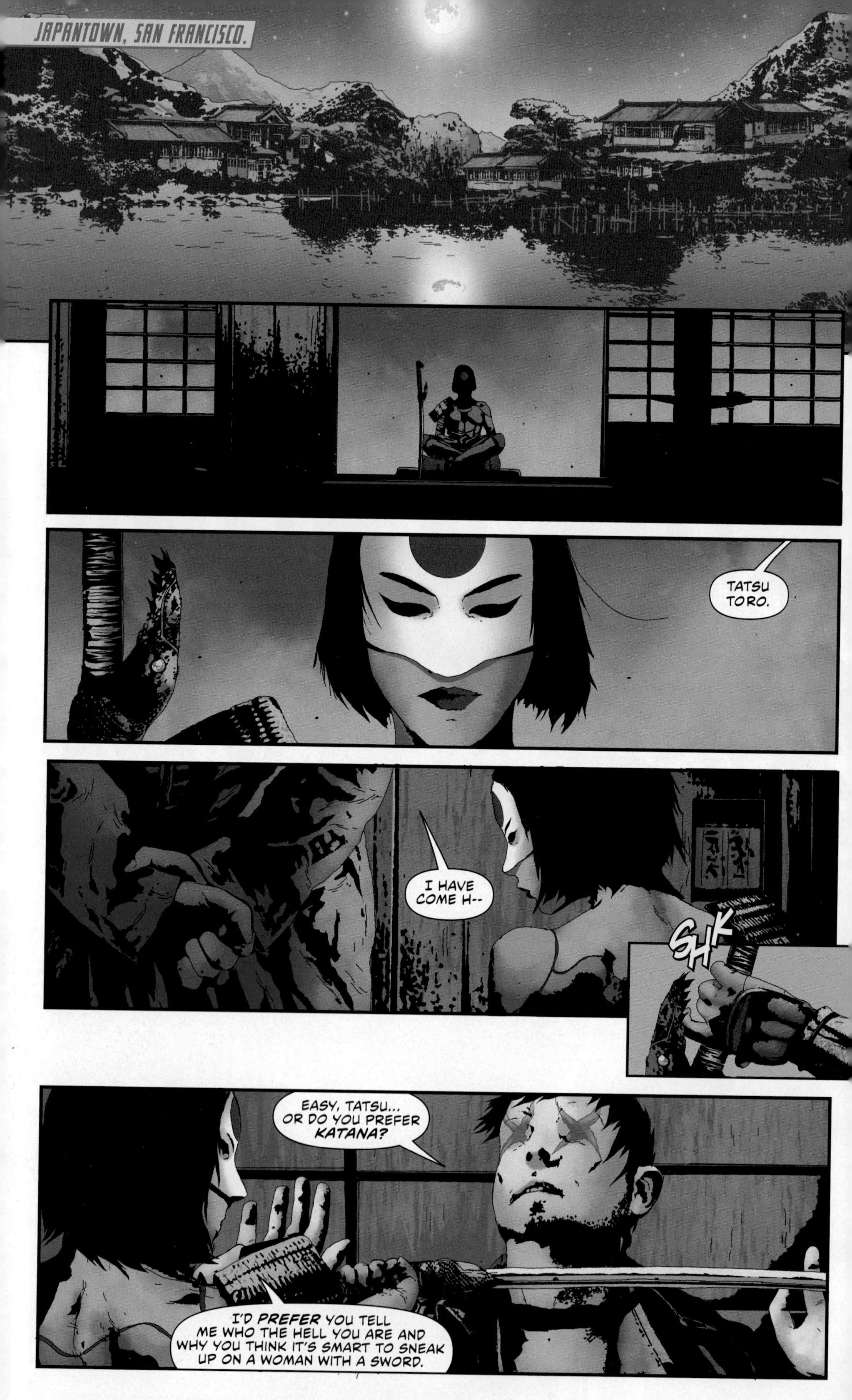
JAPANTOWN, SAN FRANCISCO.
TATSU TORO.
I HAVE COME H--
SHK
EASY, TATSU... OR DO YOU PREFER KATANA?
I'D PREFER YOU TELL ME WHO THE HELL YOU ARE AND WHY YOU THINK IT'S SMART TO SNEAK UP ON A WOMAN WITH A SWORD.

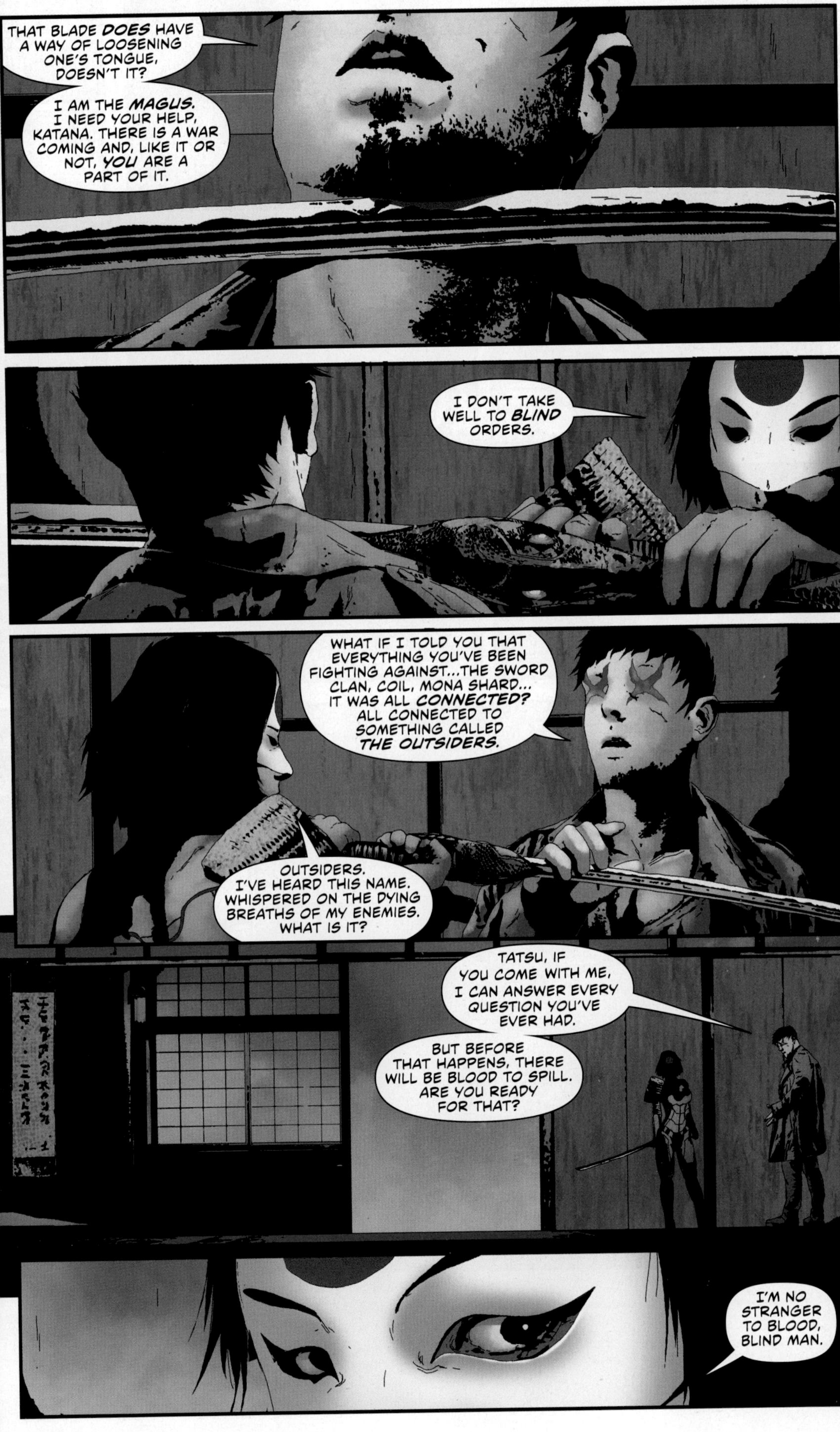
THAT BLADE *DOES* HAVE A WAY OF LOOSENING ONE'S TONGUE, DOESN'T IT?
I AM THE *MAGUS.* I NEED YOUR HELP, KATANA. THERE IS A WAR COMING AND, LIKE IT OR NOT, *YOU* ARE A PART OF IT.
I DON'T TAKE WELL TO *BLIND* ORDERS.
WHAT IF I TOLD YOU THAT EVERYTHING YOU'VE BEEN FIGHTING AGAINST...THE SWORD CLAN, COIL, MONA SHARD... IT WAS ALL *CONNECTED?* ALL CONNECTED TO SOMETHING CALLED *THE OUTSIDERS.*
OUTSIDERS. I'VE HEARD THIS NAME. WHISPERED ON THE DYING BREATHS OF MY ENEMIES. WHAT IS IT?
TATSU, IF YOU COME WITH ME, I CAN ANSWER EVERY QUESTION YOU'VE EVER HAD.
BUT BEFORE THAT HAPPENS, THERE WILL BE BLOOD TO SPILL. ARE YOU READY FOR THAT?
I'M NO STRANGER TO BLOOD, BLIND MAN.

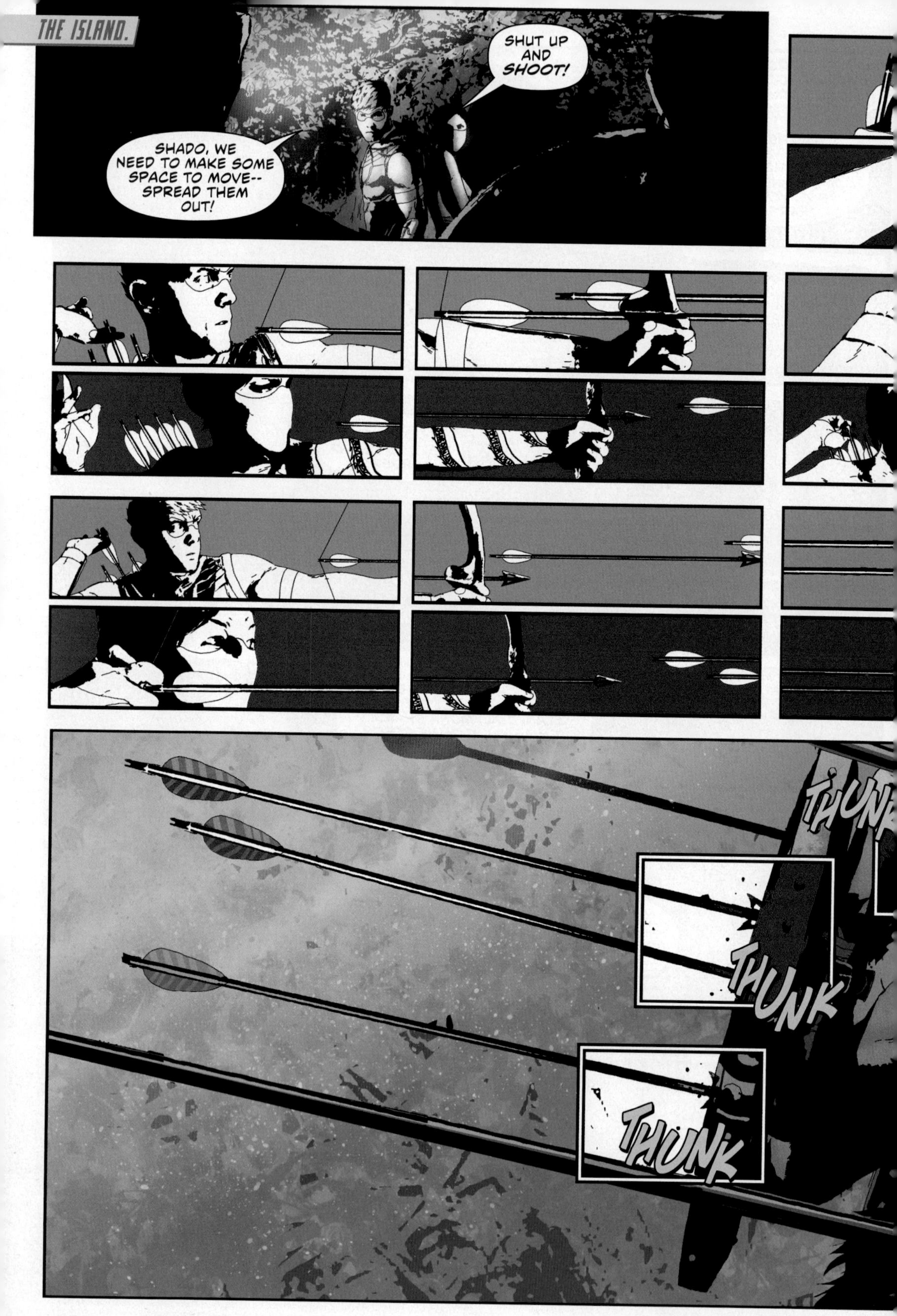
THE ISLAND.
SHADO, WE NEED TO MAKE SOME SPACE TO MOVE-- SPREAD THEM OUT!
SHUT UP AND SHOOT!
THUNK
THUNK
THUNK

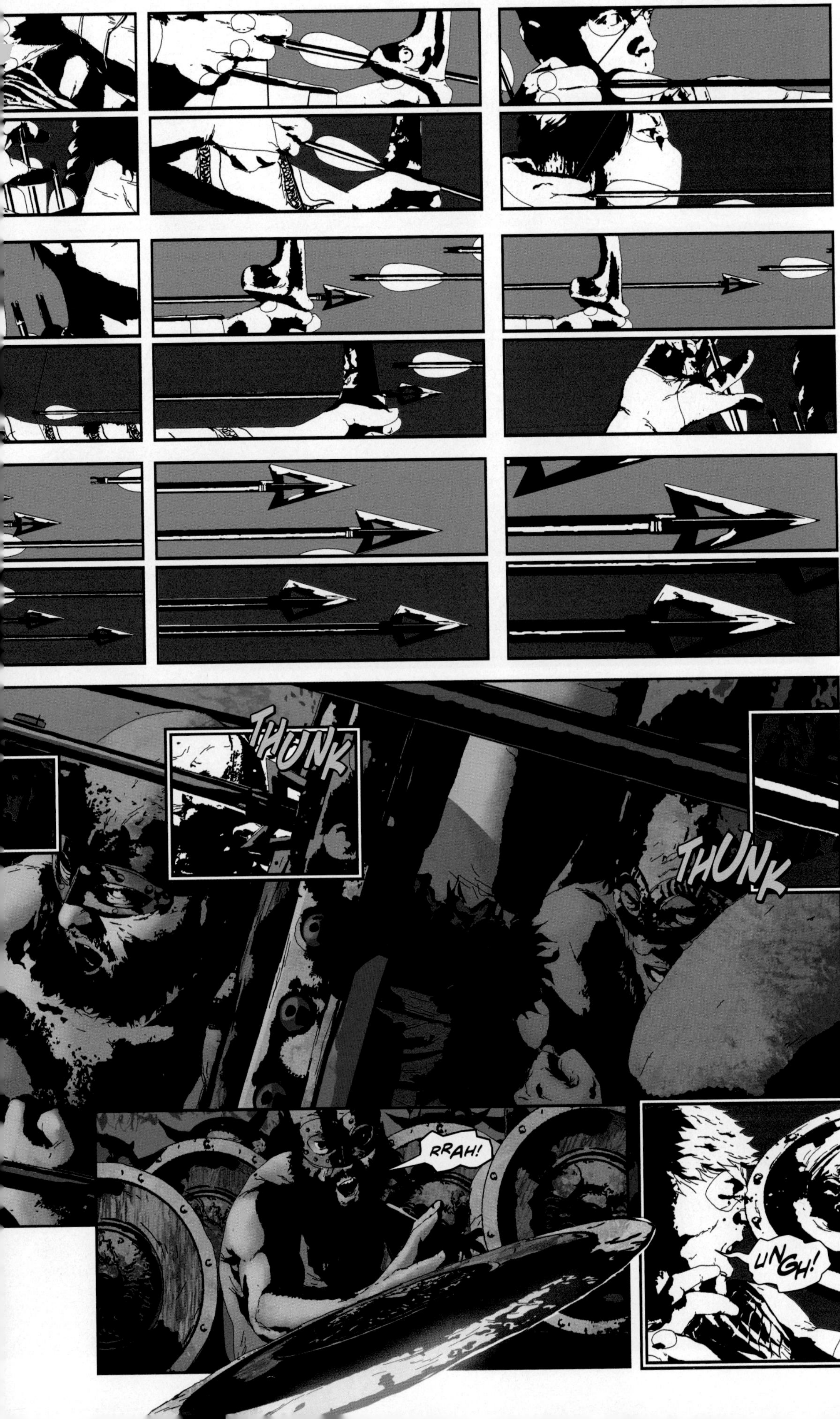
THUNK
THUNK
RRAH!
UNGH!

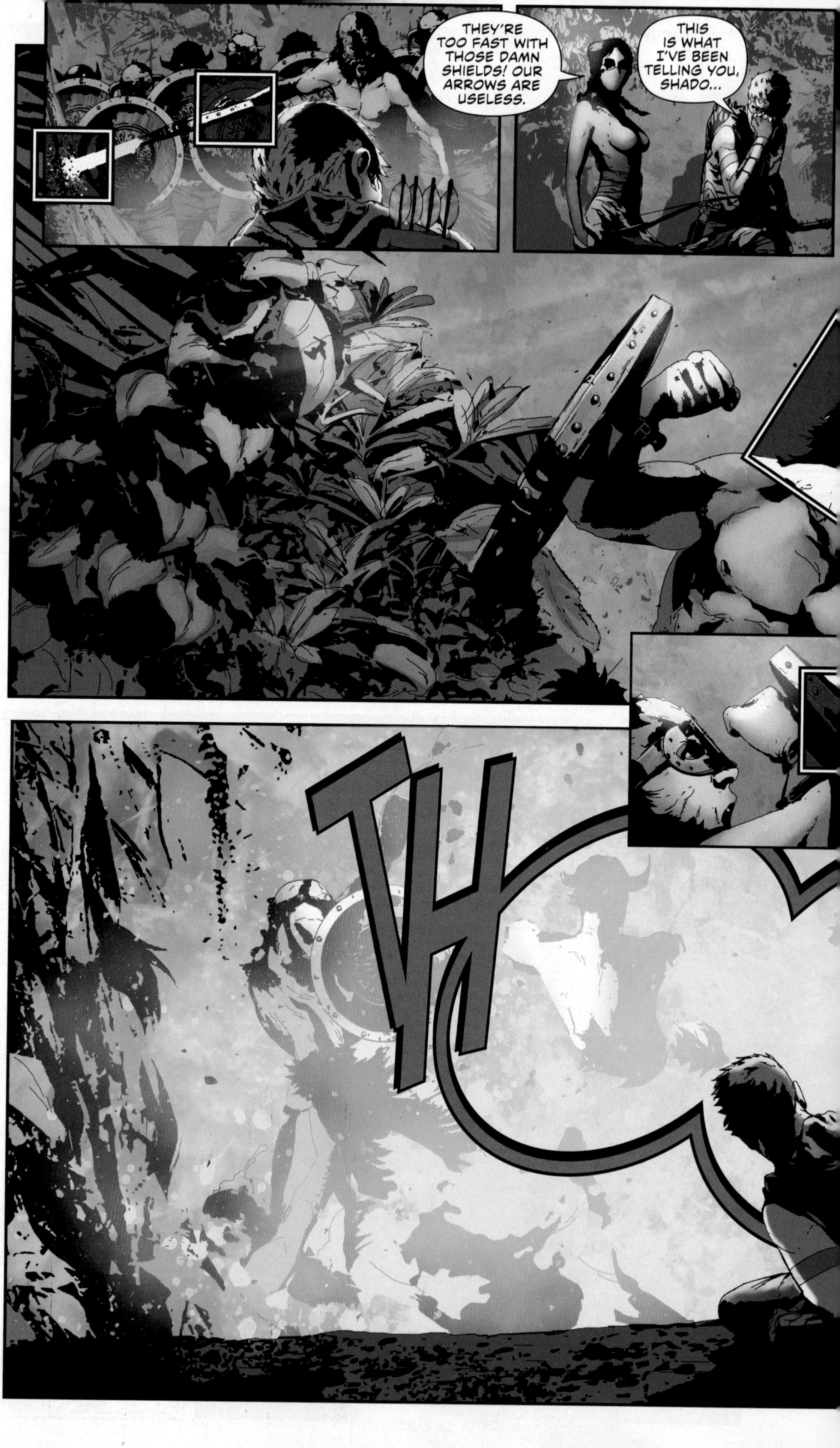
THEY'RE TOO FAST WITH THOSE DAMN SHIELDS! OUR ARROWS ARE USELESS.
THIS IS WHAT I'VE BEEN TELLING YOU, SHADO...
TH

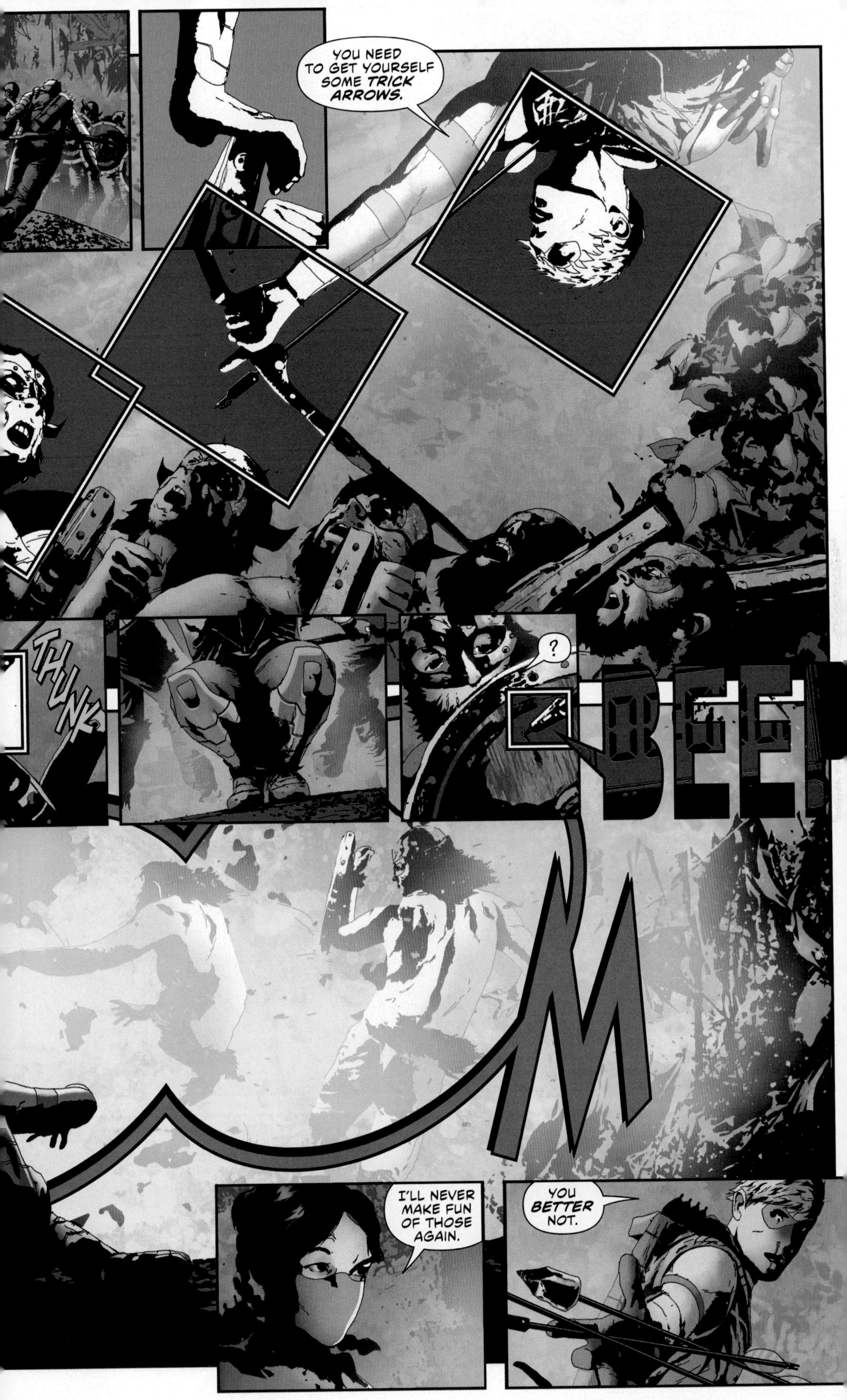
YOU NEED TO GET YOURSELF SOME TRICK ARROWS.
THUNK
?
BEEEM
I'LL NEVER MAKE FUN OF THOSE AGAIN.
YOU BETTER NOT.

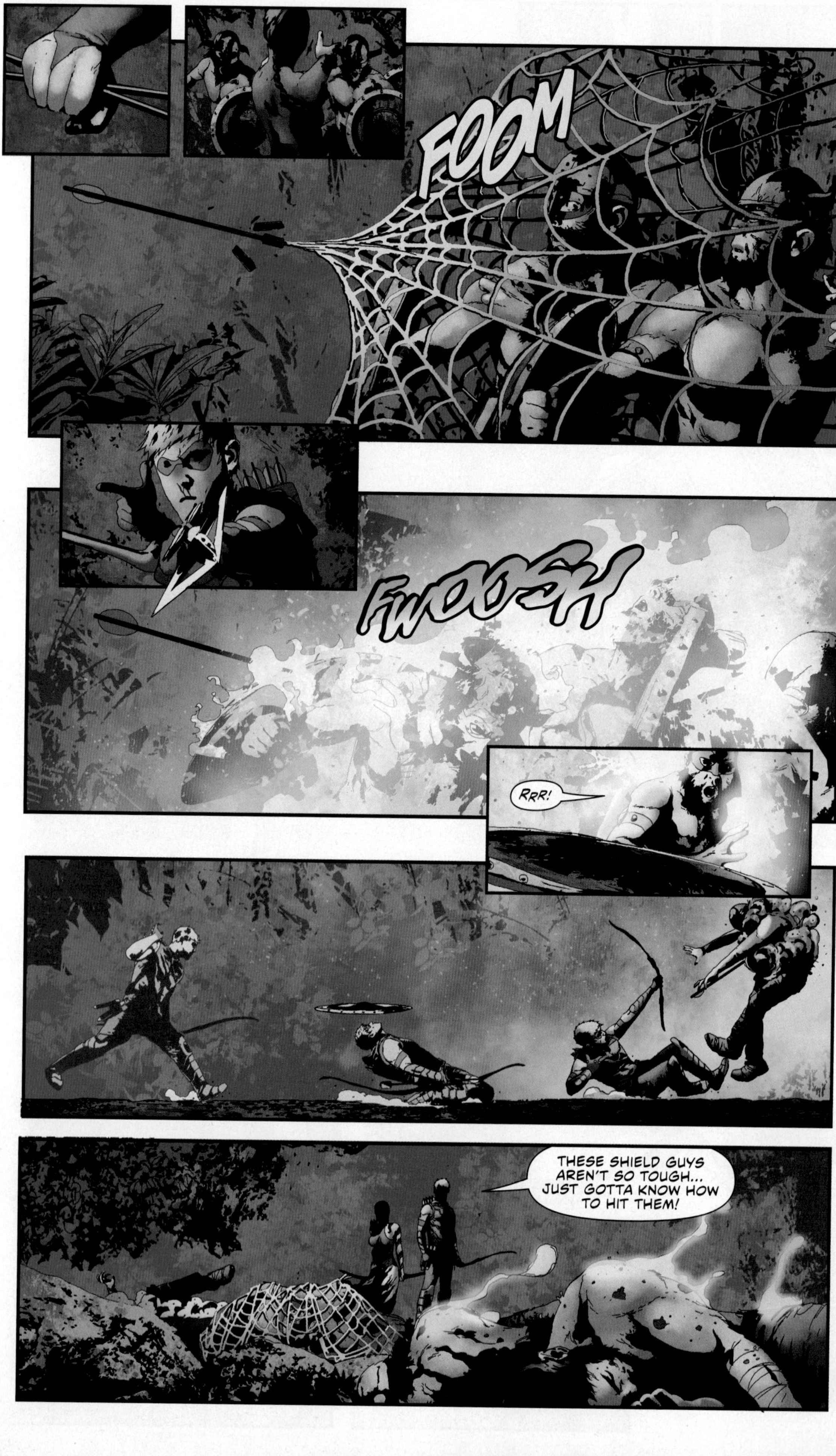
FOOM
FWOOSH
RRR!
THESE SHIELD GUYS AREN'T SO TOUGH... JUST GOTTA KNOW HOW TO HIT THEM!

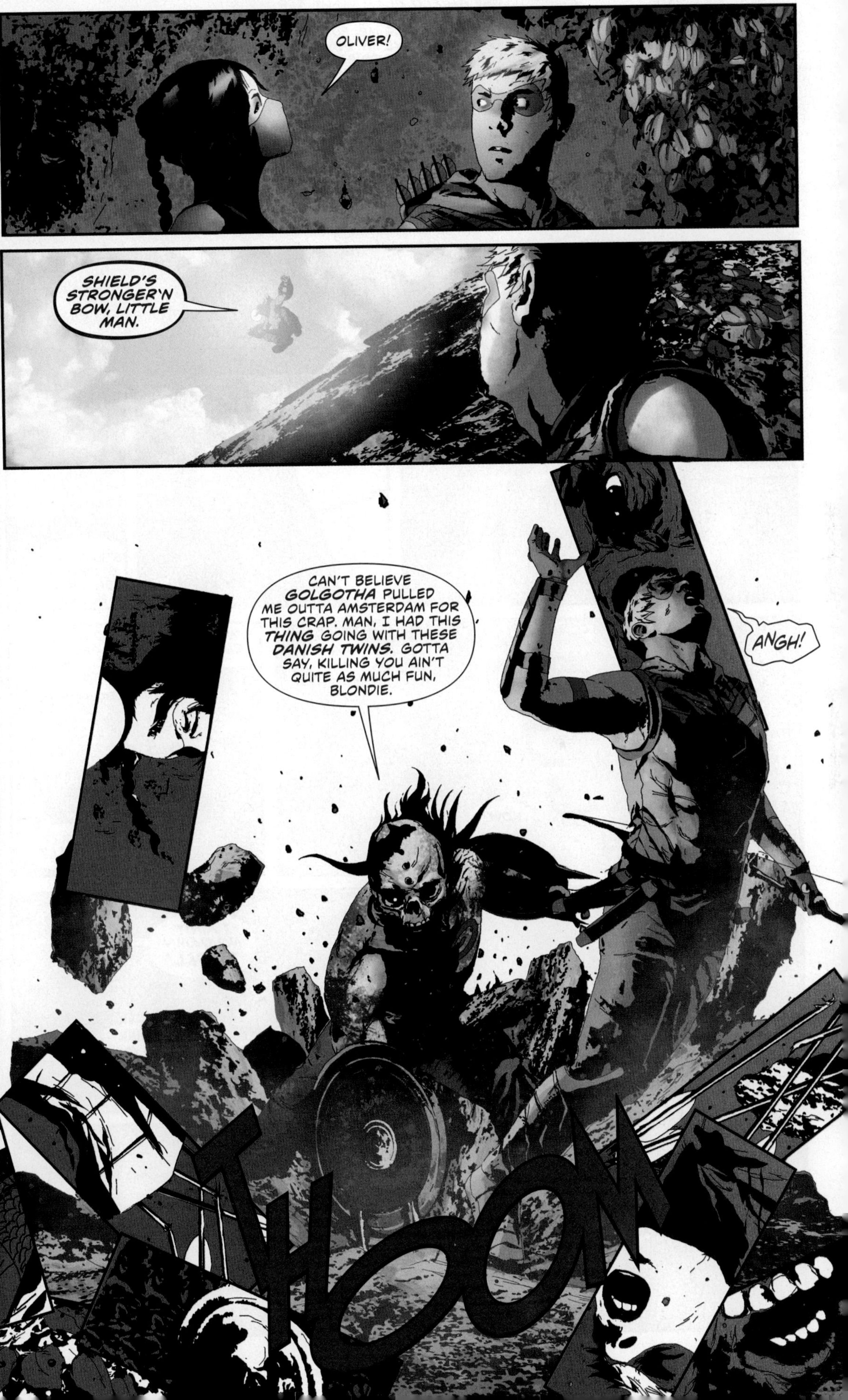
OLIVER!
SHIELD'S STRONGER'N BOW, LITTLE MAN.
CAN'T BELIEVE GOLGOTHA PULLED ME OUTTA AMSTERDAM FOR THIS CRAP. MAN, I HAD THIS THING GOING WITH THESE DANISH TWINS. GOTTA SAY, KILLING YOU AIN'T QUITE AS MUCH FUN, BLONDIE.
ANGH!
THOOM

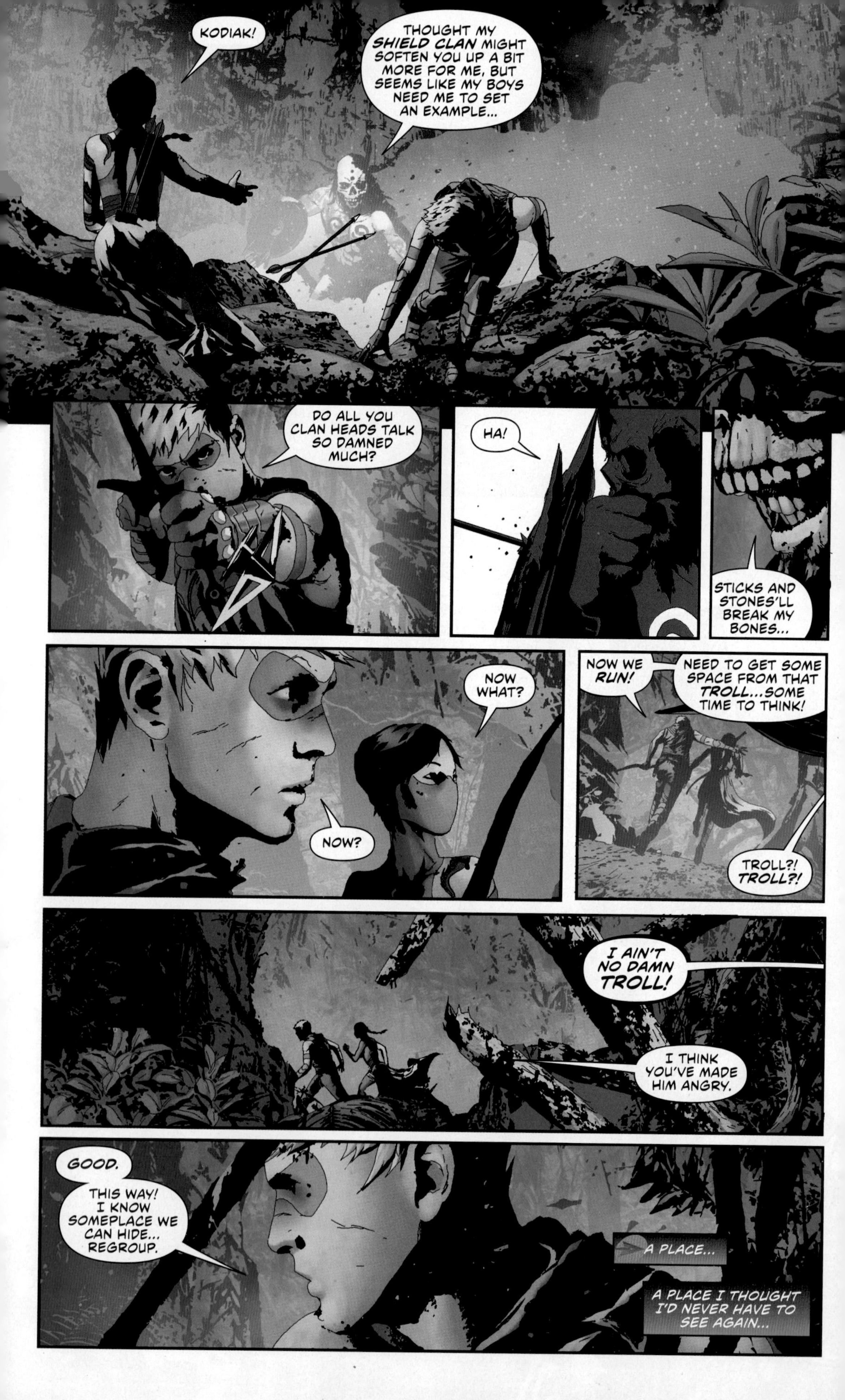
KODIAK!
THOUGHT MY SHIELD CLAN MIGHT SOFTEN YOU UP A BIT MORE FOR ME, BUT SEEMS LIKE MY BOYS NEED ME TO SET AN EXAMPLE...
DO ALL YOU CLAN HEADS TALK SO DAMNED MUCH?
HA!
STICKS AND STONES'LL BREAK MY BONES...
NOW WHAT?
NOW?
NOW WE RUN!
NEED TO GET SOME SPACE FROM THAT TROLL...SOME TIME TO THINK!
TROLL?! TROLL?!
I AIN'T NO DAMN TROLL!
I THINK YOU'VE MADE HIM ANGRY.
GOOD.
THIS WAY! I KNOW SOMEPLACE WE CAN HIDE... REGROUP.
A PLACE...
A PLACE I THOUGHT I'D NEVER HAVE TO SEE AGAIN...

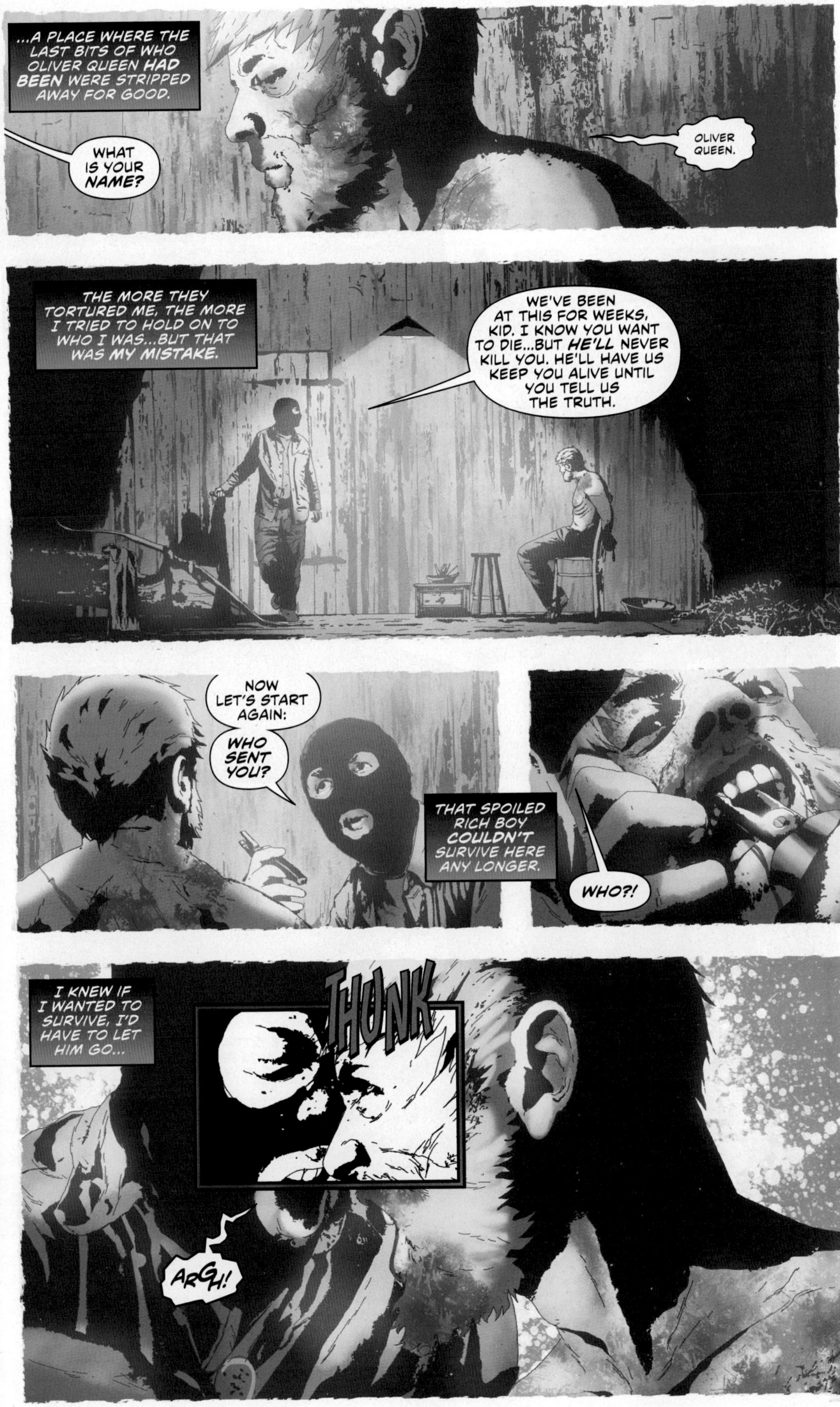
...A PLACE WHERE THE LAST BITS OF WHO OLIVER QUEEN HAD BEEN WERE STRIPPED AWAY FOR GOOD.
WHAT IS YOUR NAME?
OLIVER QUEEN.
THE MORE THEY TORTURED ME, THE MORE I TRIED TO HOLD ON TO WHO I WAS...BUT THAT WAS MY MISTAKE.
WE'VE BEEN AT THIS FOR WEEKS, KID. I KNOW YOU WANT TO DIE...BUT HE'LL NEVER KILL YOU. HE'LL HAVE US KEEP YOU ALIVE UNTIL YOU TELL US THE TRUTH.
NOW LET'S START AGAIN:
WHO SENT YOU?
THAT SPOILED RICH BOY COULDN'T SURVIVE HERE ANY LONGER.
WHO?!
I KNEW IF I WANTED TO SURVIVE, I'D HAVE TO LET HIM GO...
THUNK
ARGH!

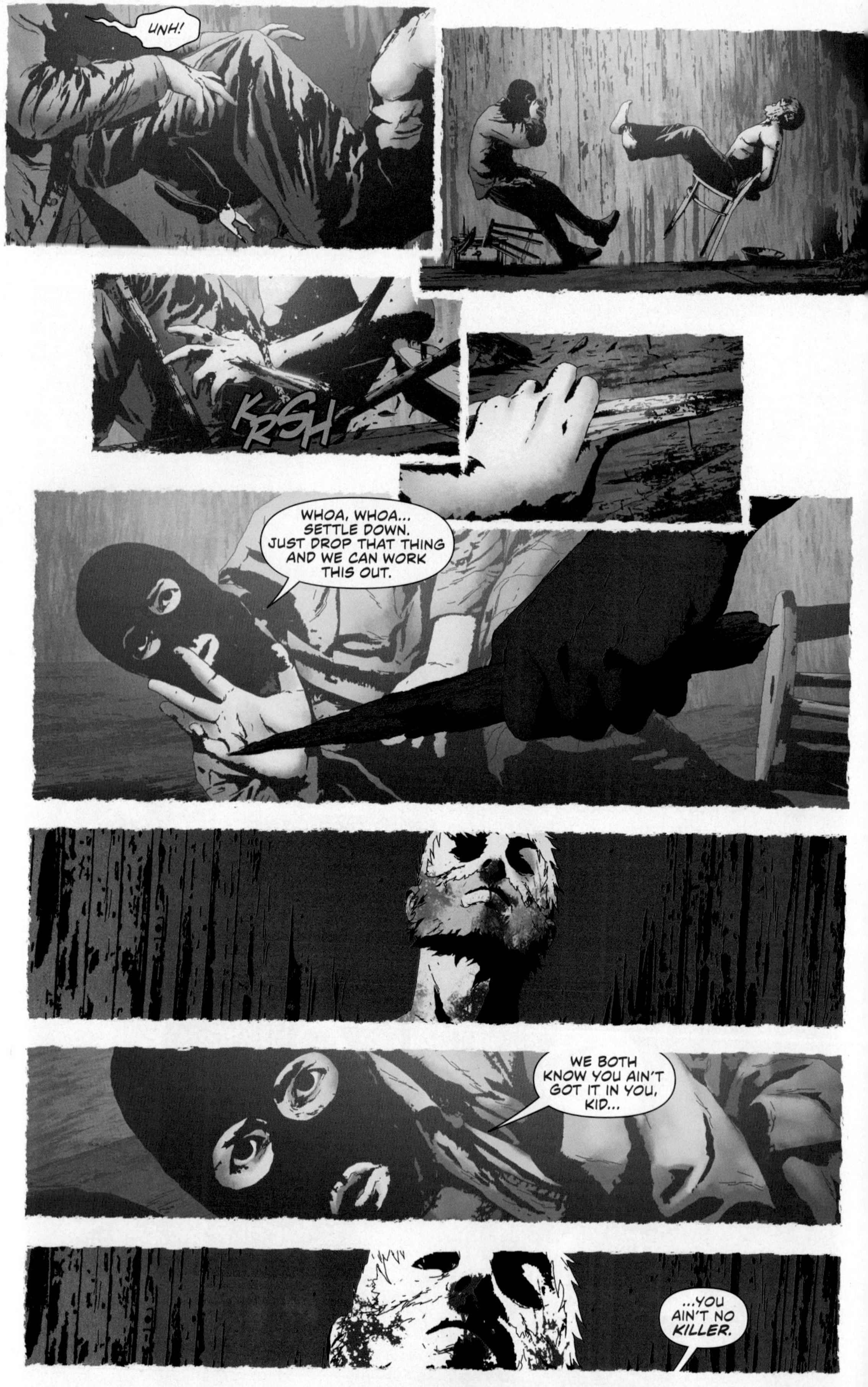
UNH!
KRSH
WHOA, WHOA... SETTLE DOWN. JUST DROP THAT THING AND WE CAN WORK THIS OUT.
WE BOTH KNOW YOU AIN'T GOT IT IN YOU, KID...
...YOU AIN'T NO KILLER.

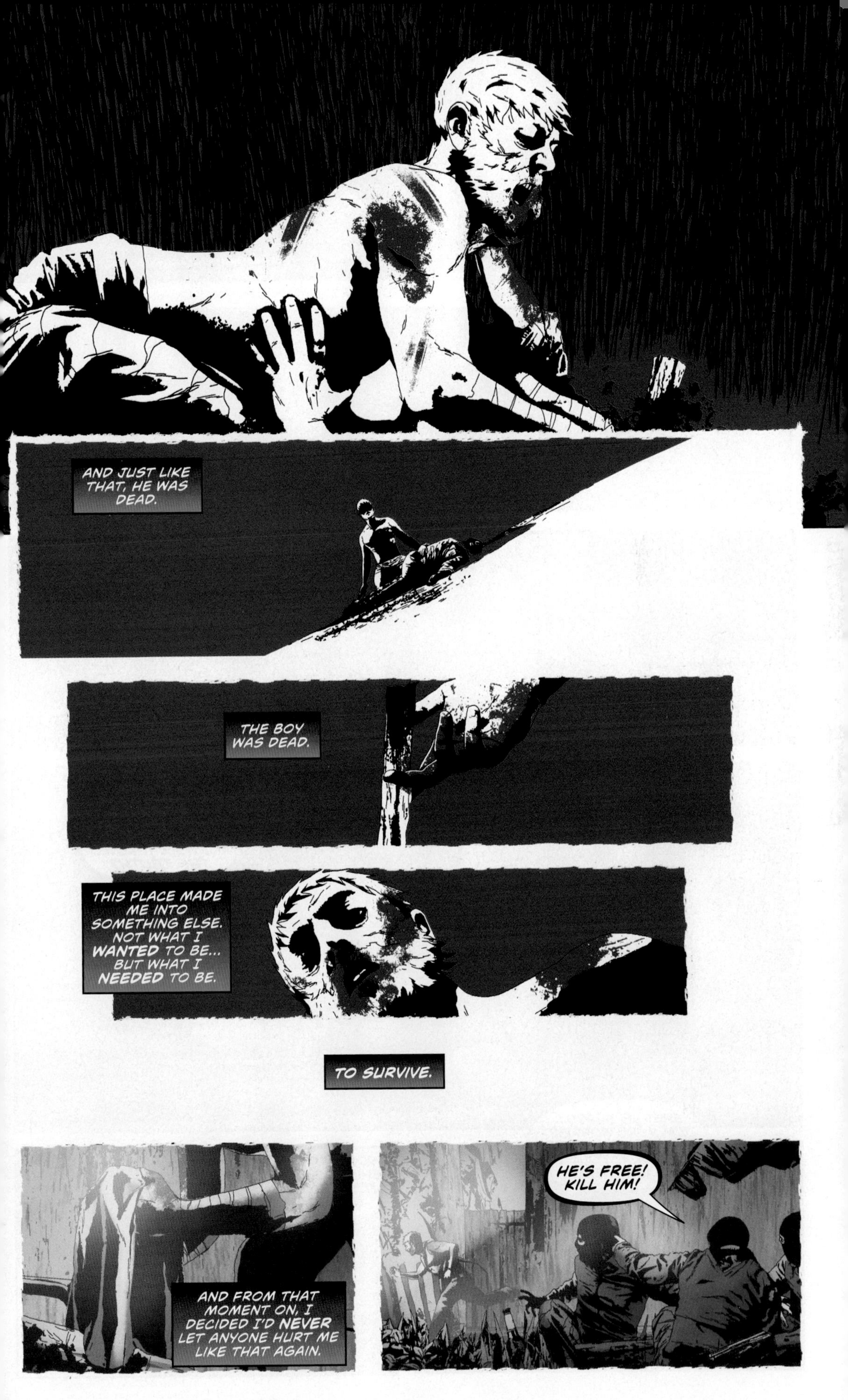

AND JUST LIKE THAT, HE WAS DEAD.
THE BOY WAS DEAD.
THIS PLACE MADE ME INTO SOMETHING ELSE. NOT WHAT I WANTED TO BE... BUT WHAT I NEEDED TO BE.
TO SURVIVE.
AND FROM THAT MOMENT ON, I DECIDED I'D NEVER LET ANYONE HURT ME LIKE THAT AGAIN.
HE'S FREE! KILL HIM!

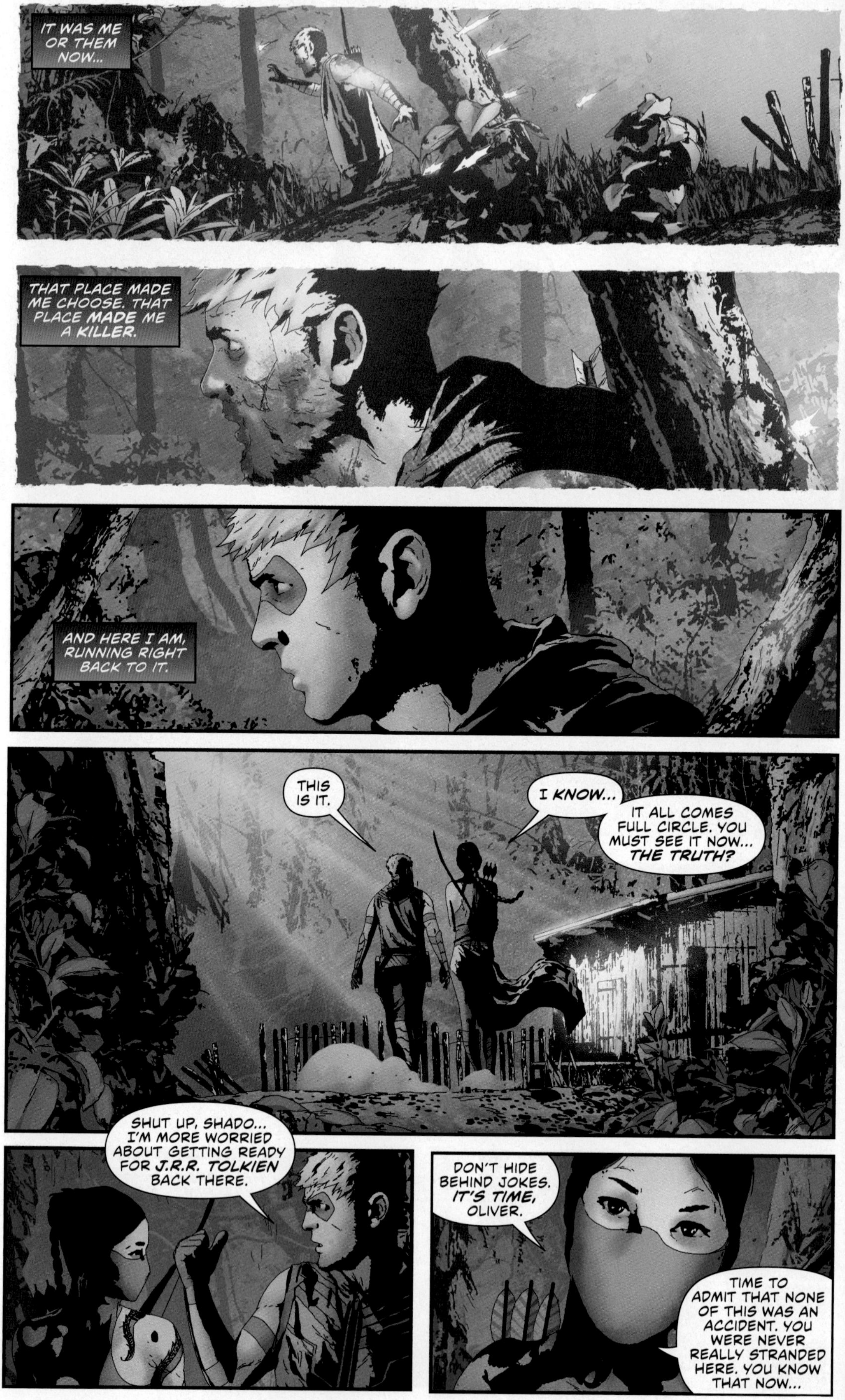
IT WAS ME OR THEM NOW...
THAT PLACE MADE ME CHOOSE. THAT PLACE MADE ME A KILLER.
AND HERE I AM, RUNNING RIGHT BACK TO IT.
THIS IS IT.
I KNOW...
IT ALL COMES FULL CIRCLE. YOU MUST SEE IT NOW... THE TRUTH?
SHUT UP, SHADO... I'M MORE WORRIED ABOUT GETTING READY FOR J.R.R. TOLKIEN BACK THERE.
DON'T HIDE BEHIND JOKES. IT'S TIME, OLIVER.
TIME TO ADMIT THAT NONE OF THIS WAS AN ACCIDENT. YOU WERE NEVER REALLY STRANDED HERE. YOU KNOW THAT NOW...

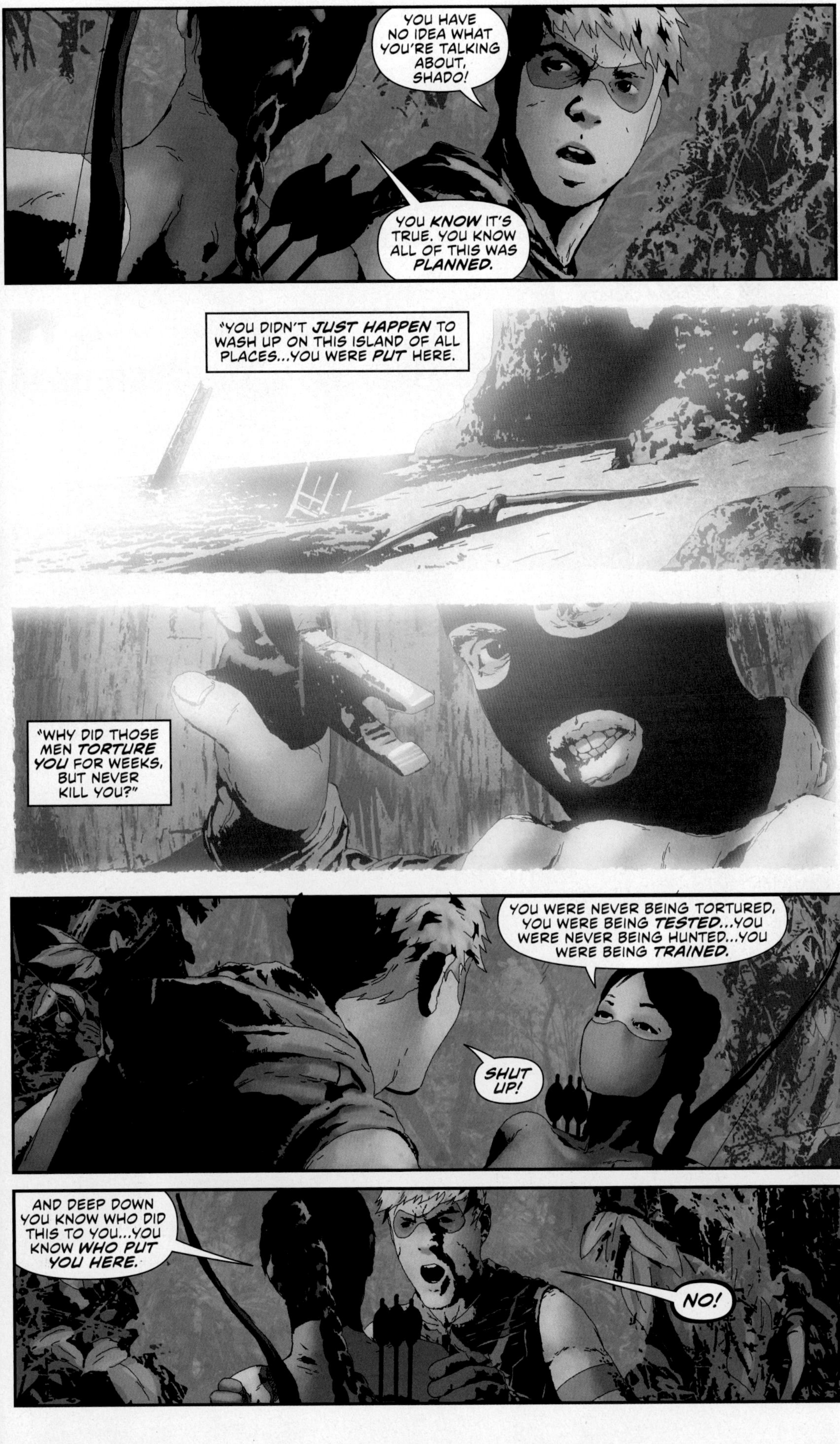
YOU HAVE NO IDEA WHAT YOU'RE TALKING ABOUT, SHADO!
YOU KNOW IT'S TRUE. YOU KNOW ALL OF THIS WAS PLANNED.
"YOU DIDN'T JUST HAPPEN TO WASH UP ON THIS ISLAND OF ALL PLACES...YOU WERE PUT HERE.
"WHY DID THOSE MEN TORTURE YOU FOR WEEKS, BUT NEVER KILL YOU?"
YOU WERE NEVER BEING TORTURED, YOU WERE BEING TESTED...YOU WERE NEVER BEING HUNTED...YOU WERE BEING TRAINED.
SHUT UP!
AND DEEP DOWN YOU KNOW WHO DID THIS TO YOU...YOU KNOW WHO PUT YOU HERE.
NO!

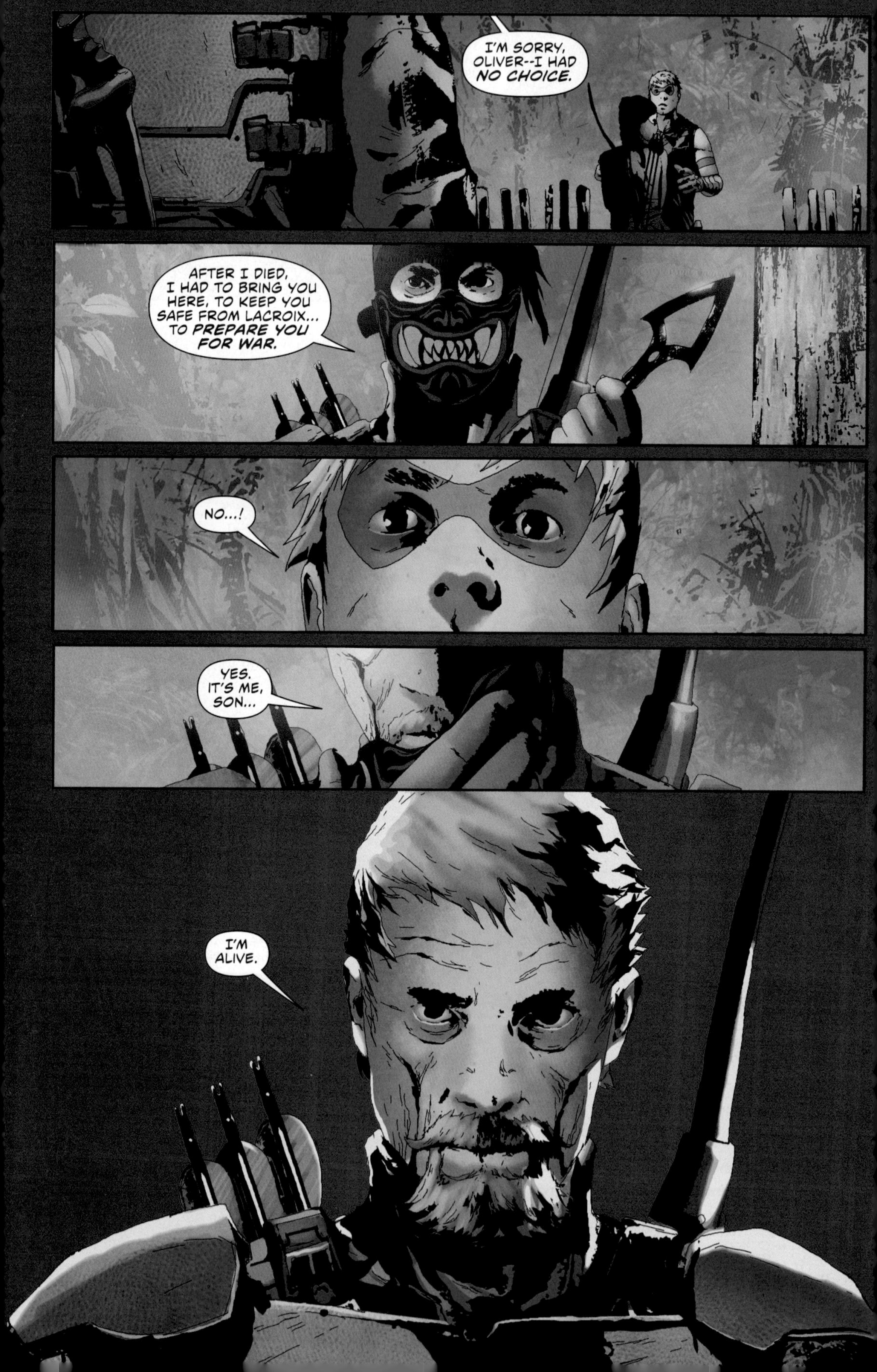
I'M SORRY, OLIVER--I HAD NO CHOICE.
AFTER I DIED, I HAD TO BRING YOU HERE, TO KEEP YOU SAFE FROM LACROIX... TO PREPARE YOU FOR WAR.
NO...!
YES. IT'S ME, SON...
I'M ALIVE.

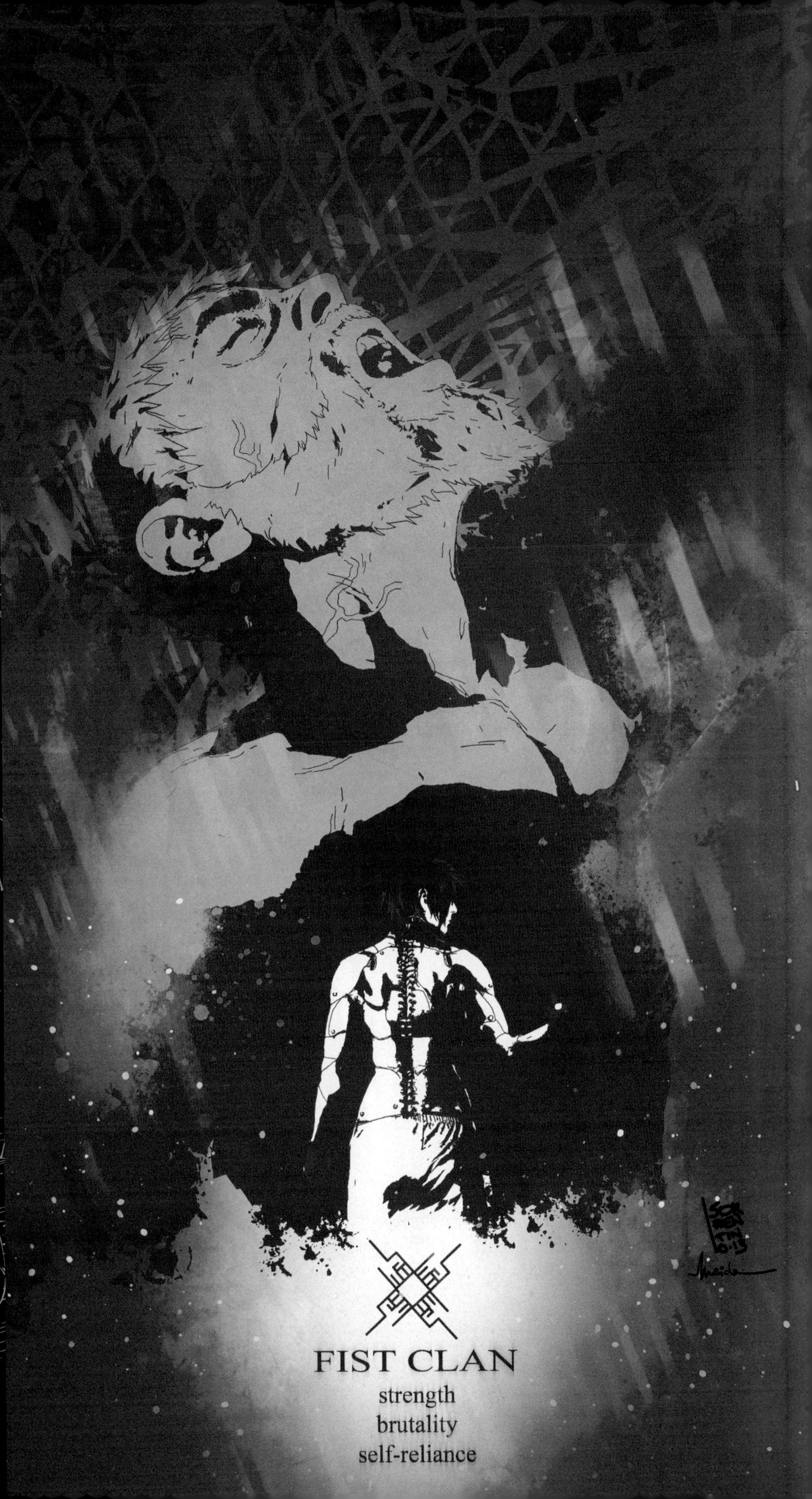
FIST CLAN
strength
brutality
self-reliance

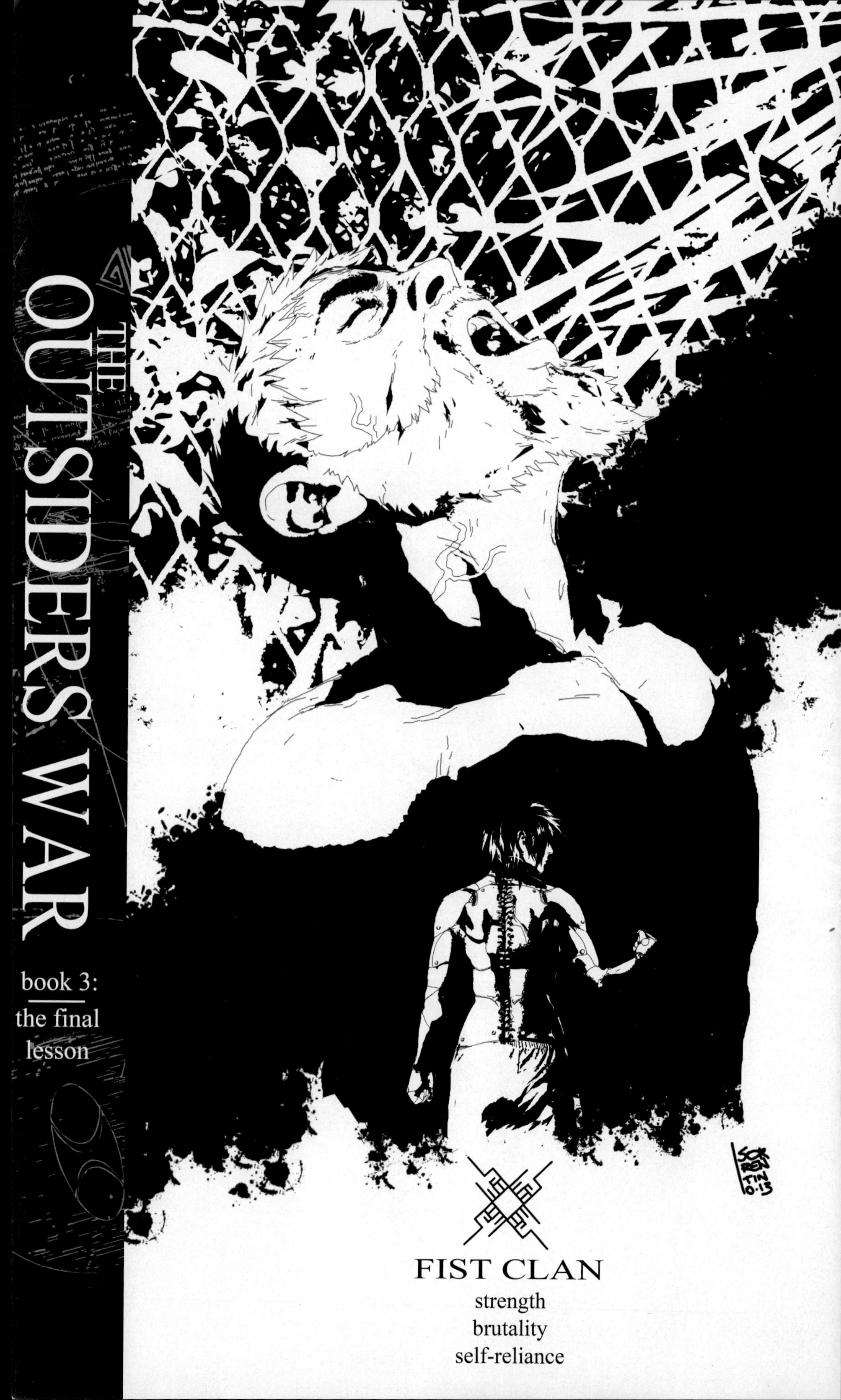
THE OUTSIDERS WAR
book 3:
the final
lesson
FIST CLAN
strength
brutality
self-reliance

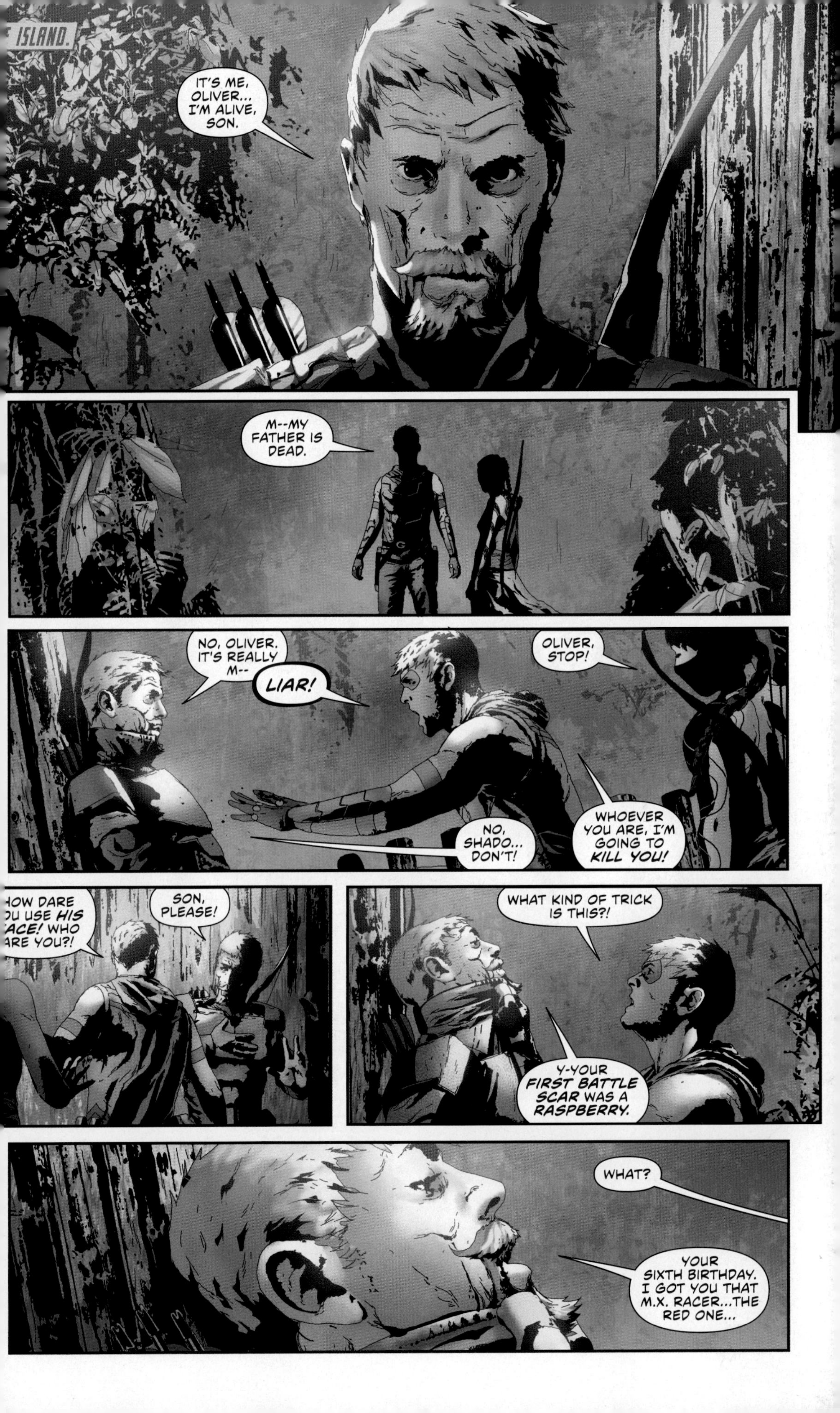
ISLAND.
IT'S ME, OLIVER... I'M ALIVE, SON.
M--MY FATHER IS DEAD.
NO, OLIVER. IT'S REALLY M--
LIAR!
OLIVER, STOP!
WHOEVER YOU ARE, I'M GOING TO KILL YOU!
NO, SHADO... DON'T!
HOW DARE YOU USE HIS FACE! WHO ARE YOU?!
SON, PLEASE!
WHAT KIND OF TRICK IS THIS?!
Y-YOUR FIRST BATTLE SCAR WAS A RASPBERRY.
WHAT?
YOUR SIXTH BIRTHDAY. I GOT YOU THAT M.X. RACER...THE RED ONE...

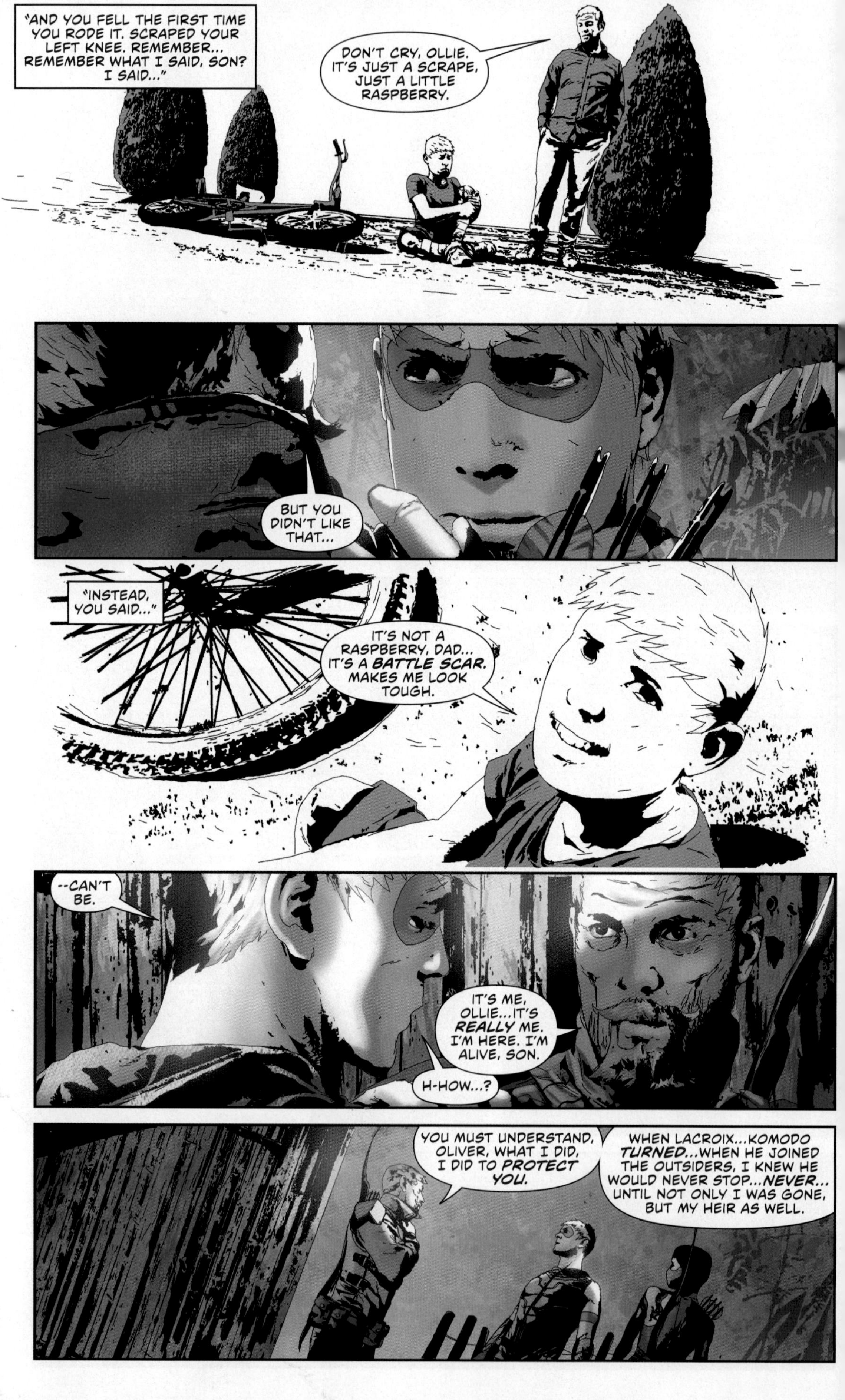
"AND YOU FELL THE FIRST TIME YOU RODE IT. SCRAPED YOUR LEFT KNEE. REMEMBER... REMEMBER WHAT I SAID, SON? I SAID..."
DON'T CRY, OLLIE. IT'S JUST A SCRAPE, JUST A LITTLE RASPBERRY.
BUT YOU DIDN'T LIKE THAT...
"INSTEAD, YOU SAID..."
IT'S NOT A RASPBERRY, DAD... IT'S A *BATTLE SCAR.* MAKES ME LOOK TOUGH.
--CAN'T BE.
IT'S ME, OLLIE...IT'S *REALLY* ME. I'M HERE. I'M ALIVE, SON.
H-HOW...?
YOU MUST UNDERSTAND, OLIVER, WHAT I DID, I DID TO *PROTECT YOU.*
WHEN LACROIX...KOMODO *TURNED*...WHEN HE JOINED THE OUTSIDERS, I KNEW HE WOULD NEVER STOP...*NEVER*... UNTIL NOT ONLY I WAS GONE, BUT MY HEIR AS WELL.

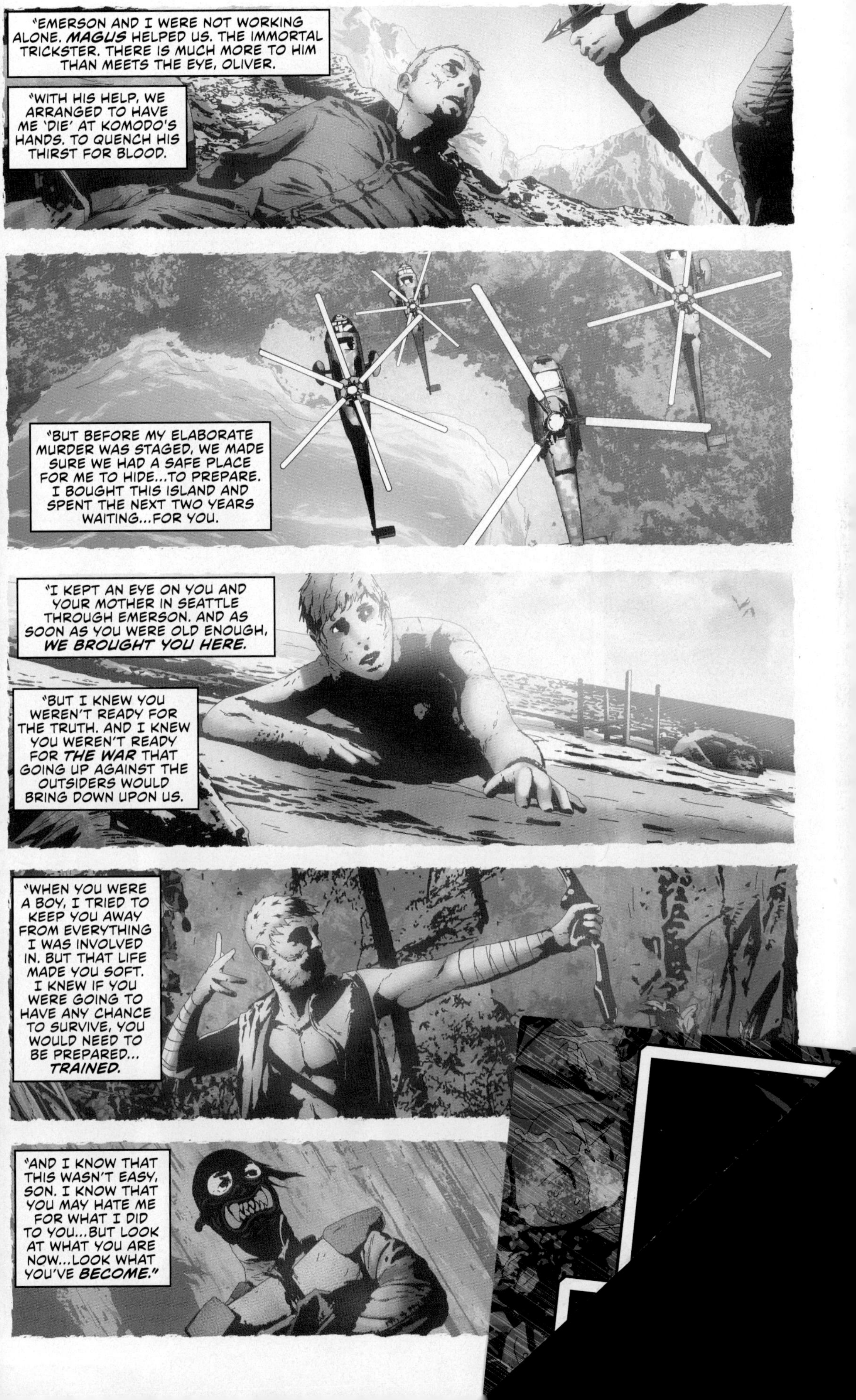
"EMERSON AND I WERE NOT WORKING ALONE. *MAGUS* HELPED US. THE IMMORTAL TRICKSTER. THERE IS MUCH MORE TO HIM THAN MEETS THE EYE, OLIVER.
"WITH HIS HELP, WE ARRANGED TO HAVE ME 'DIE' AT KOMODO'S HANDS. TO QUENCH HIS THIRST FOR BLOOD.
"BUT BEFORE MY ELABORATE MURDER WAS STAGED, WE MADE SURE WE HAD A SAFE PLACE FOR ME TO HIDE...TO PREPARE. I BOUGHT THIS ISLAND AND SPENT THE NEXT TWO YEARS WAITING...FOR YOU.
"I KEPT AN EYE ON YOU AND YOUR MOTHER IN SEATTLE THROUGH EMERSON. AND AS SOON AS YOU WERE OLD ENOUGH, *WE BROUGHT YOU HERE.*
"BUT I KNEW YOU WEREN'T READY FOR THE TRUTH. AND I KNEW YOU WEREN'T READY FOR *THE WAR* THAT GOING UP AGAINST THE OUTSIDERS WOULD BRING DOWN UPON US.
"WHEN YOU WERE A BOY, I TRIED TO KEEP YOU AWAY FROM EVERYTHING I WAS INVOLVED IN. BUT THAT LIFE MADE YOU SOFT. I KNEW IF YOU WERE GOING TO HAVE ANY CHANCE TO SURVIVE, YOU WOULD NEED TO BE PREPARED... *TRAINED.*
"AND I KNOW THAT THIS WASN'T EASY, SON. I KNOW THAT YOU MAY HATE ME FOR WHAT I DID TO YOU...BUT LOOK AT WHAT YOU ARE NOW...LOOK WHAT YOU'VE *BECOME.*"

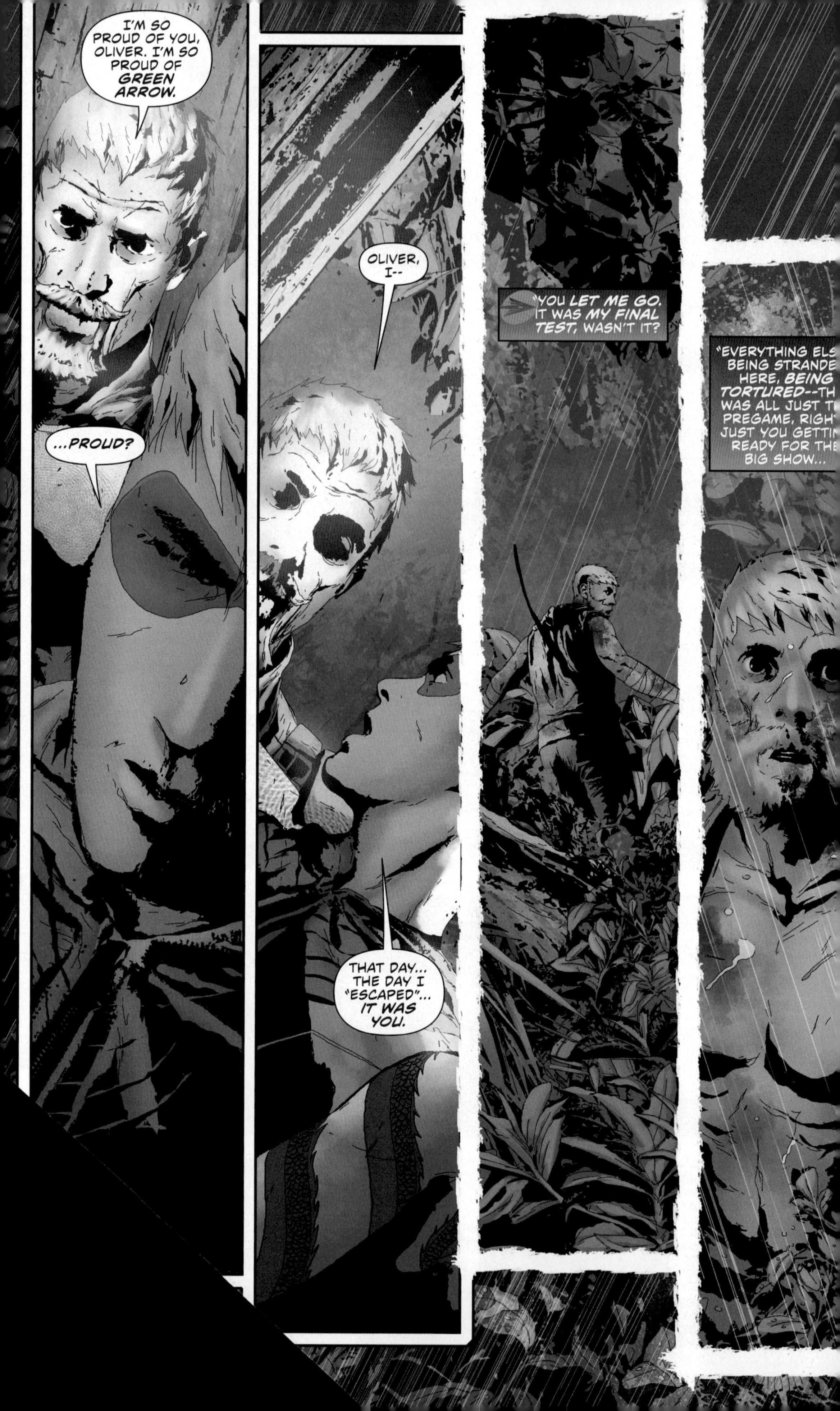
I'M SO PROUD OF YOU, OLIVER. I'M SO PROUD OF GREEN ARROW.
...PROUD?
OLIVER, I--
THAT DAY... THE DAY I "ESCAPED"... IT WAS YOU.
"YOU LET ME GO. IT WAS MY FINAL TEST, WASN'T IT?
"EVERYTHING ELS BEING STRANDE HERE, BEING TORTURED--TH WAS ALL JUST T PREGAME, RIGH JUST YOU GETTI READY FOR TH BIG SHOW...

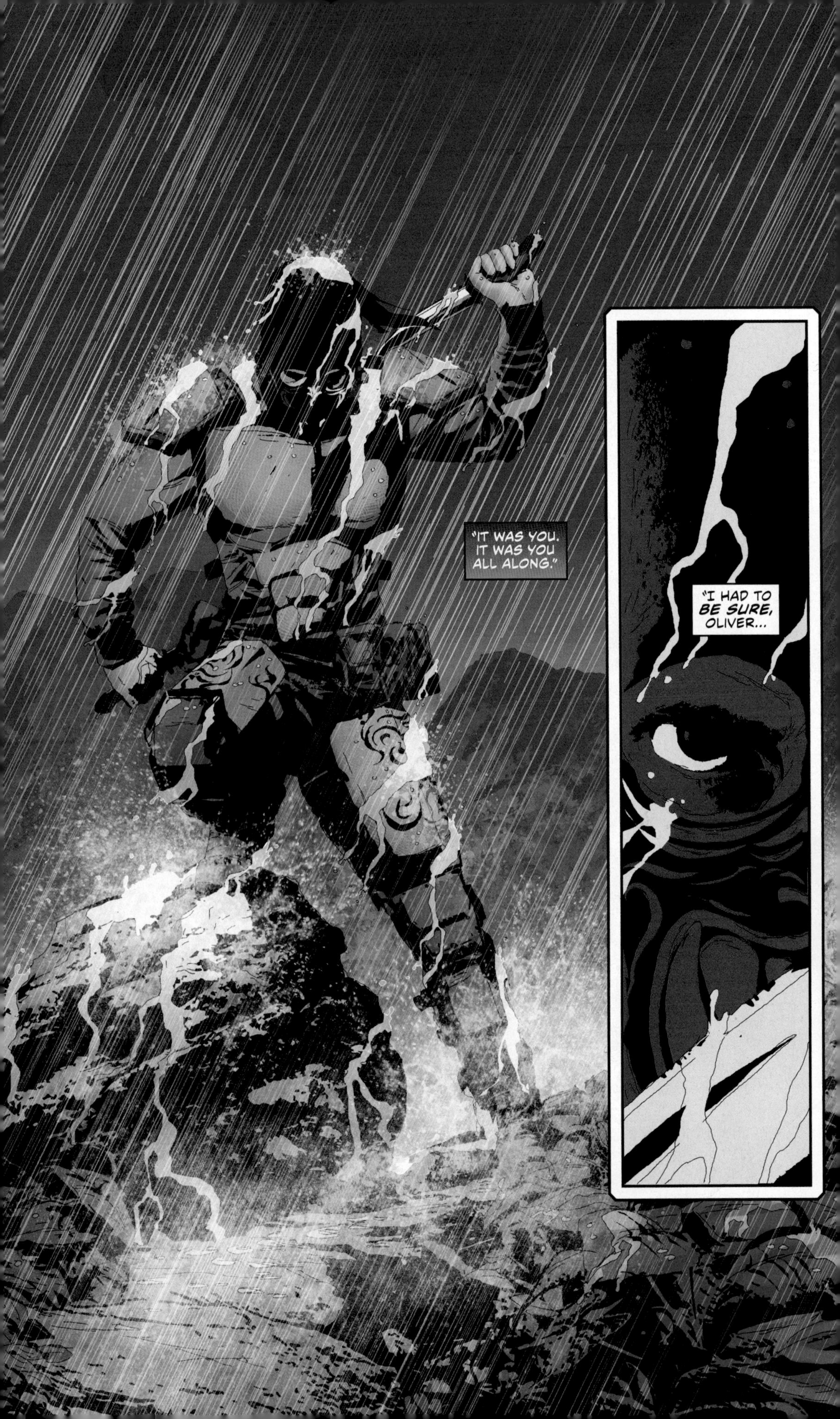
"IT WAS YOU. IT WAS YOU ALL ALONG."
"I HAD TO *BE SURE,* OLIVER...

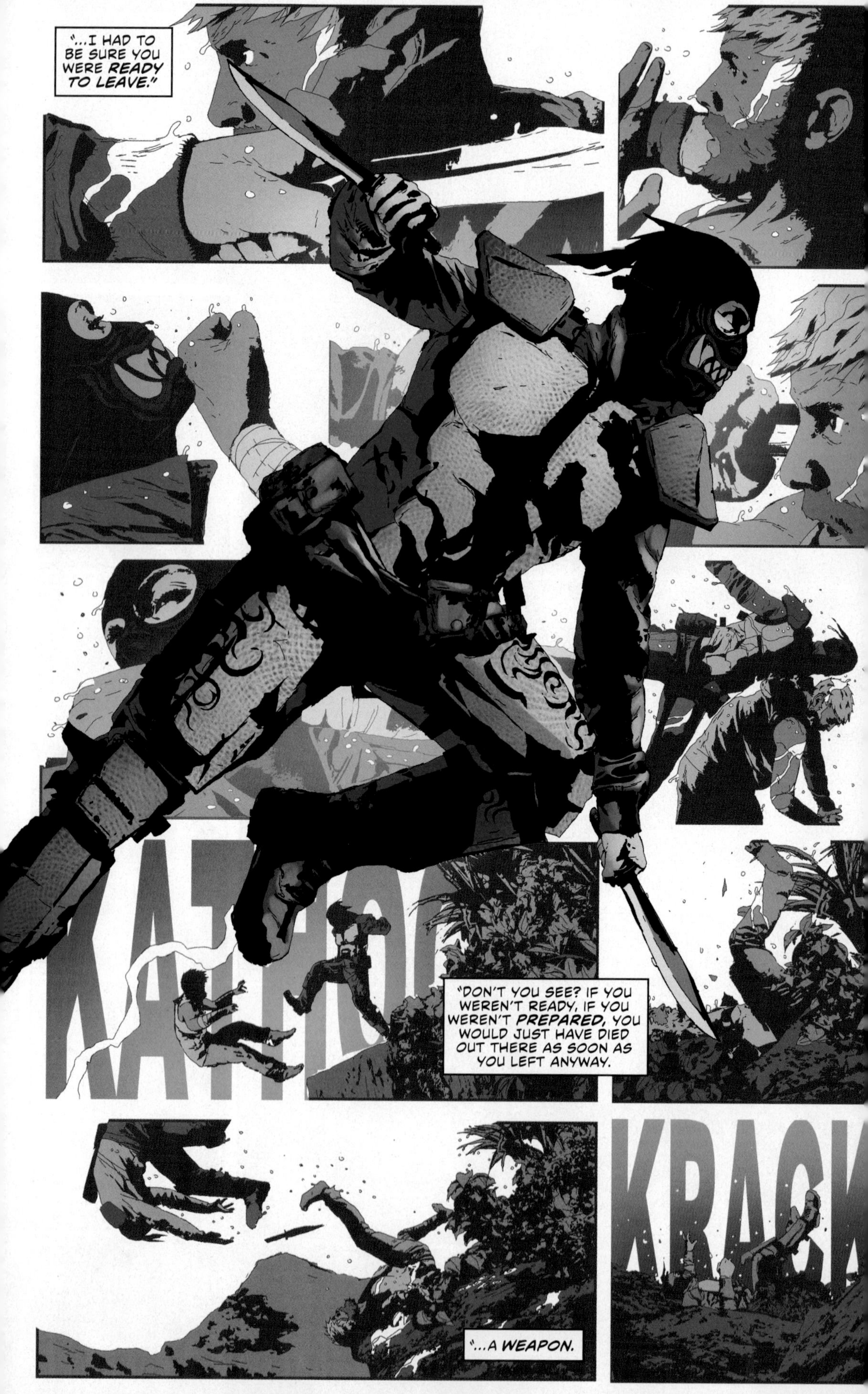
"...I HAD TO BE SURE YOU WERE READY TO LEAVE."
KATHOO
"DON'T YOU SEE? IF YOU WEREN'T READY, IF YOU WEREN'T PREPARED, YOU WOULD JUST HAVE DIED OUT THERE AS SOON AS YOU LEFT ANYWAY.
KRACK
"...A WEAPON.

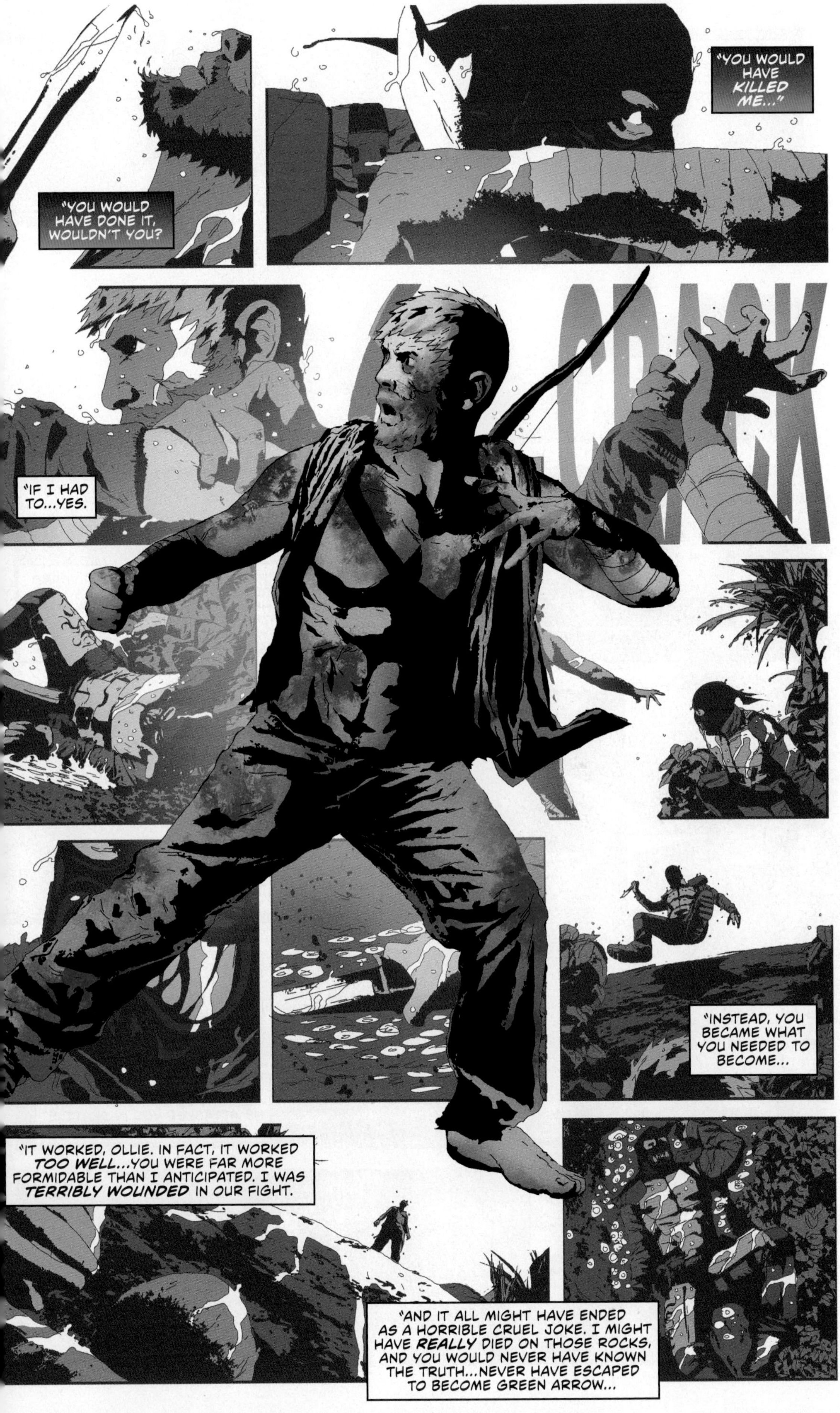
"YOU WOULD HAVE DONE IT, WOULDN'T YOU?
"YOU WOULD HAVE KILLED ME..."
CRACK
"IF I HAD TO...YES.
"INSTEAD, YOU BECAME WHAT YOU NEEDED TO BECOME...
"IT WORKED, OLLIE. IN FACT, IT WORKED TOO WELL...YOU WERE FAR MORE FORMIDABLE THAN I ANTICIPATED. I WAS TERRIBLY WOUNDED IN OUR FIGHT.
"AND IT ALL MIGHT HAVE ENDED AS A HORRIBLE CRUEL JOKE. I MIGHT HAVE REALLY DIED ON THOSE ROCKS, AND YOU WOULD NEVER HAVE KNOWN THE TRUTH...NEVER HAVE ESCAPED TO BECOME GREEN ARROW...

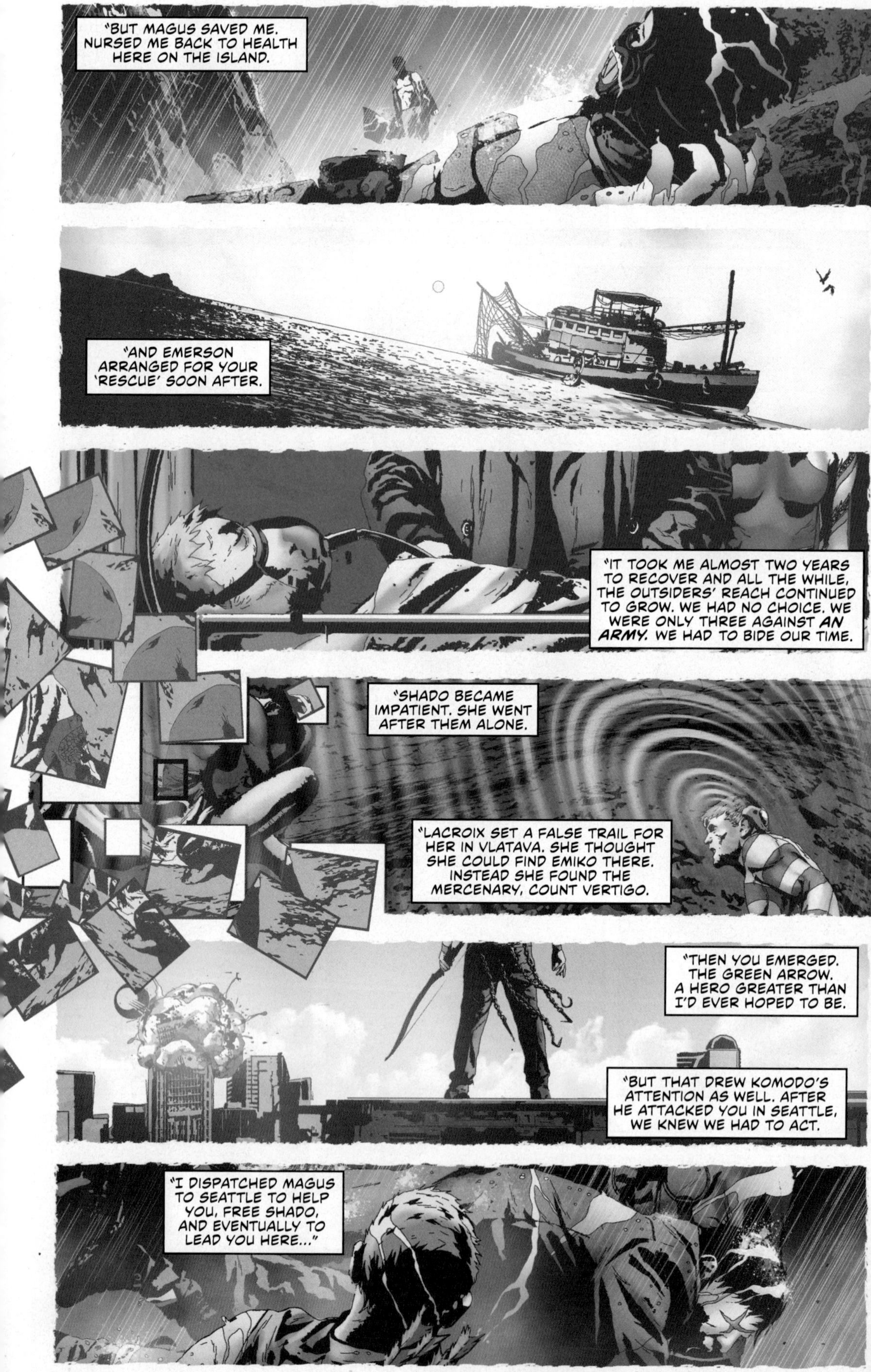
"BUT MAGUS SAVED ME. NURSED ME BACK TO HEALTH HERE ON THE ISLAND.
"AND EMERSON ARRANGED FOR YOUR 'RESCUE' SOON AFTER.
"IT TOOK ME ALMOST TWO YEARS TO RECOVER AND ALL THE WHILE, THE OUTSIDERS' REACH CONTINUED TO GROW. WE HAD NO CHOICE. WE WERE ONLY THREE AGAINST AN ARMY. WE HAD TO BIDE OUR TIME.
"SHADO BECAME IMPATIENT. SHE WENT AFTER THEM ALONE.
"LACROIX SET A FALSE TRAIL FOR HER IN VLATAVA. SHE THOUGHT SHE COULD FIND EMIKO THERE. INSTEAD SHE FOUND THE MERCENARY, COUNT VERTIGO.
"THEN YOU EMERGED. THE GREEN ARROW. A HERO GREATER THAN I'D EVER HOPED TO BE.
"BUT THAT DREW KOMODO'S ATTENTION AS WELL. AFTER HE ATTACKED YOU IN SEATTLE, WE KNEW WE HAD TO ACT.
"I DISPATCHED MAGUS TO SEATTLE TO HELP YOU, FREE SHADO, AND EVENTUALLY TO LEAD YOU HERE..."

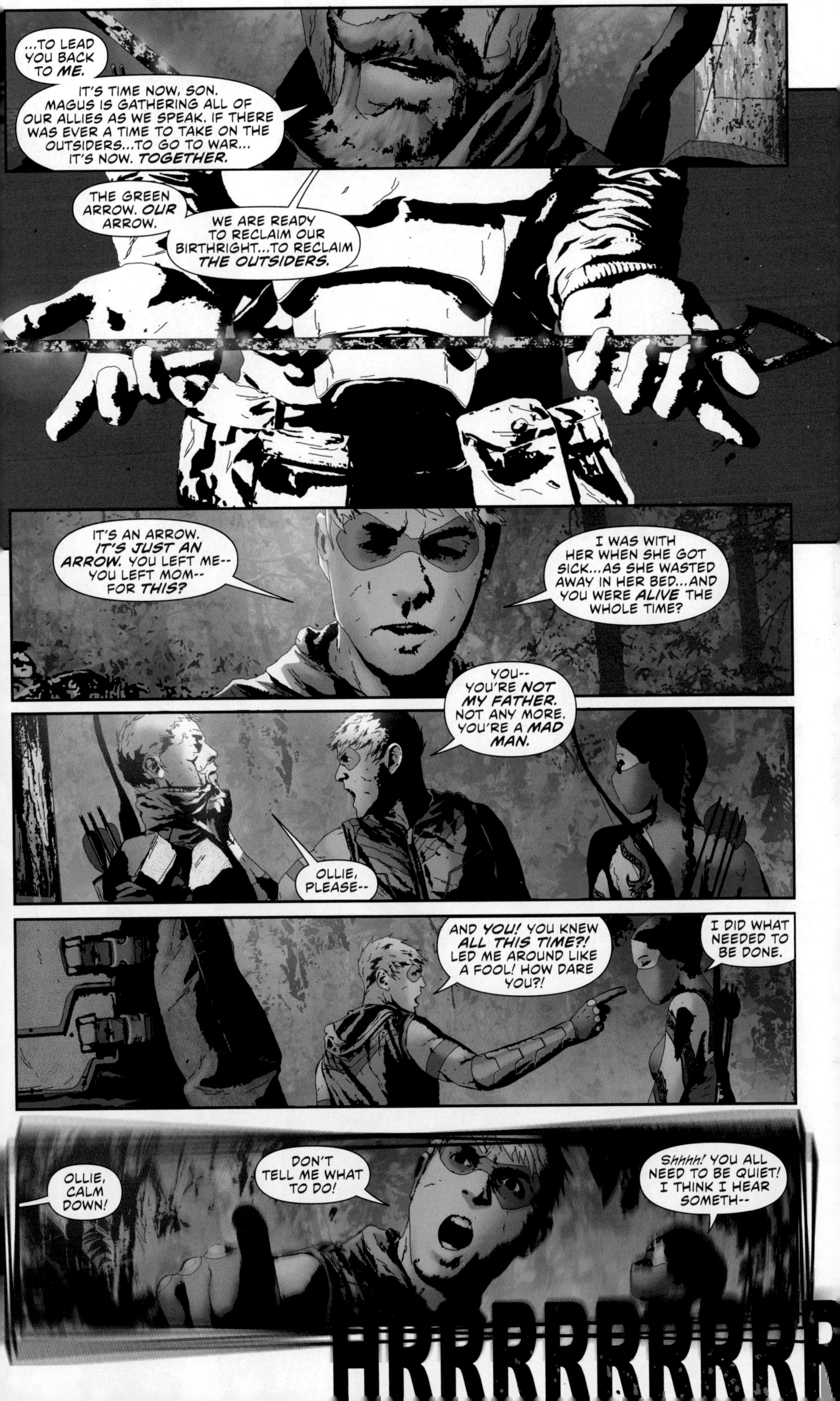
...TO LEAD YOU BACK TO ME.
IT'S TIME NOW, SON. MAGUS IS GATHERING ALL OF OUR ALLIES AS WE SPEAK. IF THERE WAS EVER A TIME TO TAKE ON THE OUTSIDERS...TO GO TO WAR... IT'S NOW. TOGETHER.
THE GREEN ARROW. OUR ARROW.
WE ARE READY TO RECLAIM OUR BIRTHRIGHT...TO RECLAIM THE OUTSIDERS.
IT'S AN ARROW. IT'S JUST AN ARROW. YOU LEFT ME-- YOU LEFT MOM-- FOR THIS?
I WAS WITH HER WHEN SHE GOT SICK...AS SHE WASTED AWAY IN HER BED...AND YOU WERE ALIVE THE WHOLE TIME?
YOU-- YOU'RE NOT MY FATHER. NOT ANY MORE. YOU'RE A MAD MAN.
OLLIE, PLEASE--
AND YOU! YOU KNEW ALL THIS TIME?! LED ME AROUND LIKE A FOOL! HOW DARE YOU?!
I DID WHAT NEEDED TO BE DONE.
OLLIE, CALM DOWN!
DON'T TELL ME WHAT TO DO!
Shhhh! YOU ALL NEED TO BE QUIET! I THINK I HEAR SOMETH--
HRRRRRRRRR

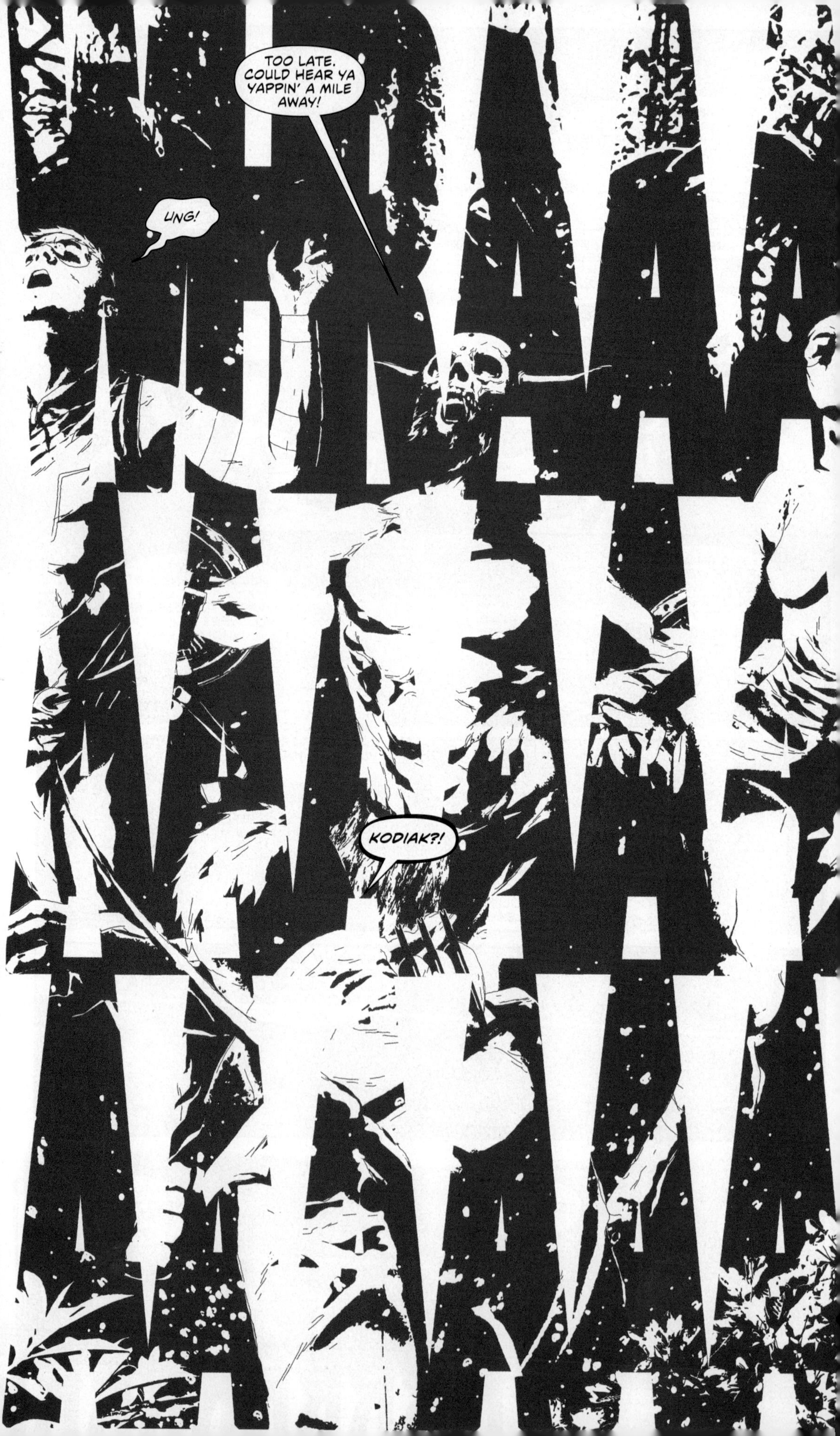
TOO LATE. COULD HEAR YA YAPPIN' A MILE AWAY!
UNG!
KODIAK?!

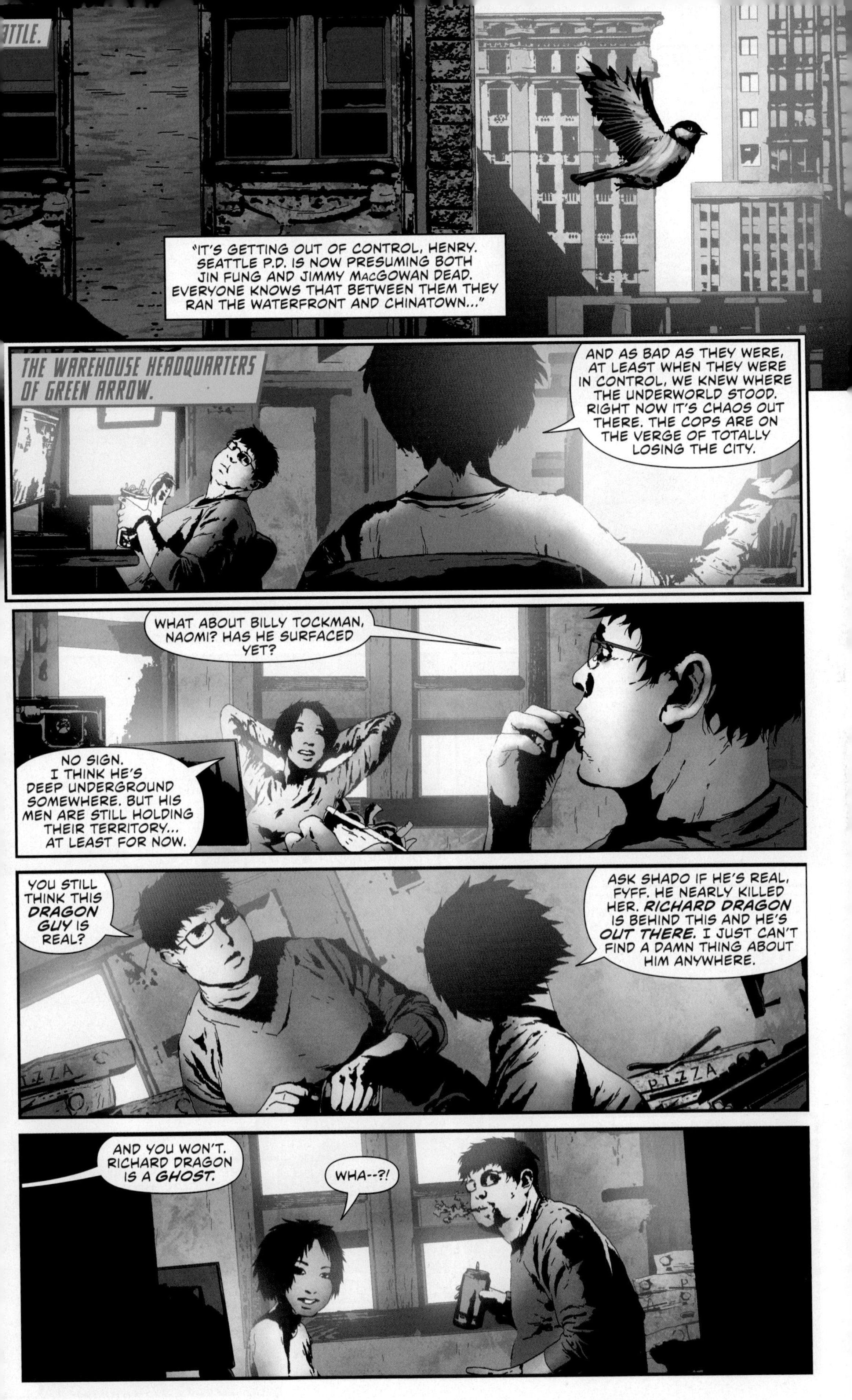

…TTLE.
"IT'S GETTING OUT OF CONTROL, HENRY. SEATTLE P.D. IS NOW PRESUMING BOTH JIN FUNG AND JIMMY MacGOWAN DEAD. EVERYONE KNOWS THAT BETWEEN THEM THEY RAN THE WATERFRONT AND CHINATOWN..."
THE WAREHOUSE HEADQUARTERS OF GREEN ARROW.
AND AS BAD AS THEY WERE, AT LEAST WHEN THEY WERE IN CONTROL, WE KNEW WHERE THE UNDERWORLD STOOD. RIGHT NOW IT'S CHAOS OUT THERE. THE COPS ARE ON THE VERGE OF TOTALLY LOSING THE CITY.
WHAT ABOUT BILLY TOCKMAN, NAOMI? HAS HE SURFACED YET?
NO SIGN. I THINK HE'S DEEP UNDERGROUND SOMEWHERE. BUT HIS MEN ARE STILL HOLDING THEIR TERRITORY... AT LEAST FOR NOW.
YOU STILL THINK THIS *DRAGON GUY* IS REAL?
ASK SHADO IF HE'S REAL, FYFF. HE NEARLY KILLED HER. *RICHARD DRAGON* IS BEHIND THIS AND HE'S *OUT THERE*. I JUST CAN'T FIND A DAMN THING ABOUT HIM ANYWHERE.
PIZZA
PIZZA
AND YOU WON'T. RICHARD DRAGON IS A *GHOST*.
WHA--?!

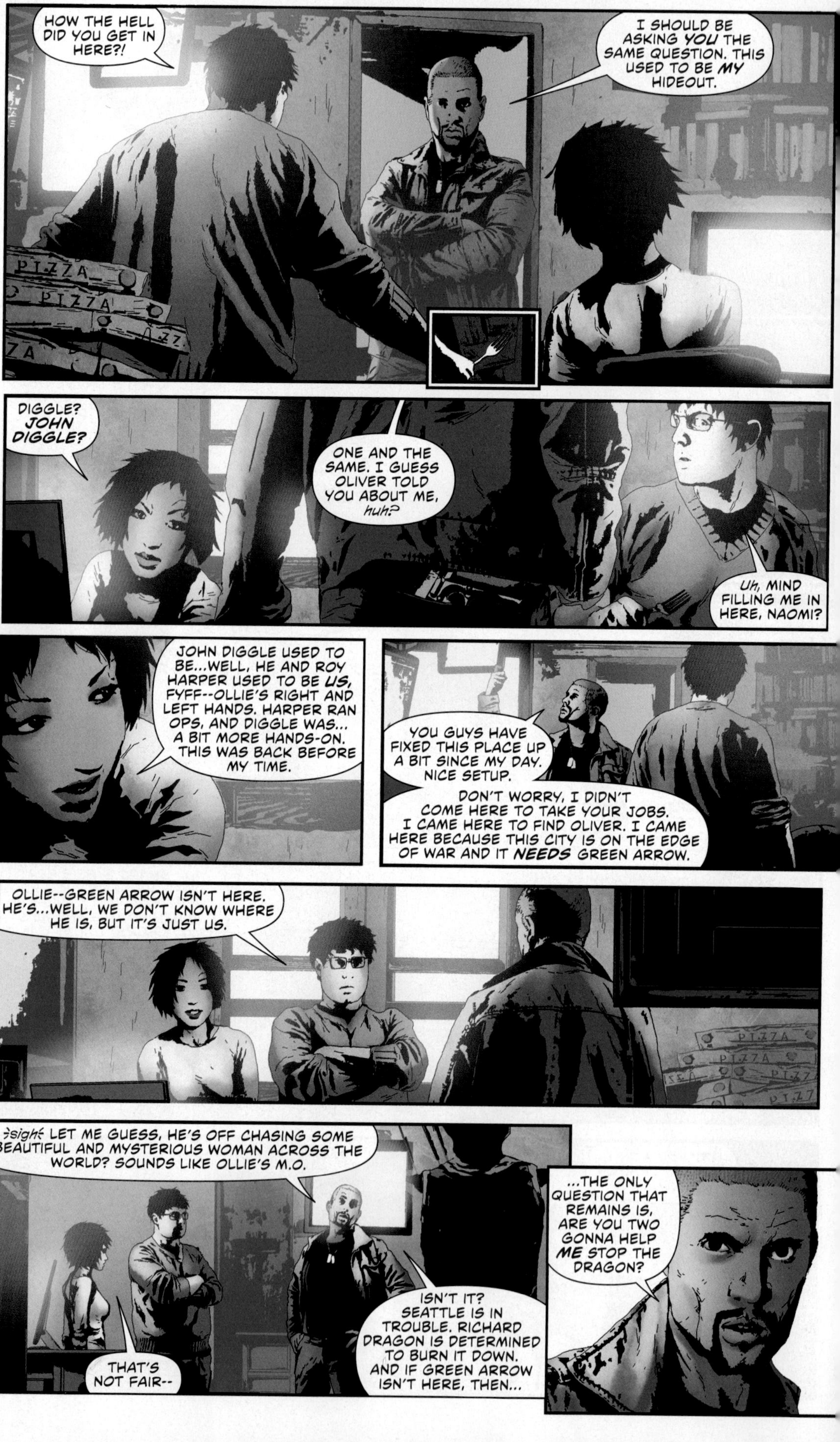

HOW THE HELL DID YOU GET IN HERE?!
I SHOULD BE ASKING *YOU* THE SAME QUESTION. THIS USED TO BE *MY* HIDEOUT.
PIZZA
PIZZA
DIGGLE? *JOHN DIGGLE?*
ONE AND THE SAME. I GUESS OLIVER TOLD YOU ABOUT ME, *huh?*
Uh, MIND FILLING ME IN HERE, NAOMI?
JOHN DIGGLE USED TO BE...WELL, HE AND ROY HARPER USED TO BE *US,* FYFF--OLLIE'S RIGHT AND LEFT HANDS. HARPER RAN OPS, AND DIGGLE WAS... A BIT MORE HANDS-ON. THIS WAS BACK BEFORE MY TIME.
YOU GUYS HAVE FIXED THIS PLACE UP A BIT SINCE MY DAY. NICE SETUP.
DON'T WORRY, I DIDN'T COME HERE TO TAKE YOUR JOBS. I CAME HERE TO FIND OLIVER. I CAME HERE BECAUSE THIS CITY IS ON THE EDGE OF WAR AND IT *NEEDS* GREEN ARROW.
OLLIE--GREEN ARROW ISN'T HERE. HE'S...WELL, WE DON'T KNOW WHERE HE IS, BUT IT'S JUST US.
PIZZA
PIZZA
sigh LET ME GUESS, HE'S OFF CHASING SOME BEAUTIFUL AND MYSTERIOUS WOMAN ACROSS THE WORLD? SOUNDS LIKE OLLIE'S M.O.
THAT'S NOT FAIR--
ISN'T IT? SEATTLE IS IN TROUBLE. RICHARD DRAGON IS DETERMINED TO BURN IT DOWN. AND IF GREEN ARROW ISN'T HERE, THEN...
...THE ONLY QUESTION THAT REMAINS IS, ARE YOU TWO GONNA HELP *ME* STOP THE DRAGON?

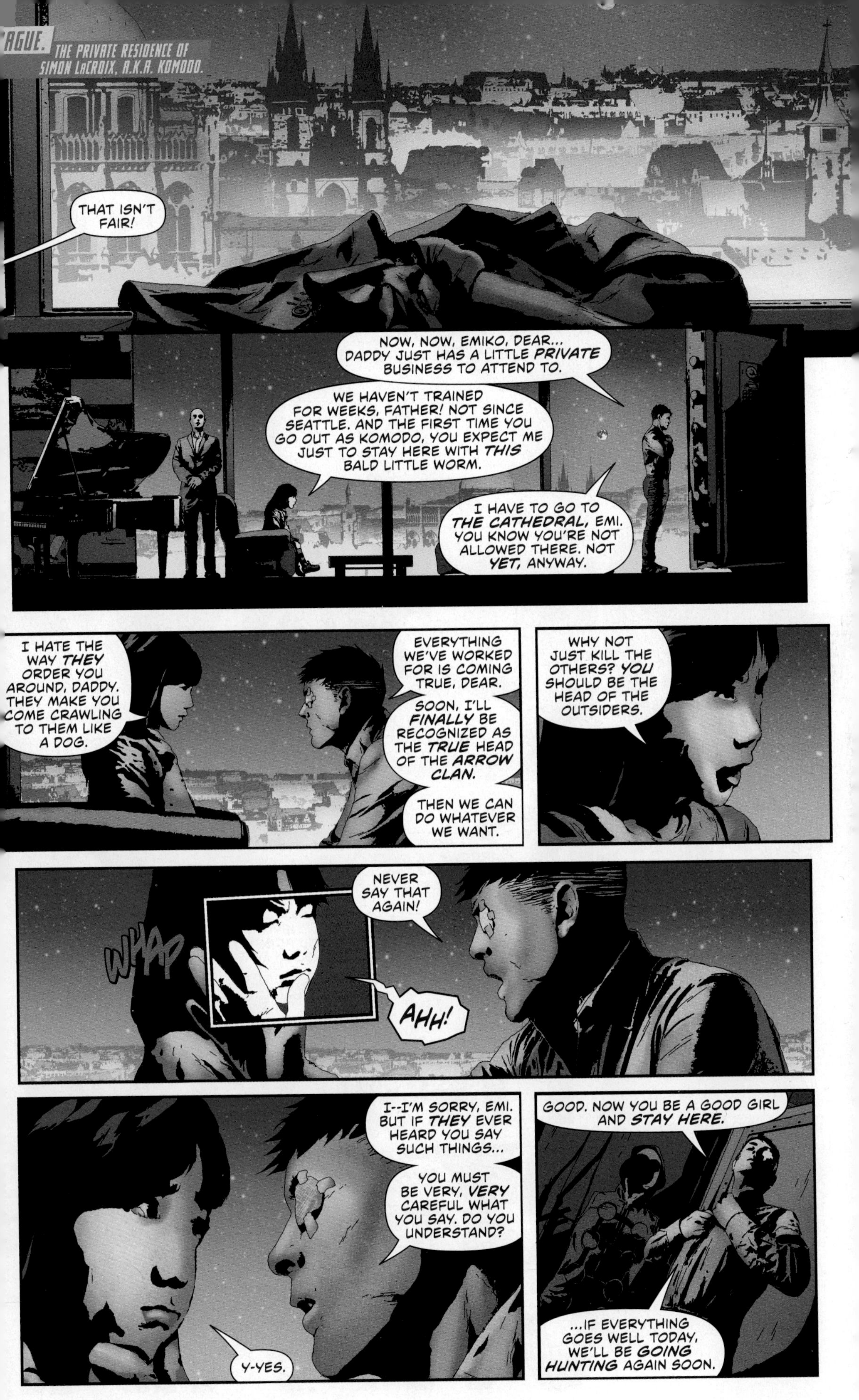
AGUE. THE PRIVATE RESIDENCE OF SIMON LaCROIX, A.K.A. KOMODO.
THAT ISN'T FAIR!
NOW, NOW, EMIKO, DEAR... DADDY JUST HAS A LITTLE PRIVATE BUSINESS TO ATTEND TO.
WE HAVEN'T TRAINED FOR WEEKS, FATHER! NOT SINCE SEATTLE. AND THE FIRST TIME YOU GO OUT AS KOMODO, YOU EXPECT ME JUST TO STAY HERE WITH THIS BALD LITTLE WORM.
I HAVE TO GO TO THE CATHEDRAL, EMI. YOU KNOW YOU'RE NOT ALLOWED THERE. NOT YET, ANYWAY.
I HATE THE WAY THEY ORDER YOU AROUND, DADDY. THEY MAKE YOU COME CRAWLING TO THEM LIKE A DOG.
EVERYTHING WE'VE WORKED FOR IS COMING TRUE, DEAR.
SOON, I'LL FINALLY BE RECOGNIZED AS THE TRUE HEAD OF THE ARROW CLAN.
THEN WE CAN DO WHATEVER WE WANT.
WHY NOT JUST KILL THE OTHERS? YOU SHOULD BE THE HEAD OF THE OUTSIDERS.
WHAP
NEVER SAY THAT AGAIN!
AHH!
I--I'M SORRY, EMI. BUT IF THEY EVER HEARD YOU SAY SUCH THINGS...
YOU MUST BE VERY, VERY CAREFUL WHAT YOU SAY. DO YOU UNDERSTAND?
Y-YES.
GOOD. NOW YOU BE A GOOD GIRL AND STAY HERE.
...IF EVERYTHING GOES WELL TODAY, WE'LL BE GOING HUNTING AGAIN SOON.

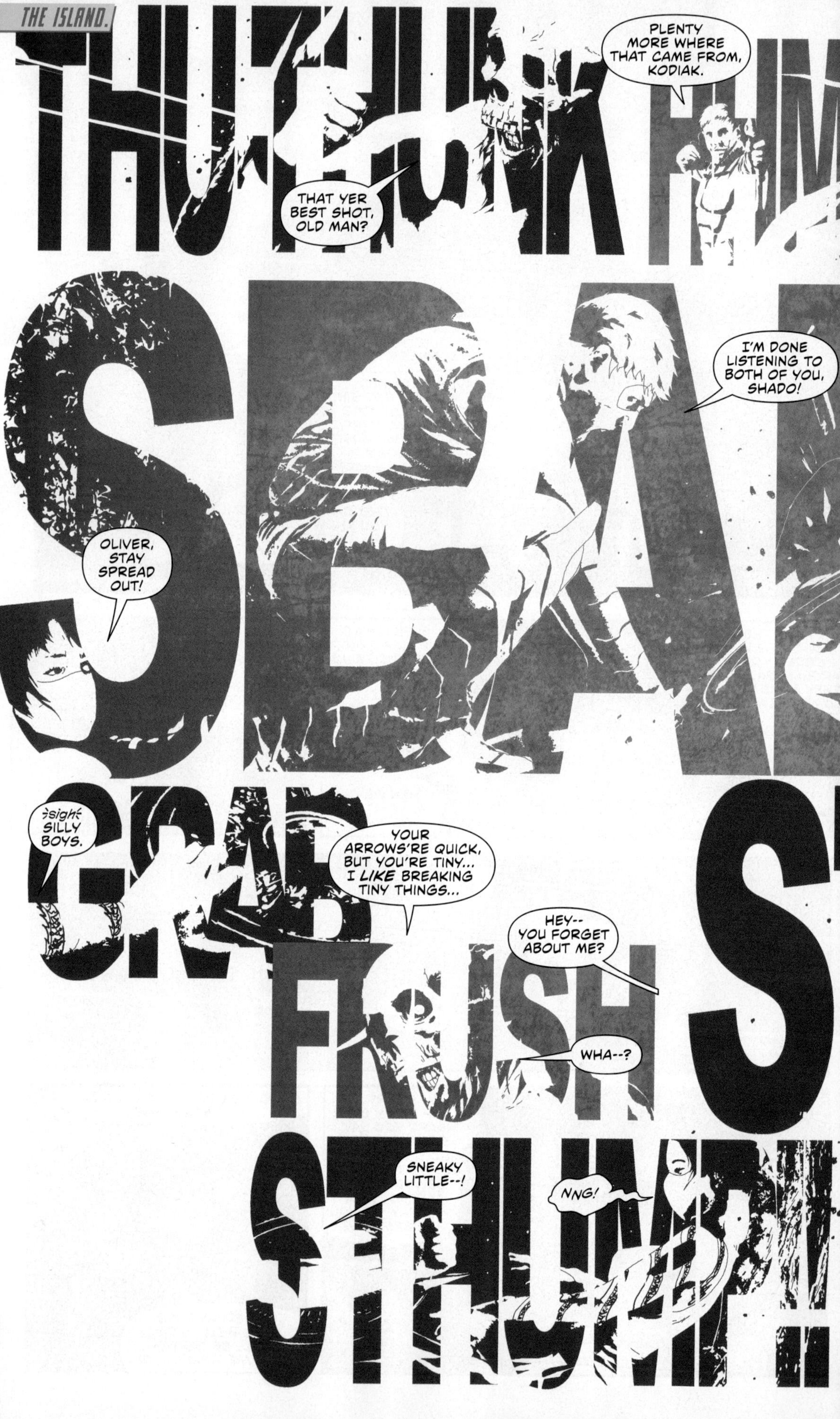
THUTHUNK
PLENTY MORE WHERE THAT CAME FROM, KODIAK.
THAT YER BEST SHOT, OLD MAN?
I'M DONE LISTENING TO BOTH OF YOU, SHADO!
OLIVER, STAY SPREAD OUT!
sigh SILLY BOYS.
YOUR ARROWS'RE QUICK, BUT YOU'RE TINY... I *LIKE* BREAKING TINY THINGS...
HEY-- YOU FORGET ABOUT ME?
FRUSH
WHA--?
SNEAKY LITTLE--!
NNG!
STHUMP!!

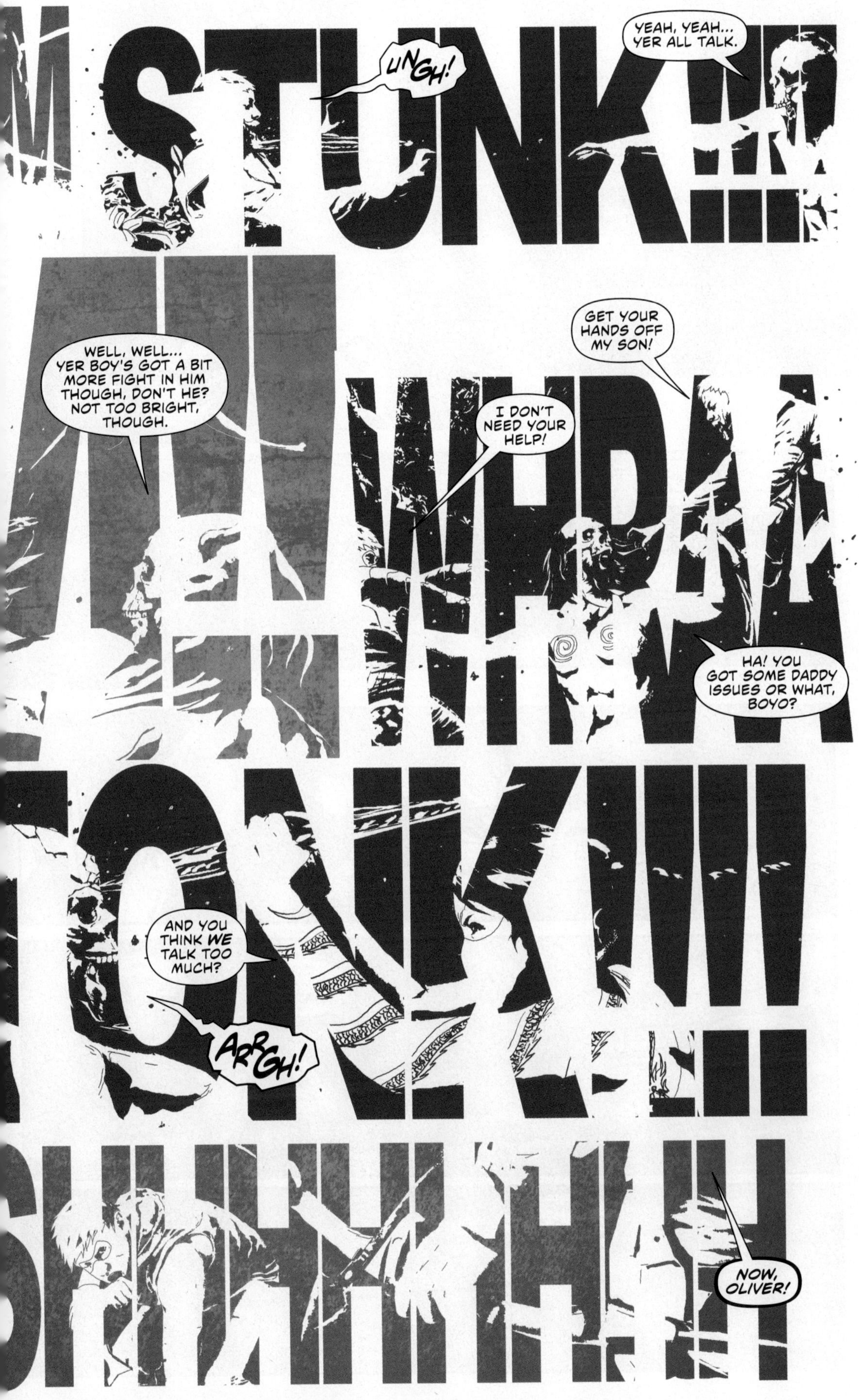
STUNK!!!
UNGH!
YEAH, YEAH... YER ALL TALK.
WELL, WELL... YER BOY'S GOT A BIT MORE FIGHT IN HIM THOUGH, DON'T HE? NOT TOO BRIGHT, THOUGH.
I DON'T NEED YOUR HELP!
GET YOUR HANDS OFF MY SON!
HA! YOU GOT SOME DADDY ISSUES OR WHAT, BOYO?
AND YOU THINK WE TALK TOO MUCH?
ARRGH!
NOW, OLIVER!

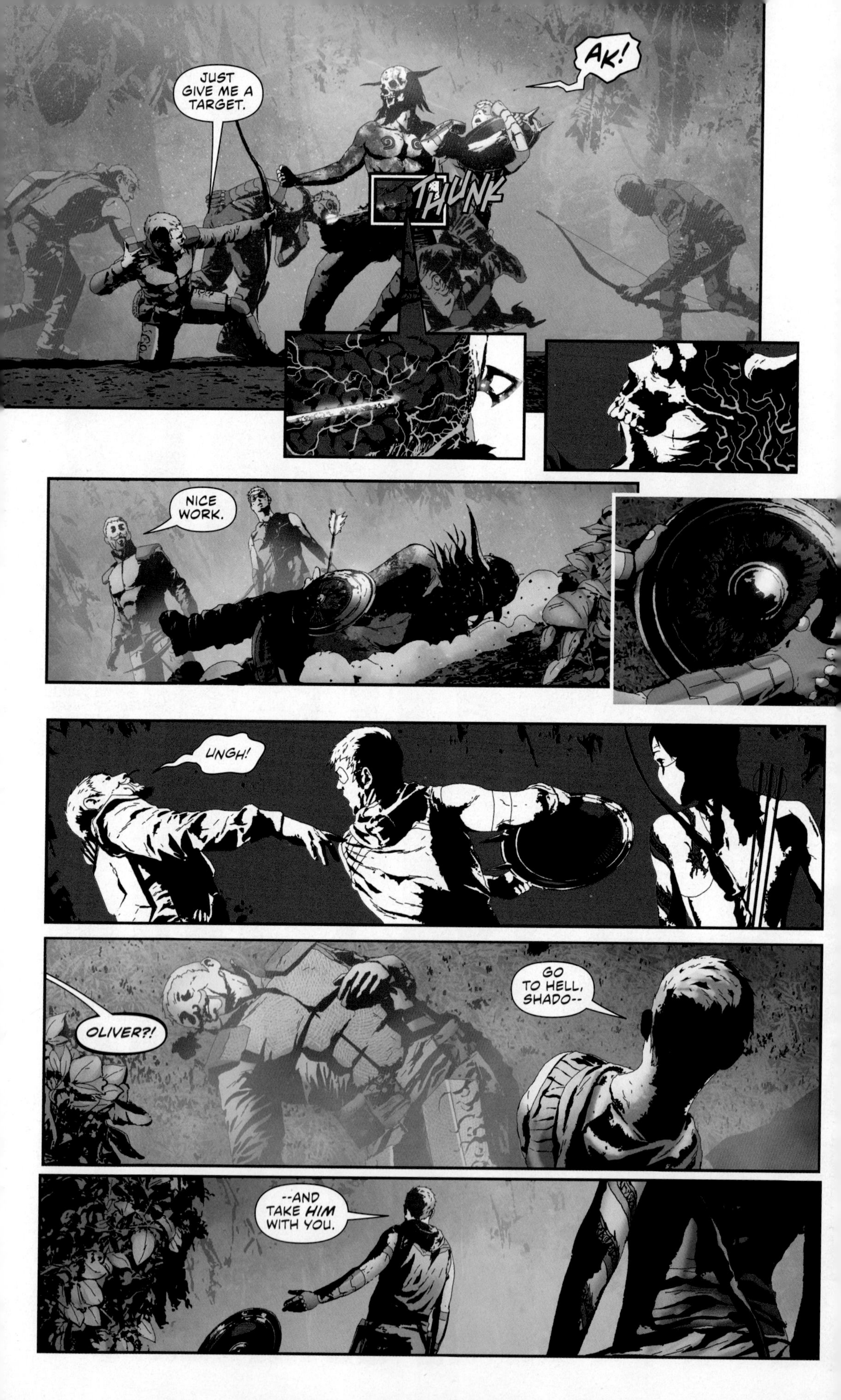
JUST GIVE ME A TARGET.
AK!
THUNK
NICE WORK.
UNGH!
GO TO HELL, SHADO--
OLIVER?!
--AND TAKE HIM WITH YOU.

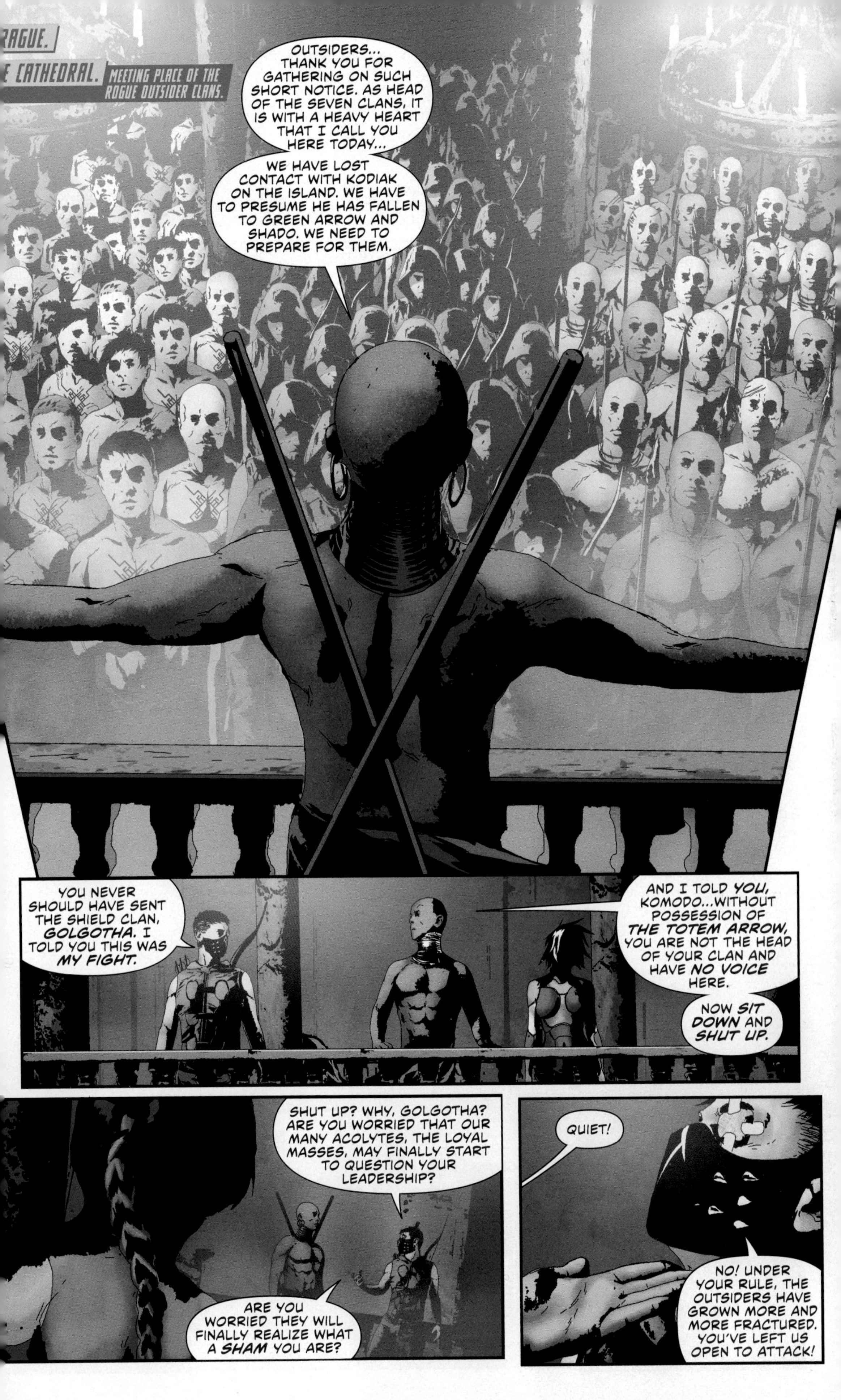
RAGUE.
E CATHEDRAL.
MEETING PLACE OF THE ROGUE OUTSIDER CLANS.
OUTSIDERS... THANK YOU FOR GATHERING ON SUCH SHORT NOTICE. AS HEAD OF THE SEVEN CLANS, IT IS WITH A HEAVY HEART THAT I CALL YOU HERE TODAY...
WE HAVE LOST CONTACT WITH KODIAK ON THE ISLAND. WE HAVE TO PRESUME HE HAS FALLEN TO GREEN ARROW AND SHADO. WE NEED TO PREPARE FOR THEM.
YOU NEVER SHOULD HAVE SENT THE SHIELD CLAN, GOLGOTHA. I TOLD YOU THIS WAS MY FIGHT.
AND I TOLD YOU, KOMODO...WITHOUT POSSESSION OF THE TOTEM ARROW, YOU ARE NOT THE HEAD OF YOUR CLAN AND HAVE NO VOICE HERE.
NOW SIT DOWN AND SHUT UP.
SHUT UP? WHY, GOLGOTHA? ARE YOU WORRIED THAT OUR MANY ACOLYTES, THE LOYAL MASSES, MAY FINALLY START TO QUESTION YOUR LEADERSHIP?
ARE YOU WORRIED THEY WILL FINALLY REALIZE WHAT A SHAM YOU ARE?
QUIET!
NO! UNDER YOUR RULE, THE OUTSIDERS HAVE GROWN MORE AND MORE FRACTURED. YOU'VE LEFT US OPEN TO ATTACK!

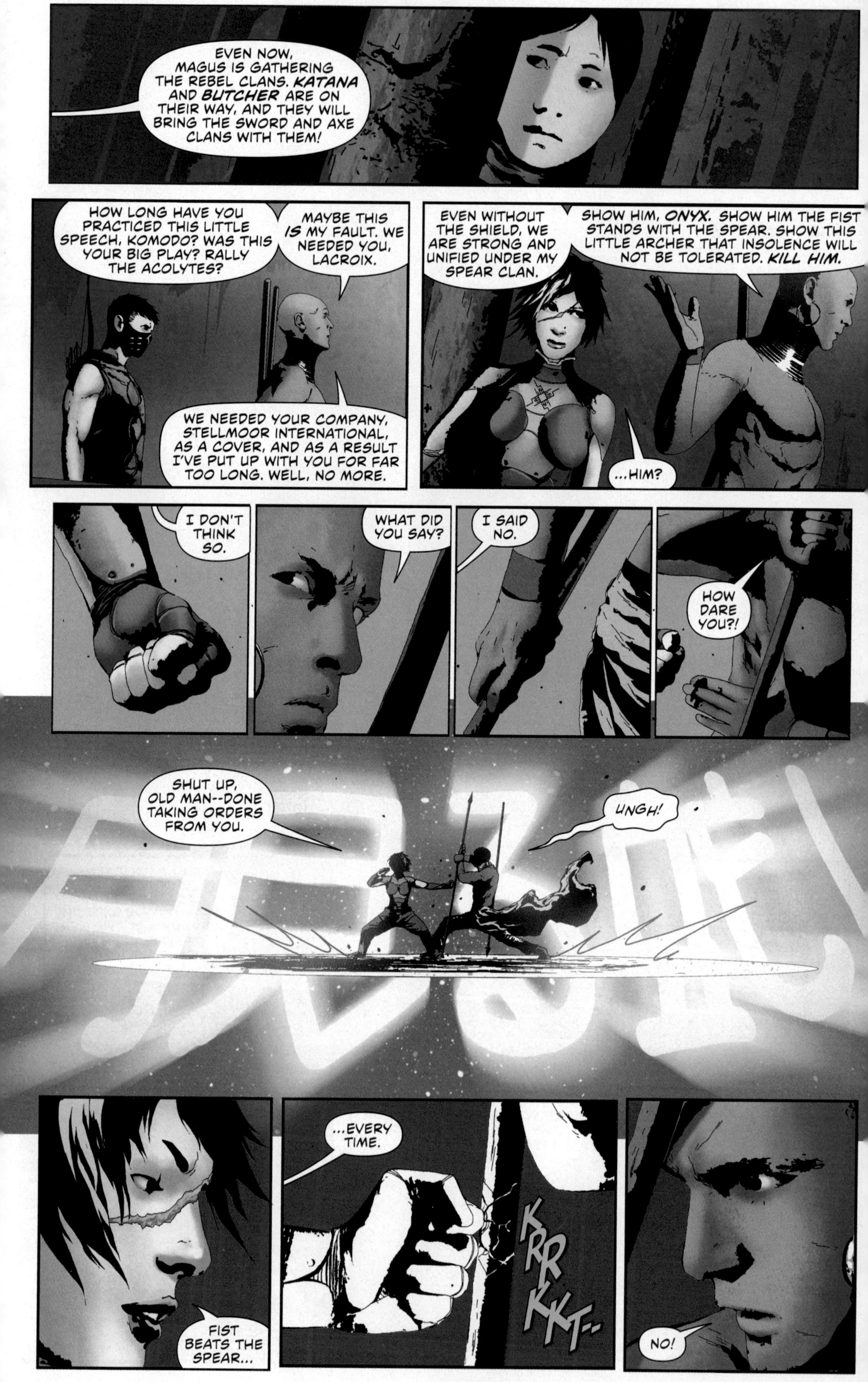
EVEN NOW, MAGUS IS GATHERING THE REBEL CLANS. *KATANA* AND *BUTCHER* ARE ON THEIR WAY, AND THEY WILL BRING THE SWORD AND AXE CLANS WITH THEM!
HOW LONG HAVE YOU PRACTICED THIS LITTLE SPEECH, KOMODO? WAS THIS YOUR BIG PLAY? RALLY THE ACOLYTES?
MAYBE THIS *IS* MY FAULT. WE NEEDED YOU, LACROIX.
WE NEEDED YOUR COMPANY, STELLMOOR INTERNATIONAL, AS A COVER, AND AS A RESULT I'VE PUT UP WITH YOU FOR FAR TOO LONG. WELL, NO MORE.
EVEN WITHOUT THE SHIELD, WE ARE STRONG AND UNIFIED UNDER MY SPEAR CLAN.
SHOW HIM, *ONYX.* SHOW HIM THE FIST STANDS WITH THE SPEAR. SHOW THIS LITTLE ARCHER THAT INSOLENCE WILL NOT BE TOLERATED. *KILL HIM.*
...HIM?
I DON'T THINK SO.
WHAT DID YOU SAY?
I SAID NO.
HOW DARE YOU?!
SHUT UP, OLD MAN--DONE TAKING ORDERS FROM YOU.
UNGH!
FIST BEATS THE SPEAR...
...EVERY TIME.
KRRKKT--
NO!

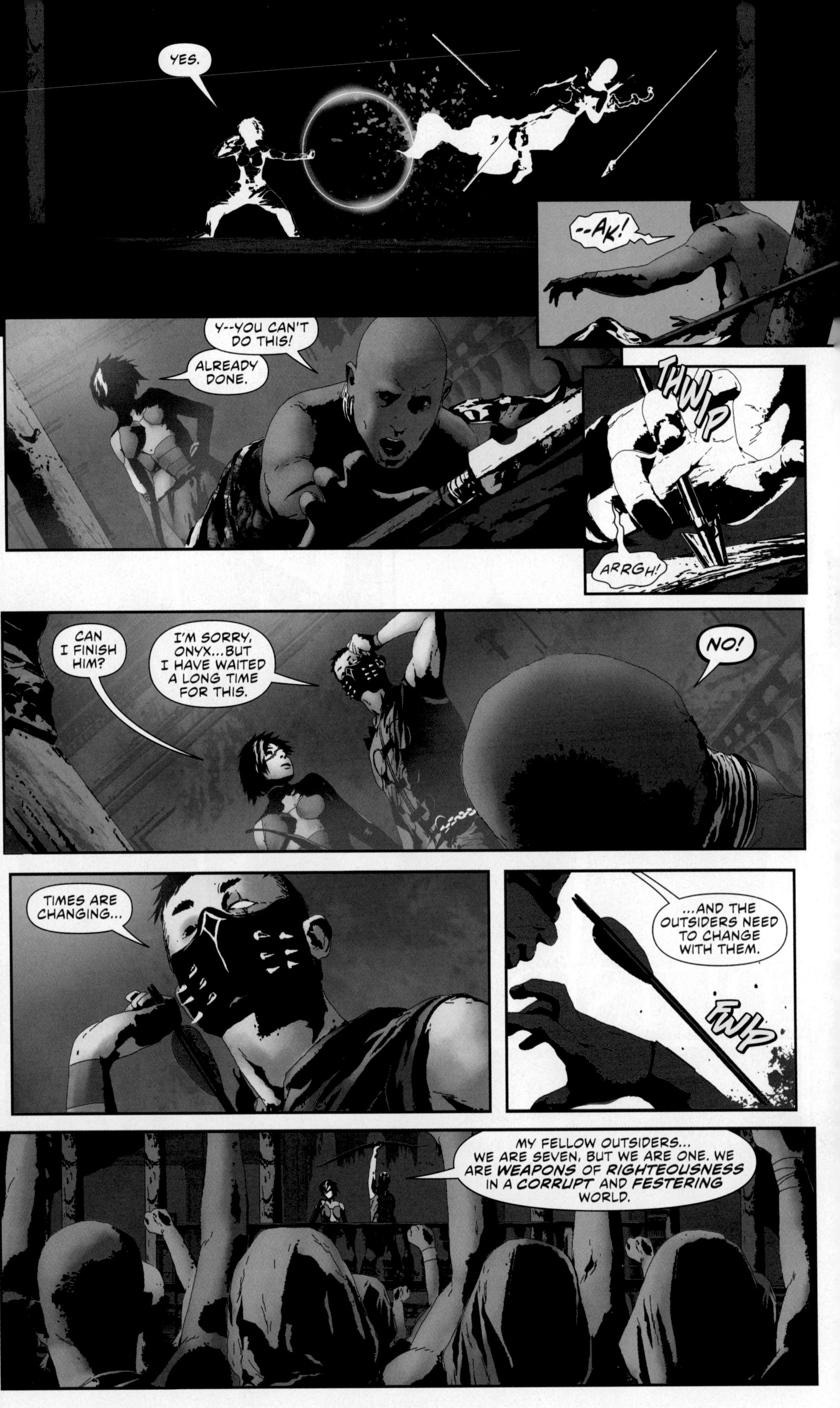
YES.
--AK!
Y--YOU CAN'T DO THIS!
ALREADY DONE.
THWIP
ARRGH!
CAN I FINISH HIM?
I'M SORRY, ONYX...BUT I HAVE WAITED A LONG TIME FOR THIS.
NO!
TIMES ARE CHANGING...
...AND THE OUTSIDERS NEED TO CHANGE WITH THEM.
FWIP
MY FELLOW OUTSIDERS... WE ARE SEVEN, BUT WE ARE ONE. WE ARE WEAPONS OF RIGHTEOUSNESS IN A CORRUPT AND FESTERING WORLD.

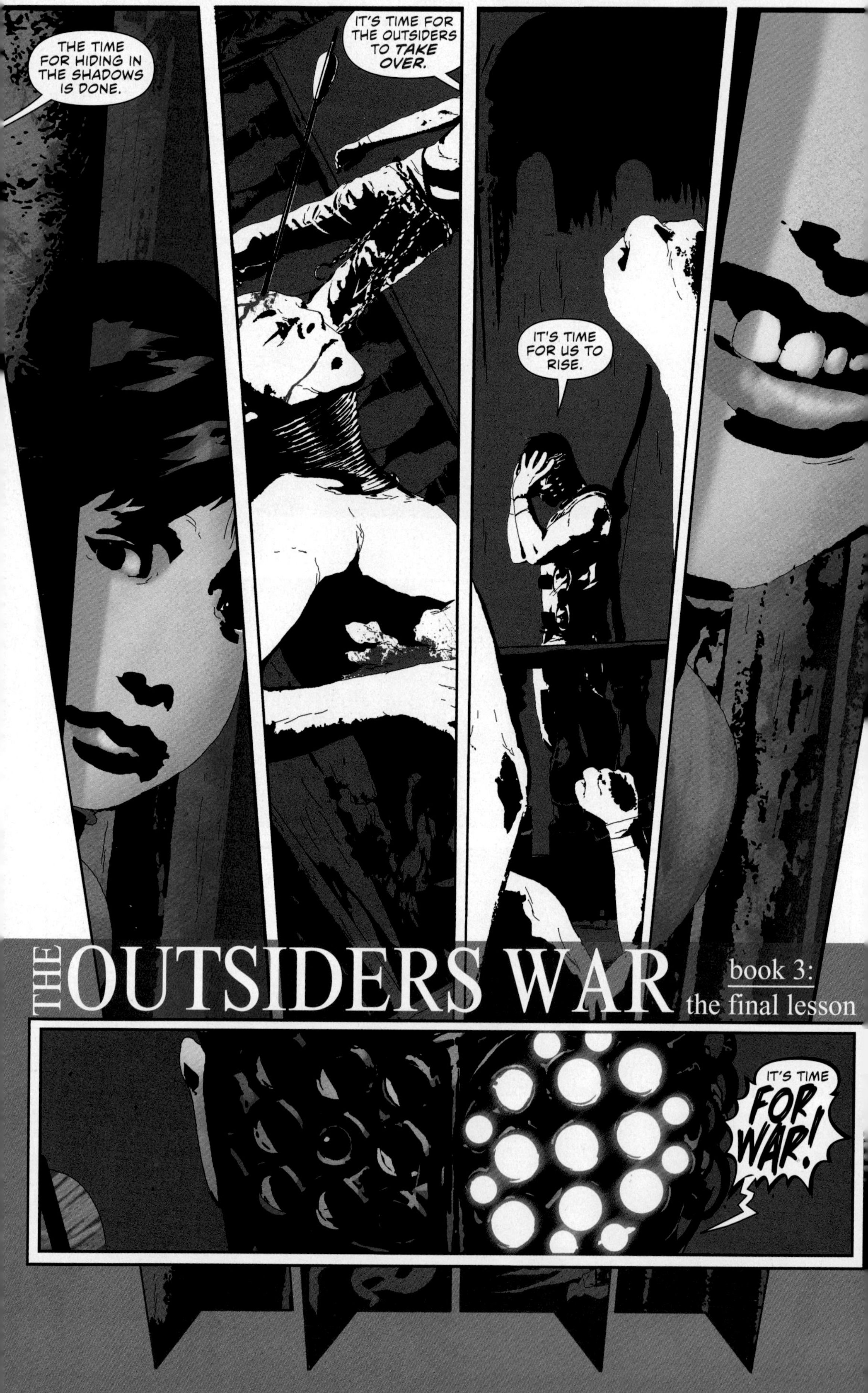
THE TIME FOR HIDING IN THE SHADOWS IS DONE.
IT'S TIME FOR THE OUTSIDERS TO TAKE OVER.
IT'S TIME FOR US TO RISE.
THE OUTSIDERS WAR
book 3:
the final lesson
IT'S TIME FOR WAR!

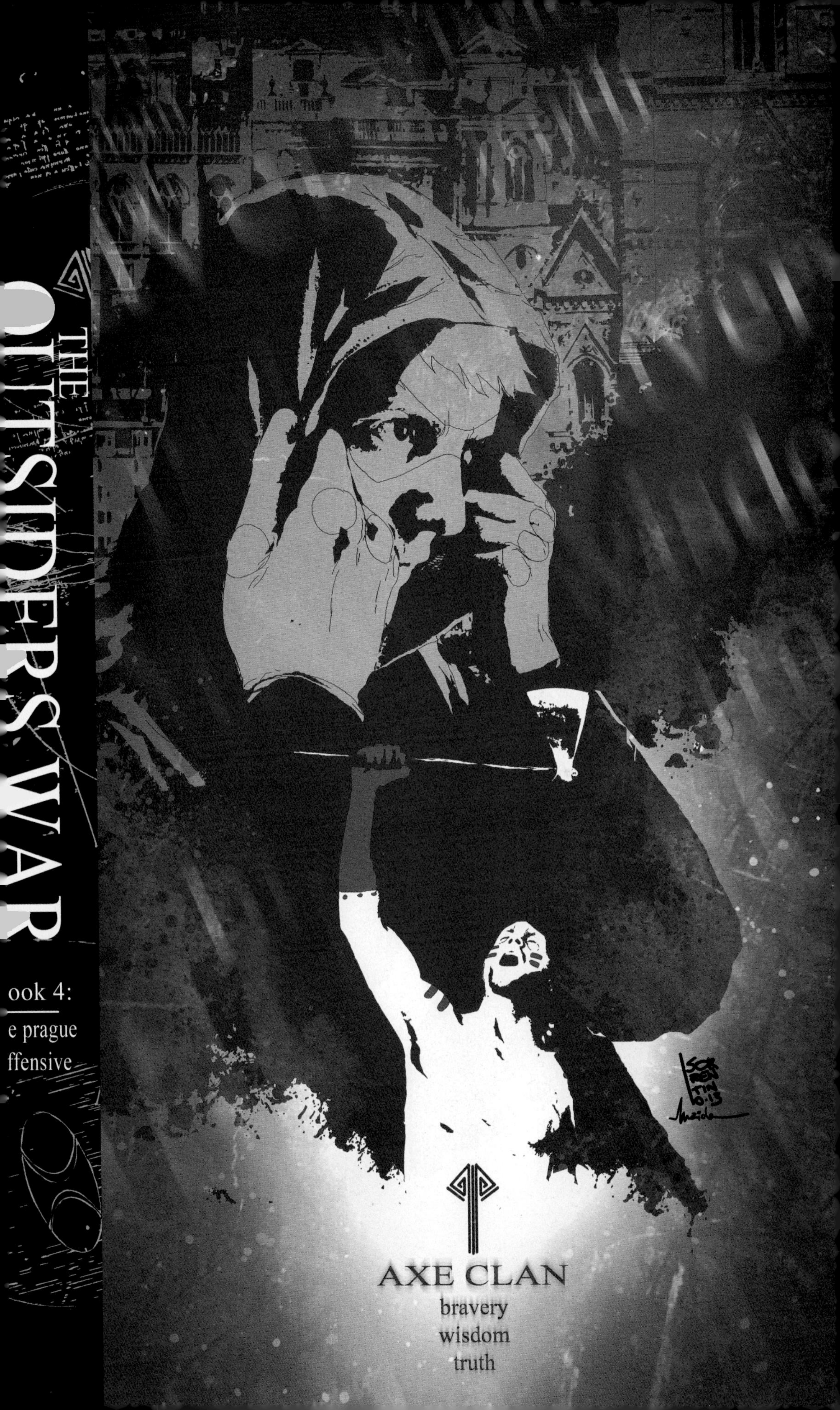
THE
ook 4:
e prague
ffensive
AXE CLAN
bravery
wisdom
truth

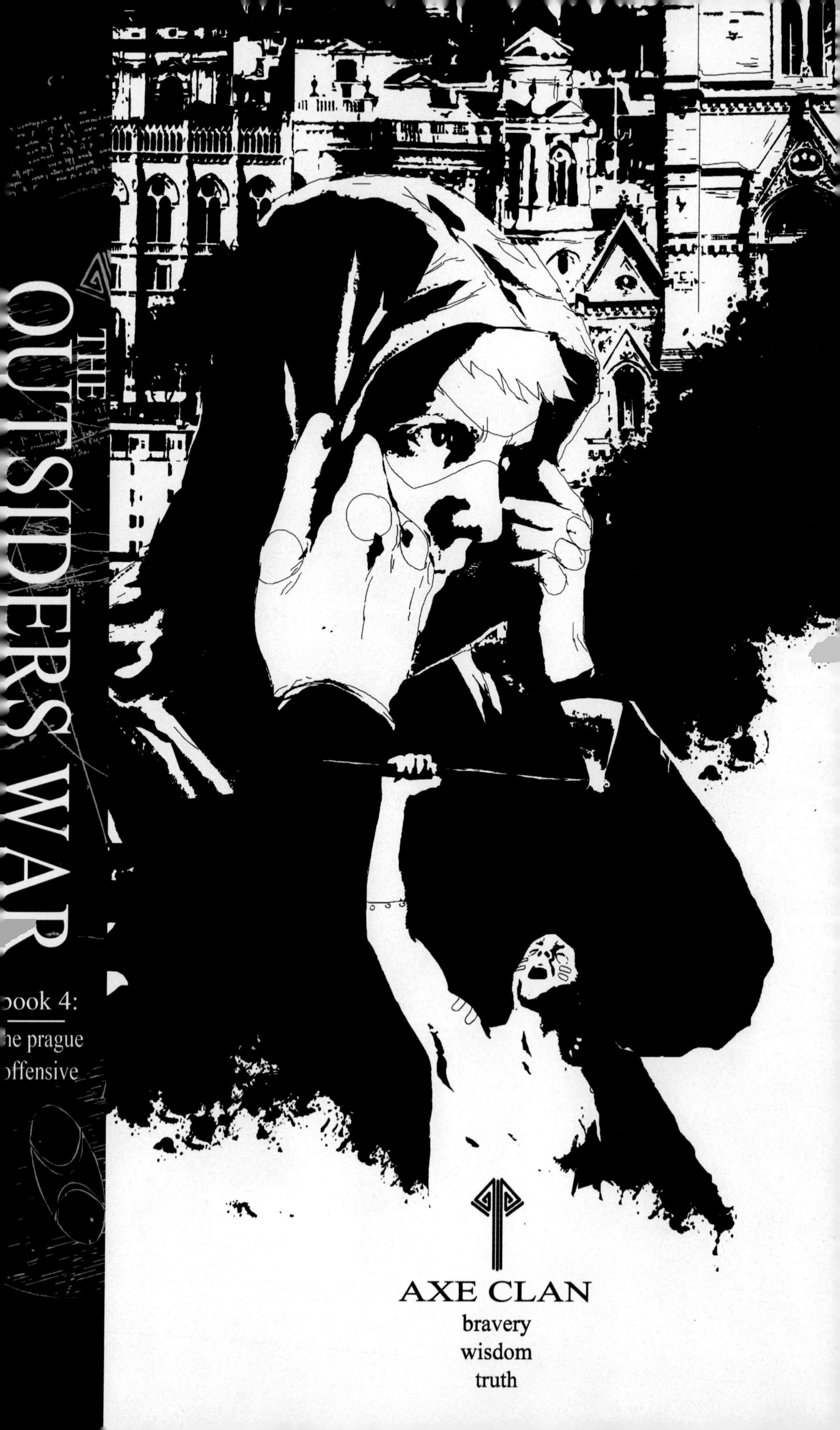
THE OUTSIDERS WAR
ook 4:
he prague
ffensive
AXE CLAN
bravery
wisdom
truth

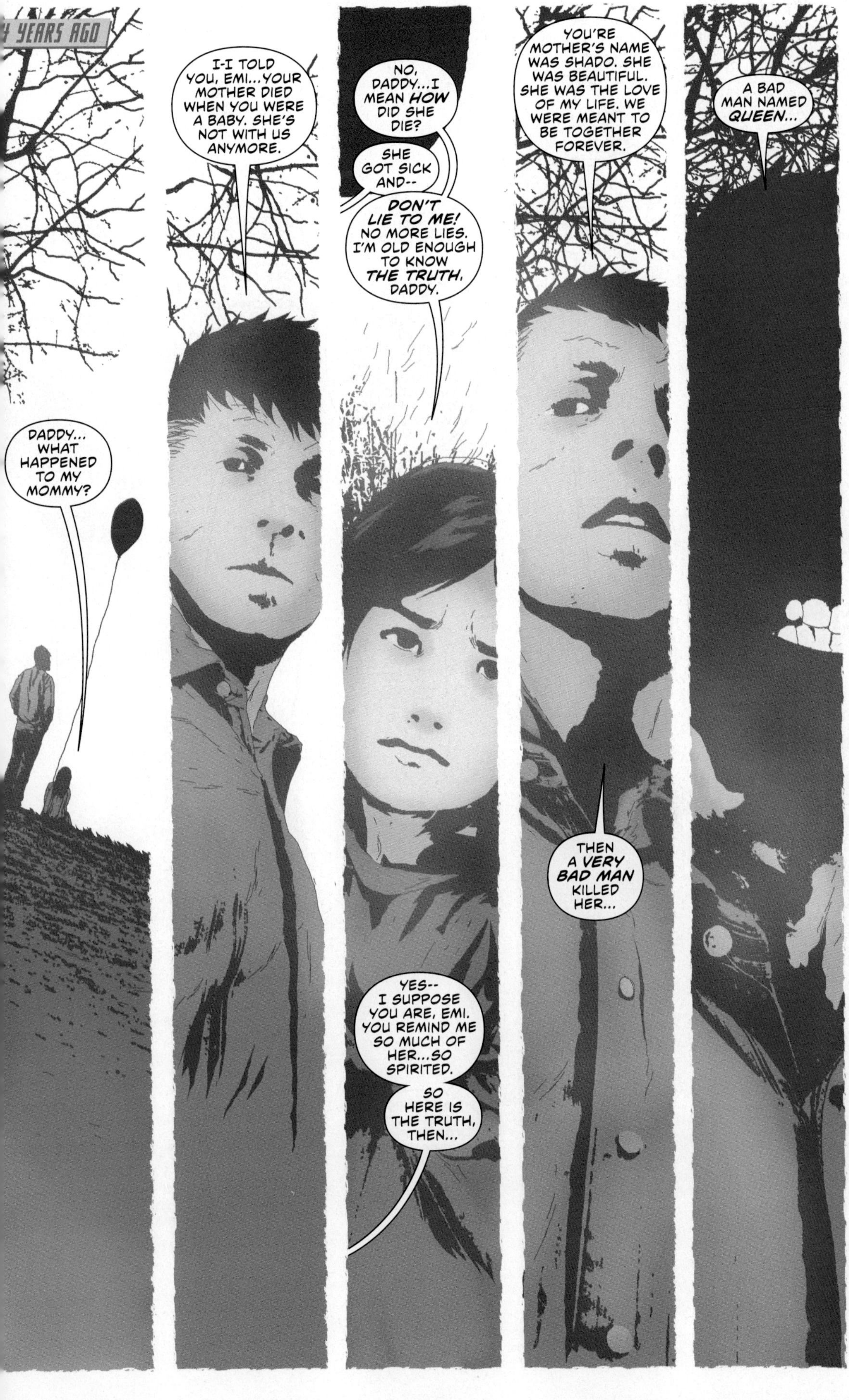
4 YEARS AGO
DADDY... WHAT HAPPENED TO MY MOMMY?
I-I TOLD YOU, EMI...YOUR MOTHER DIED WHEN YOU WERE A BABY. SHE'S NOT WITH US ANYMORE.
NO, DADDY...I MEAN HOW DID SHE DIE?
SHE GOT SICK AND--
DON'T LIE TO ME! NO MORE LIES. I'M OLD ENOUGH TO KNOW THE TRUTH, DADDY.
YES-- I SUPPOSE YOU ARE, EMI. YOU REMIND ME SO MUCH OF HER...SO SPIRITED.
SO HERE IS THE TRUTH, THEN...
YOU'RE MOTHER'S NAME WAS SHADO. SHE WAS BEAUTIFUL. SHE WAS THE LOVE OF MY LIFE. WE WERE MEANT TO BE TOGETHER FOREVER.
THEN A VERY BAD MAN KILLED HER...
A BAD MAN NAMED QUEEN...

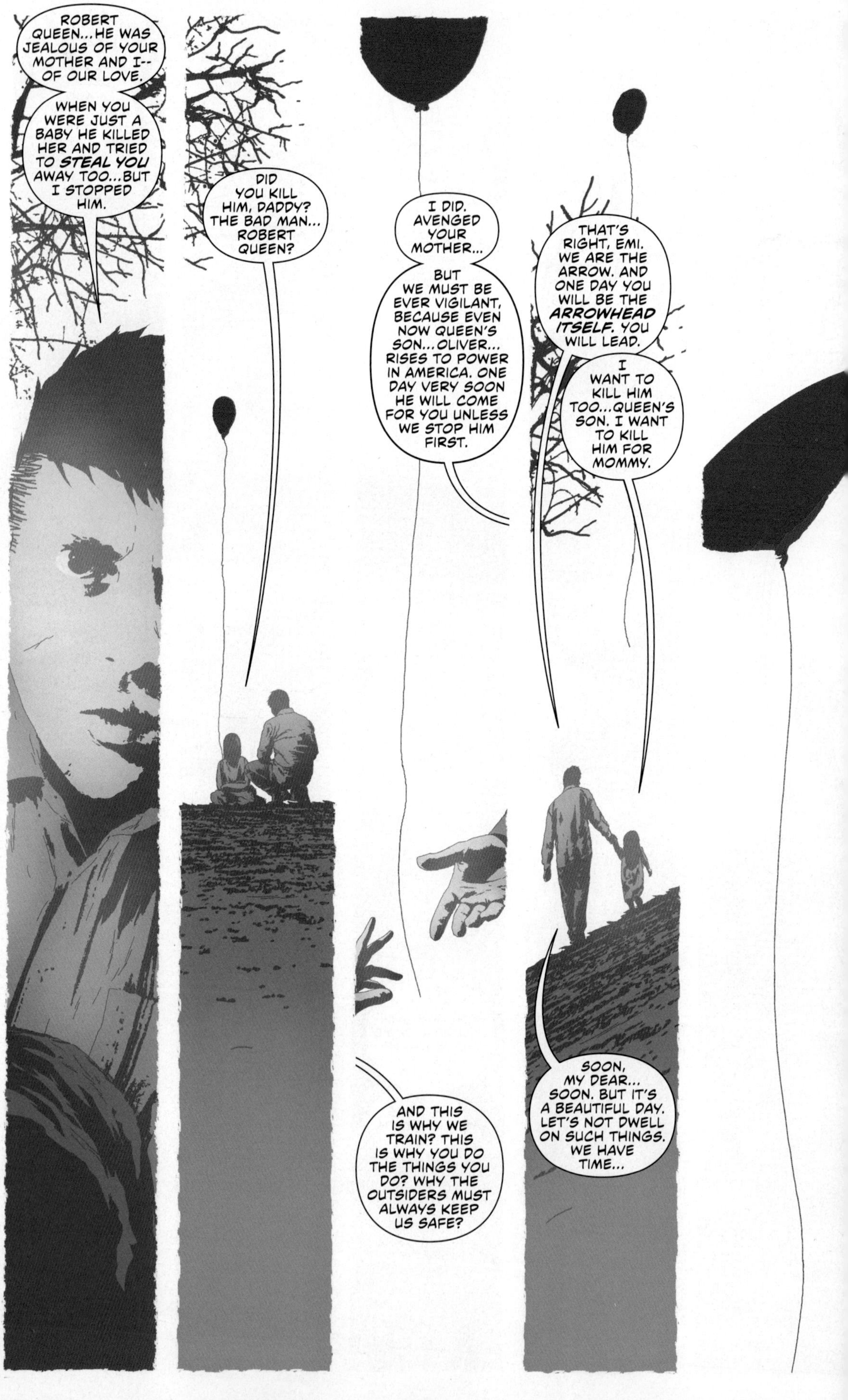
ROBERT QUEEN...HE WAS JEALOUS OF YOUR MOTHER AND I-- OF OUR LOVE.
WHEN YOU WERE JUST A BABY HE KILLED HER AND TRIED TO **STEAL YOU** AWAY TOO...BUT I STOPPED HIM.
DID YOU KILL HIM, DADDY? THE BAD MAN... ROBERT QUEEN?
I DID. AVENGED YOUR MOTHER...
BUT WE MUST BE EVER VIGILANT, BECAUSE EVEN NOW QUEEN'S SON...OLIVER... RISES TO POWER IN AMERICA. ONE DAY VERY SOON HE WILL COME FOR YOU UNLESS WE STOP HIM FIRST.
AND THIS IS WHY WE TRAIN? THIS IS WHY YOU DO THE THINGS YOU DO? WHY THE OUTSIDERS MUST ALWAYS KEEP US SAFE?
THAT'S RIGHT, EMI. WE ARE THE ARROW. AND ONE DAY YOU WILL BE THE ***ARROWHEAD ITSELF.*** YOU WILL LEAD.
I WANT TO KILL HIM TOO...QUEEN'S SON. I WANT TO KILL HIM FOR MOMMY.
SOON, MY DEAR... SOON. BUT IT'S A BEAUTIFUL DAY. LET'S NOT DWELL ON SUCH THINGS. WE HAVE TIME...

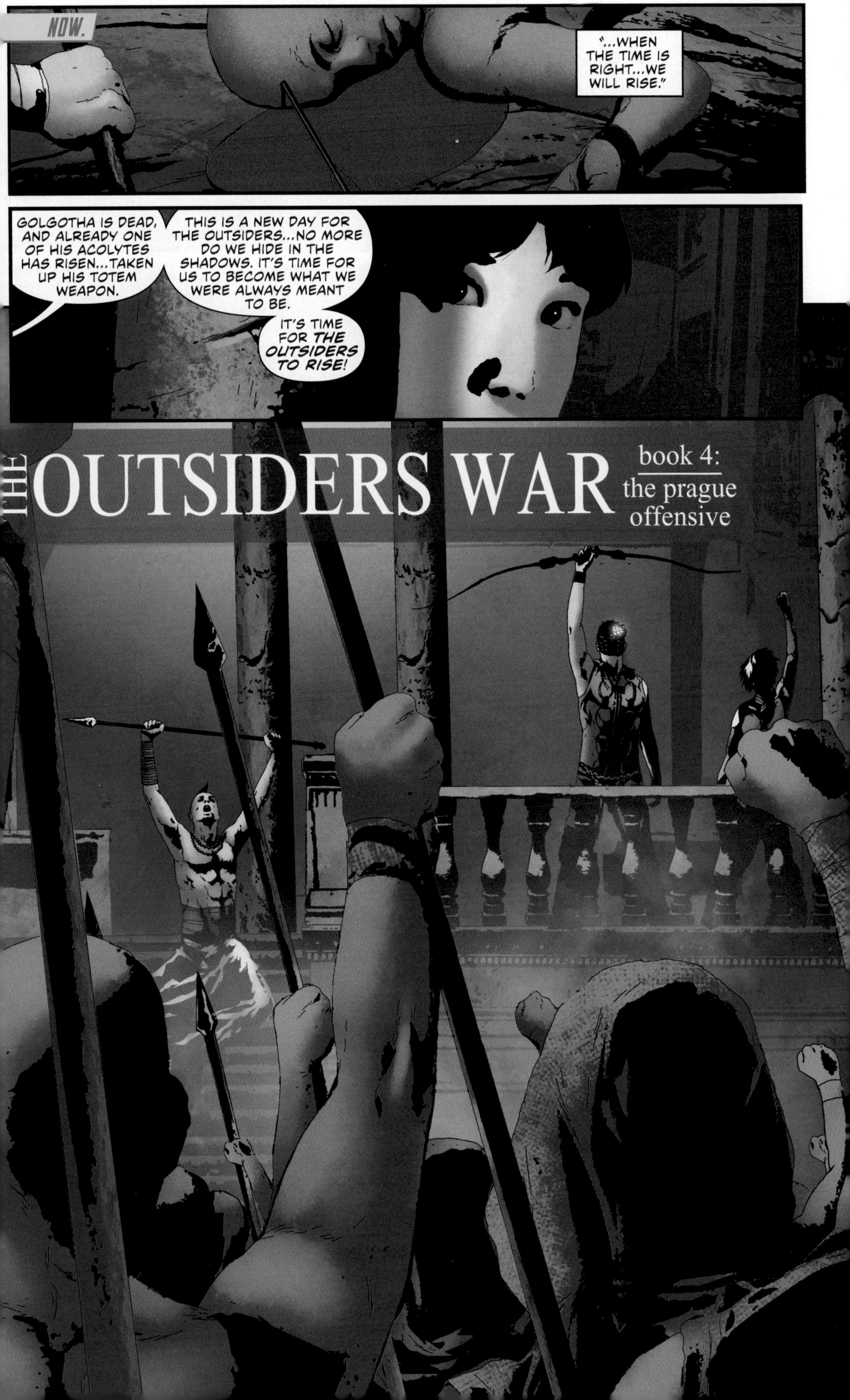
NOW.
"...WHEN THE TIME IS RIGHT...WE WILL RISE."
GOLGOTHA IS DEAD, AND ALREADY ONE OF HIS ACOLYTES HAS RISEN...TAKEN UP HIS TOTEM WEAPON.
THIS IS A NEW DAY FOR THE OUTSIDERS...NO MORE DO WE HIDE IN THE SHADOWS. IT'S TIME FOR US TO BECOME WHAT WE WERE ALWAYS MEANT TO BE.
IT'S TIME FOR THE OUTSIDERS TO RISE!
THE OUTSIDERS WAR
book 4: the prague offensive

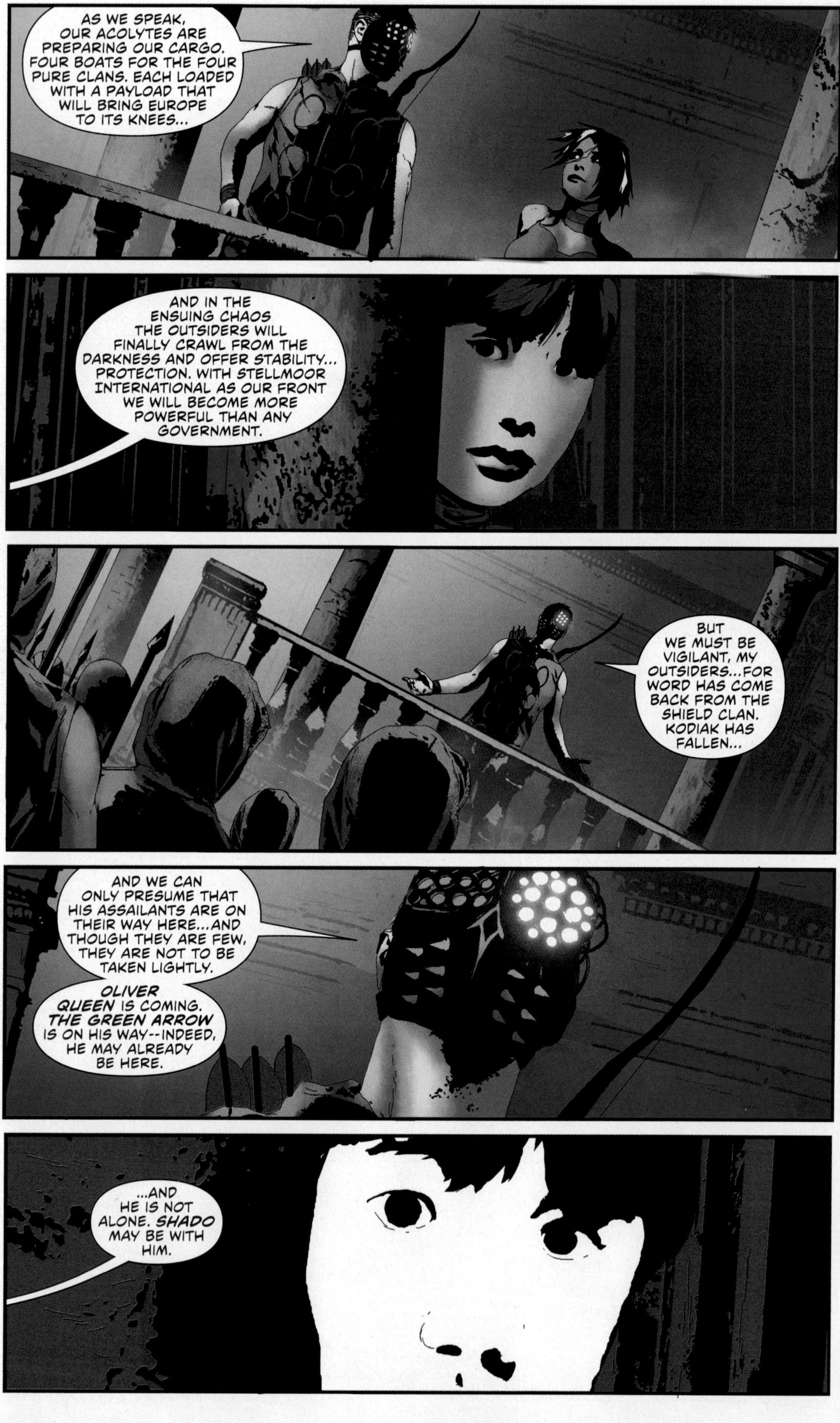
AS WE SPEAK, OUR ACOLYTES ARE PREPARING OUR CARGO. FOUR BOATS FOR THE FOUR PURE CLANS. EACH LOADED WITH A PAYLOAD THAT WILL BRING EUROPE TO ITS KNEES...
AND IN THE ENSUING CHAOS THE OUTSIDERS WILL FINALLY CRAWL FROM THE DARKNESS AND OFFER STABILITY... PROTECTION. WITH STELLMOOR INTERNATIONAL AS OUR FRONT WE WILL BECOME MORE POWERFUL THAN ANY GOVERNMENT.
BUT WE MUST BE VIGILANT, MY OUTSIDERS...FOR WORD HAS COME BACK FROM THE SHIELD CLAN. KODIAK HAS FALLEN...
AND WE CAN ONLY PRESUME THAT HIS ASSAILANTS ARE ON THEIR WAY HERE...AND THOUGH THEY ARE FEW, THEY ARE NOT TO BE TAKEN LIGHTLY.
OLIVER QUEEN IS COMING. *THE GREEN ARROW* IS ON HIS WAY--INDEED, HE MAY ALREADY BE HERE.
...AND HE IS NOT ALONE. *SHADO* MAY BE WITH HIM.

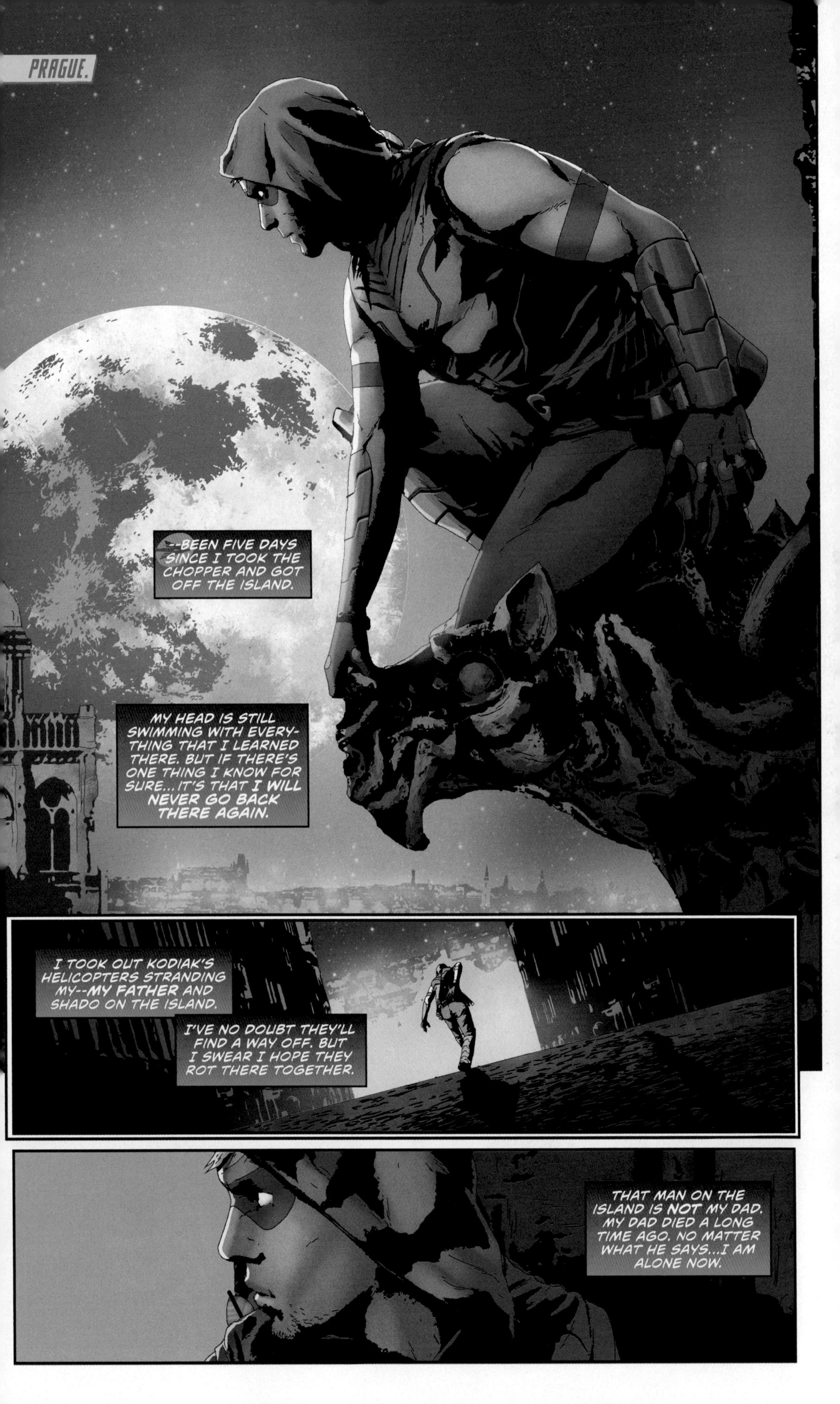
PRAGUE.
--BEEN FIVE DAYS SINCE I TOOK THE CHOPPER AND GOT OFF THE ISLAND.
MY HEAD IS STILL SWIMMING WITH EVERYTHING THAT I LEARNED THERE. BUT IF THERE'S ONE THING I KNOW FOR SURE...IT'S THAT I WILL NEVER GO BACK THERE AGAIN.
I TOOK OUT KODIAK'S HELICOPTERS STRANDING MY--MY FATHER AND SHADO ON THE ISLAND.
I'VE NO DOUBT THEY'LL FIND A WAY OFF. BUT I SWEAR I HOPE THEY ROT THERE TOGETHER.
THAT MAN ON THE ISLAND IS NOT MY DAD. MY DAD DIED A LONG TIME AGO. NO MATTER WHAT HE SAYS...I AM ALONE NOW.

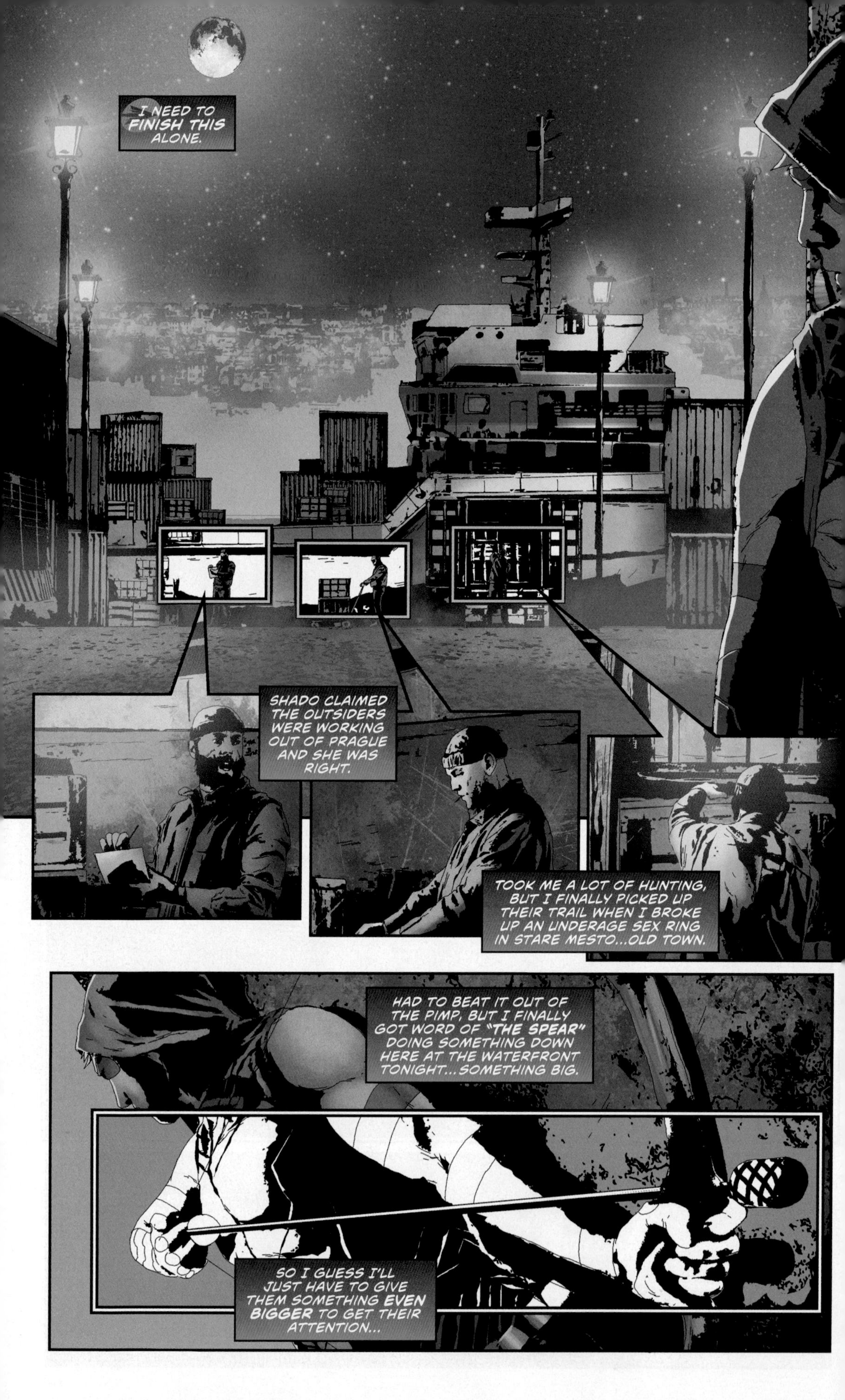
I NEED TO FINISH THIS ALONE.
SHADO CLAIMED THE OUTSIDERS WERE WORKING OUT OF PRAGUE AND SHE WAS RIGHT.
TOOK ME A LOT OF HUNTING, BUT I FINALLY PICKED UP THEIR TRAIL WHEN I BROKE UP AN UNDERAGE SEX RING IN STARE MESTO...OLD TOWN.
HAD TO BEAT IT OUT OF THE PIMP, BUT I FINALLY GOT WORD OF "THE SPEAR" DOING SOMETHING DOWN HERE AT THE WATERFRONT TONIGHT...SOMETHING BIG.
SO I GUESS I'LL JUST HAVE TO GIVE THEM SOMETHING EVEN BIGGER TO GET THEIR ATTENTION...

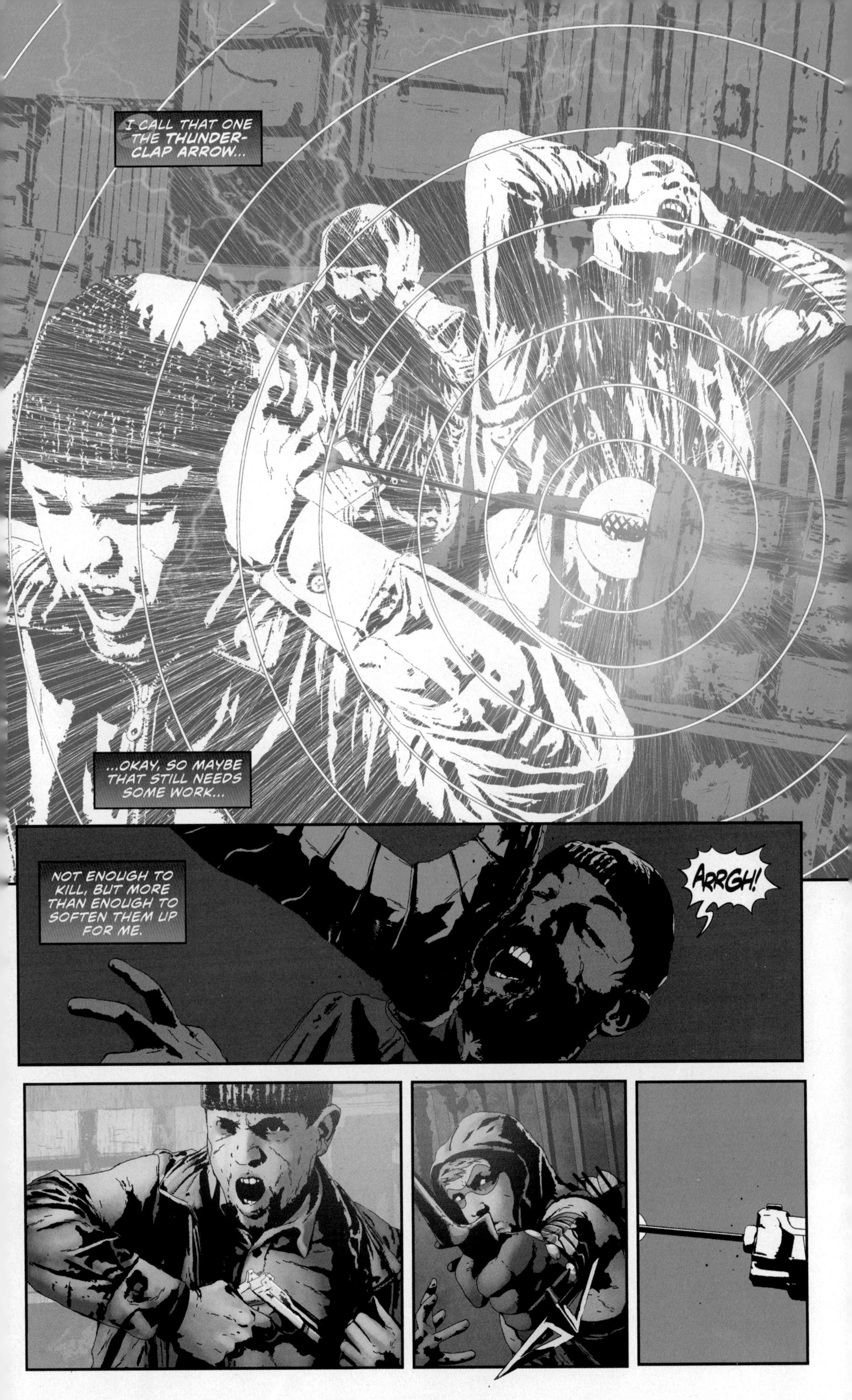
I CALL THAT ONE THE THUNDER-CLAP ARROW...
...OKAY, SO MAYBE THAT STILL NEEDS SOME WORK...
NOT ENOUGH TO KILL, BUT MORE THAN ENOUGH TO SOFTEN THEM UP FOR ME.
ARRGH!

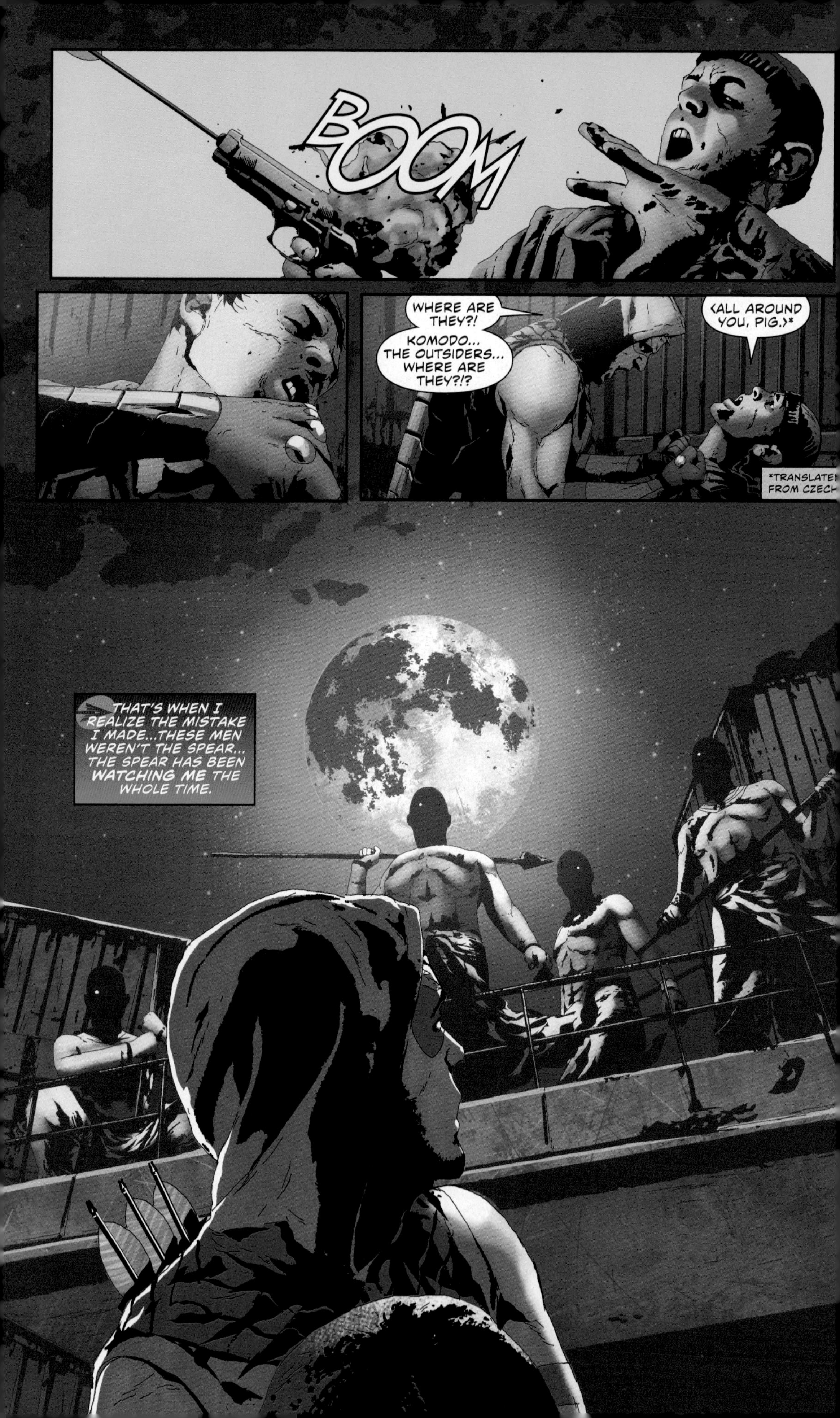
BOOM
WHERE ARE THEY?!
KOMODO... THE OUTSIDERS... WHERE ARE THEY?!?
<ALL AROUND YOU, PIG.>*
*TRANSLATE FROM CZECH
THAT'S WHEN I REALIZE THE MISTAKE I MADE...THESE MEN WEREN'T THE SPEAR... THE SPEAR HAS BEEN WATCHING ME THE WHOLE TIME.

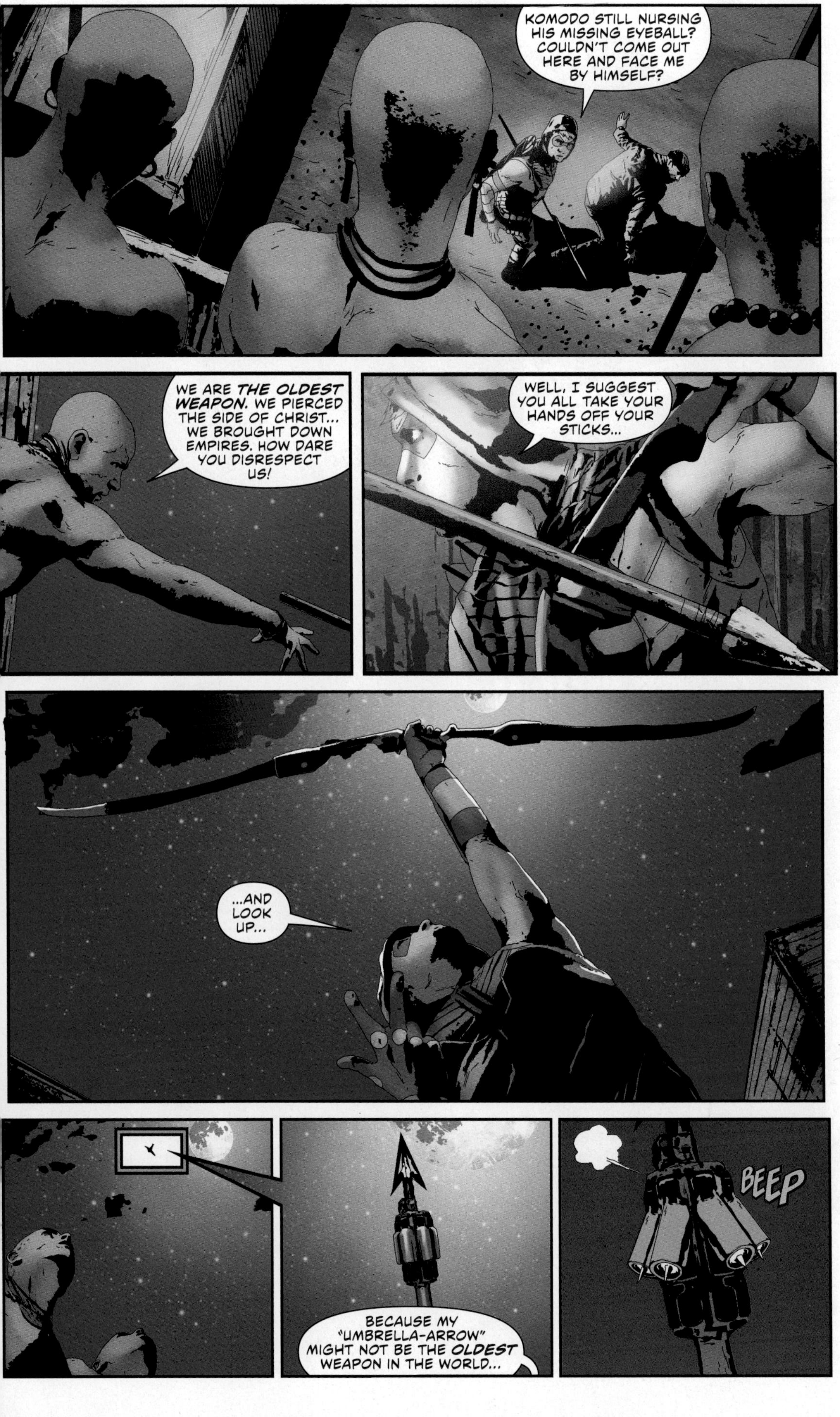
KOMODO STILL NURSING HIS MISSING EYEBALL? COULDN'T COME OUT HERE AND FACE ME BY HIMSELF?
WE ARE THE OLDEST WEAPON. WE PIERCED THE SIDE OF CHRIST... WE BROUGHT DOWN EMPIRES. HOW DARE YOU DISRESPECT US!
WELL, I SUGGEST YOU ALL TAKE YOUR HANDS OFF YOUR STICKS...
...AND LOOK UP...
BECAUSE MY "UMBRELLA-ARROW" MIGHT NOT BE THE OLDEST WEAPON IN THE WORLD...
BEEP

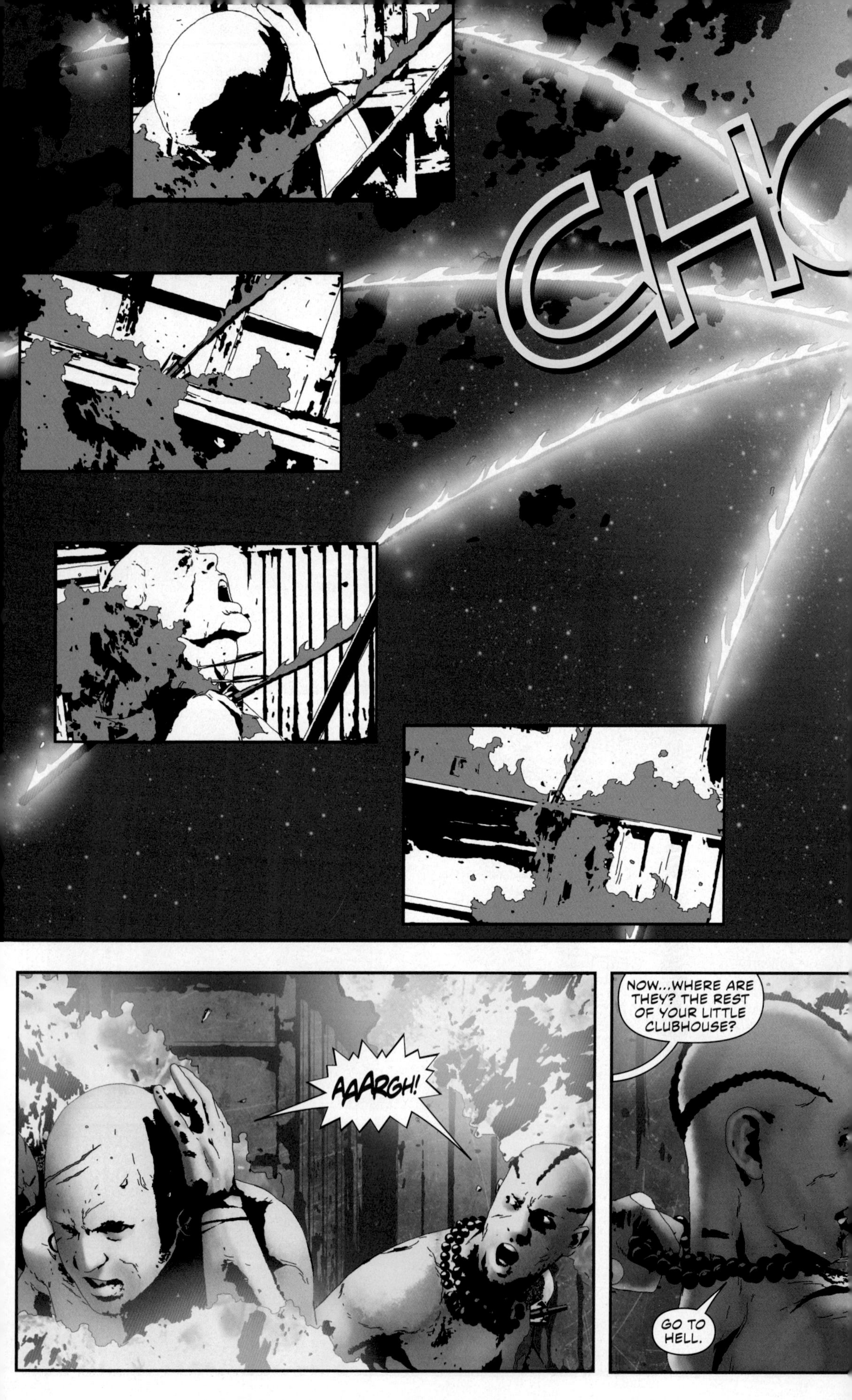
CHO
AAARGH!
NOW...WHERE ARE THEY? THE REST OF YOUR LITTLE CLUBHOUSE?
GO TO HELL.

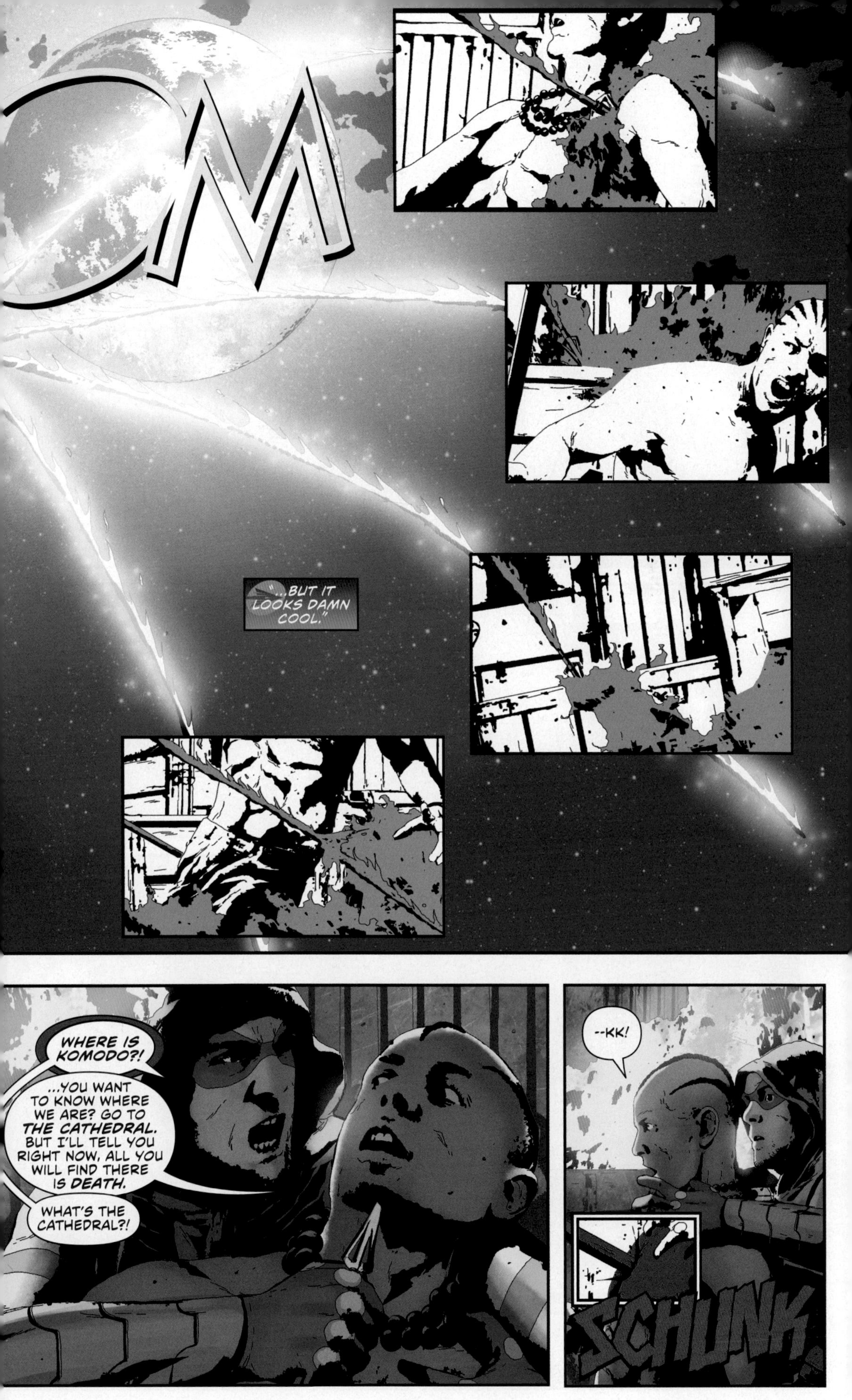

"...BUT IT LOOKS DAMN COOL."
WHERE IS KOMODO?!
...YOU WANT TO KNOW WHERE WE ARE? GO TO THE CATHEDRAL. BUT I'LL TELL YOU RIGHT NOW, ALL YOU WILL FIND THERE IS DEATH.
WHAT'S THE CATHEDRAL?!
--KK!
SCHUNK

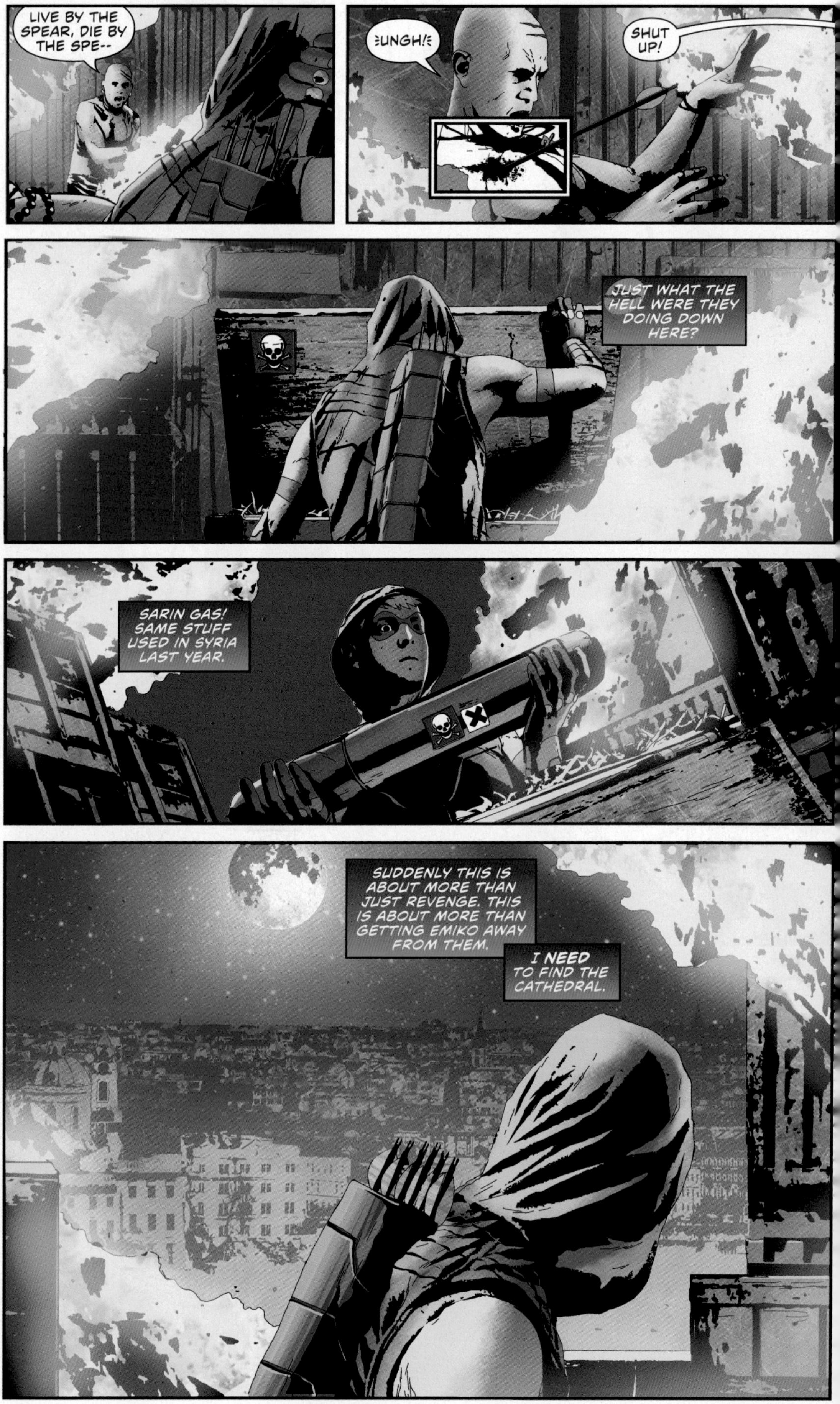
LIVE BY THE SPEAR, DIE BY THE SPE--
UNGH!
SHUT UP!
JUST WHAT THE HELL WERE THEY DOING DOWN HERE?
SARIN GAS! SAME STUFF USED IN SYRIA LAST YEAR.
SUDDENLY THIS IS ABOUT MORE THAN JUST REVENGE. THIS IS ABOUT MORE THAN GETTING EMIKO AWAY FROM THEM.
I NEED TO FIND THE CATHEDRAL.

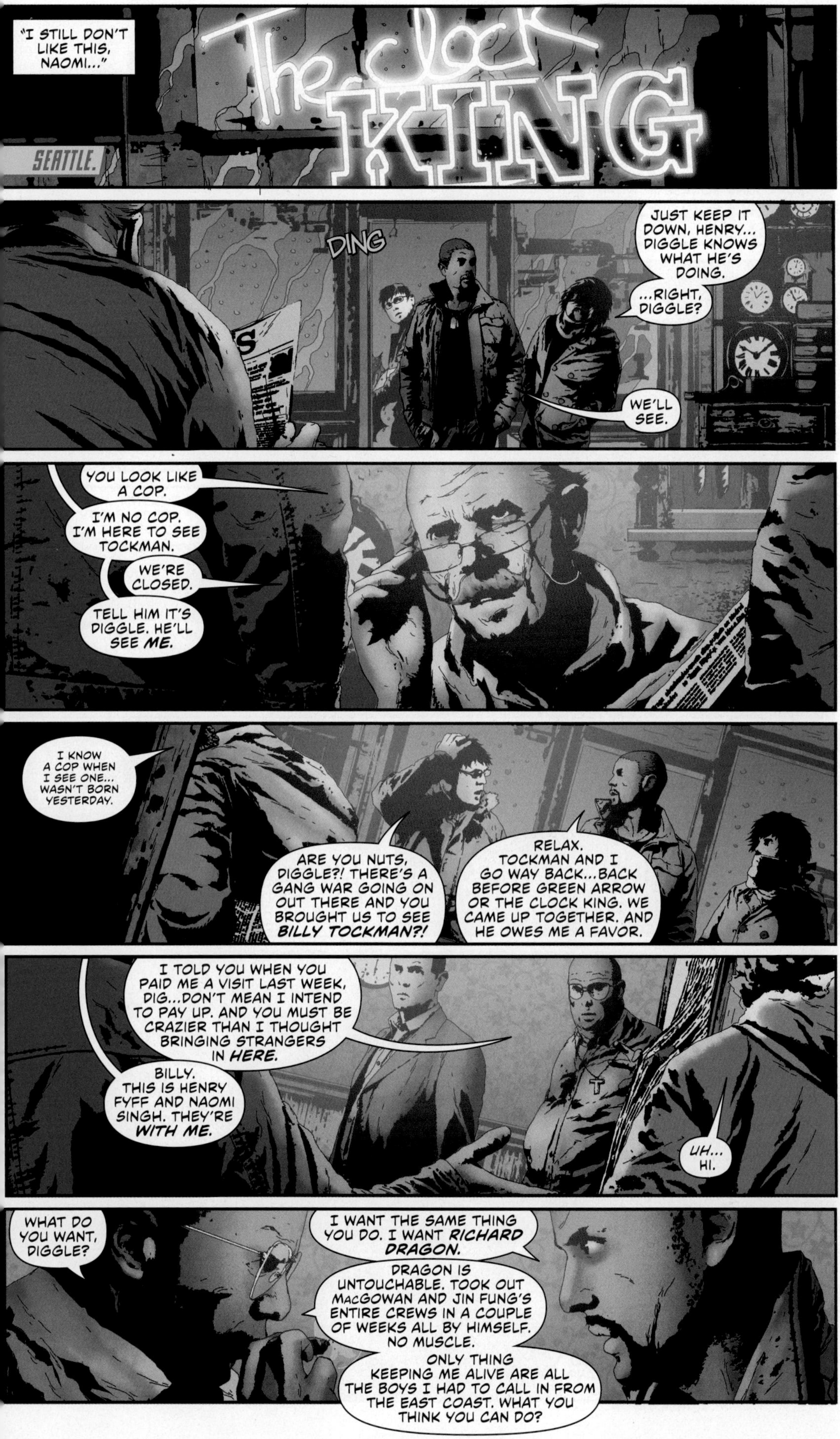

"I STILL DON'T LIKE THIS, NAOMI..."
The clock KING
SEATTLE.
DING
JUST KEEP IT DOWN, HENRY... DIGGLE KNOWS WHAT HE'S DOING.
...RIGHT, DIGGLE?
WE'LL SEE.
YOU LOOK LIKE A COP.
I'M NO COP. I'M HERE TO SEE TOCKMAN.
WE'RE CLOSED.
TELL HIM IT'S DIGGLE. HE'LL SEE *ME.*
I KNOW A COP WHEN I SEE ONE... WASN'T BORN YESTERDAY.
ARE YOU NUTS, DIGGLE?! THERE'S A GANG WAR GOING ON OUT THERE AND YOU BROUGHT US TO SEE *BILLY TOCKMAN?!*
RELAX. TOCKMAN AND I GO WAY BACK...BACK BEFORE GREEN ARROW OR THE CLOCK KING. WE CAME UP TOGETHER. AND HE OWES ME A FAVOR.
I TOLD YOU WHEN YOU PAID ME A VISIT LAST WEEK, DIG...DON'T MEAN I INTEND TO PAY UP. AND YOU MUST BE CRAZIER THAN I THOUGHT BRINGING STRANGERS IN *HERE.*
BILLY. THIS IS HENRY FYFF AND NAOMI SINGH. THEY'RE *WITH ME.*
UH... HI.
WHAT DO YOU WANT, DIGGLE?
I WANT THE SAME THING YOU DO. I WANT *RICHARD DRAGON.*
DRAGON IS UNTOUCHABLE. TOOK OUT MacGOWAN AND JIN FUNG'S ENTIRE CREWS IN A COUPLE OF WEEKS ALL BY HIMSELF. NO MUSCLE.
ONLY THING KEEPING ME ALIVE ARE ALL THE BOYS I HAD TO CALL IN FROM THE EAST COAST. WHAT YOU THINK YOU CAN DO?

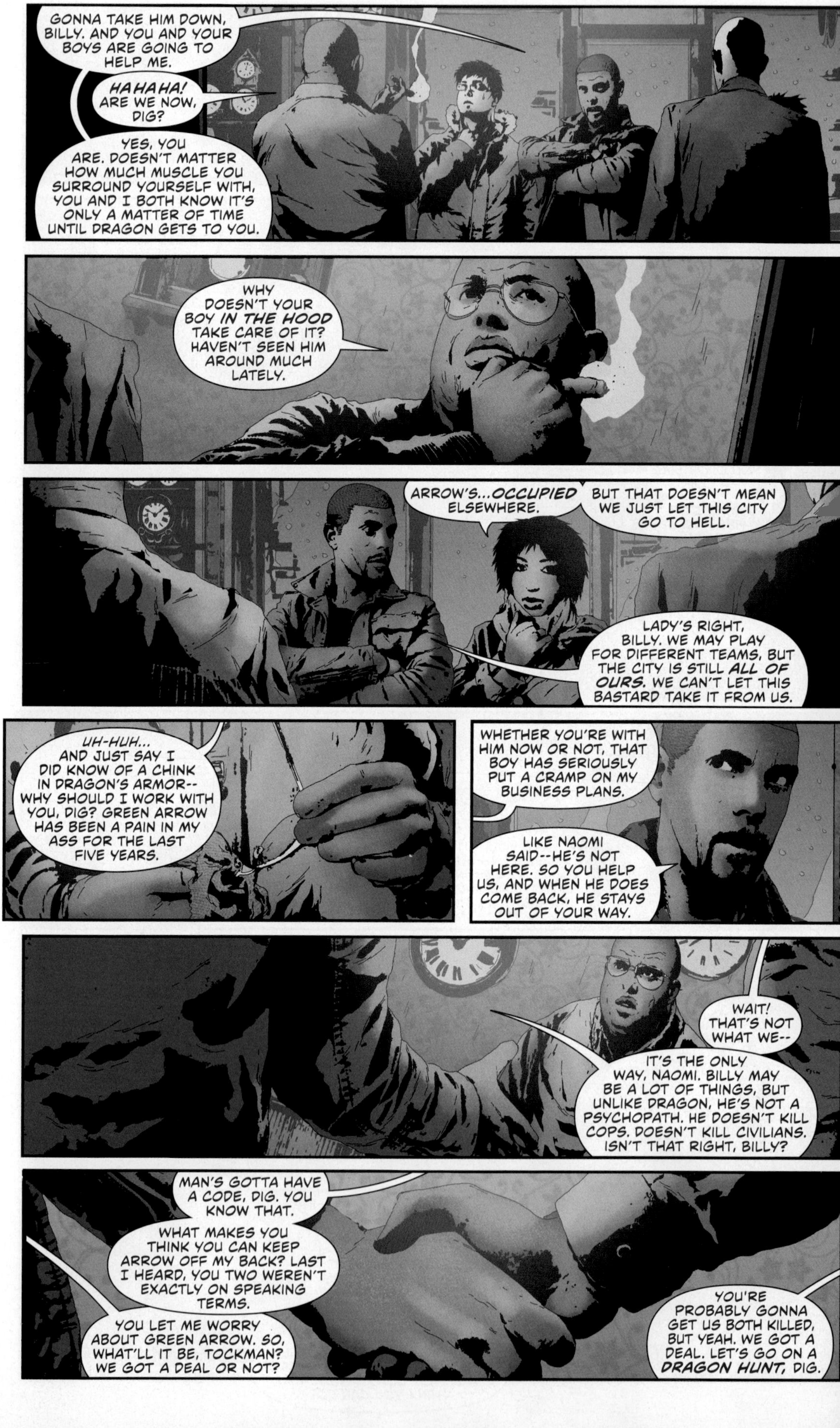
GONNA TAKE HIM DOWN, BILLY. AND YOU AND YOUR BOYS ARE GOING TO HELP ME.
HAHAHA! ARE WE NOW, DIG?
YES, YOU ARE. DOESN'T MATTER HOW MUCH MUSCLE YOU SURROUND YOURSELF WITH, YOU AND I BOTH KNOW IT'S ONLY A MATTER OF TIME UNTIL DRAGON GETS TO YOU.
WHY DOESN'T YOUR BOY IN THE HOOD TAKE CARE OF IT? HAVEN'T SEEN HIM AROUND MUCH LATELY.
ARROW'S...OCCUPIED ELSEWHERE.
BUT THAT DOESN'T MEAN WE JUST LET THIS CITY GO TO HELL.
LADY'S RIGHT, BILLY. WE MAY PLAY FOR DIFFERENT TEAMS, BUT THE CITY IS STILL ALL OF OURS. WE CAN'T LET THIS BASTARD TAKE IT FROM US.
UH-HUH... AND JUST SAY I DID KNOW OF A CHINK IN DRAGON'S ARMOR--WHY SHOULD I WORK WITH YOU, DIG? GREEN ARROW HAS BEEN A PAIN IN MY ASS FOR THE LAST FIVE YEARS.
WHETHER YOU'RE WITH HIM NOW OR NOT, THAT BOY HAS SERIOUSLY PUT A CRAMP ON MY BUSINESS PLANS.
LIKE NAOMI SAID--HE'S NOT HERE. SO YOU HELP US, AND WHEN HE DOES COME BACK, HE STAYS OUT OF YOUR WAY.
WAIT! THAT'S NOT WHAT WE--
IT'S THE ONLY WAY, NAOMI. BILLY MAY BE A LOT OF THINGS, BUT UNLIKE DRAGON, HE'S NOT A PSYCHOPATH. HE DOESN'T KILL COPS. DOESN'T KILL CIVILIANS. ISN'T THAT RIGHT, BILLY?
MAN'S GOTTA HAVE A CODE, DIG. YOU KNOW THAT.
WHAT MAKES YOU THINK YOU CAN KEEP ARROW OFF MY BACK? LAST I HEARD, YOU TWO WEREN'T EXACTLY ON SPEAKING TERMS.
YOU LET ME WORRY ABOUT GREEN ARROW. SO, WHAT'LL IT BE, TOCKMAN? WE GOT A DEAL OR NOT?
YOU'RE PROBABLY GONNA GET US BOTH KILLED, BUT YEAH. WE GOT A DEAL. LET'S GO ON A DRAGON HUNT, DIG.

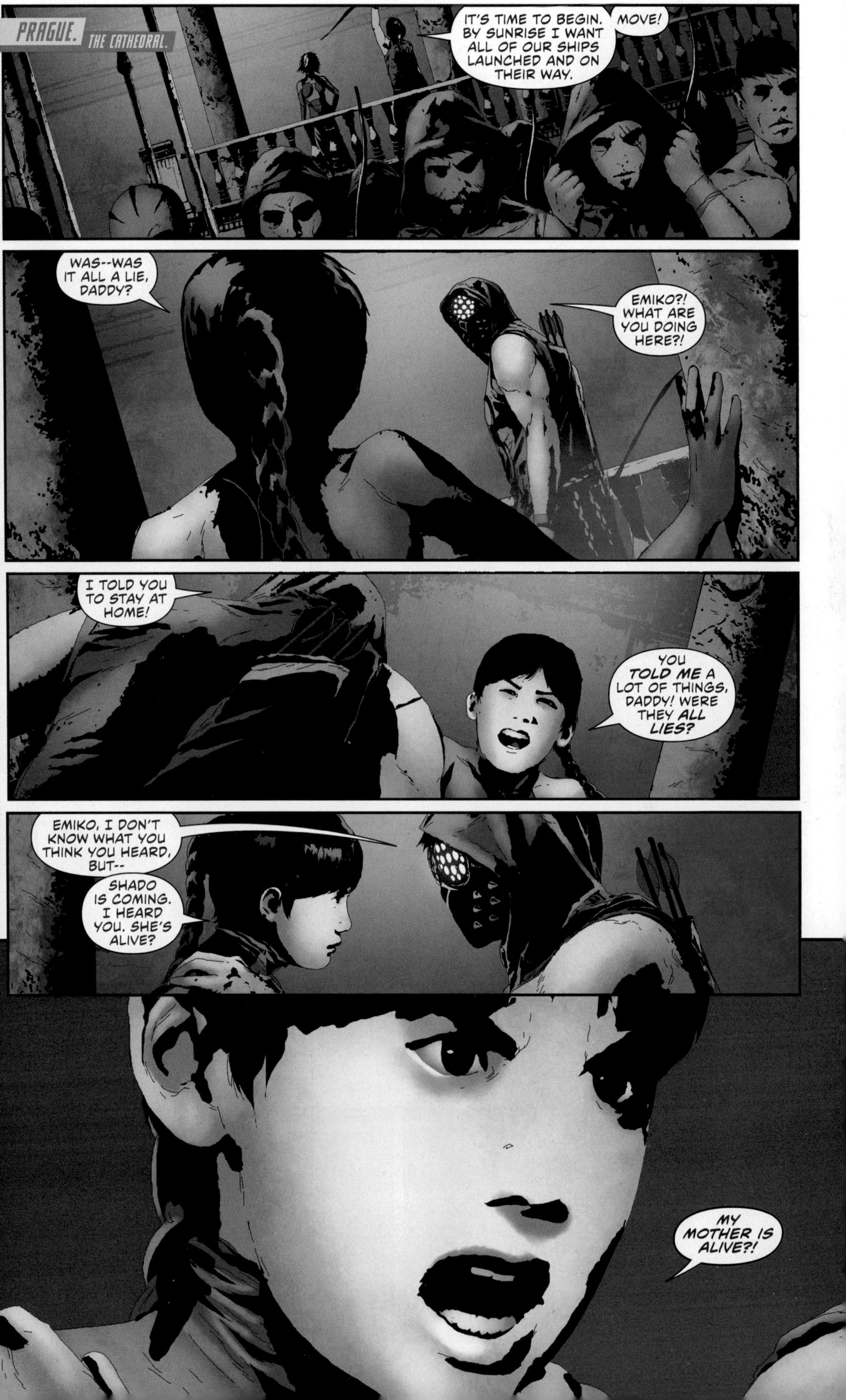
PRAGUE. THE CATHEDRAL.
IT'S TIME TO BEGIN. BY SUNRISE I WANT ALL OF OUR SHIPS LAUNCHED AND ON THEIR WAY.
MOVE!
WAS--WAS IT ALL A LIE, DADDY?
EMIKO?! WHAT ARE YOU DOING HERE?!
I TOLD YOU TO STAY AT HOME!
YOU TOLD ME A LOT OF THINGS, DADDY! WERE THEY ALL LIES?
EMIKO, I DON'T KNOW WHAT YOU THINK YOU HEARD, BUT--
SHADO IS COMING. I HEARD YOU. SHE'S ALIVE?
MY MOTHER IS ALIVE?!

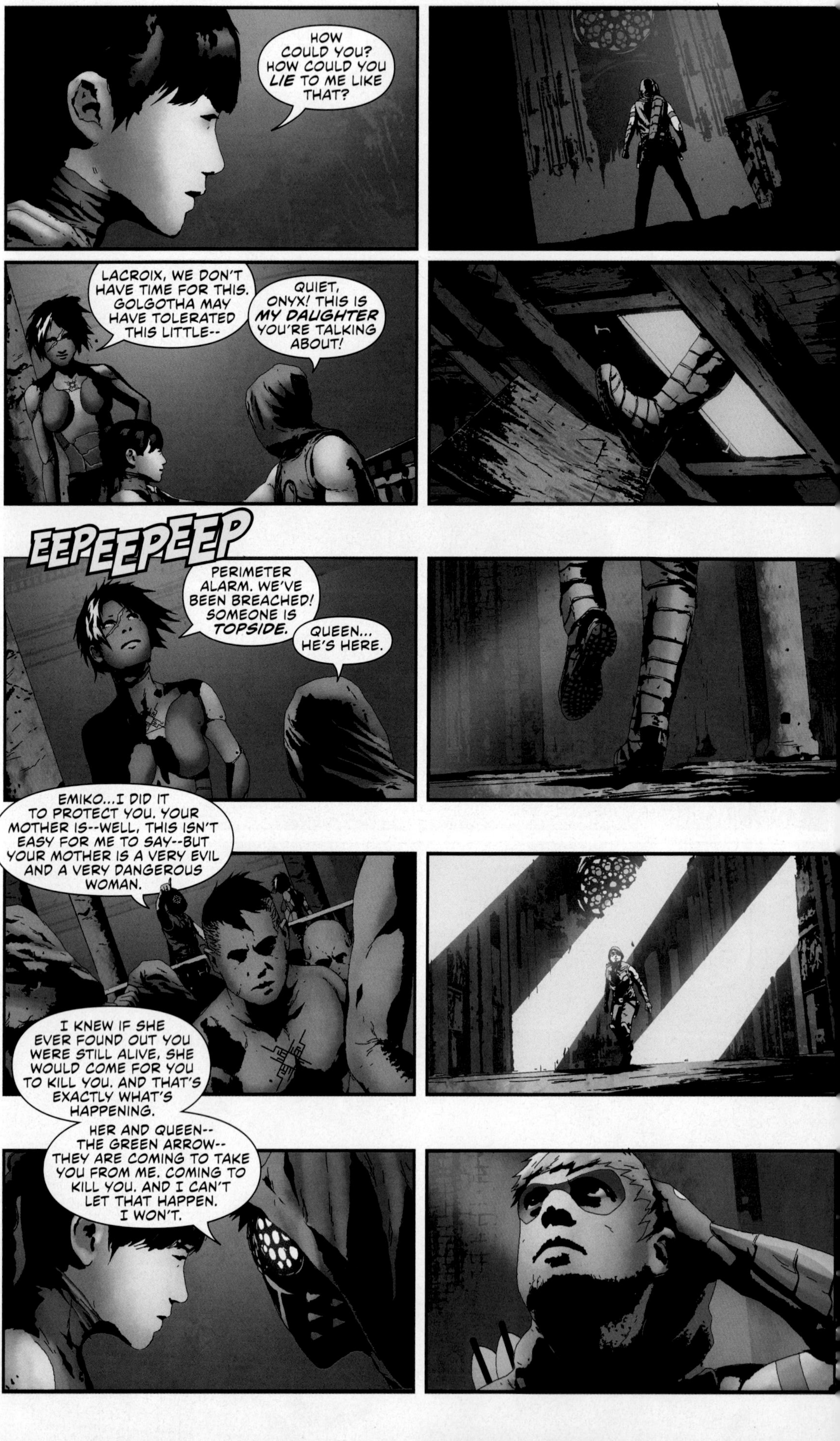
HOW COULD YOU? HOW COULD YOU LIE TO ME LIKE THAT?
LACROIX, WE DON'T HAVE TIME FOR THIS. GOLGOTHA MAY HAVE TOLERATED THIS LITTLE--
QUIET, ONYX! THIS IS MY DAUGHTER YOU'RE TALKING ABOUT!
EEPEEPEEP
PERIMETER ALARM. WE'VE BEEN BREACHED! SOMEONE IS TOPSIDE.
QUEEN... HE'S HERE.
EMIKO...I DID IT TO PROTECT YOU. YOUR MOTHER IS--WELL, THIS ISN'T EASY FOR ME TO SAY--BUT YOUR MOTHER IS A VERY EVIL AND A VERY DANGEROUS WOMAN.
I KNEW IF SHE EVER FOUND OUT YOU WERE STILL ALIVE, SHE WOULD COME FOR YOU TO KILL YOU. AND THAT'S EXACTLY WHAT'S HAPPENING.
HER AND QUEEN-- THE GREEN ARROW-- THEY ARE COMING TO TAKE YOU FROM ME. COMING TO KILL YOU. AND I CAN'T LET THAT HAPPEN. I WON'T.

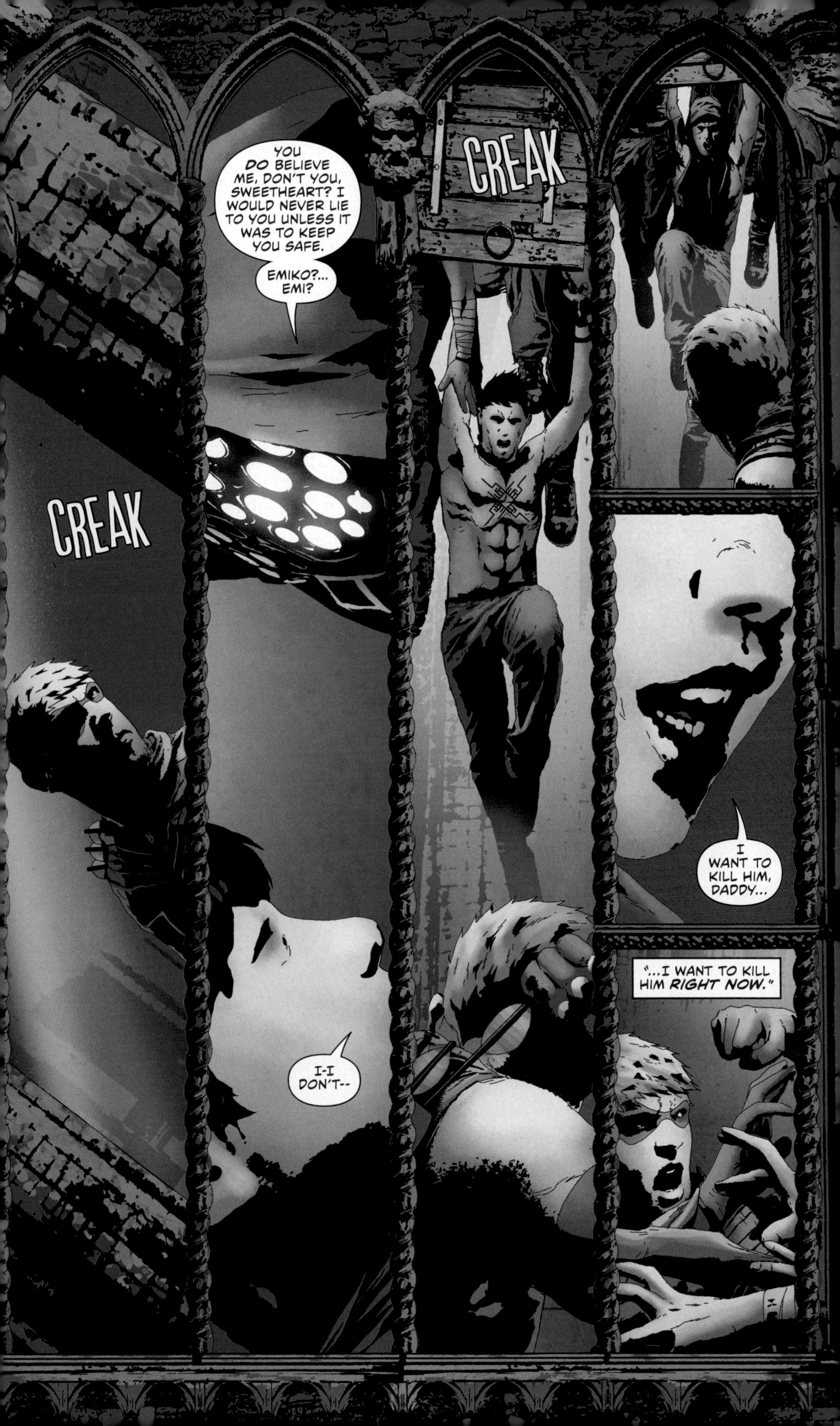
CREAK
YOU DO BELIEVE ME, DON'T YOU, SWEETHEART? I WOULD NEVER LIE TO YOU UNLESS IT WAS TO KEEP YOU SAFE.
EMIKO?... EMI?
CREAK
I-I DON'T--
I WANT TO KILL HIM, DADDY...
"...I WANT TO KILL HIM RIGHT NOW."

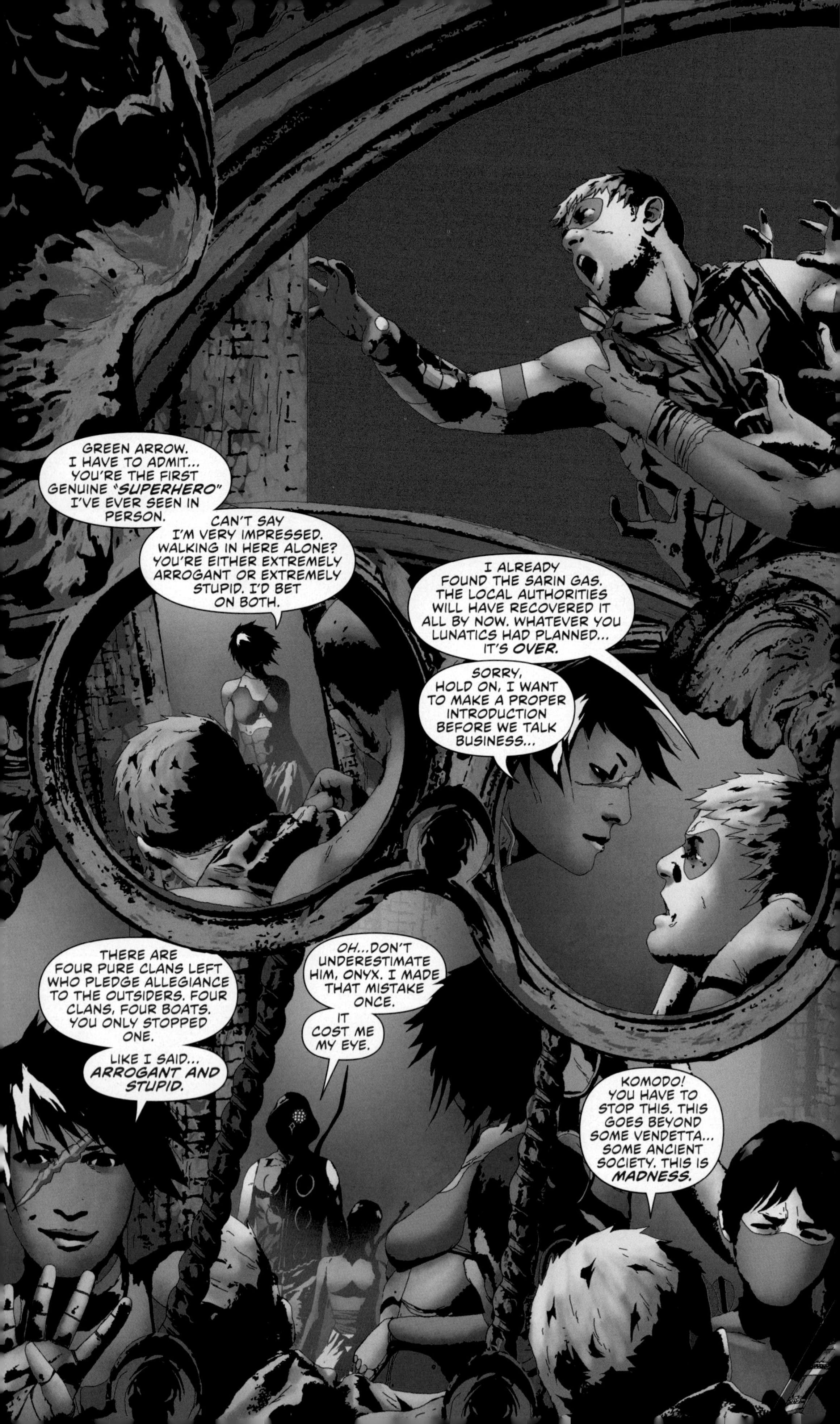
GREEN ARROW. I HAVE TO ADMIT... YOU'RE THE FIRST GENUINE "SUPERHERO" I'VE EVER SEEN IN PERSON.
CAN'T SAY I'M VERY IMPRESSED. WALKING IN HERE ALONE? YOU'RE EITHER EXTREMELY ARROGANT OR EXTREMELY STUPID. I'D BET ON BOTH.
I ALREADY FOUND THE SARIN GAS. THE LOCAL AUTHORITIES WILL HAVE RECOVERED IT ALL BY NOW. WHATEVER YOU LUNATICS HAD PLANNED... IT'S OVER.
SORRY, HOLD ON, I WANT TO MAKE A PROPER INTRODUCTION BEFORE WE TALK BUSINESS...
THERE ARE FOUR PURE CLANS LEFT WHO PLEDGE ALLEGIANCE TO THE OUTSIDERS. FOUR CLANS, FOUR BOATS. YOU ONLY STOPPED ONE.
LIKE I SAID... ARROGANT AND STUPID.
OH...DON'T UNDERESTIMATE HIM, ONYX. I MADE THAT MISTAKE ONCE.
IT COST ME MY EYE.
KOMODO! YOU HAVE TO STOP THIS. THIS GOES BEYOND SOME VENDETTA... SOME ANCIENT SOCIETY. THIS IS MADNESS.

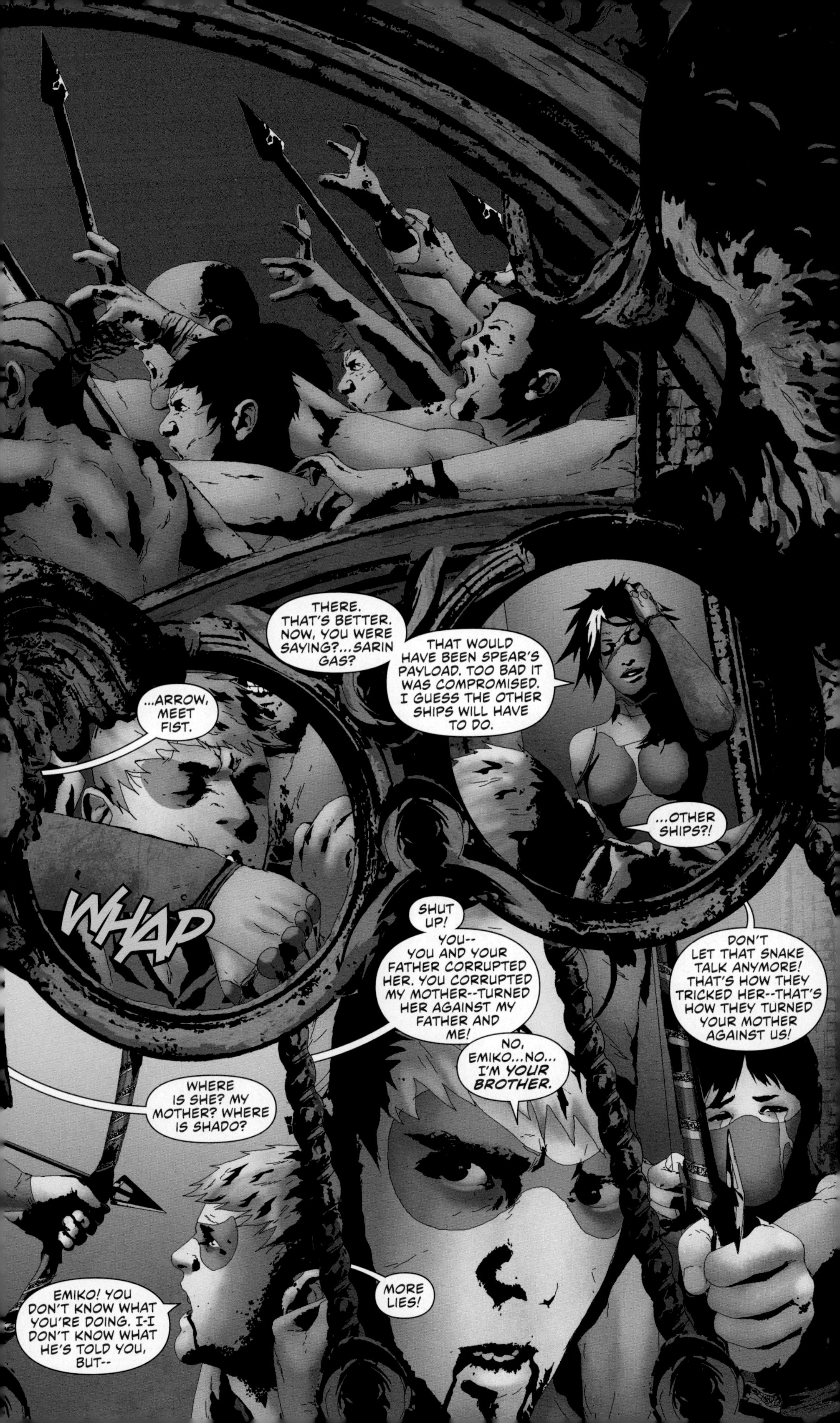
THERE. THAT'S BETTER. NOW, YOU WERE SAYING?...SARIN GAS?
...ARROW, MEET FIST.
THAT WOULD HAVE BEEN SPEAR'S PAYLOAD. TOO BAD IT WAS COMPROMISED. I GUESS THE OTHER SHIPS WILL HAVE TO DO.
WHAP
...OTHER SHIPS?!
SHUT UP!
YOU-- YOU AND YOUR FATHER CORRUPTED HER. YOU CORRUPTED MY MOTHER--TURNED HER AGAINST MY FATHER AND ME!
DON'T LET THAT SNAKE TALK ANYMORE! THAT'S HOW THEY TRICKED HER--THAT'S HOW THEY TURNED YOUR MOTHER AGAINST US!
NO, EMIKO...NO... I'M *YOUR BROTHER.*
WHERE IS SHE? MY MOTHER? WHERE IS SHADO?
EMIKO! YOU DON'T KNOW WHAT YOU'RE DOING. I-I DON'T KNOW WHAT HE'S TOLD YOU, BUT--
MORE LIES!

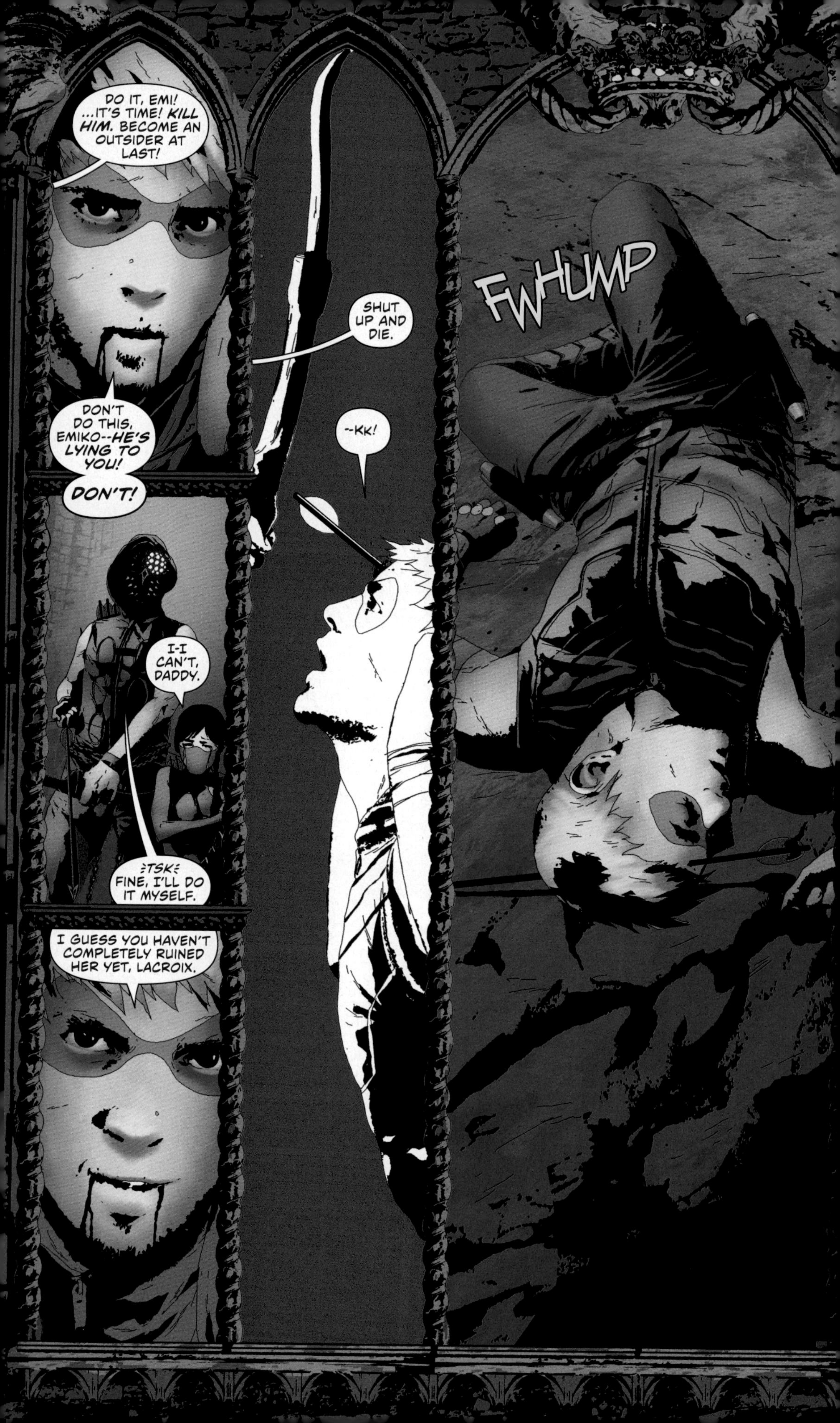
DO IT, EMI! ...IT'S TIME! KILL HIM. BECOME AN OUTSIDER AT LAST!
SHUT UP AND DIE.
DON'T DO THIS, EMIKO--HE'S LYING TO YOU!
DON'T!
--KK!
FWHUMP
I-I CAN'T, DADDY.
TSK
FINE, I'LL DO IT MYSELF.
I GUESS YOU HAVEN'T COMPLETELY RUINED HER YET, LACROIX.

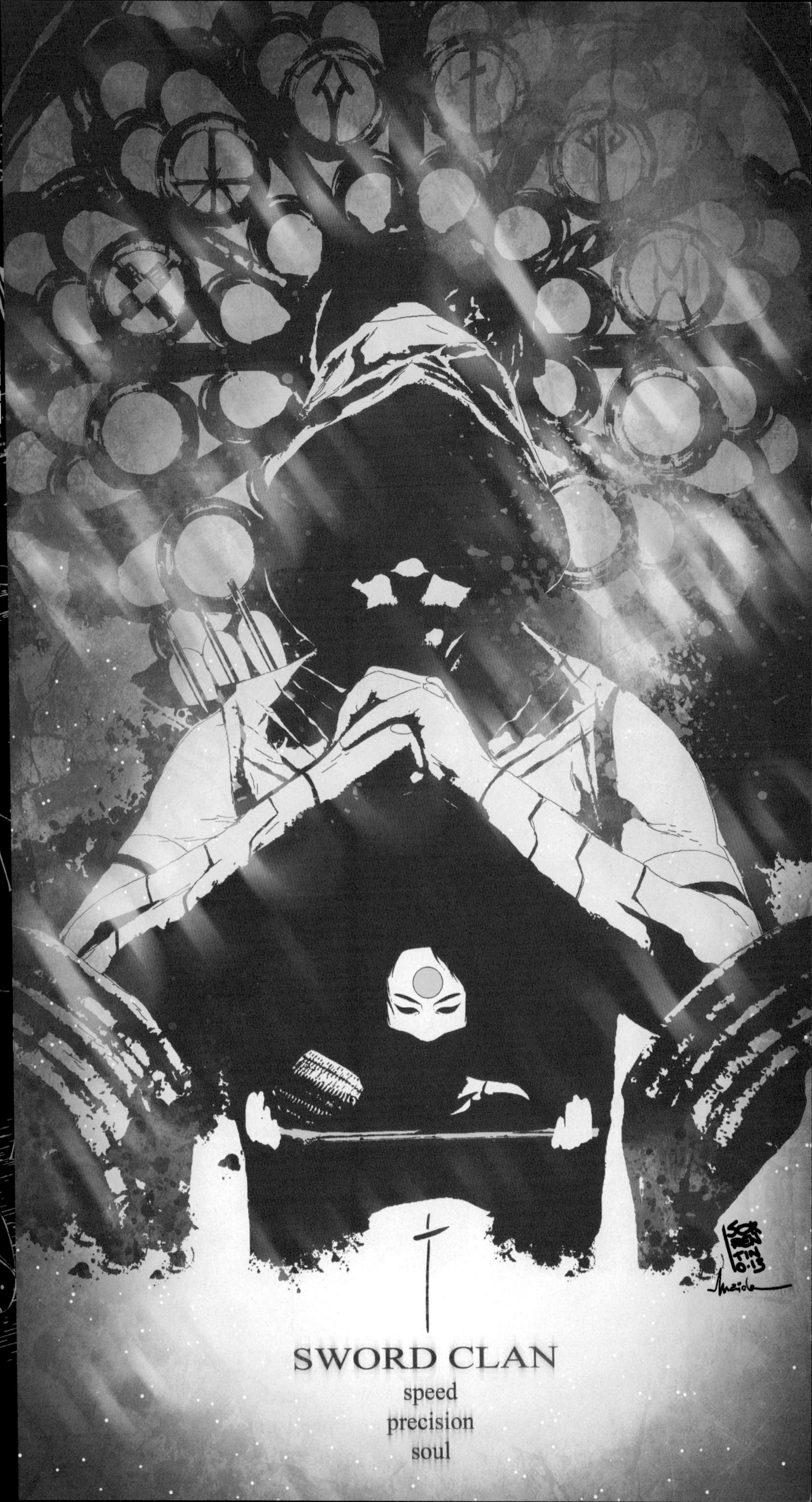
SWORD CLAN
speed
precision
soul

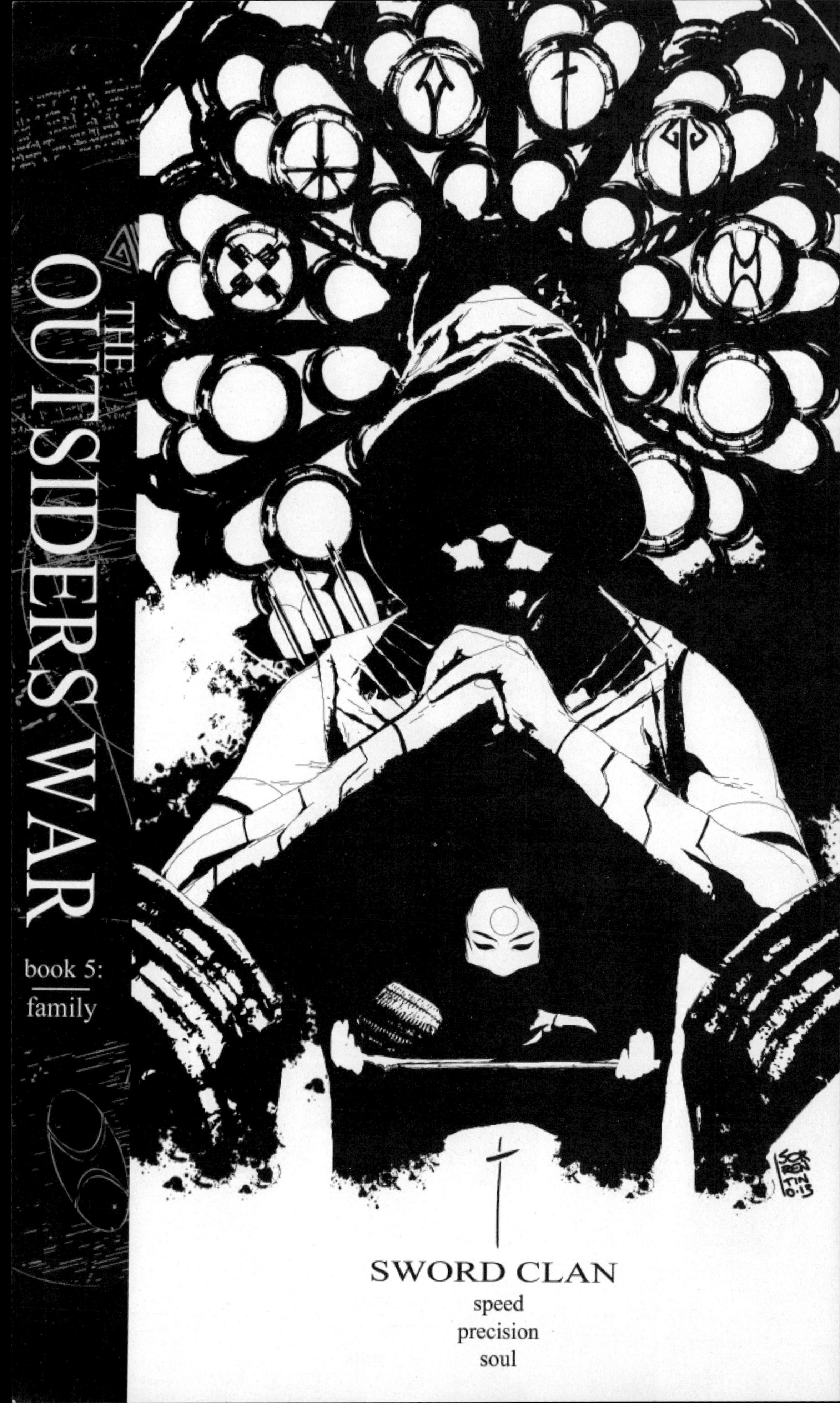
THE OUTSIDERS WAR
book 5:
family
SWORD CLAN
speed
precision
soul

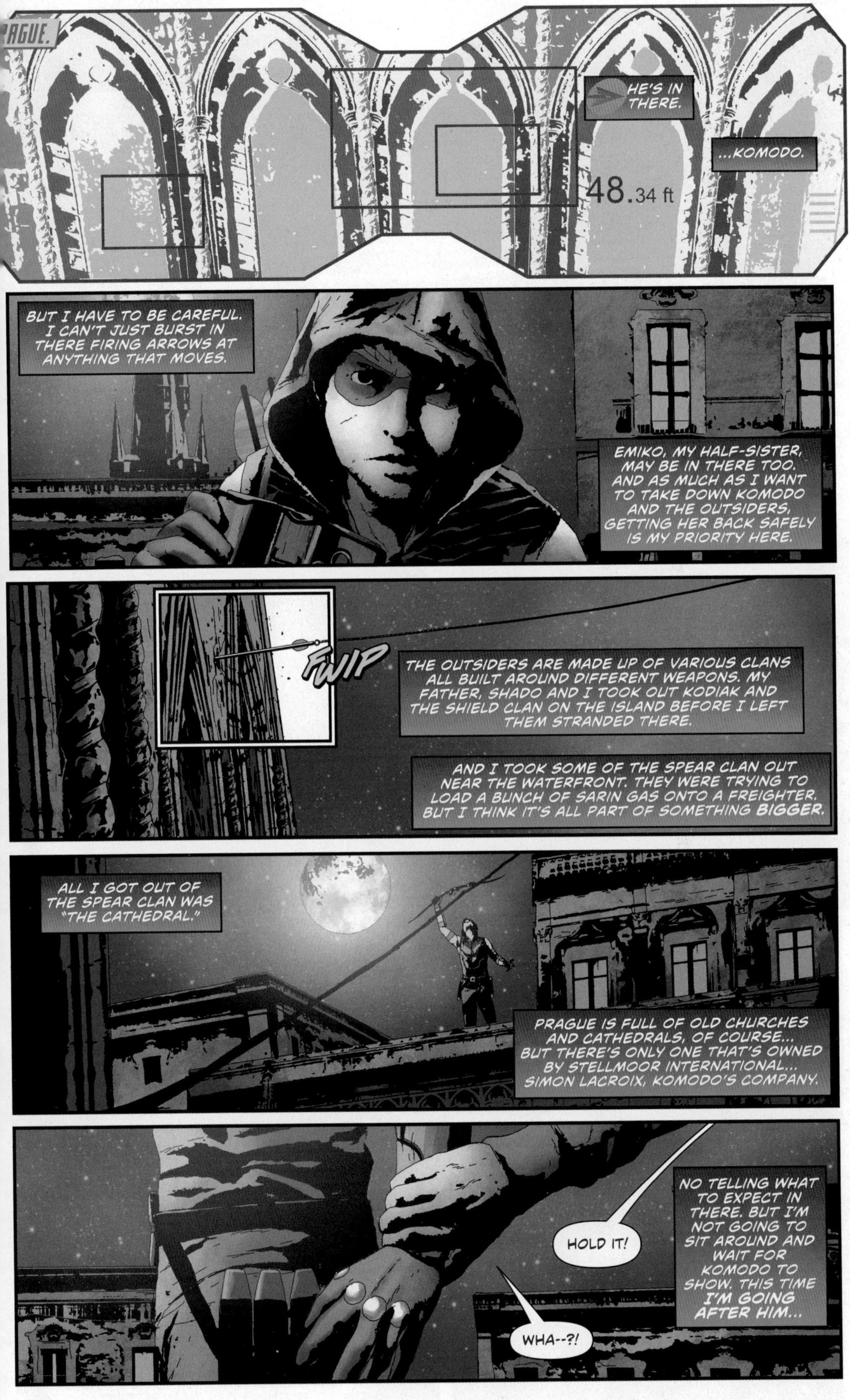
PRAGUE.
HE'S IN THERE.
...KOMODO.
48.34 ft
BUT I HAVE TO BE CAREFUL. I CAN'T JUST BURST IN THERE FIRING ARROWS AT ANYTHING THAT MOVES.
EMIKO, MY HALF-SISTER, MAY BE IN THERE TOO. AND AS MUCH AS I WANT TO TAKE DOWN KOMODO AND THE OUTSIDERS, GETTING HER BACK SAFELY IS MY PRIORITY HERE.
FWIP
THE OUTSIDERS ARE MADE UP OF VARIOUS CLANS ALL BUILT AROUND DIFFERENT WEAPONS. MY FATHER, SHADO AND I TOOK OUT KODIAK AND THE SHIELD CLAN ON THE ISLAND BEFORE I LEFT THEM STRANDED THERE.
AND I TOOK SOME OF THE SPEAR CLAN OUT NEAR THE WATERFRONT. THEY WERE TRYING TO LOAD A BUNCH OF SARIN GAS ONTO A FREIGHTER. BUT I THINK IT'S ALL PART OF SOMETHING **BIGGER**.
ALL I GOT OUT OF THE SPEAR CLAN WAS "THE CATHEDRAL."
PRAGUE IS FULL OF OLD CHURCHES AND CATHEDRALS, OF COURSE... BUT THERE'S ONLY ONE THAT'S OWNED BY STELLMOOR INTERNATIONAL... SIMON LACROIX, KOMODO'S COMPANY.
NO TELLING WHAT TO EXPECT IN THERE. BUT I'M NOT GOING TO SIT AROUND AND WAIT FOR KOMODO TO SHOW. THIS TIME **I'M GOING AFTER HIM...**
HOLD IT!
WHA--?!

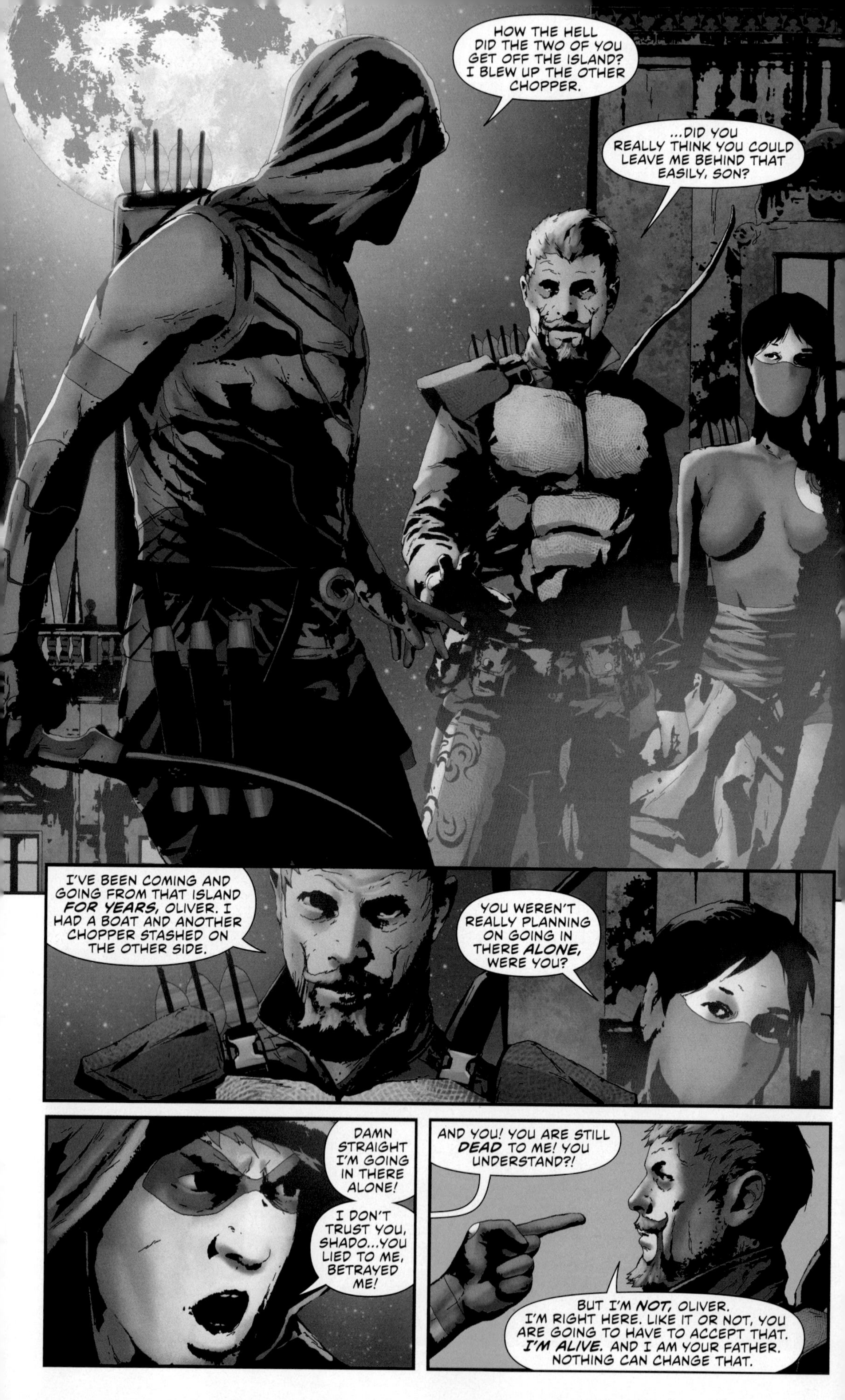
HOW THE HELL DID THE TWO OF YOU GET OFF THE ISLAND? I BLEW UP THE OTHER CHOPPER.
...DID YOU REALLY THINK YOU COULD LEAVE ME BEHIND THAT EASILY, SON?
I'VE BEEN COMING AND GOING FROM THAT ISLAND FOR YEARS, OLIVER. I HAD A BOAT AND ANOTHER CHOPPER STASHED ON THE OTHER SIDE.
YOU WEREN'T REALLY PLANNING ON GOING IN THERE ALONE, WERE YOU?
DAMN STRAIGHT I'M GOING IN THERE ALONE!
I DON'T TRUST YOU, SHADO...YOU LIED TO ME, BETRAYED ME!
AND YOU! YOU ARE STILL DEAD TO ME! YOU UNDERSTAND?!
BUT I'M NOT, OLIVER. I'M RIGHT HERE. LIKE IT OR NOT, YOU ARE GOING TO HAVE TO ACCEPT THAT. I'M ALIVE. AND I AM YOUR FATHER. NOTHING CAN CHANGE THAT.

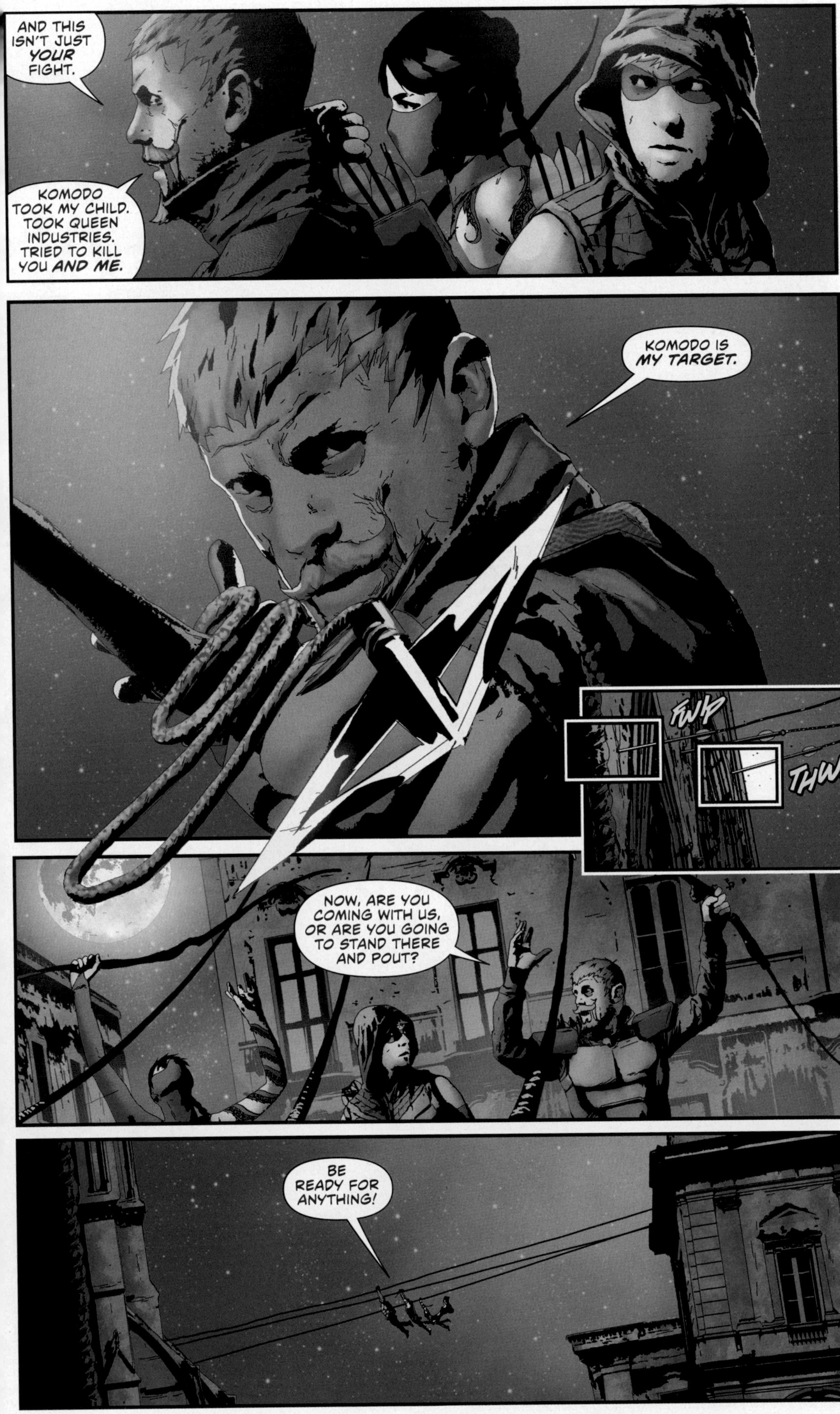
AND THIS ISN'T JUST YOUR FIGHT.
KOMODO TOOK MY CHILD. TOOK QUEEN INDUSTRIES. TRIED TO KILL YOU AND ME.
KOMODO IS MY TARGET.
FWIP
THWIP
NOW, ARE YOU COMING WITH US, OR ARE YOU GOING TO STAND THERE AND POUT?
BE READY FOR ANYTHING!

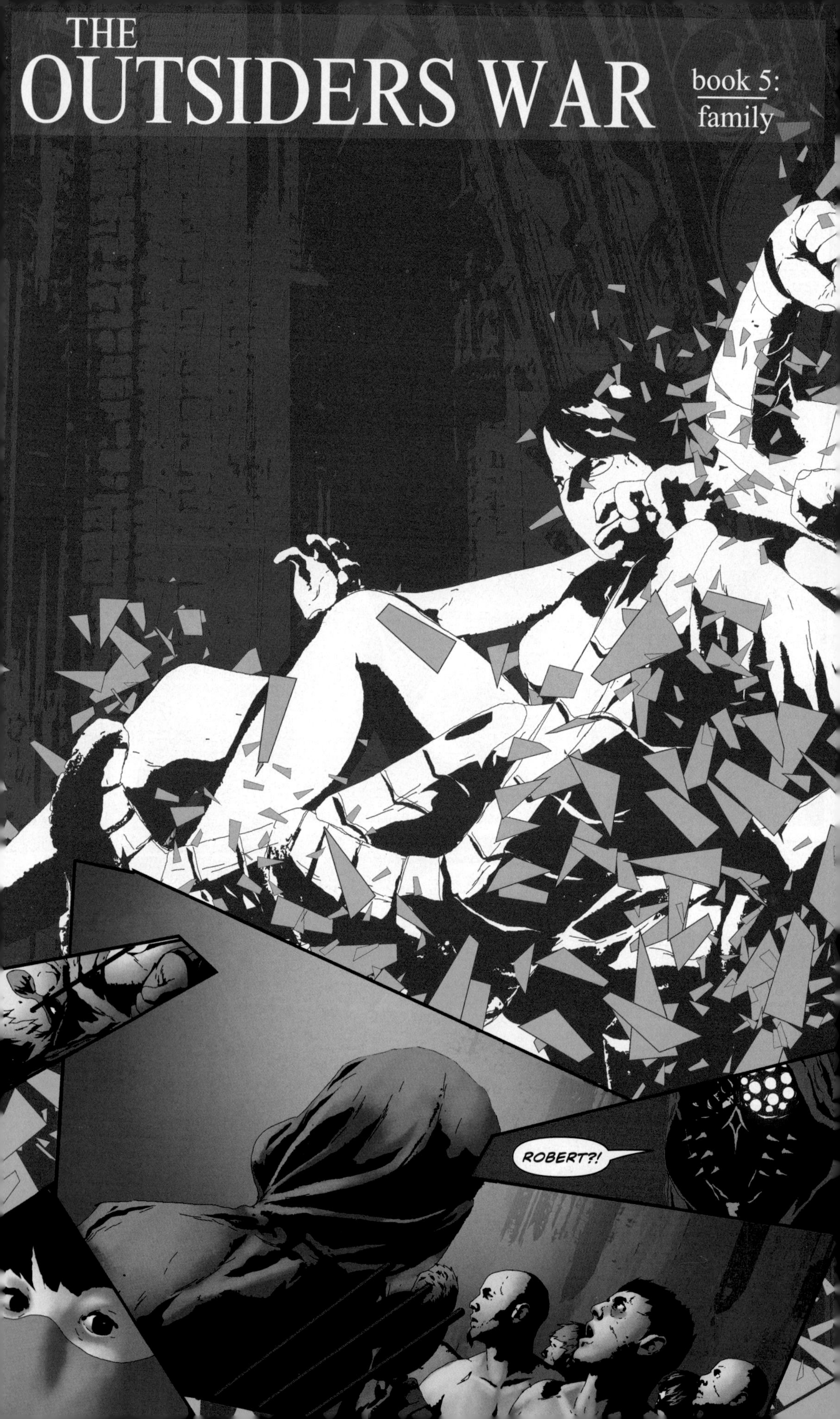
THE
OUTSIDERS WAR
book 5:
family
ROBERT?!

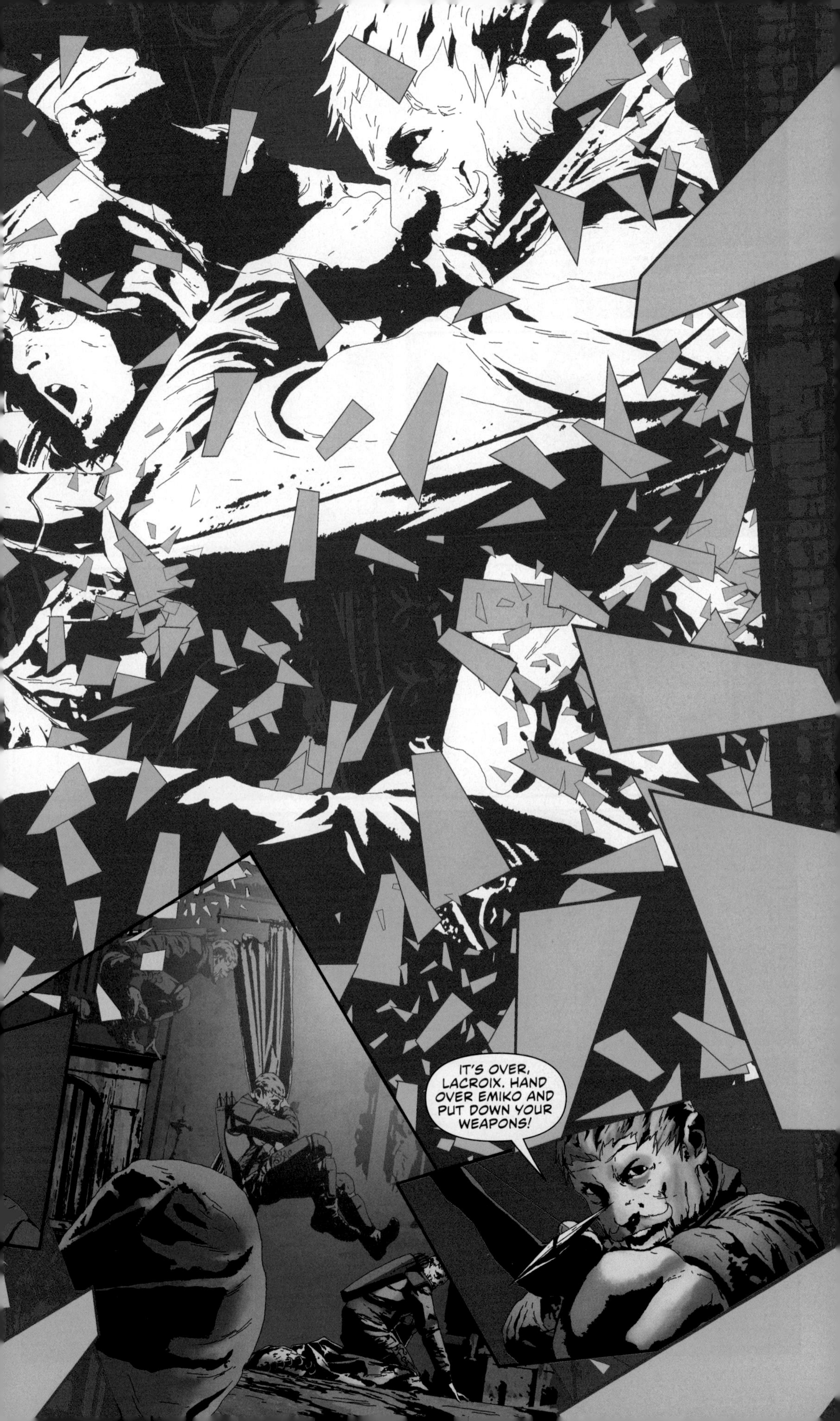
IT'S OVER, LACROIX. HAND OVER EMIKO AND PUT DOWN YOUR WEAPONS!

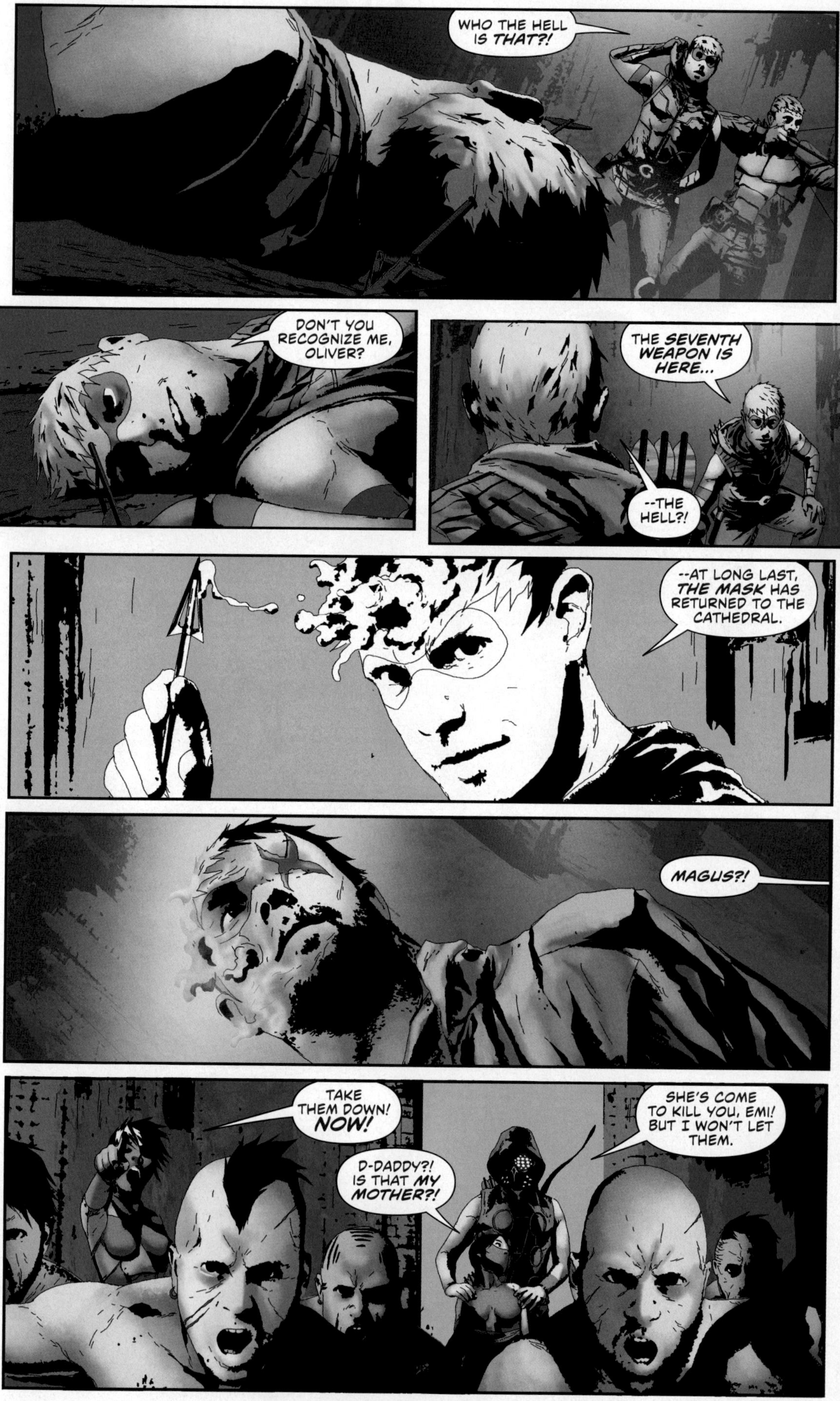
WHO THE HELL IS THAT?!
DON'T YOU RECOGNIZE ME, OLIVER?
THE SEVENTH WEAPON IS HERE...
--THE HELL?!
--AT LONG LAST, THE MASK HAS RETURNED TO THE CATHEDRAL.
MAGUS?!
TAKE THEM DOWN! NOW!
D-DADDY?! IS THAT MY MOTHER?!
SHE'S COME TO KILL YOU, EMI! BUT I WON'T LET THEM.

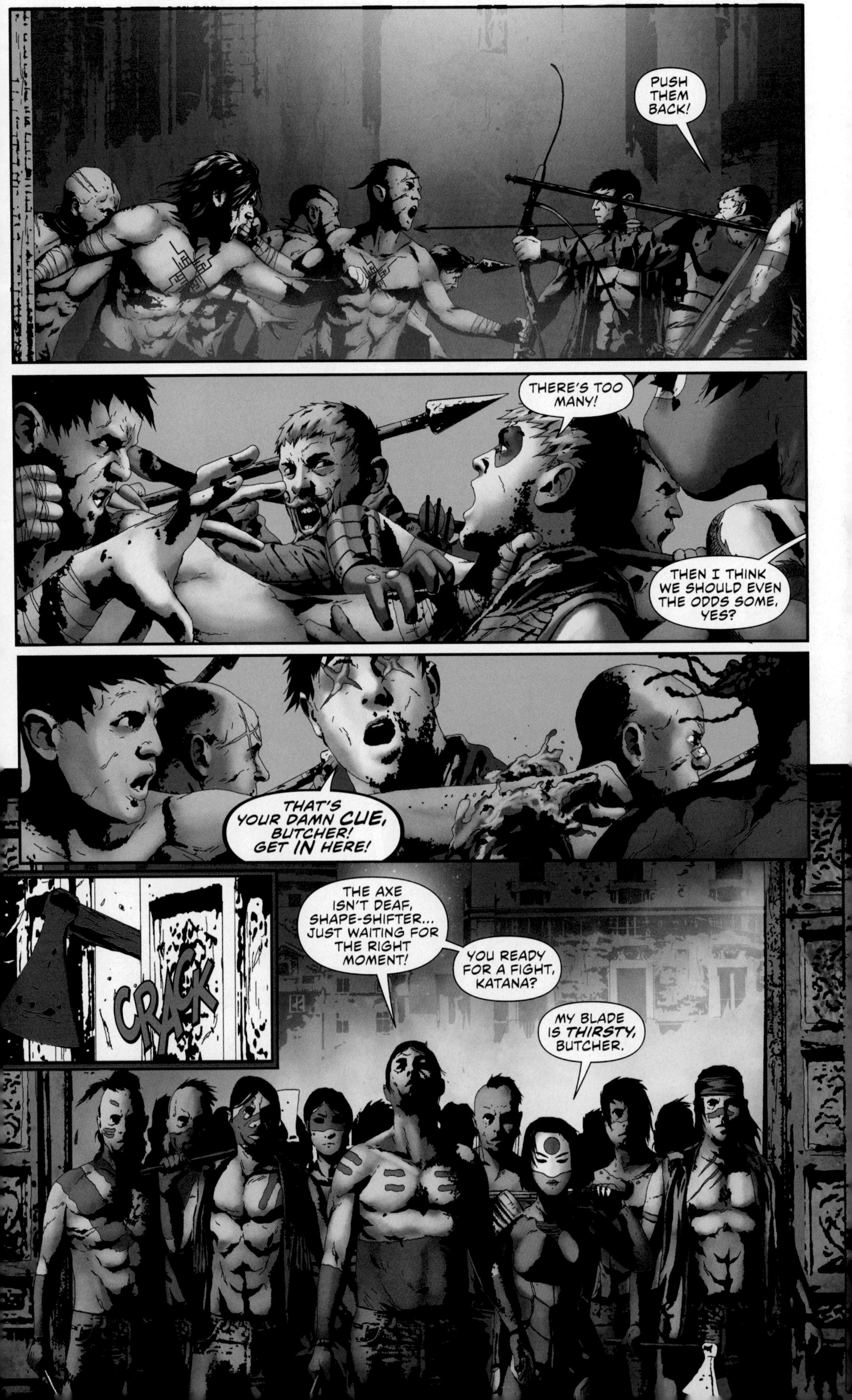
PUSH THEM BACK!
THERE'S TOO MANY!
THEN I THINK WE SHOULD EVEN THE ODDS SOME, YES?
THAT'S YOUR DAMN CUE, BUTCHER! GET IN HERE!
CRACK
THE AXE ISN'T DEAF, SHAPE-SHIFTER... JUST WAITING FOR THE RIGHT MOMENT!
YOU READY FOR A FIGHT, KATANA?
MY BLADE IS THIRSTY, BUTCHER.

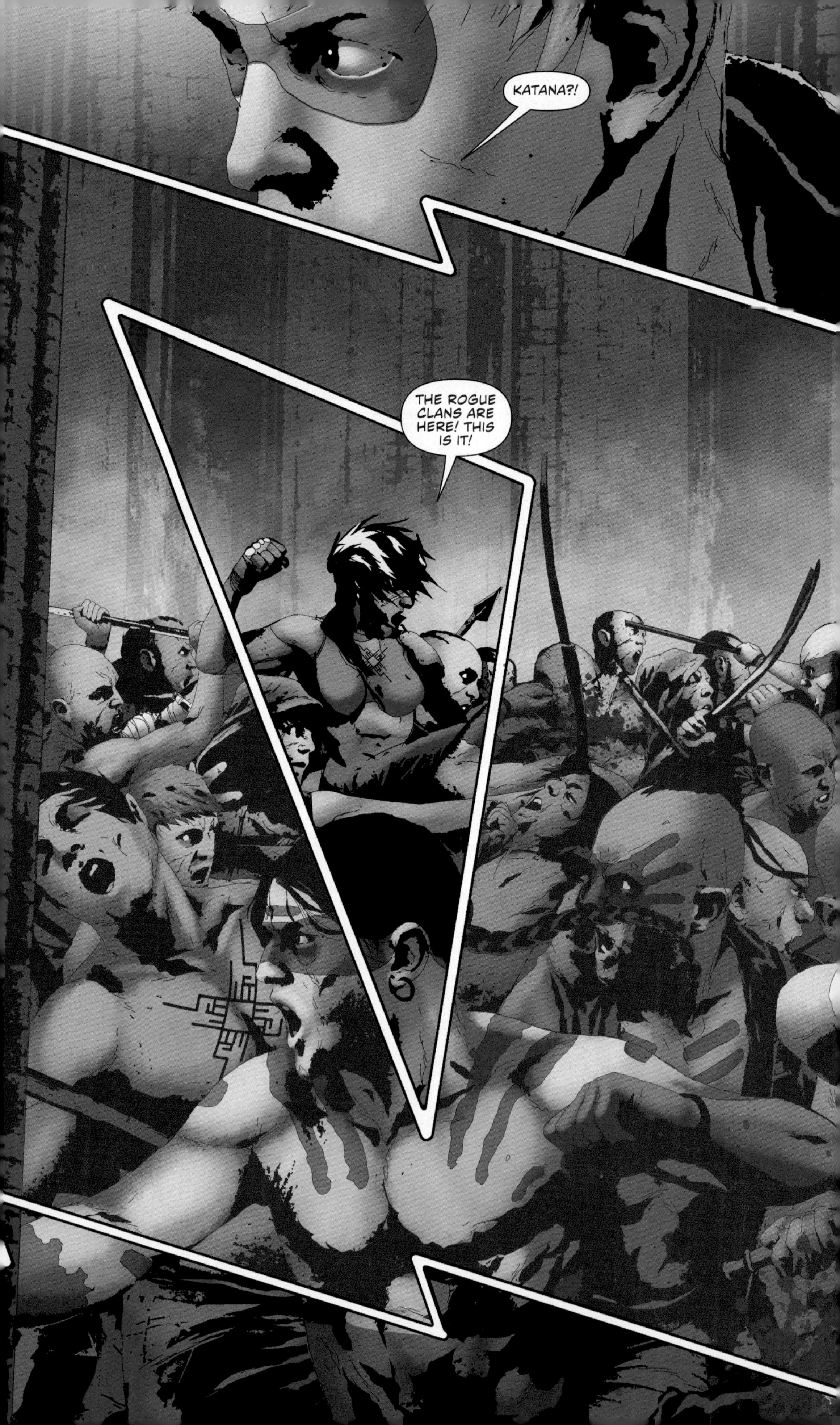
KATANA?!
THE ROGUE CLANS ARE HERE! THIS IS IT!

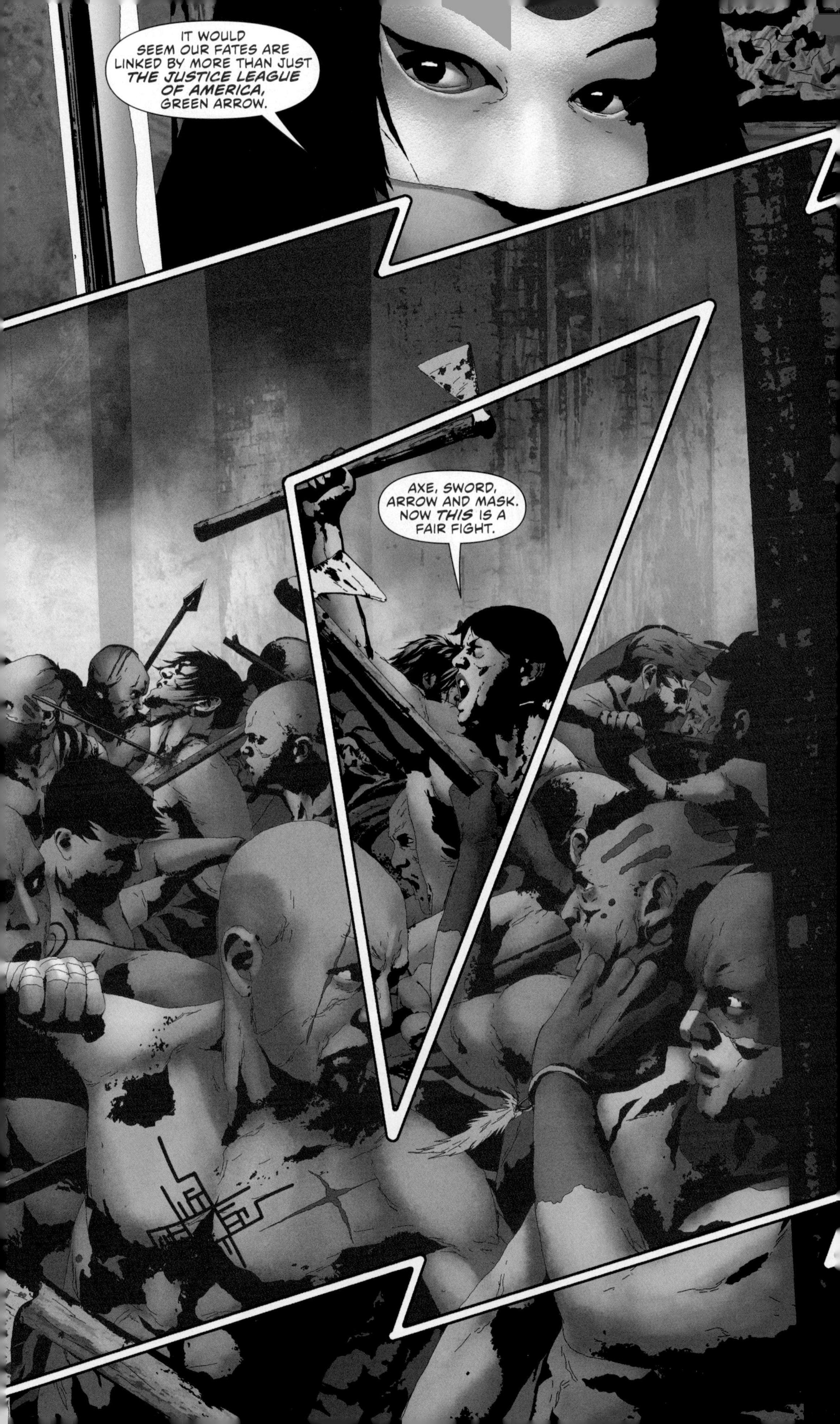
IT WOULD SEEM OUR FATES ARE LINKED BY MORE THAN JUST *THE JUSTICE LEAGUE OF AMERICA,* GREEN ARROW.
AXE, SWORD, ARROW AND MASK. NOW *THIS* IS A FAIR FIGHT.

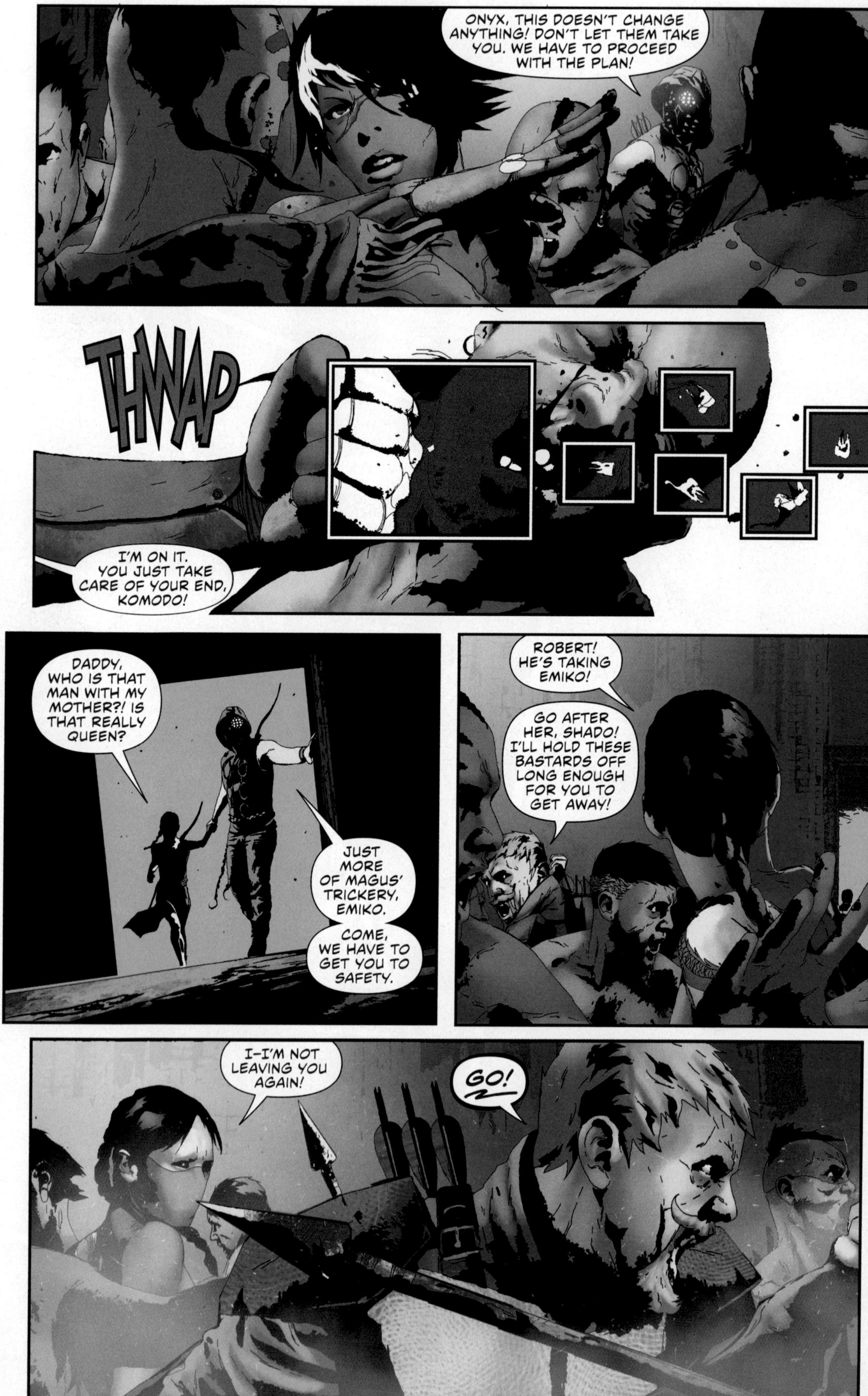
ONYX, THIS DOESN'T CHANGE ANYTHING! DON'T LET THEM TAKE YOU. WE HAVE TO PROCEED WITH THE PLAN!
THWAP
I'M ON IT. YOU JUST TAKE CARE OF YOUR END, KOMODO!
DADDY, WHO IS THAT MAN WITH MY MOTHER?! IS THAT REALLY QUEEN?
JUST MORE OF MAGUS' TRICKERY, EMIKO.
COME, WE HAVE TO GET YOU TO SAFETY.
ROBERT! HE'S TAKING EMIKO!
GO AFTER HER, SHADO! I'LL HOLD THESE BASTARDS OFF LONG ENOUGH FOR YOU TO GET AWAY!
I-I'M NOT LEAVING YOU AGAIN!
GO!

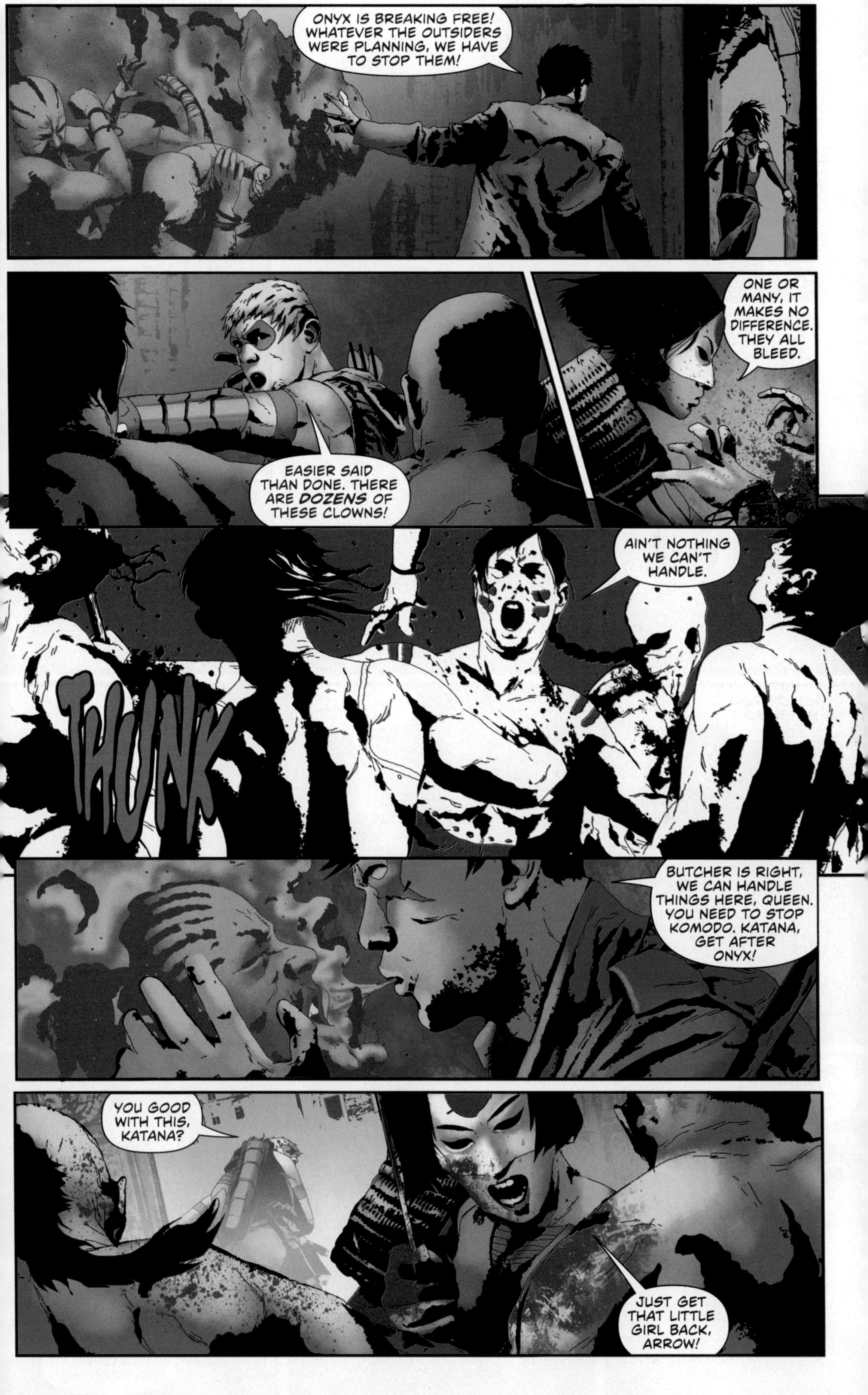
ONYX IS BREAKING FREE! WHATEVER THE OUTSIDERS WERE PLANNING, WE HAVE TO STOP THEM!
EASIER SAID THAN DONE. THERE ARE *DOZENS* OF THESE CLOWNS!
ONE OR MANY, IT MAKES NO DIFFERENCE. THEY ALL BLEED.
THUNK
AIN'T NOTHING WE CAN'T HANDLE.
BUTCHER IS RIGHT, WE CAN HANDLE THINGS HERE, QUEEN. YOU NEED TO STOP KOMODO. KATANA, GET AFTER ONYX!
YOU GOOD WITH THIS, KATANA?
JUST GET THAT LITTLE GIRL BACK, ARROW!

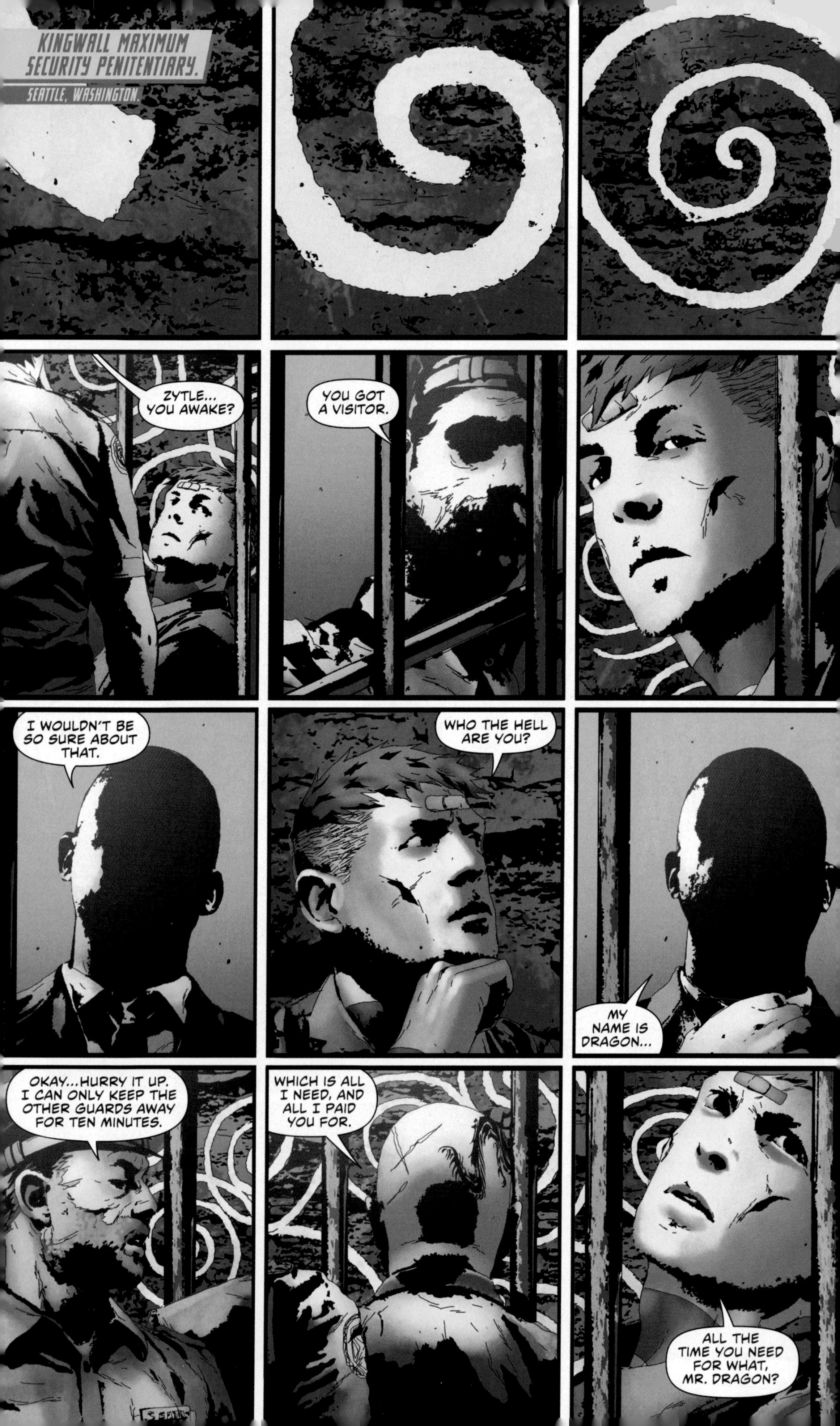
KINGWALL MAXIMUM SECURITY PENITENTIARY.
SEATTLE, WASHINGTON.
ZYTLE... YOU AWAKE?
YOU GOT A VISITOR.
I WOULDN'T BE SO SURE ABOUT THAT.
WHO THE HELL ARE YOU?
MY NAME IS DRAGON...
OKAY...HURRY IT UP. I CAN ONLY KEEP THE OTHER GUARDS AWAY FOR TEN MINUTES.
WHICH IS ALL I NEED, AND ALL I PAID YOU FOR.
ALL THE TIME YOU NEED FOR WHAT, MR. DRAGON?

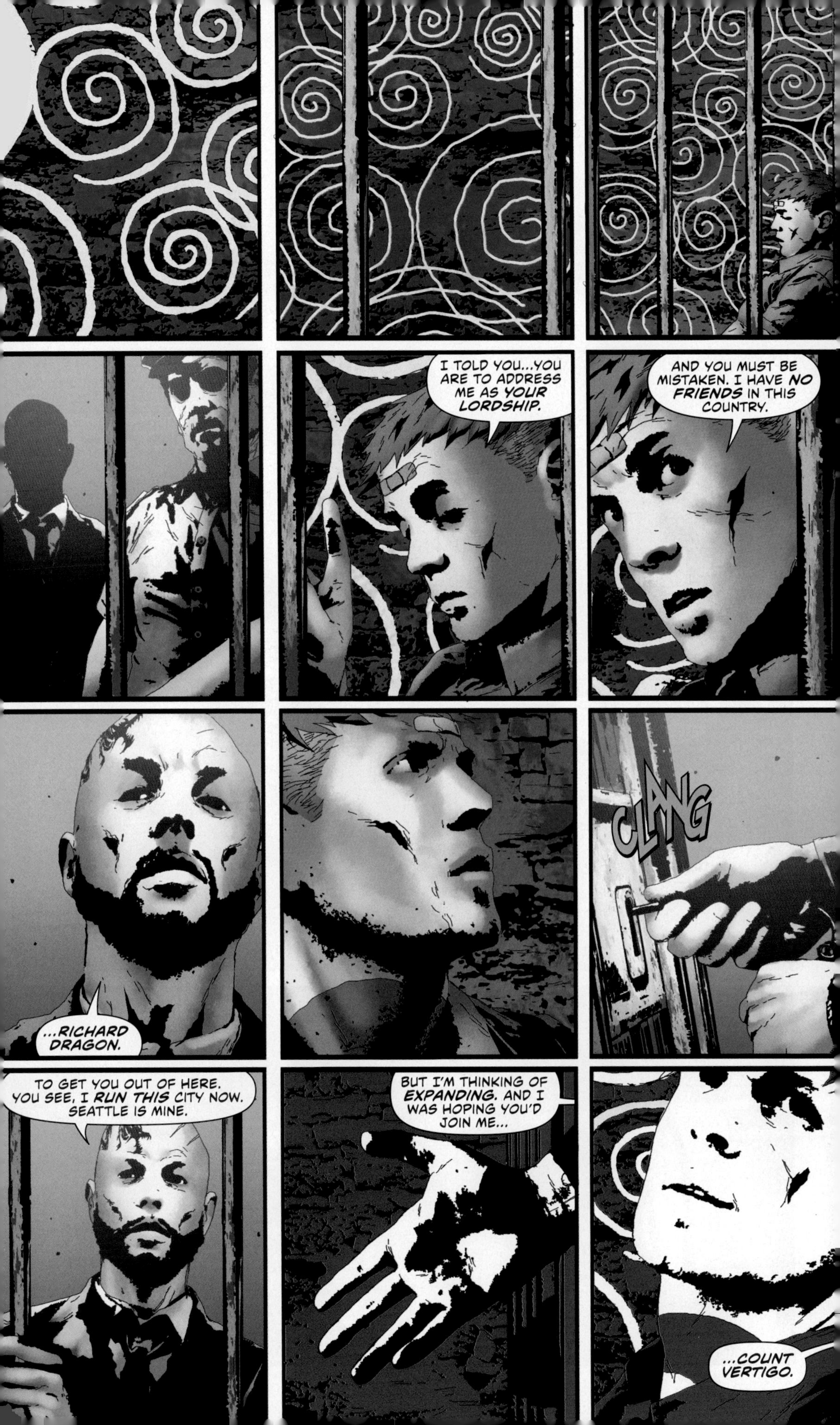
I TOLD YOU...YOU ARE TO ADDRESS ME AS YOUR LORDSHIP.
AND YOU MUST BE MISTAKEN. I HAVE NO FRIENDS IN THIS COUNTRY.
...RICHARD DRAGON.
CLANG
TO GET YOU OUT OF HERE. YOU SEE, I RUN THIS CITY NOW. SEATTLE IS MINE.
BUT I'M THINKING OF EXPANDING. AND I WAS HOPING YOU'D JOIN ME...
...COUNT VERTIGO.

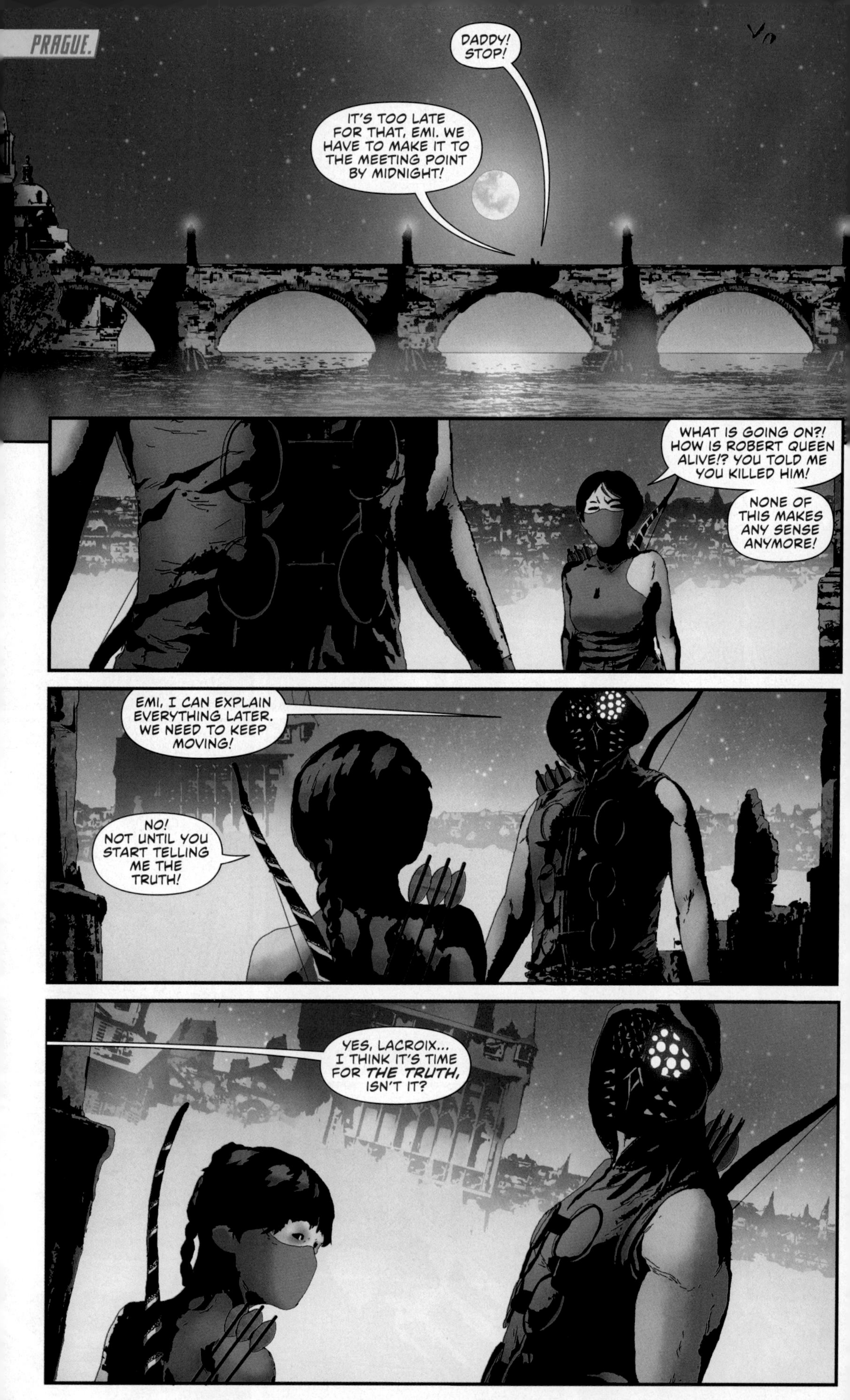
PRAGUE.
DADDY! STOP!
IT'S TOO LATE FOR THAT, EMI. WE HAVE TO MAKE IT TO THE MEETING POINT BY MIDNIGHT!
WHAT IS GOING ON?! HOW IS ROBERT QUEEN ALIVE!? YOU TOLD ME YOU KILLED HIM!
NONE OF THIS MAKES ANY SENSE ANYMORE!
EMI, I CAN EXPLAIN EVERYTHING LATER. WE NEED TO KEEP MOVING!
NO! NOT UNTIL YOU START TELLING ME THE TRUTH!
YES, LACROIX... I THINK IT'S TIME FOR THE TRUTH, ISN'T IT?

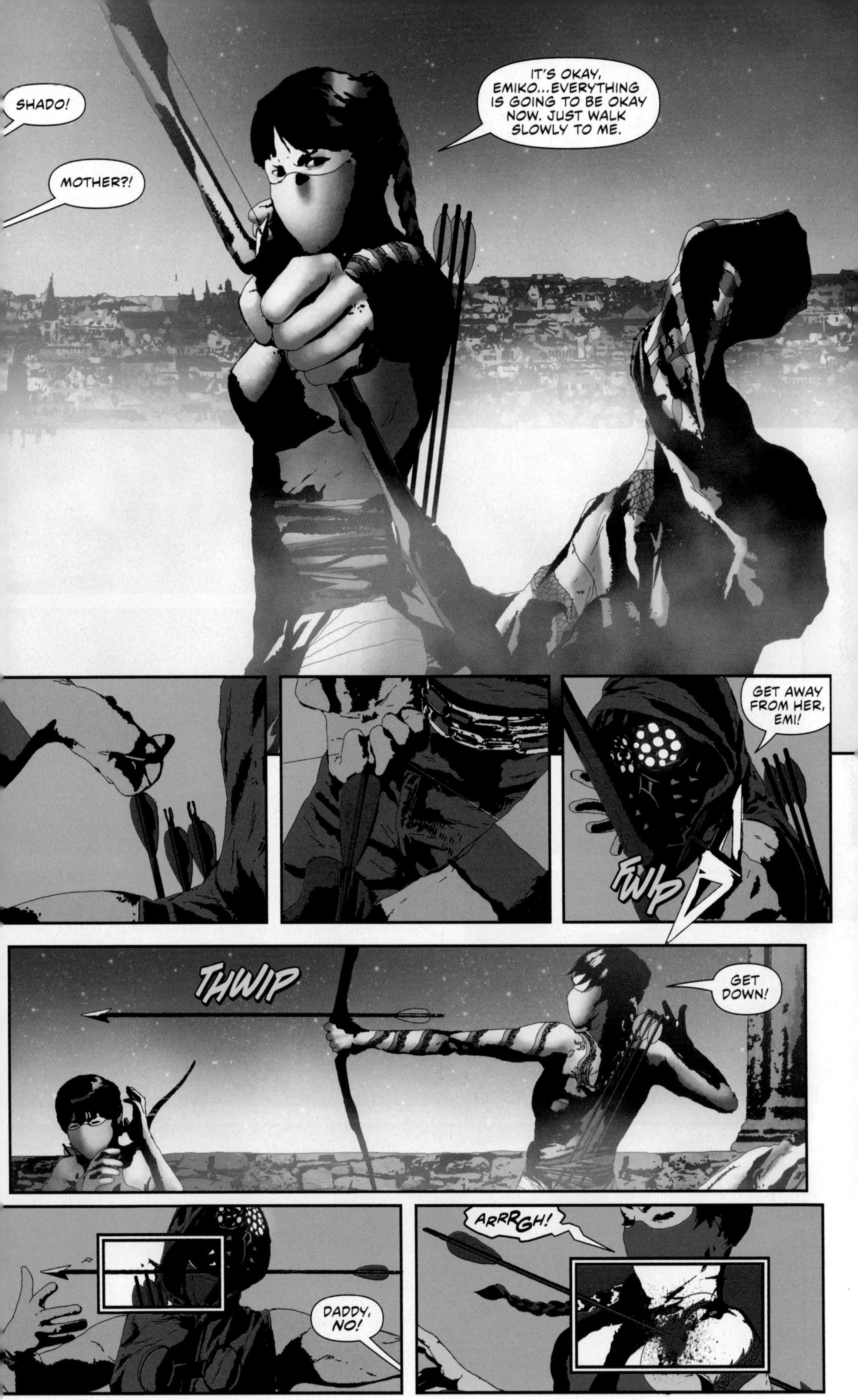
SHADO!
MOTHER?!
IT'S OKAY, EMIKO...EVERYTHING IS GOING TO BE OKAY NOW. JUST WALK SLOWLY TO ME.
GET AWAY FROM HER, EMI!
FWIP
THWIP
GET DOWN!
DADDY, NO!
ARRRGH!

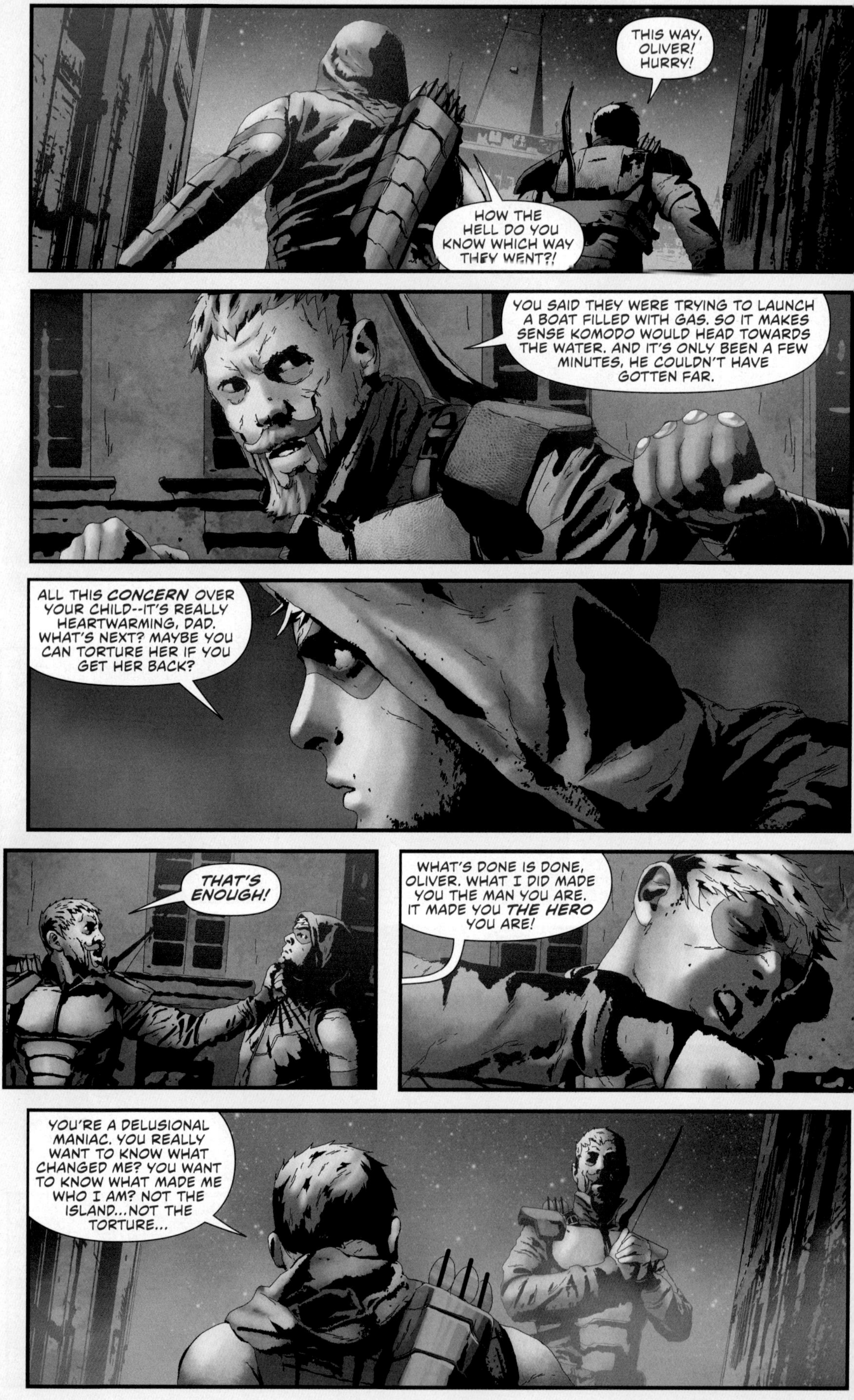
THIS WAY, OLIVER! HURRY!
HOW THE HELL DO YOU KNOW WHICH WAY THEY WENT?!
YOU SAID THEY WERE TRYING TO LAUNCH A BOAT FILLED WITH GAS. SO IT MAKES SENSE KOMODO WOULD HEAD TOWARDS THE WATER. AND IT'S ONLY BEEN A FEW MINUTES, HE COULDN'T HAVE GOTTEN FAR.
ALL THIS CONCERN OVER YOUR CHILD--IT'S REALLY HEARTWARMING, DAD. WHAT'S NEXT? MAYBE YOU CAN TORTURE HER IF YOU GET HER BACK?
THAT'S ENOUGH!
WHAT'S DONE IS DONE, OLIVER. WHAT I DID MADE YOU THE MAN YOU ARE. IT MADE YOU THE HERO YOU ARE!
YOU'RE A DELUSIONAL MANIAC. YOU REALLY WANT TO KNOW WHAT CHANGED ME? YOU WANT TO KNOW WHAT MADE ME WHO I AM? NOT THE ISLAND...NOT THE TORTURE...

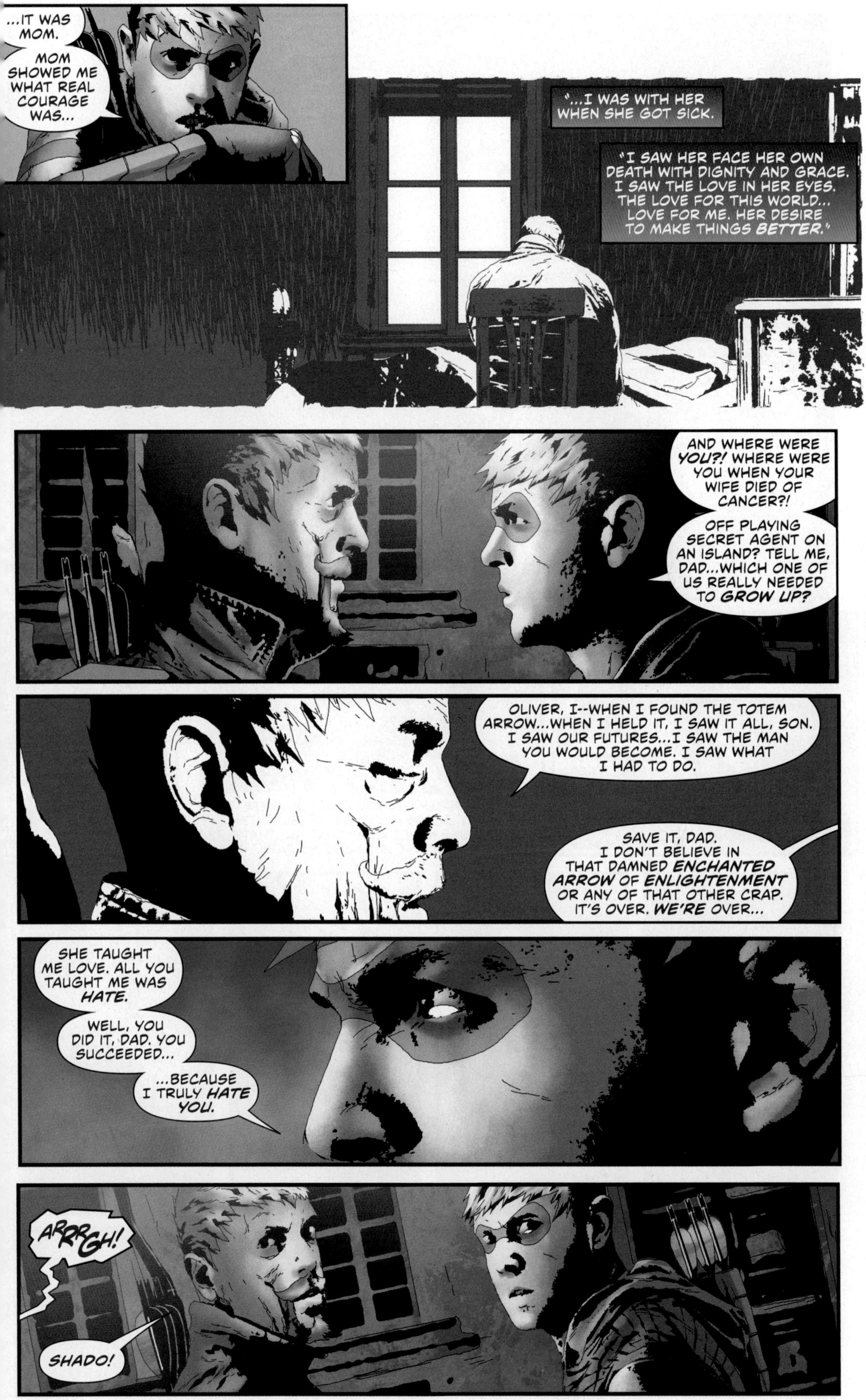
...IT WAS MOM.
MOM SHOWED ME WHAT REAL COURAGE WAS...
"...I WAS WITH HER WHEN SHE GOT SICK.
"I SAW HER FACE HER OWN DEATH WITH DIGNITY AND GRACE. I SAW THE LOVE IN HER EYES. THE LOVE FOR THIS WORLD... LOVE FOR ME. HER DESIRE TO MAKE THINGS *BETTER.*"
AND WHERE WERE *YOU?!* WHERE WERE YOU WHEN YOUR WIFE DIED OF CANCER?!
OFF PLAYING SECRET AGENT ON AN ISLAND? TELL ME, DAD...WHICH ONE OF US REALLY NEEDED TO ***GROW UP?***
OLIVER, I--WHEN I FOUND THE TOTEM ARROW...WHEN I HELD IT, I SAW IT ALL, SON. I SAW OUR FUTURES...I SAW THE MAN YOU WOULD BECOME. I SAW WHAT I HAD TO DO.
SAVE IT, DAD. I DON'T BELIEVE IN THAT DAMNED ***ENCHANTED ARROW*** OF ***ENLIGHTENMENT*** OR ANY OF THAT OTHER CRAP. IT'S OVER. ***WE'RE*** OVER...
SHE TAUGHT ME LOVE. ALL YOU TAUGHT ME WAS ***HATE.***
WELL, YOU DID IT, DAD. YOU SUCCEEDED...
...BECAUSE I TRULY ***HATE YOU.***
ARRRGH!
SHADO!

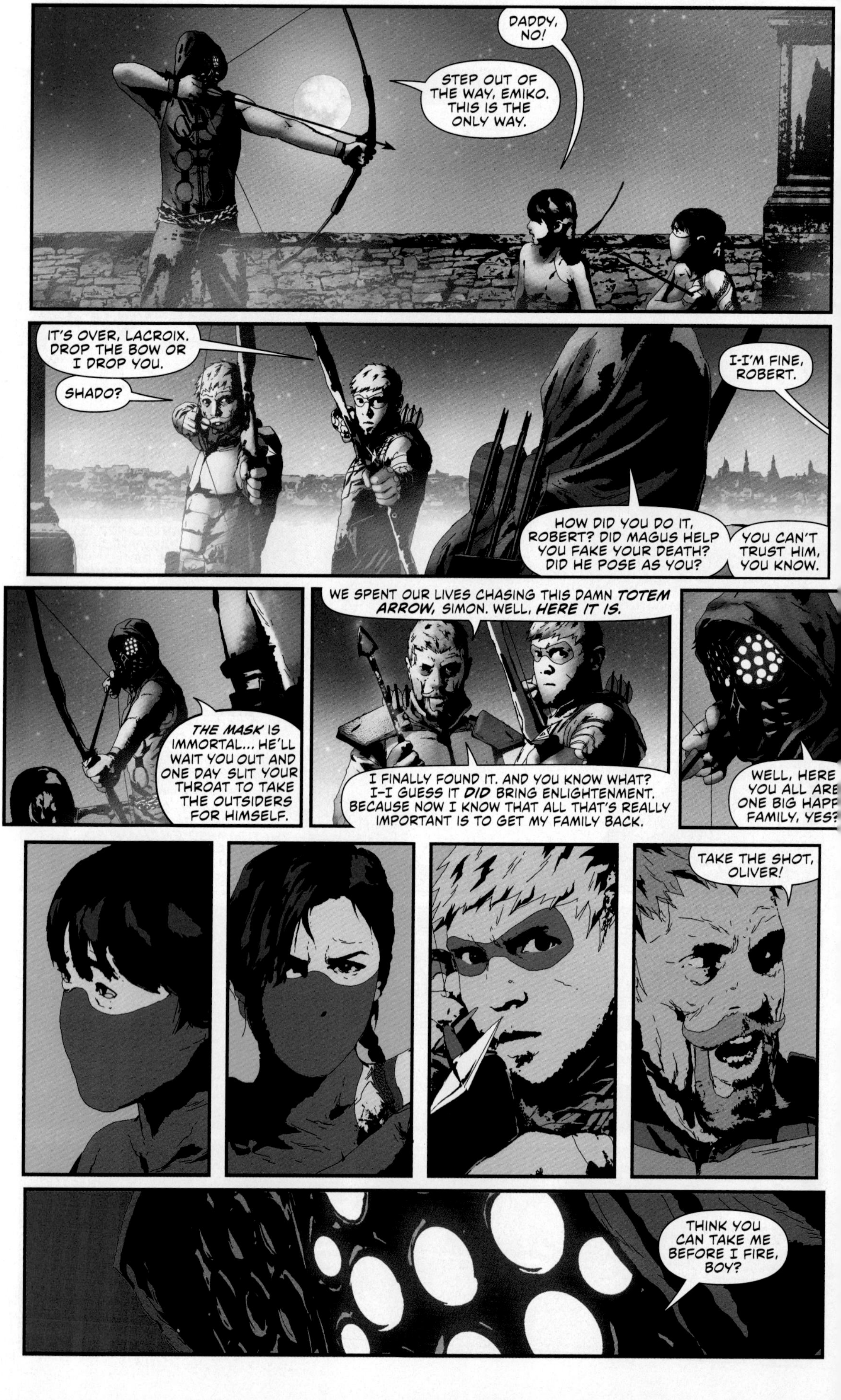
DADDY, NO!
STEP OUT OF THE WAY, EMIKO. THIS IS THE ONLY WAY.
IT'S OVER, LACROIX. DROP THE BOW OR I DROP YOU.
SHADO?
I-I'M FINE, ROBERT.
HOW DID YOU DO IT, ROBERT? DID MAGUS HELP YOU FAKE YOUR DEATH? DID HE POSE AS YOU?
YOU CAN'T TRUST HIM, YOU KNOW.
THE MASK IS IMMORTAL... HE'LL WAIT YOU OUT AND ONE DAY SLIT YOUR THROAT TO TAKE THE OUTSIDERS FOR HIMSELF.
WE SPENT OUR LIVES CHASING THIS DAMN TOTEM ARROW, SIMON. WELL, HERE IT IS.
I FINALLY FOUND IT. AND YOU KNOW WHAT? I-I GUESS IT DID BRING ENLIGHTENMENT. BECAUSE NOW I KNOW THAT ALL THAT'S REALLY IMPORTANT IS TO GET MY FAMILY BACK.
WELL, HERE YOU ALL ARE ONE BIG HAPP FAMILY, YES?
TAKE THE SHOT, OLIVER!
THINK YOU CAN TAKE ME BEFORE I FIRE, BOY?

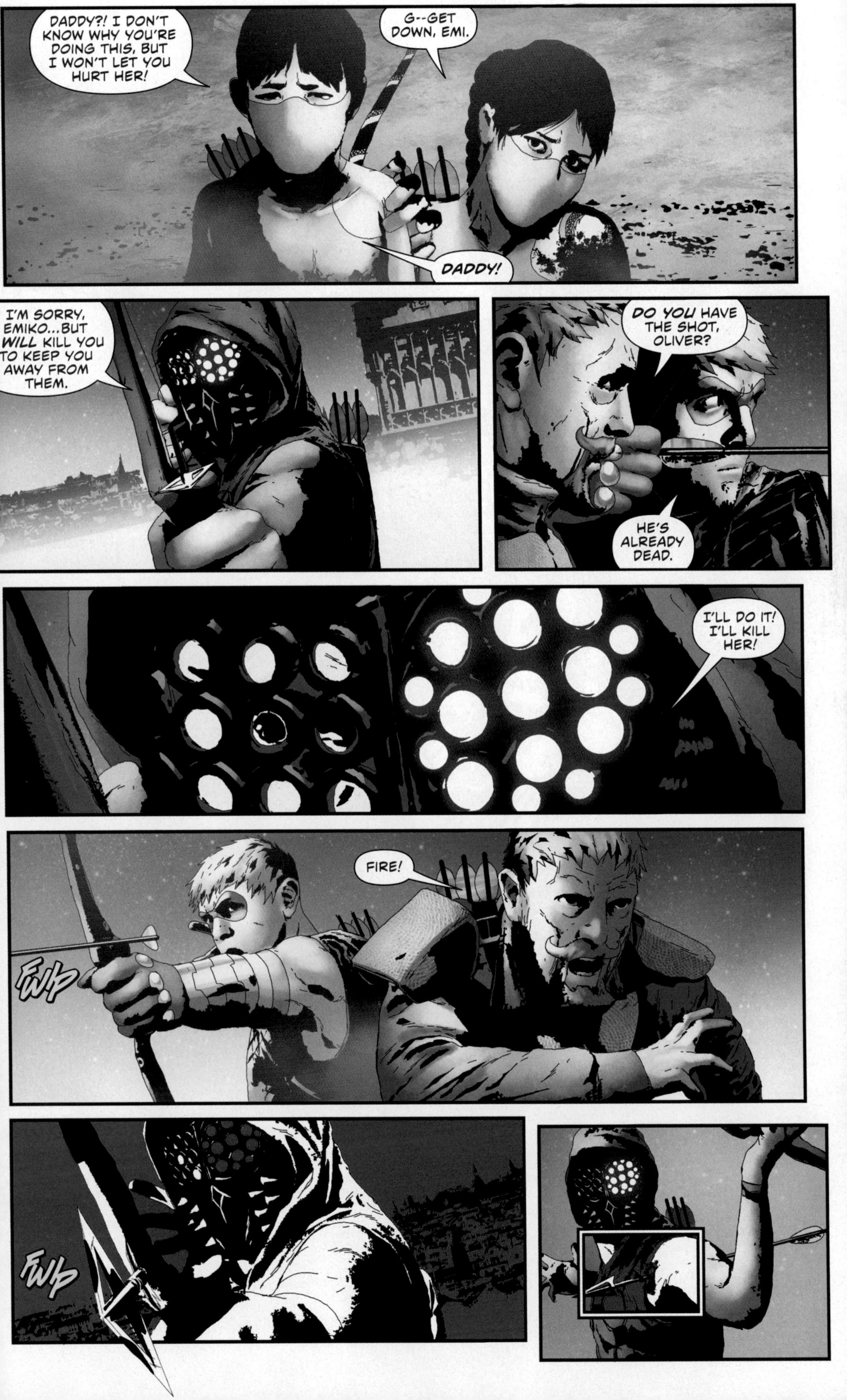
DADDY?! I DON'T KNOW WHY YOU'RE DOING THIS, BUT I WON'T LET YOU HURT HER!
G--GET DOWN, EMI.
DADDY!
I'M SORRY, EMIKO...BUT WILL KILL YOU TO KEEP YOU AWAY FROM THEM.
DO YOU HAVE THE SHOT, OLIVER?
HE'S ALREADY DEAD.
I'LL DO IT! I'LL KILL HER!
FIRE!
FWIP
FWIP

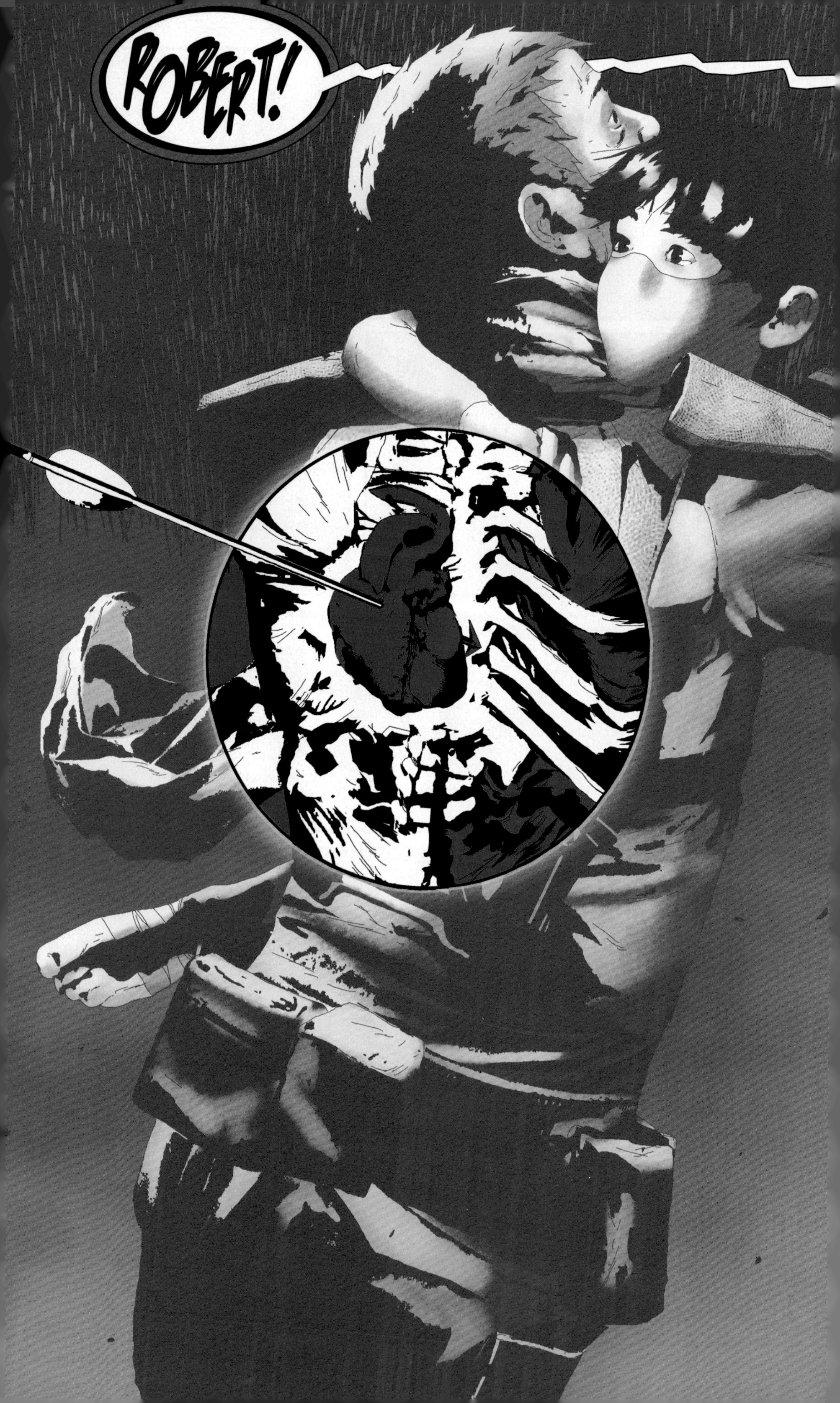
ROBERT!

THE OUTSIDERS WAR

book 6:
spoils of
war

ARROW CLAN
enlightenment
steadfastness
lineage

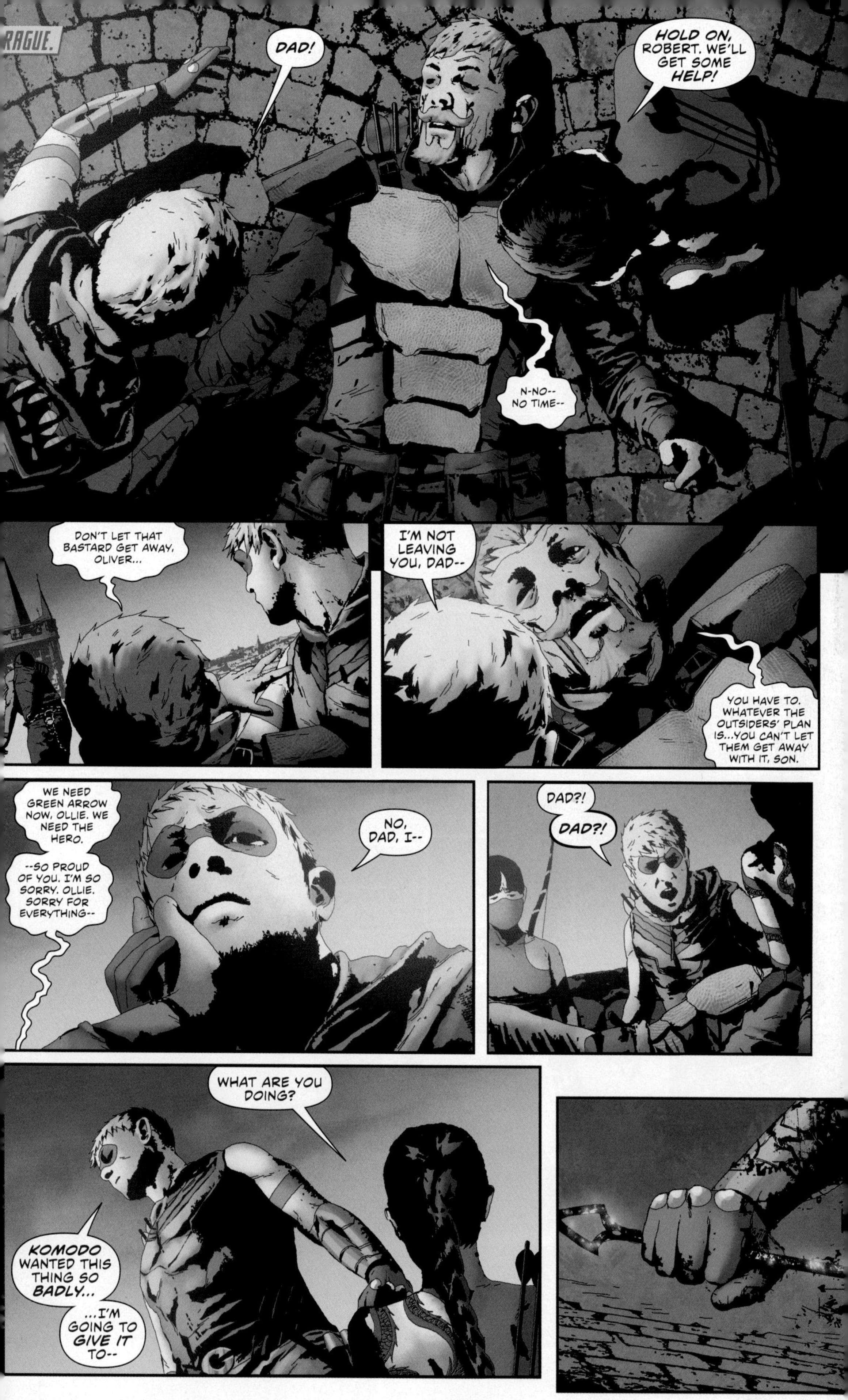
RAGUE.
DAD!
HOLD ON, ROBERT. WE'LL GET SOME HELP!
N-NO-- NO TIME--
DON'T LET THAT BASTARD GET AWAY, OLIVER...
I'M NOT LEAVING YOU, DAD--
YOU HAVE TO. WHATEVER THE OUTSIDERS' PLAN IS...YOU CAN'T LET THEM GET AWAY WITH IT, SON.
WE NEED GREEN ARROW NOW, OLLIE. WE NEED THE HERO.
NO, DAD, I--
--SO PROUD OF YOU. I'M SO SORRY. OLLIE. SORRY FOR EVERYTHING--
DAD?!
DAD?!
WHAT ARE YOU DOING?
KOMODO WANTED THIS THING SO BADLY...
...I'M GOING TO GIVE IT TO--

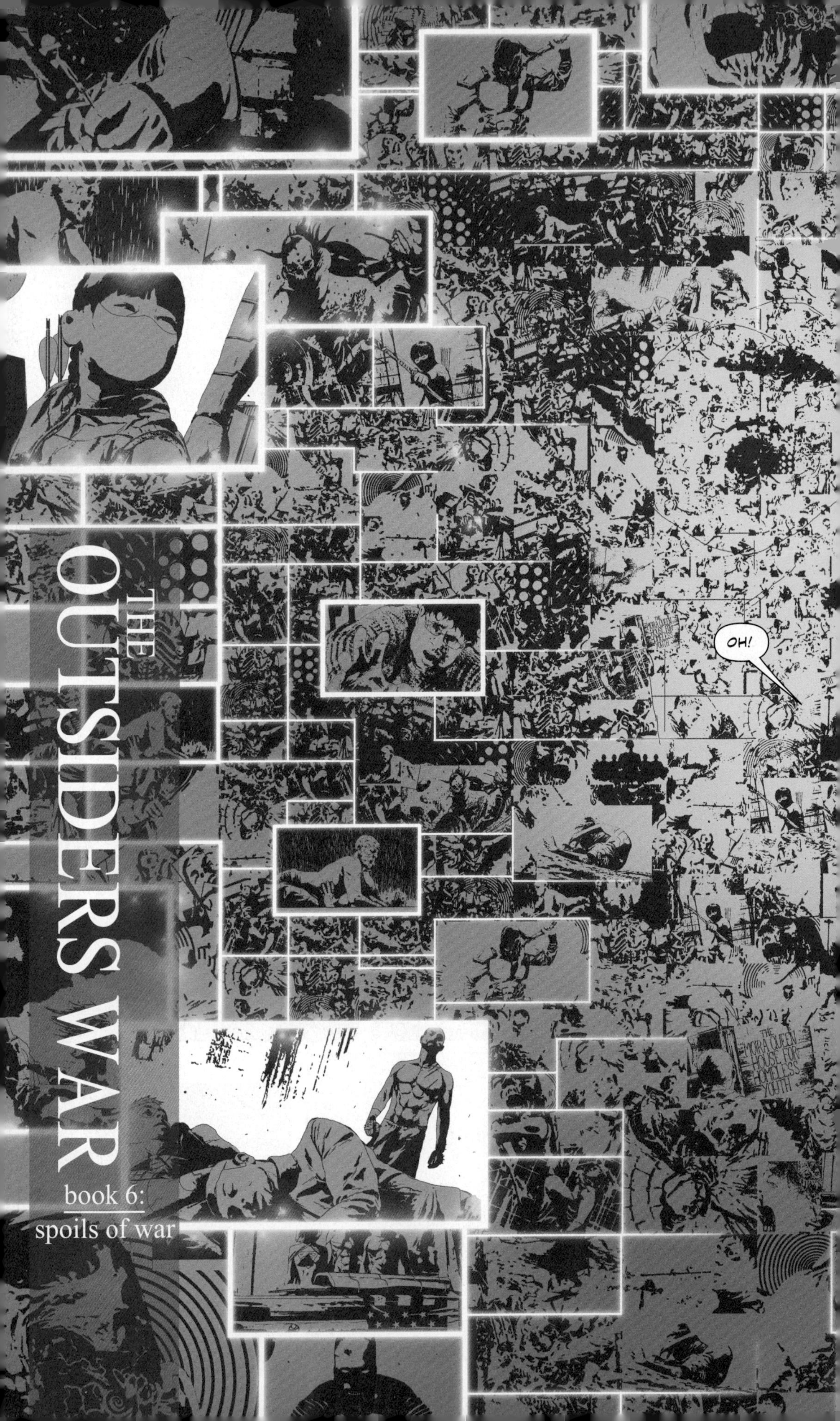
THE OUTSIDERS WAR
book 6:
spoils of war
OH!
THE MOIRA QUEEN HOUSE FOR HOMELESS YOUTH

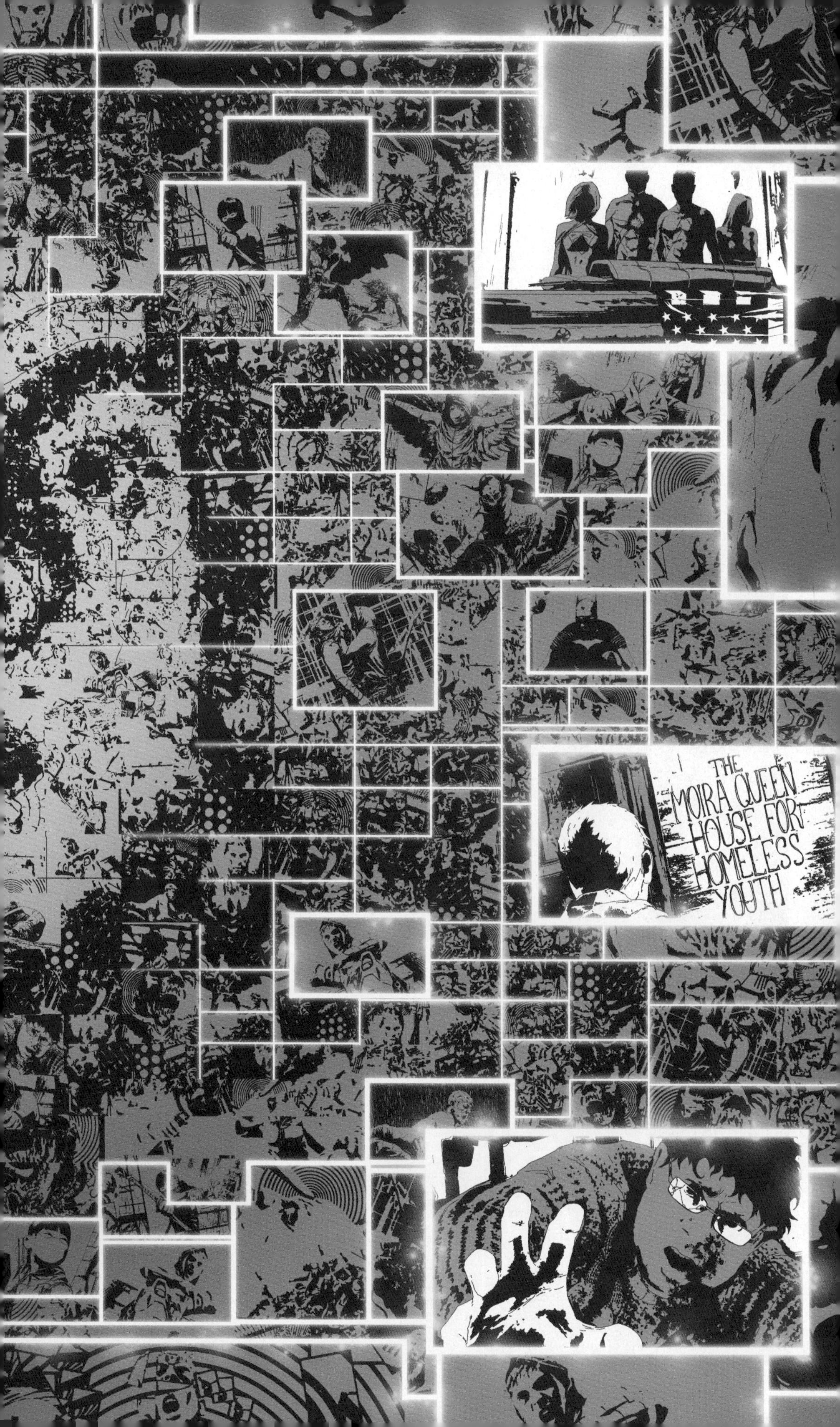
THE
MOIRA QUEEN
HOUSE FOR
HOMELESS
YOUTH

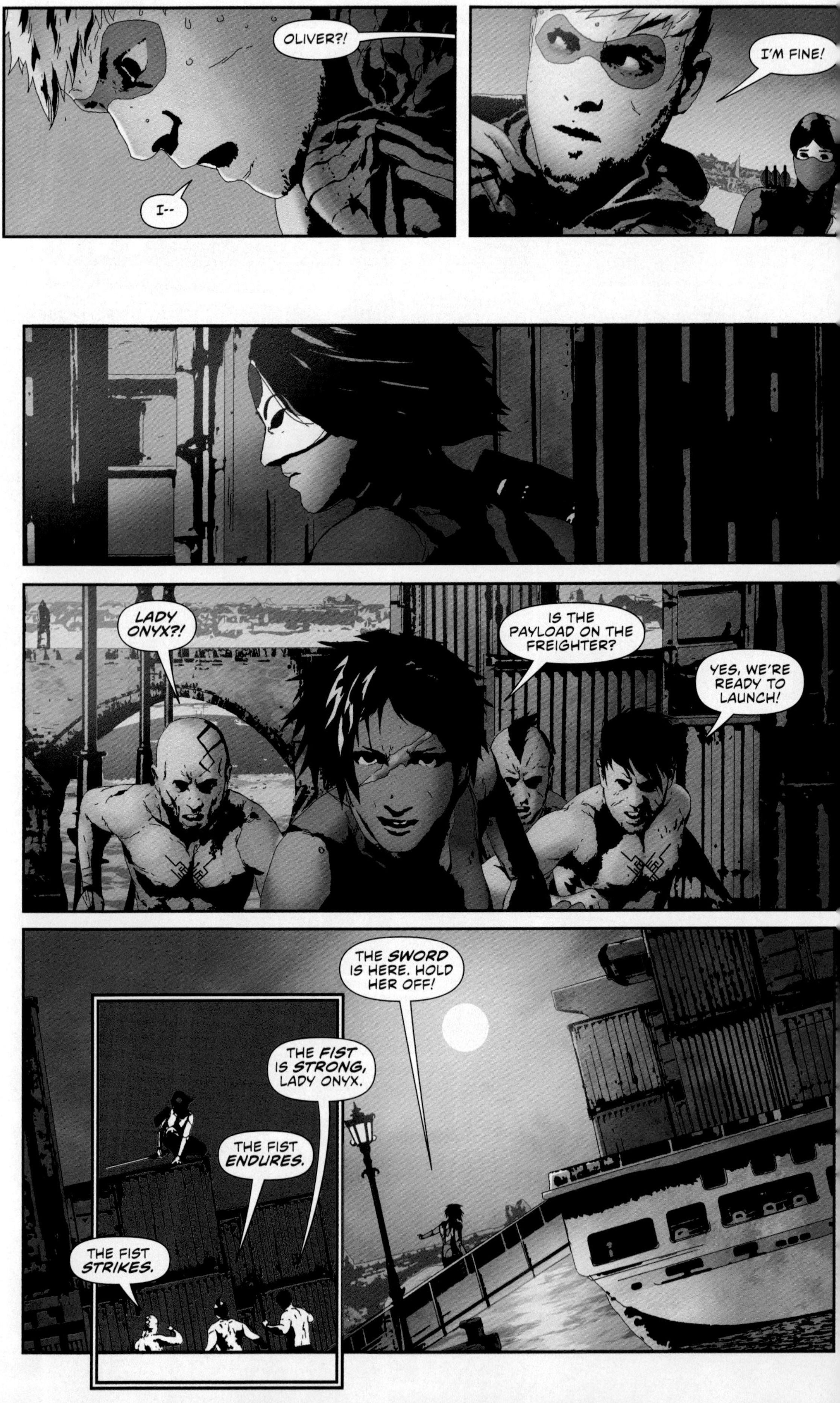
OLIVER?!
I--
I'M FINE!
LADY ONYX?!
IS THE PAYLOAD ON THE FREIGHTER?
YES, WE'RE READY TO LAUNCH!
THE SWORD IS HERE. HOLD HER OFF!
THE FIST IS STRONG, LADY ONYX.
THE FIST ENDURES.
THE FIST STRIKES.

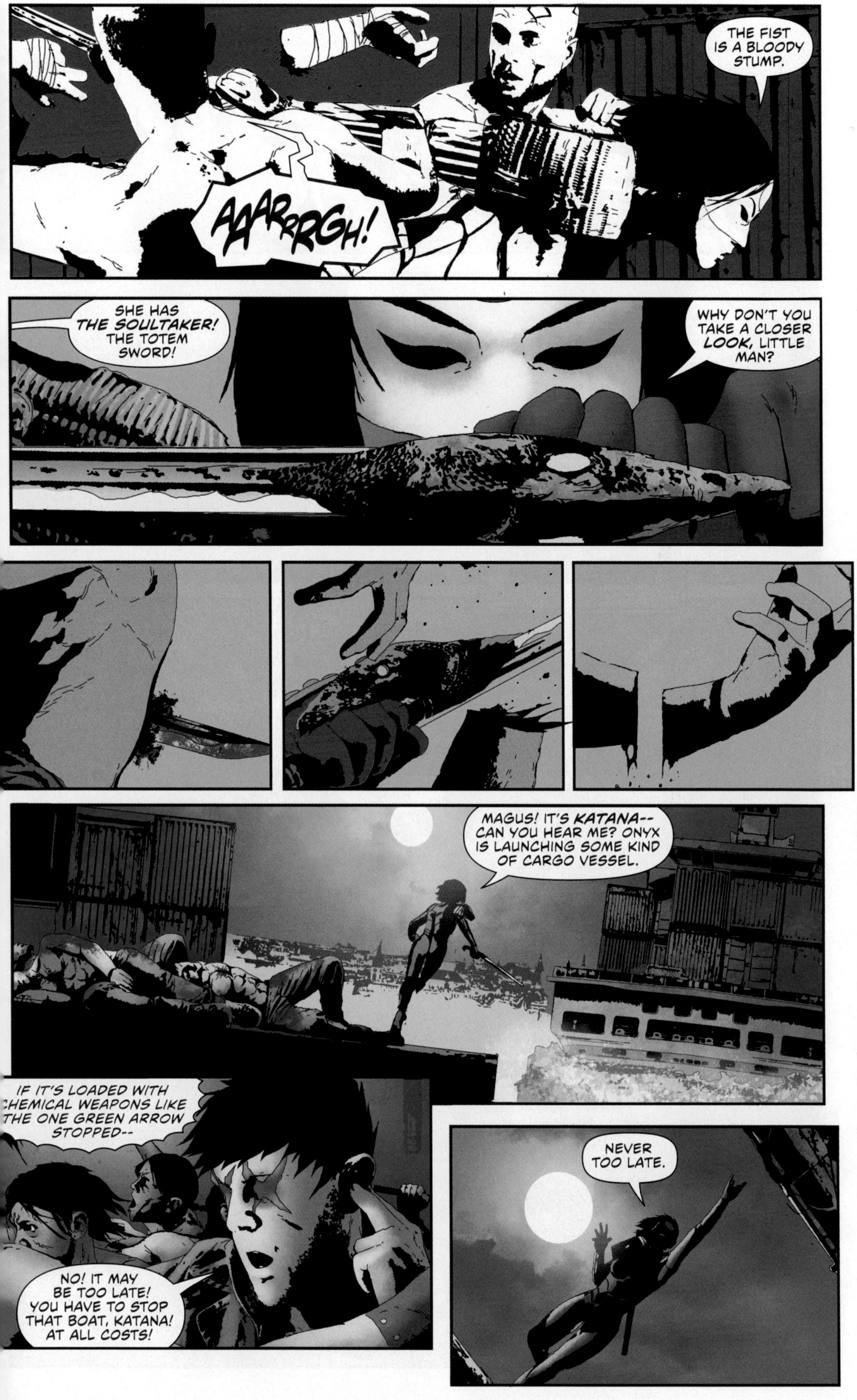
THE FIST IS A BLOODY STUMP.
AAARRRGH!
SHE HAS THE SOULTAKER! THE TOTEM SWORD!
WHY DON'T YOU TAKE A CLOSER LOOK, LITTLE MAN?
MAGUS! IT'S KATANA-- CAN YOU HEAR ME? ONYX IS LAUNCHING SOME KIND OF CARGO VESSEL.
IF IT'S LOADED WITH CHEMICAL WEAPONS LIKE THE ONE GREEN ARROW STOPPED--
NO! IT MAY BE TOO LATE! YOU HAVE TO STOP THAT BOAT, KATANA! AT ALL COSTS!
NEVER TOO LATE.

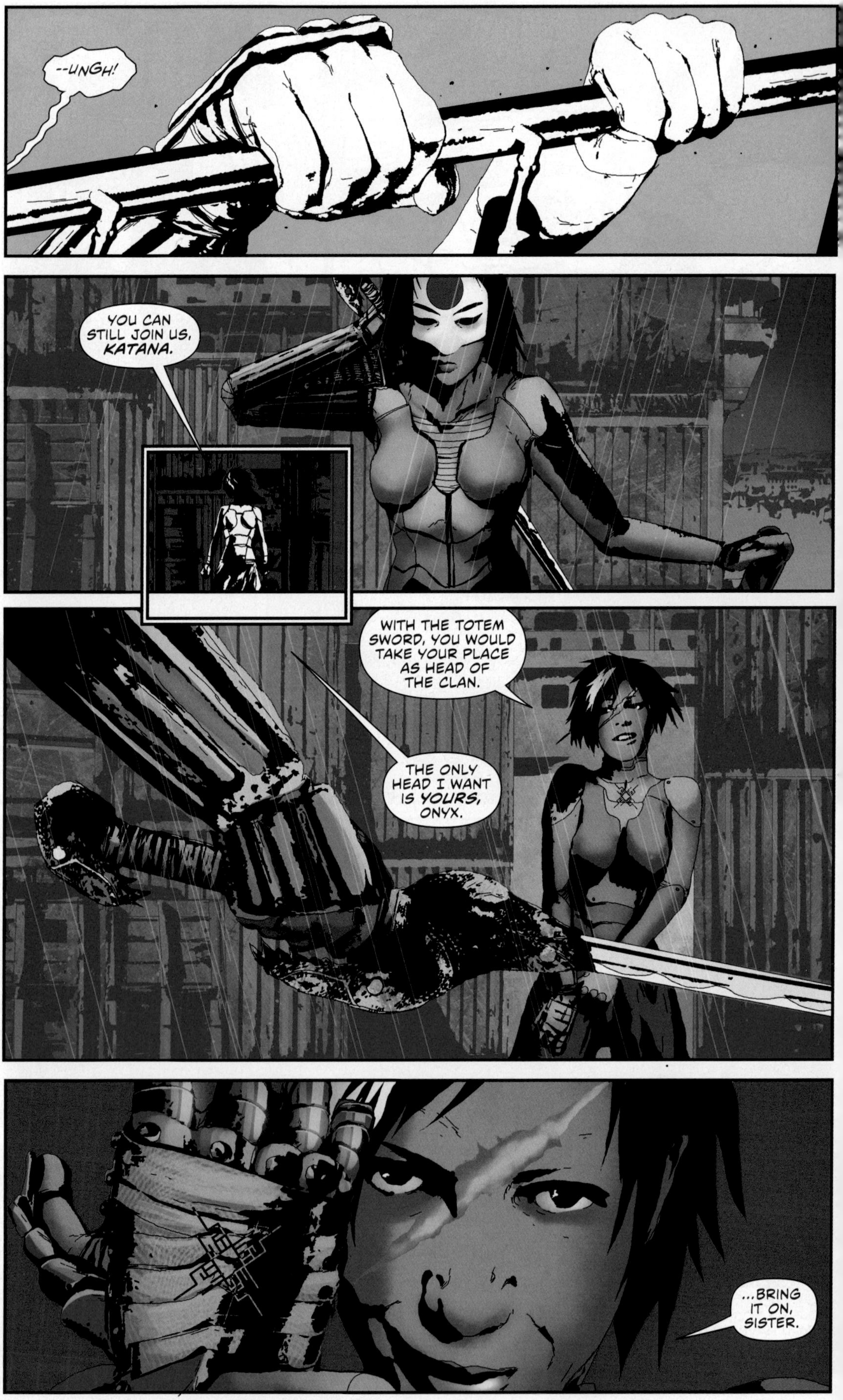
--UNGH!
YOU CAN STILL JOIN US, KATANA.
WITH THE TOTEM SWORD, YOU WOULD TAKE YOUR PLACE AS HEAD OF THE CLAN.
THE ONLY HEAD I WANT IS YOURS, ONYX.
...BRING IT ON, SISTER.

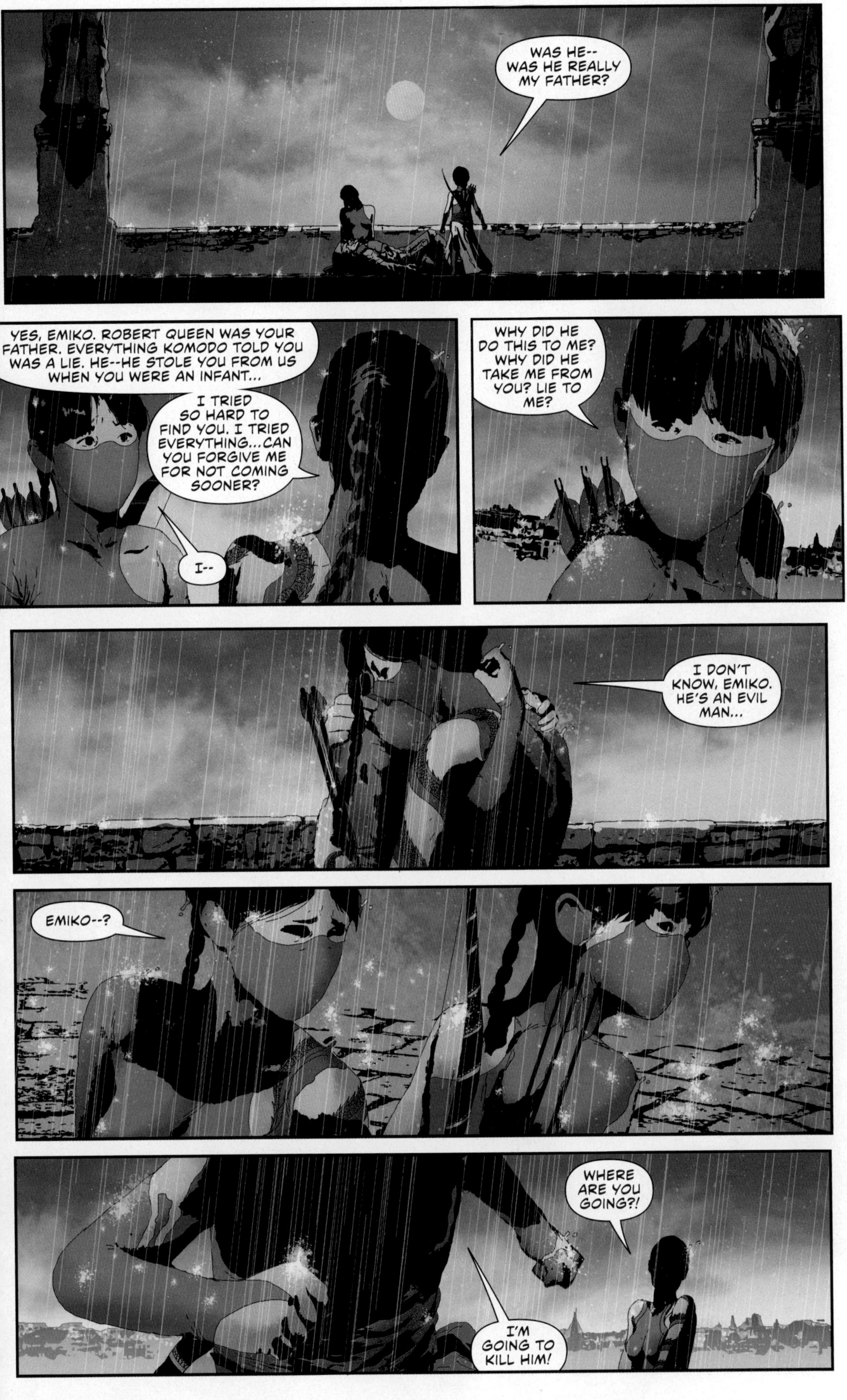

WAS HE-- WAS HE REALLY MY FATHER?
YES, EMIKO. ROBERT QUEEN WAS YOUR FATHER. EVERYTHING KOMODO TOLD YOU WAS A LIE. HE--HE STOLE YOU FROM US WHEN YOU WERE AN INFANT...
I TRIED SO HARD TO FIND YOU. I TRIED EVERYTHING...CAN YOU FORGIVE ME FOR NOT COMING SOONER?
I--
WHY DID HE DO THIS TO ME? WHY DID HE TAKE ME FROM YOU? LIE TO ME?
I DON'T KNOW, EMIKO. HE'S AN EVIL MAN...
EMIKO--?
WHERE ARE YOU GOING?!
I'M GOING TO KILL HIM!

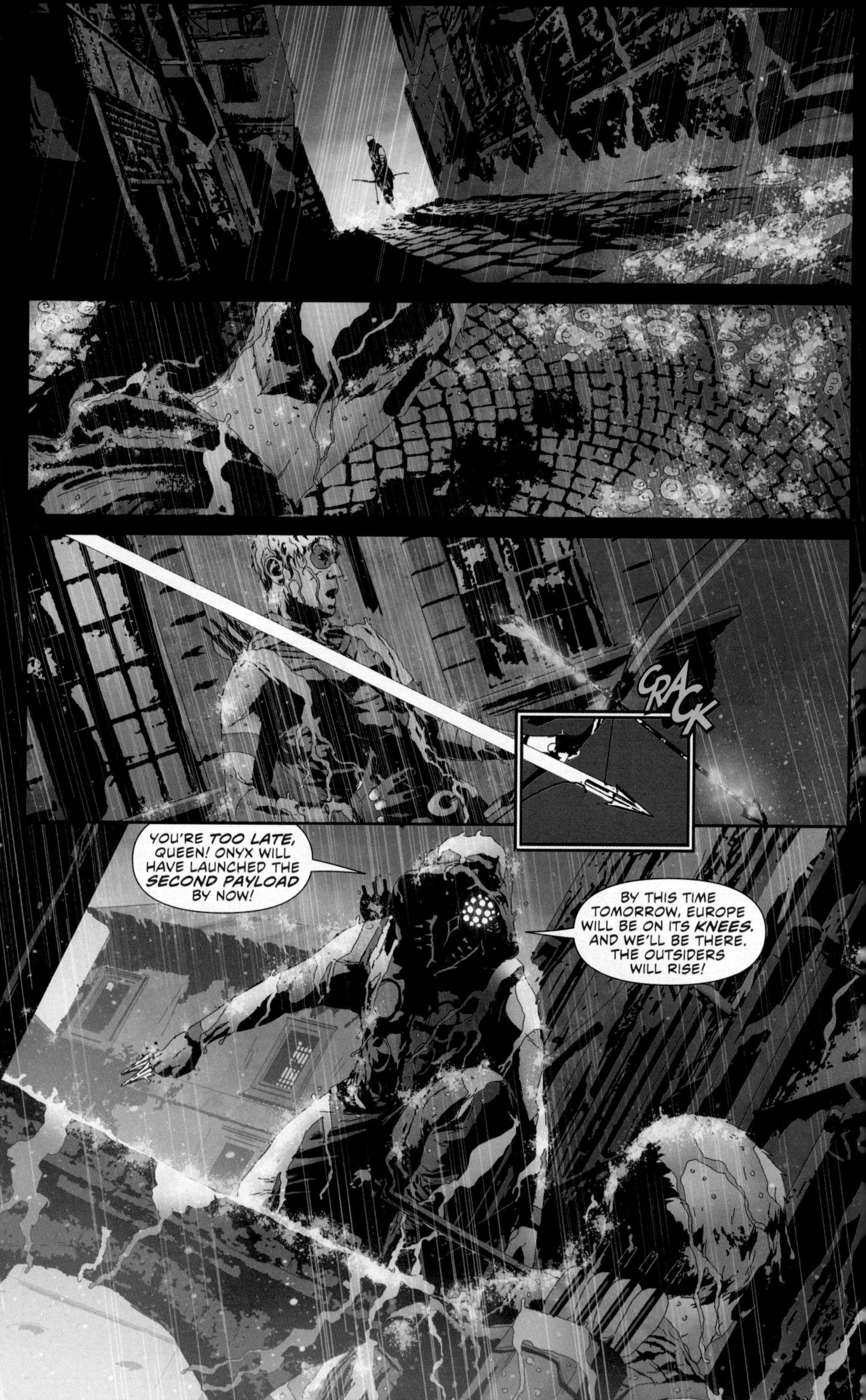
CRACK
YOU'RE TOO LATE, QUEEN! ONYX WILL HAVE LAUNCHED THE SECOND PAYLOAD BY NOW!
BY THIS TIME TOMORROW, EUROPE WILL BE ON ITS KNEES. AND WE'LL BE THERE. THE OUTSIDERS WILL RISE!

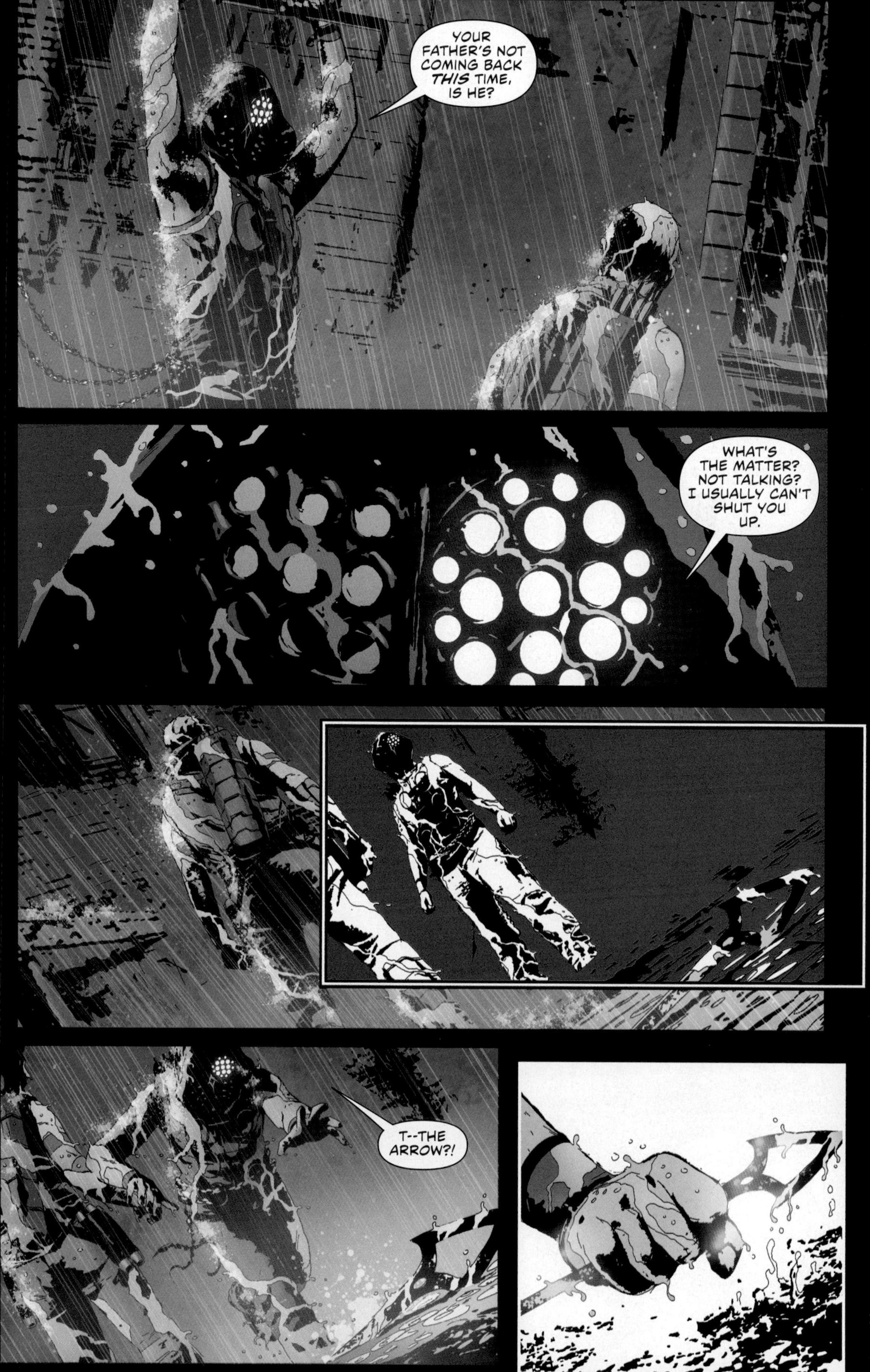
YOUR FATHER'S NOT COMING BACK *THIS* TIME, IS HE?
WHAT'S THE MATTER? NOT TALKING? I USUALLY CAN'T SHUT YOU UP.
T--THE ARROW?!

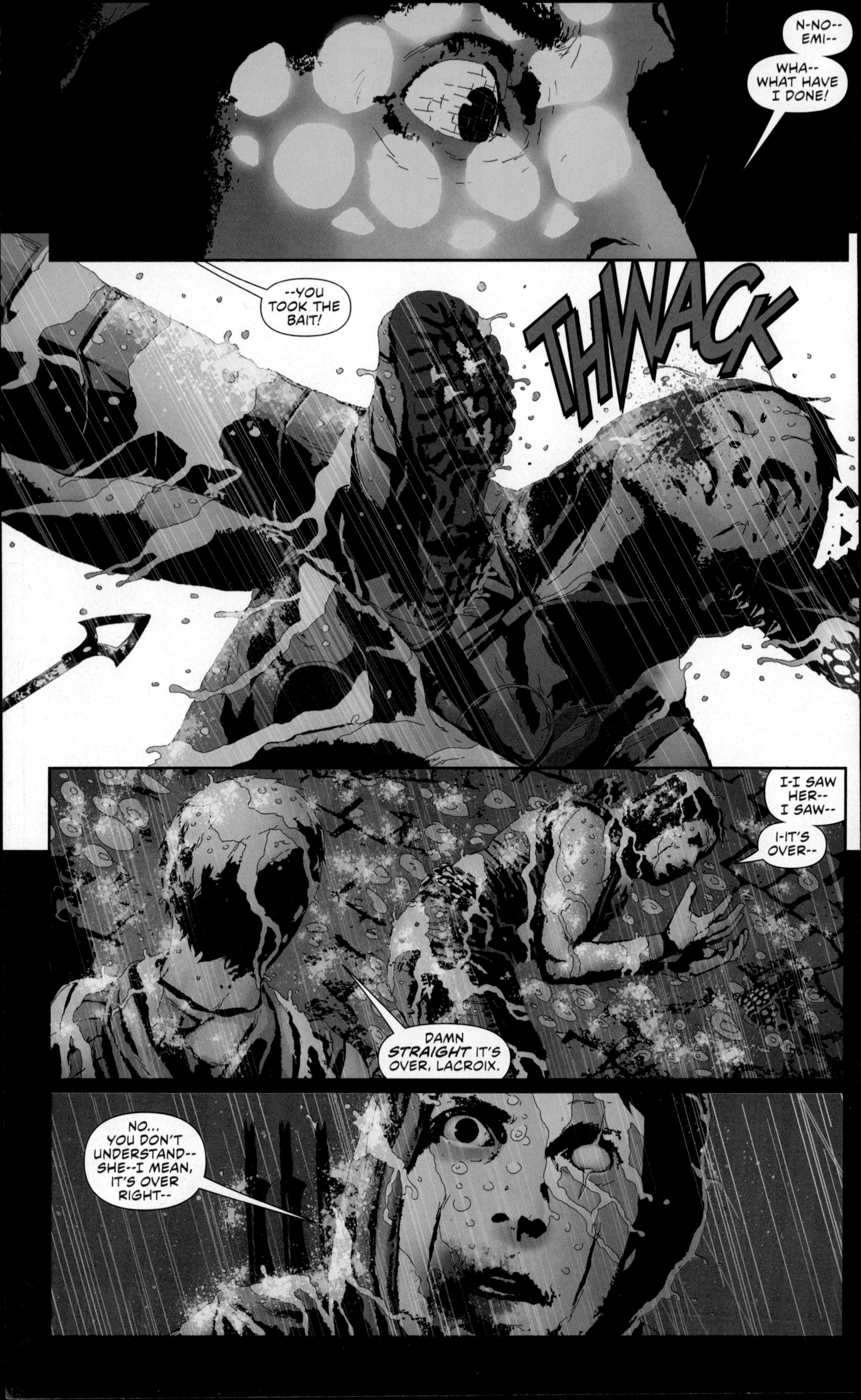
N-NO-- EMI--
WHA-- WHAT HAVE I DONE!
--YOU TOOK THE BAIT!
THWACK
I-I SAW HER-- I SAW--
I-IT'S OVER--
DAMN *STRAIGHT* IT'S OVER, LACROIX.
NO... YOU DON'T UNDERSTAND-- SHE--I MEAN, IT'S OVER RIGHT--

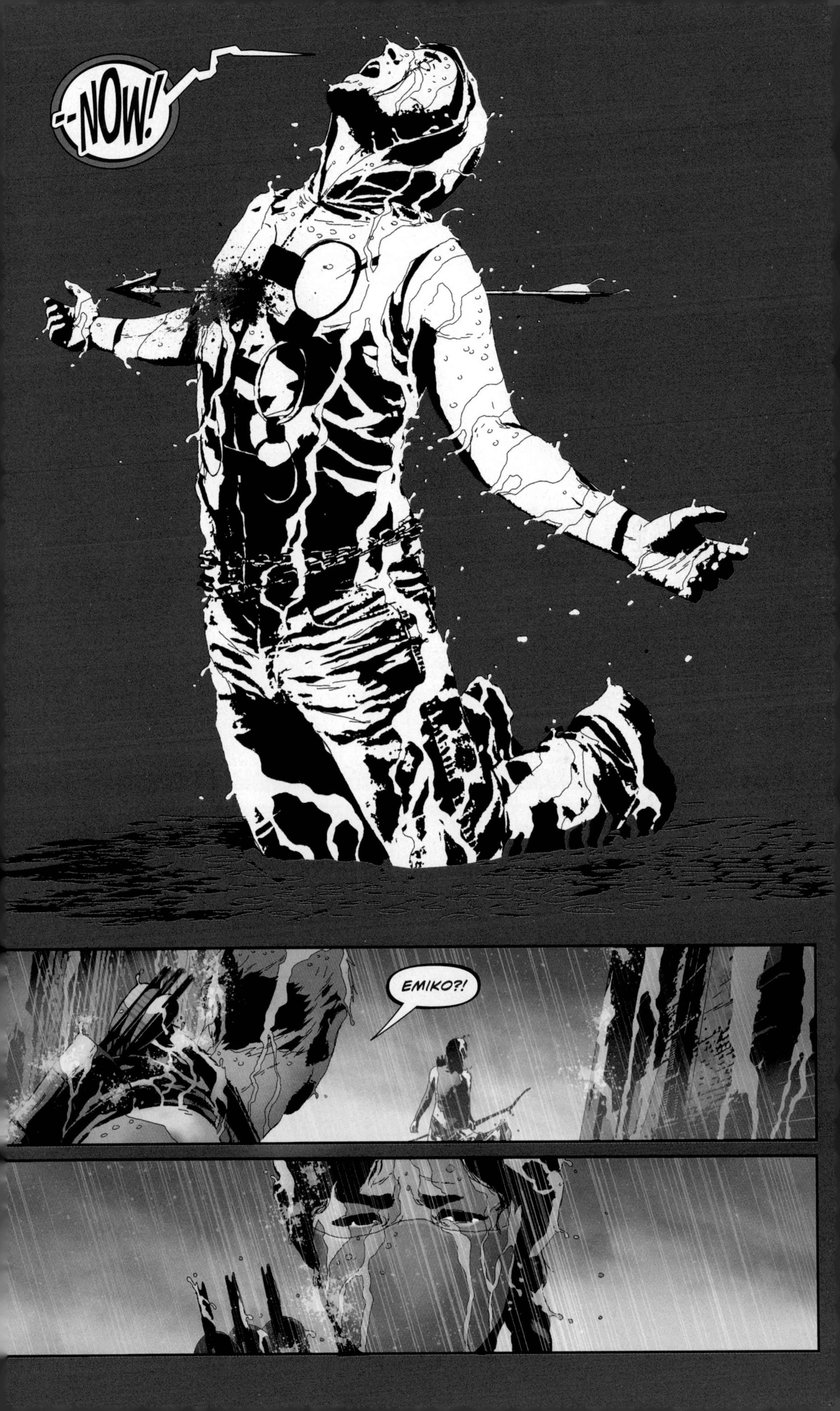
--NOW!
EMIKO?!

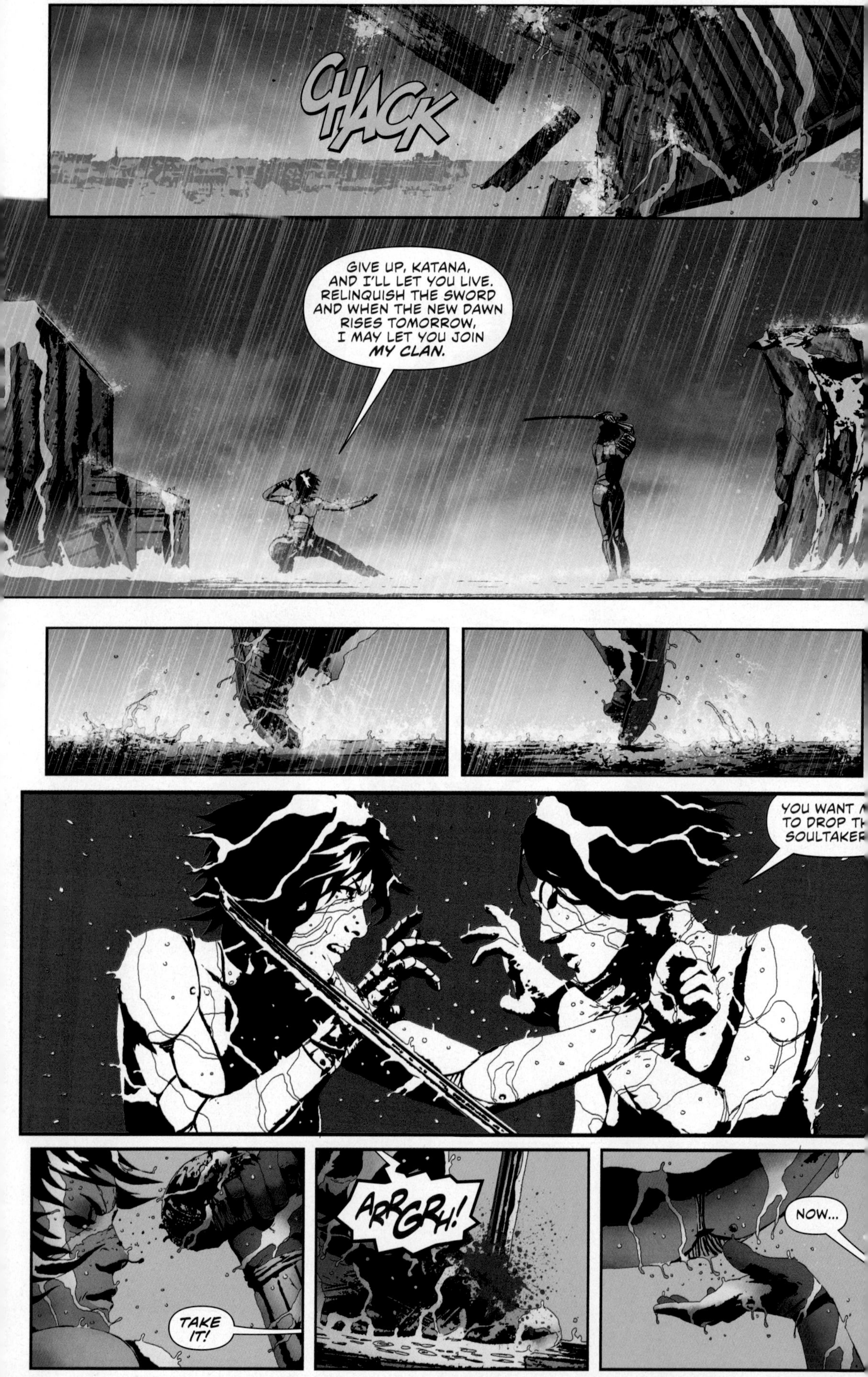
CHACK
GIVE UP, KATANA, AND I'LL LET YOU LIVE. RELINQUISH THE SWORD AND WHEN THE NEW DAWN RISES TOMORROW, I MAY LET YOU JOIN MY CLAN.
YOU WANT TO DROP TH SOULTAKER
TAKE IT!
ARRGRH!
NOW...

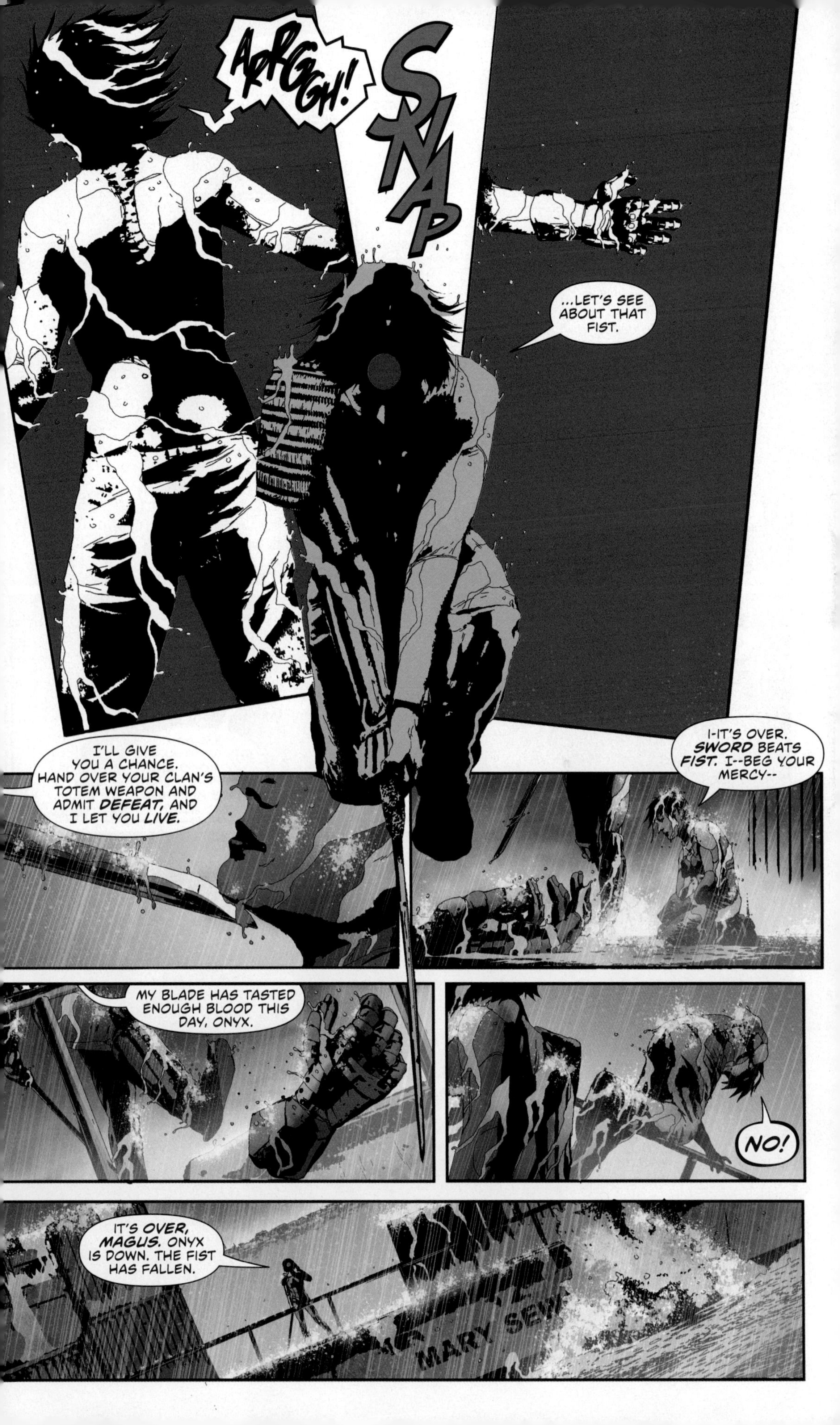

ARRGGGH!
SNAP
...LET'S SEE ABOUT THAT FIST.
I'LL GIVE YOU A CHANCE. HAND OVER YOUR CLAN'S TOTEM WEAPON AND ADMIT *DEFEAT,* AND I LET YOU *LIVE.*
I-IT'S OVER. *SWORD* BEATS *FIST.* I--BEG YOUR MERCY--
MY BLADE HAS TASTED ENOUGH BLOOD THIS DAY, ONYX.
NO!
IT'S *OVER, MAGUS.* ONYX IS DOWN. THE FIST HAS FALLEN.
MARY SEW

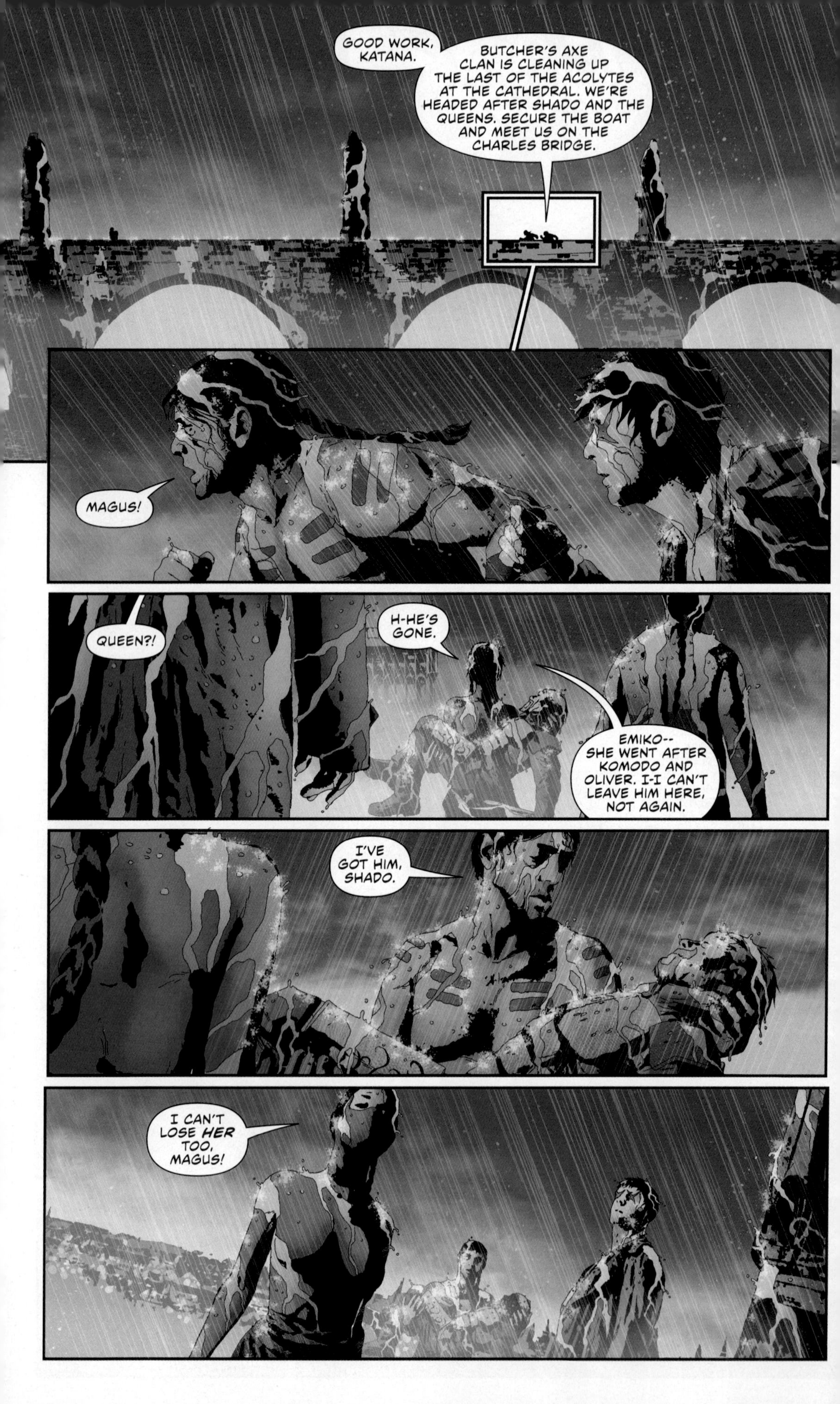
GOOD WORK, KATANA.
BUTCHER'S AXE CLAN IS CLEANING UP THE LAST OF THE ACOLYTES AT THE CATHEDRAL. WE'RE HEADED AFTER SHADO AND THE QUEENS. SECURE THE BOAT AND MEET US ON THE CHARLES BRIDGE.
MAGUS!
QUEEN?!
H-HE'S GONE.
EMIKO-- SHE WENT AFTER KOMODO AND OLIVER. I-I CAN'T LEAVE HIM HERE, NOT AGAIN.
I'VE GOT HIM, SHADO.
I CAN'T LOSE **HER** TOO, MAGUS!

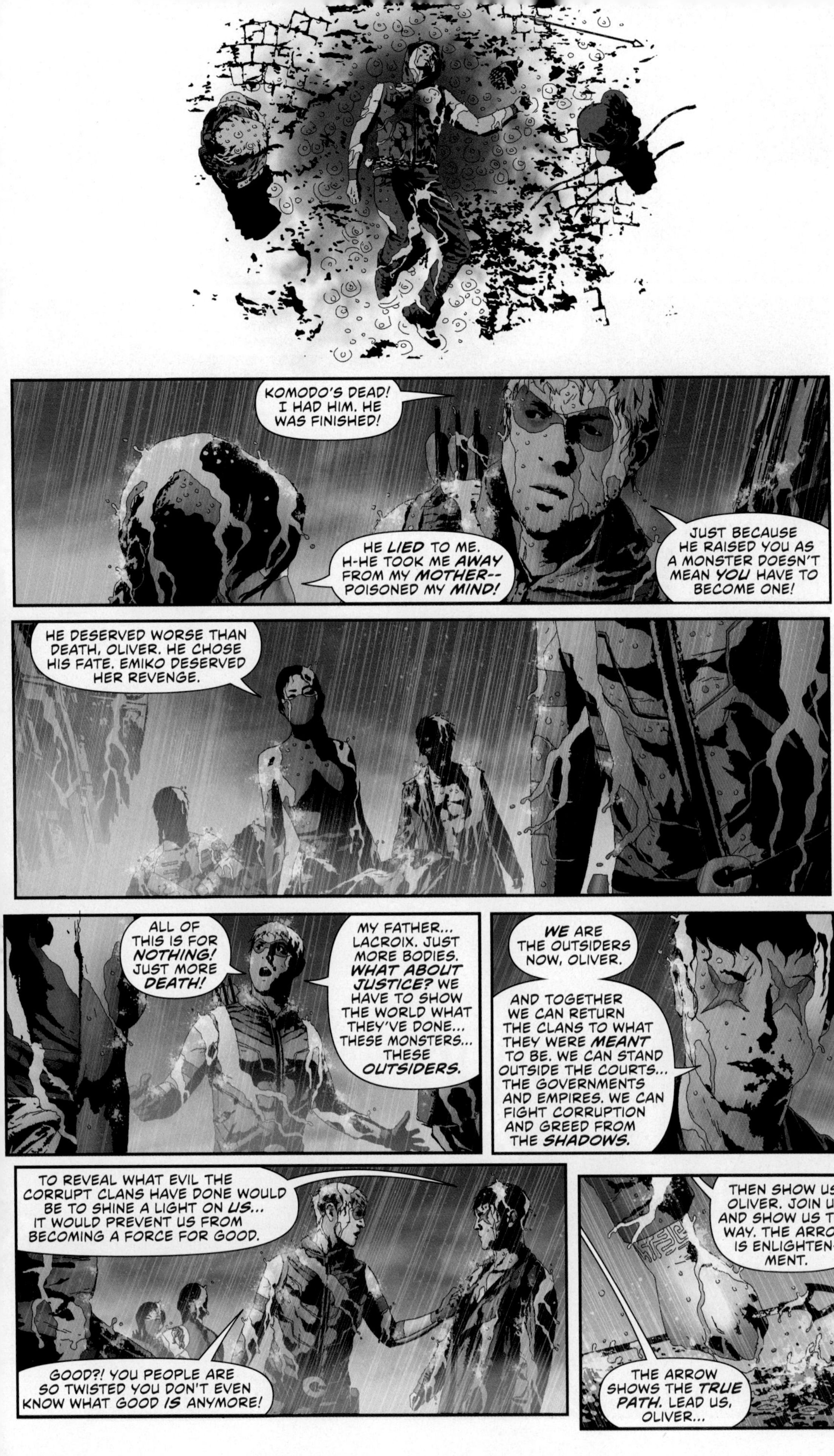
KOMODO'S DEAD! I HAD HIM. HE WAS FINISHED!
HE LIED TO ME. H-HE TOOK ME AWAY FROM MY MOTHER-- POISONED MY MIND!
JUST BECAUSE HE RAISED YOU AS A MONSTER DOESN'T MEAN YOU HAVE TO BECOME ONE!
HE DESERVED WORSE THAN DEATH, OLIVER. HE CHOSE HIS FATE. EMIKO DESERVED HER REVENGE.
ALL OF THIS IS FOR NOTHING! JUST MORE DEATH!
MY FATHER... LACROIX. JUST MORE BODIES. WHAT ABOUT JUSTICE? WE HAVE TO SHOW THE WORLD WHAT THEY'VE DONE... THESE MONSTERS... THESE OUTSIDERS.
WE ARE THE OUTSIDERS NOW, OLIVER.
AND TOGETHER WE CAN RETURN THE CLANS TO WHAT THEY WERE MEANT TO BE. WE CAN STAND OUTSIDE THE COURTS... THE GOVERNMENTS AND EMPIRES. WE CAN FIGHT CORRUPTION AND GREED FROM THE SHADOWS.
TO REVEAL WHAT EVIL THE CORRUPT CLANS HAVE DONE WOULD BE TO SHINE A LIGHT ON US... IT WOULD PREVENT US FROM BECOMING A FORCE FOR GOOD.
GOOD?! YOU PEOPLE ARE SO TWISTED YOU DON'T EVEN KNOW WHAT GOOD IS ANYMORE!
THEN SHOW US, OLIVER. JOIN US AND SHOW US THE WAY. THE ARROW IS ENLIGHTEN-MENT.
THE ARROW SHOWS THE TRUE PATH. LEAD US, OLIVER...

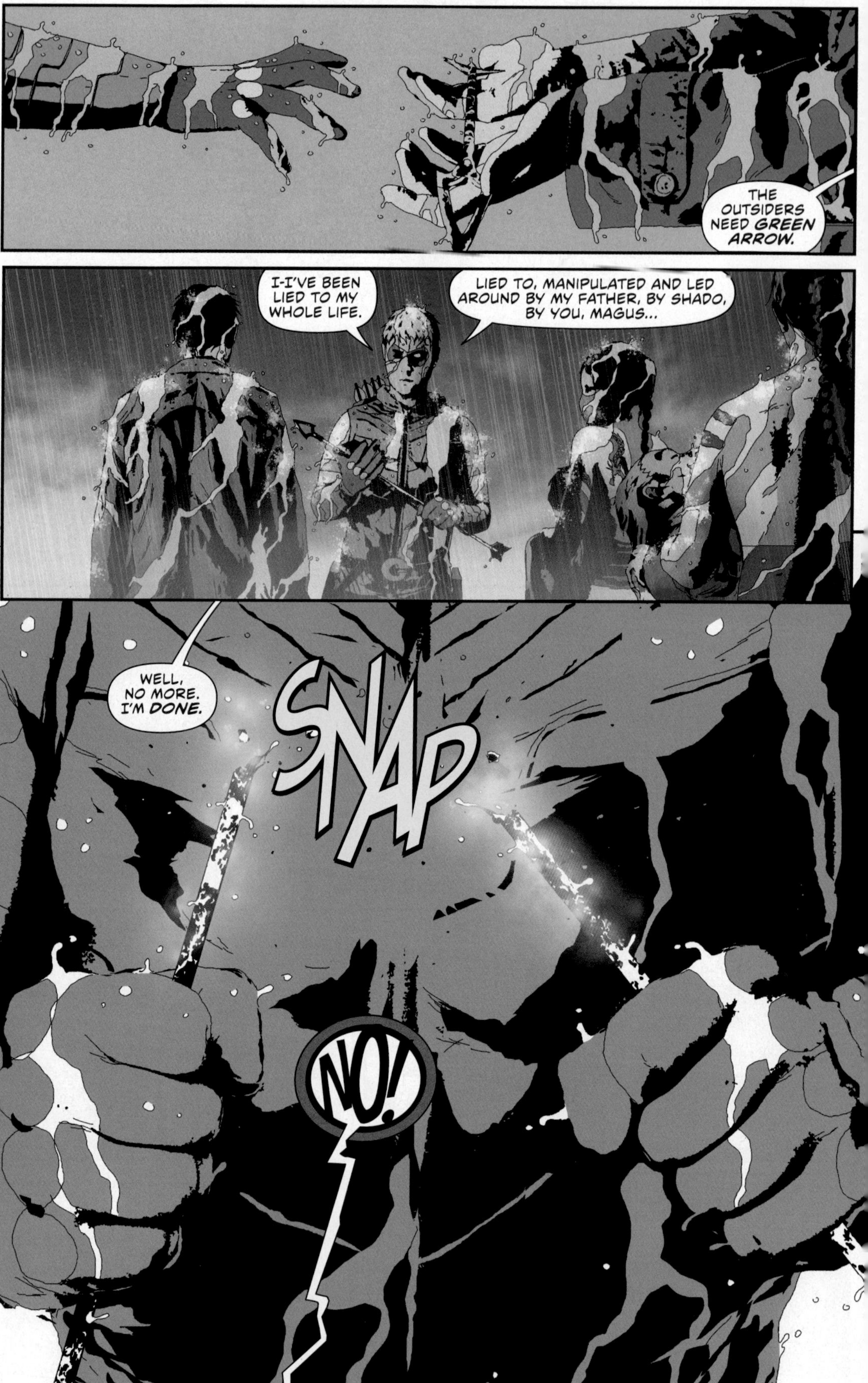
THE OUTSIDERS NEED GREEN ARROW.
I-I'VE BEEN LIED TO MY WHOLE LIFE.
LIED TO, MANIPULATED AND LED AROUND BY MY FATHER, BY SHADO, BY YOU, MAGUS...
WELL, NO MORE. I'M DONE.
SNAP
NO!

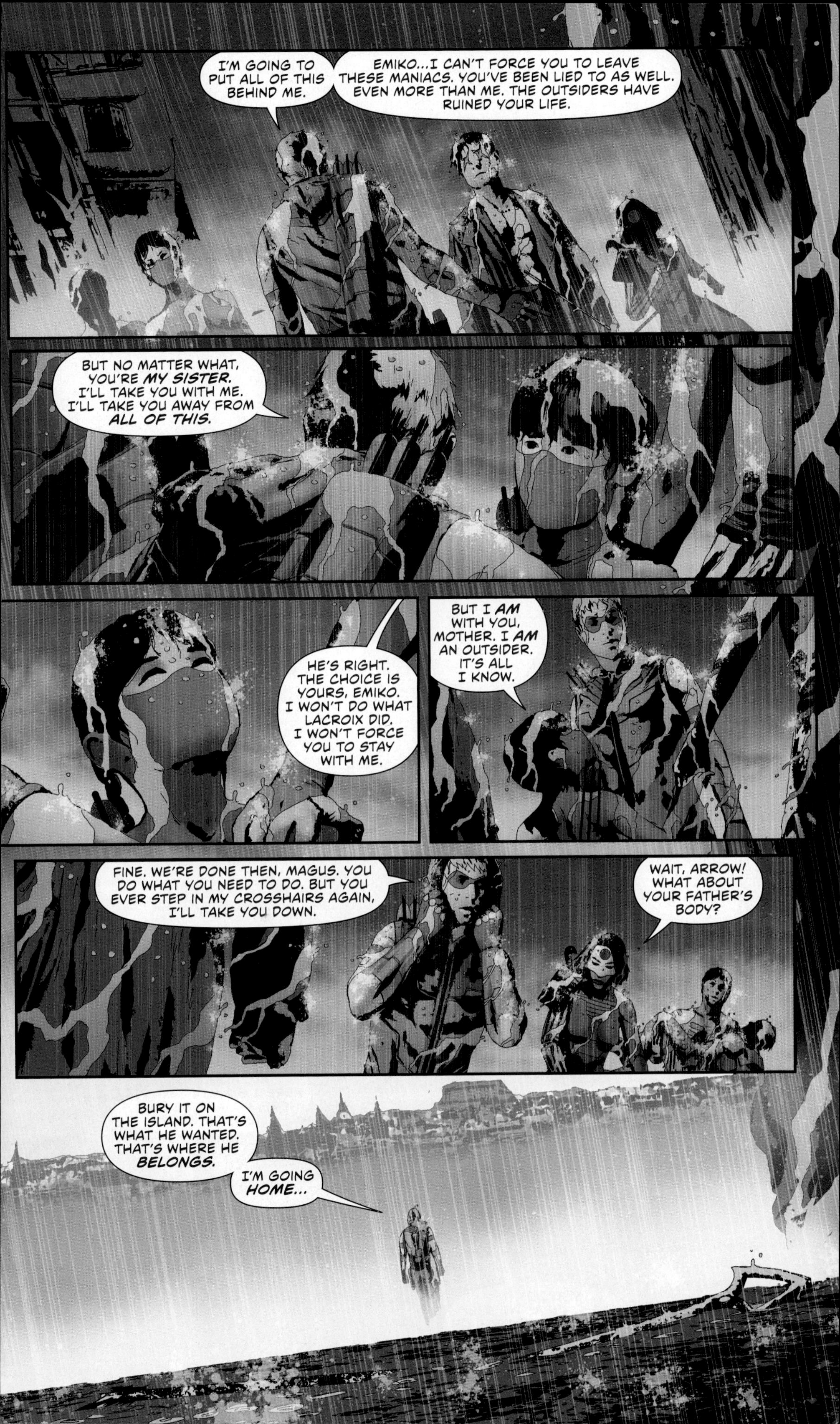

I'M GOING TO PUT ALL OF THIS BEHIND ME.
EMIKO...I CAN'T FORCE YOU TO LEAVE THESE MANIACS. YOU'VE BEEN LIED TO AS WELL. EVEN MORE THAN ME. THE OUTSIDERS HAVE RUINED YOUR LIFE.
BUT NO MATTER WHAT, YOU'RE **MY SISTER.** I'LL TAKE YOU WITH ME. I'LL TAKE YOU AWAY FROM **ALL OF THIS.**
HE'S RIGHT. THE CHOICE IS YOURS, EMIKO. I WON'T DO WHAT LACROIX DID. I WON'T FORCE YOU TO STAY WITH ME.
BUT I **AM** WITH YOU, MOTHER. I **AM** AN OUTSIDER. IT'S ALL I KNOW.
FINE. WE'RE DONE THEN, MAGUS. YOU DO WHAT YOU NEED TO DO. BUT YOU EVER STEP IN MY CROSSHAIRS AGAIN, I'LL TAKE YOU DOWN.
WAIT, ARROW! WHAT ABOUT YOUR FATHER'S BODY?
BURY IT ON THE ISLAND. THAT'S WHAT HE WANTED. THAT'S WHERE HE **BELONGS.**
I'M GOING **HOME...**

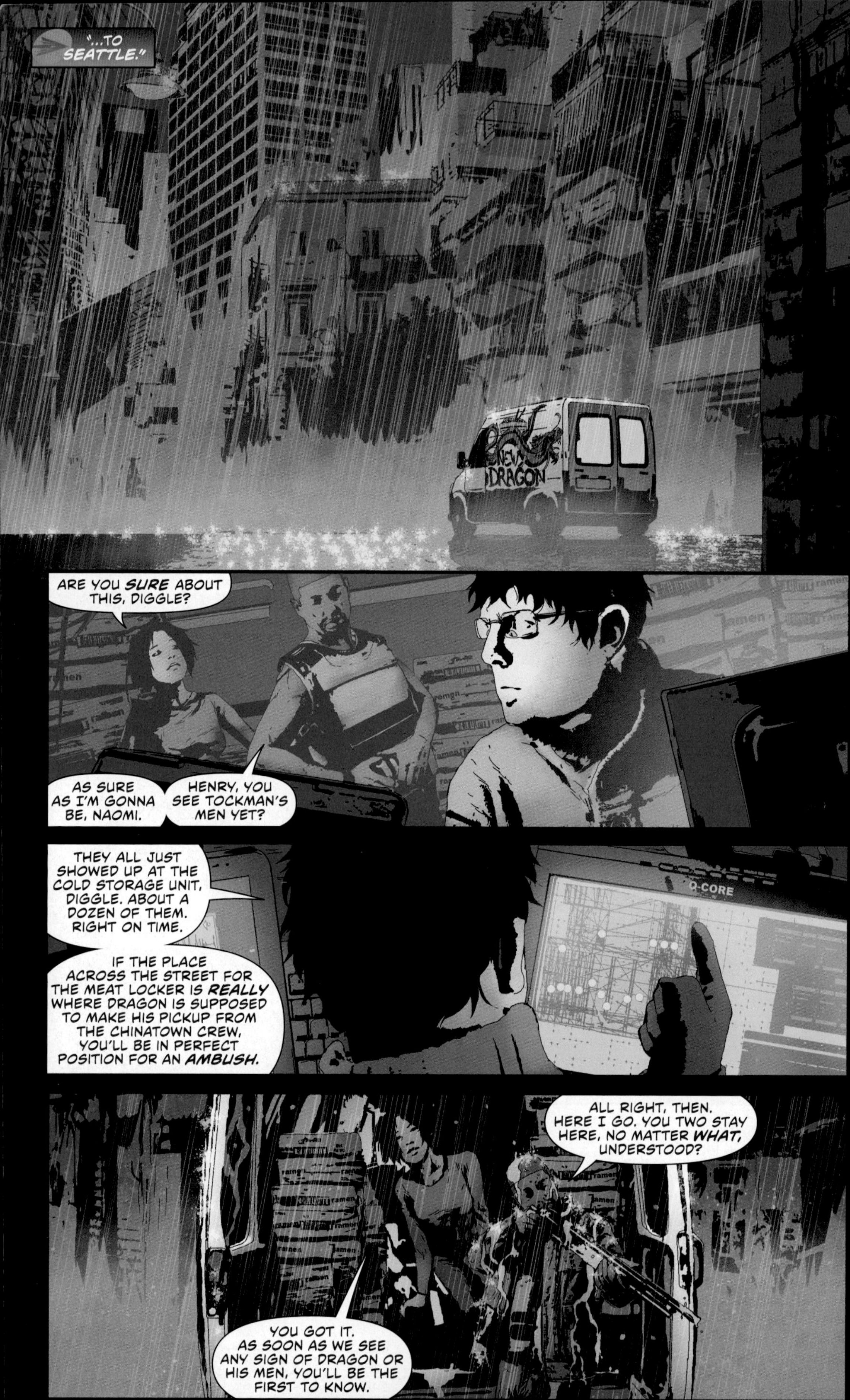
"...TO SEATTLE."
NEW DRAGON
ARE YOU SURE ABOUT THIS, DIGGLE?
AS SURE AS I'M GONNA BE, NAOMI.
HENRY, YOU SEE TOCKMAN'S MEN YET?
THEY ALL JUST SHOWED UP AT THE COLD STORAGE UNIT, DIGGLE. ABOUT A DOZEN OF THEM. RIGHT ON TIME.
IF THE PLACE ACROSS THE STREET FOR THE MEAT LOCKER IS REALLY WHERE DRAGON IS SUPPOSED TO MAKE HIS PICKUP FROM THE CHINATOWN CREW, YOU'LL BE IN PERFECT POSITION FOR AN AMBUSH.
Q-CORE
ALL RIGHT, THEN. HERE I GO. YOU TWO STAY HERE, NO MATTER WHAT, UNDERSTOOD?
YOU GOT IT. AS SOON AS WE SEE ANY SIGN OF DRAGON OR HIS MEN, YOU'LL BE THE FIRST TO KNOW.

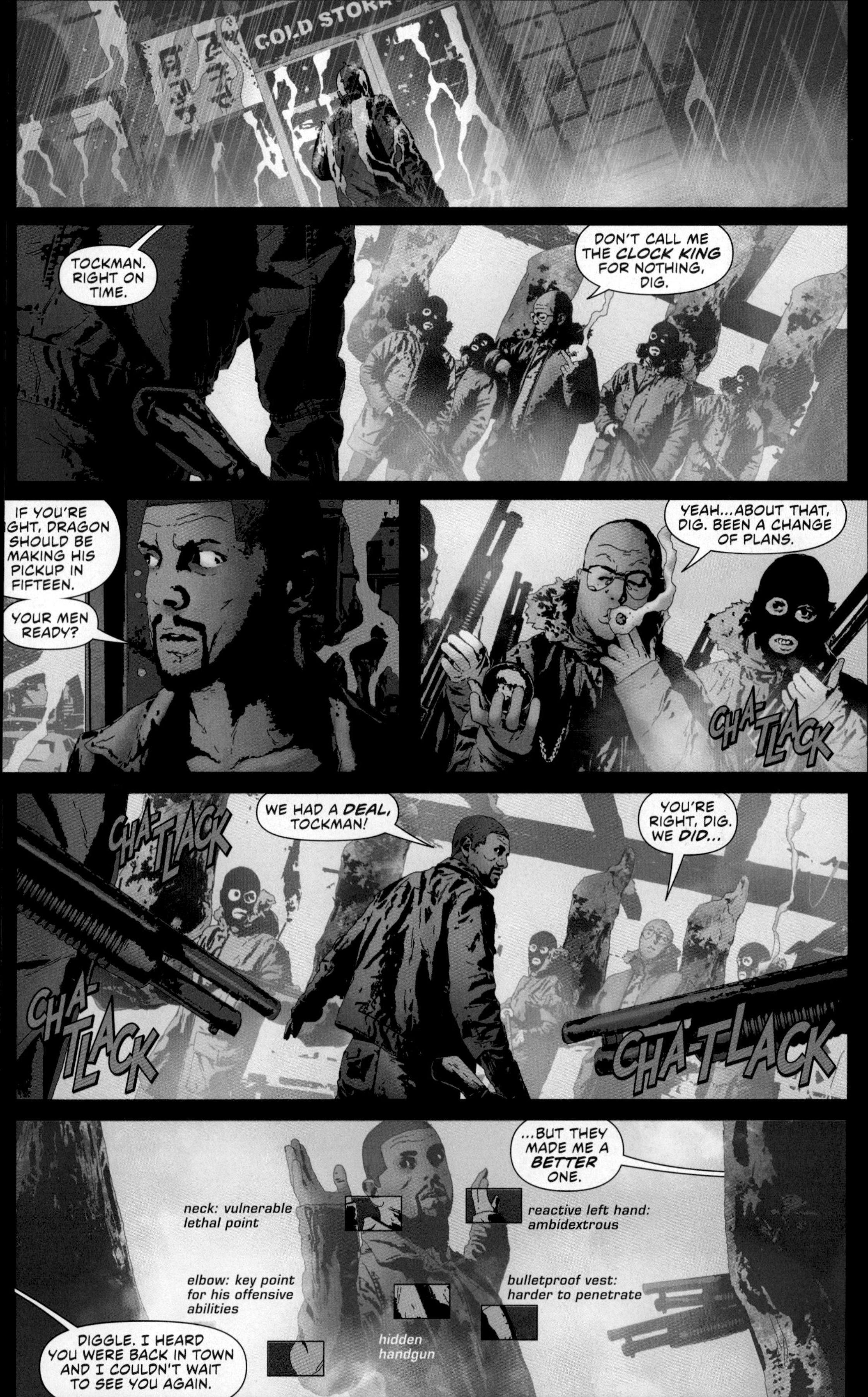
COLD STORA
TOCKMAN. RIGHT ON TIME.
DON'T CALL ME THE CLOCK KING FOR NOTHING, DIG.
IF YOU'RE IGHT, DRAGON SHOULD BE MAKING HIS PICKUP IN FIFTEEN.
YOUR MEN READY?
YEAH...ABOUT THAT, DIG. BEEN A CHANGE OF PLANS.
CHA-TLACK
CHA-TLACK
WE HAD A DEAL, TOCKMAN!
YOU'RE RIGHT, DIG. WE DID...
CHA-TLACK
CHA-T-LACK
...BUT THEY MADE ME A BETTER ONE.
neck: vulnerable lethal point
reactive left hand: ambidextrous
elbow: key point for his offensive abilities
bulletproof vest: harder to penetrate
hidden handgun
DIGGLE. I HEARD YOU WERE BACK IN TOWN AND I COULDN'T WAIT TO SEE YOU AGAIN.

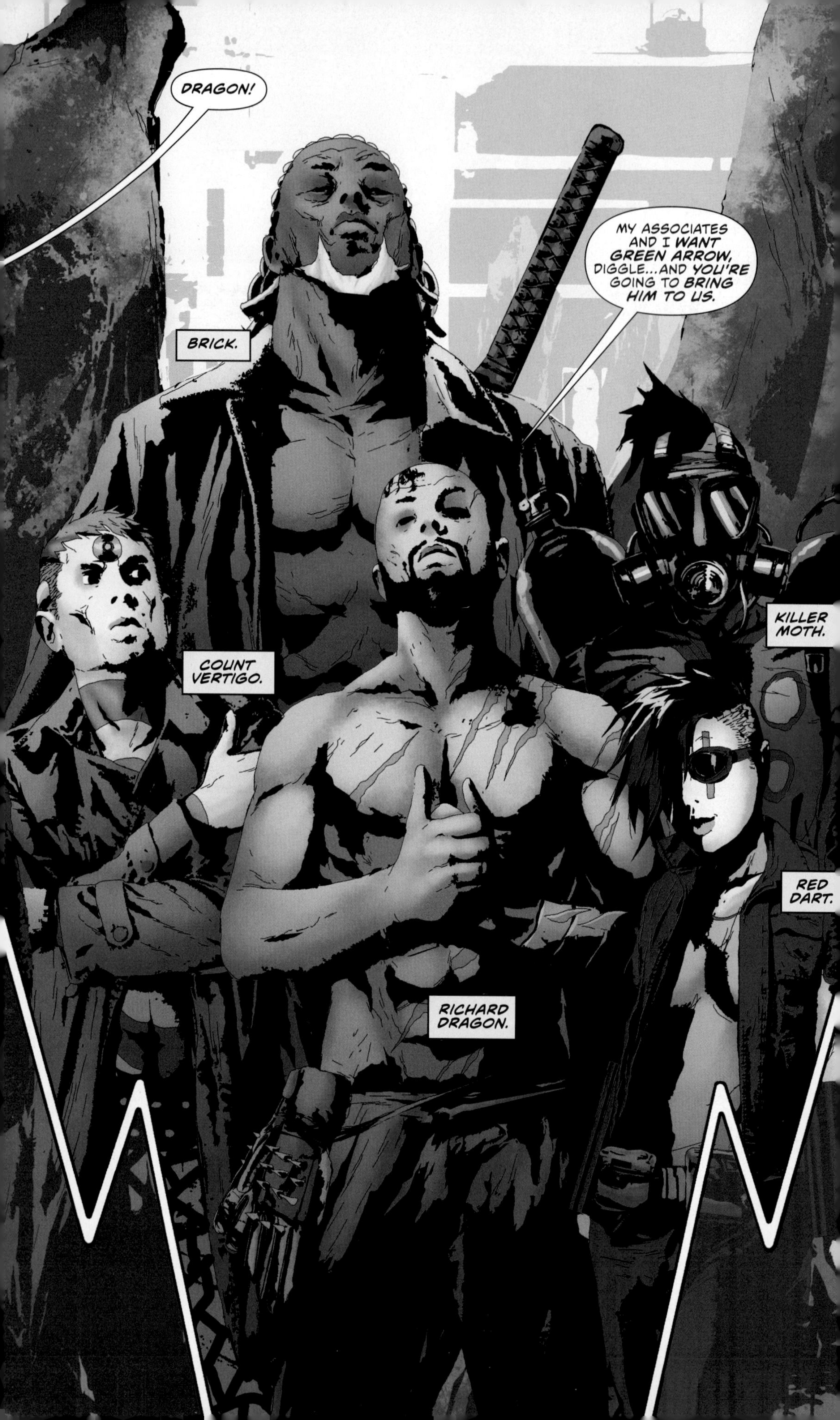
DRAGON!
BRICK.
MY ASSOCIATES AND I WANT GREEN ARROW, DIGGLE...AND YOU'RE GOING TO BRING HIM TO US.
KILLER MOTH.
COUNT VERTIGO.
RED DART.
RICHARD DRAGON.

Richard Dragon character sketches

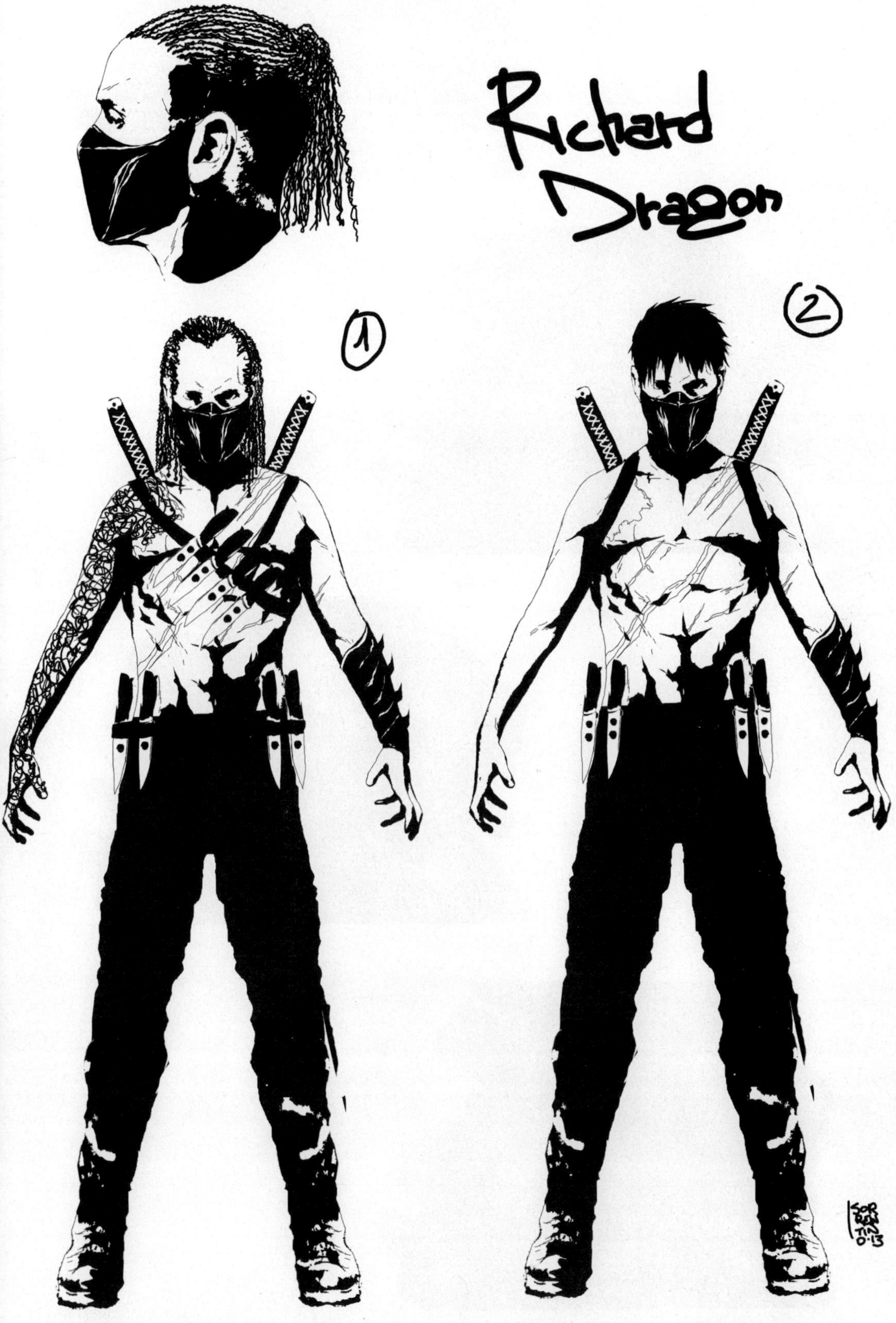
Richard
Dragon
1
2
SORRENTINO 0·13

Variations on Komodo's design

Cover layout ideas for GREEN ARROW #26

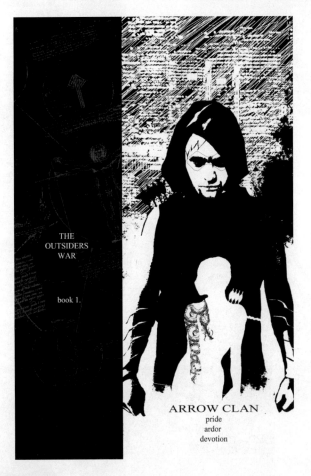

THE
OUTSIDERS
WAR

book 1.

ARROW CLAN
pride
ardor
devotion

THE OUTSIDERS WAR
book 1.

ARROW CLAN
pride
ardor
devotion

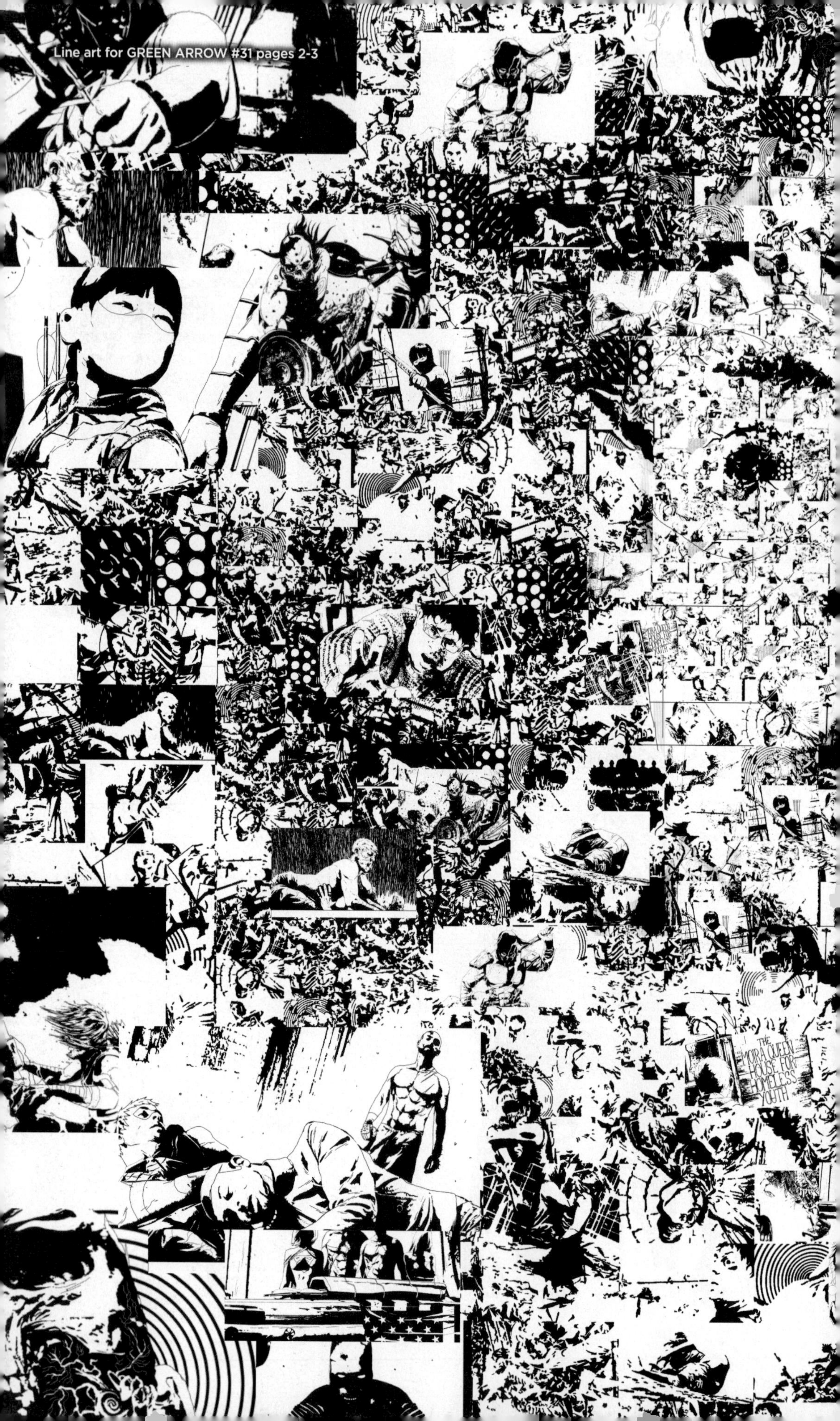
THE MOIRA QUEEN HOUSE FOR HOMELESS YOUTH

Line art for GREEN ARROW #31 pages 2-3

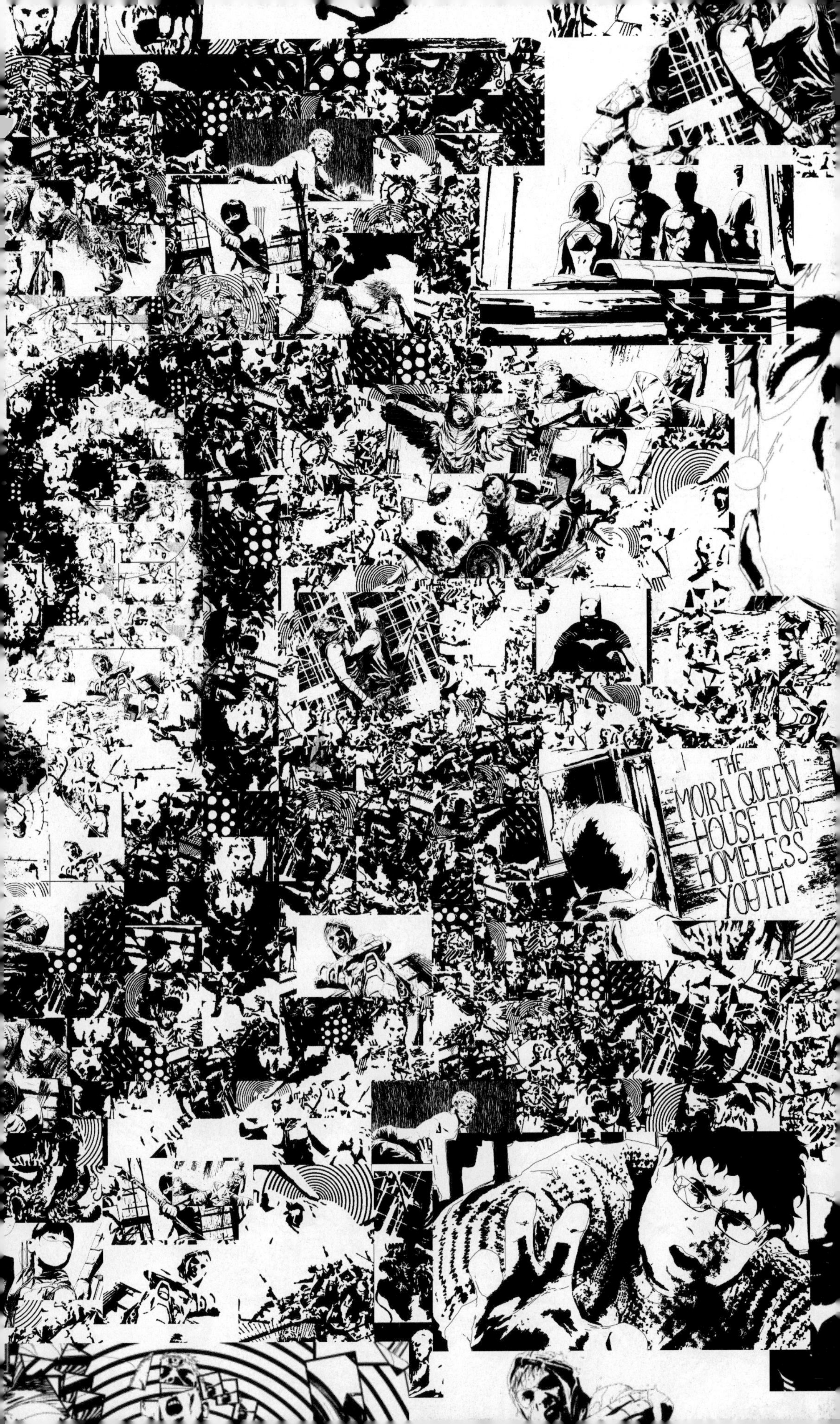
THE
MOIRA QUEEN
HOUSE FOR
HOMELESS
YOUTH

Line art for GREEN ARROW #27 page 13

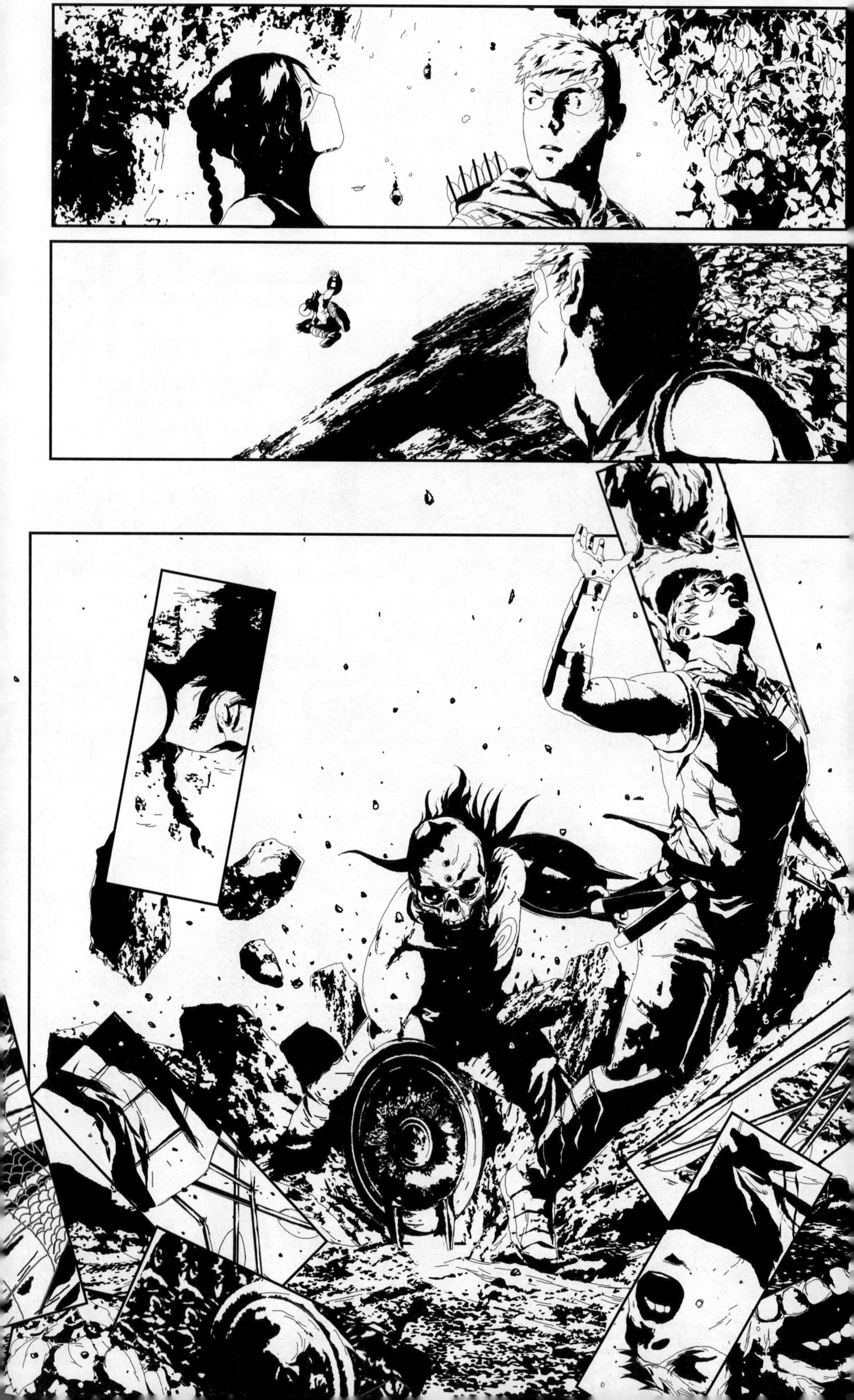

"Writer Geoff Johns and artist Jim Lee toss you–and their heroes–into the action from the very start and don't put on the brakes. DC's über-creative team craft an inviting world for those who are trying out a comic for the first time. Lee's art is stunning."—USA TODAY

"A fun ride."—IGN

START AT THE BEGINNING!
JUSTICE LEAGUE
VOLUME 1: ORIGIN
GEOFF JOHNS and JIM LEE

JUSTICE LEAGUE VOL. 2: THE VILLAIN'S JOURNEY

JUSTICE LEAGUE VOL. 3: THRONE OF ATLANTIS

JUSTICE LEAGUE OF AMERICA VOL. 1: WORLD'S MOST DANGEROUS